Hans Jonas

This book offers new perspectives on the early and formative years of the German-Jewish philosopher Hans Jonas, through innovative studies of his German and Hebrew work in pre-war Germany and Palestine.

Covering all facets of Jonas' early work, the book brings together leading scholars to explore key conceptual, historical, genealogical, and biographical contexts. Some of the main topics examined include his deep intellectual history of Western thought and its origins in late antiquity through the category of *Gnosis*, the intellectual influence of Heidegger, Bultmann, Husserl, and Spengler, his relation to Christian theology, and his interest in Judaism and Zionism. Existing research on his early work is not only limited in size but also often methodologically problematic, for it is common to interpret the early in light of the late and as teleologically leading to it. By introducing new materials and addressing new questions, this book offers innovative perspectives on Jonas' intellectual project as a whole and provides a historical and conceptual foundation for further scholarly explorations of his *oeuvre*.

Providing fresh insights into the work of one of the twentieth century's most influential philosophers, the book will appeal to students and researchers working in intellectual history, Jewish studies, and religion.

Daniel M. Herskowitz is the Smart Family Associate Professor at the Department of Religious Studies at Duke University. Before this he taught theology and religion at the University of Oxford. His first book, *Heidegger and His Jewish Reception* (2021) was awarded the Salo W. and Jeannette M. Baron Young Scholars Award. His second book, *The Judeo-Christian Thought of Franz Rosenzweig*, is forthcoming.

Elad Lapidot is a Professor for Jewish Thought at the University of Lille, France. Among his publications: *Jews Out of the Question. A Critique of Anti-Anti-Semitism* (2020), *Heidegger and Jewish Thought. Difficult Others,* edited with M. Brumlik (2018).

Christian Wiese is the Martin-Buber-Chair in Jewish Thought and Philosophy at Goethe University Frankfurt, Germany. His research focuses on Modern and Contemporary Jewish intellectual and cultural history. His publications include the biography *The Life and Thought of Hans Jonas: Jewish Dimensions* (2007).

Routledge Jewish Studies Series
Series Editor: Oliver Leaman,
University of Kentucky

Jewish Studies, which are interpreted to cover the disciplines of history, sociology, anthropology, culture, politics, philosophy, theology, religion, as they relate to Jewish affairs. The remit includes texts which have as their primary focus issues, ideas, personalities and events of relevance to Jews, Jewish life and the concepts which have characterised Jewish culture both in the past and today. The series is interested in receiving appropriate scripts or proposals.

Bialik, the Hebrew Bible and the Literature of Nationalism
David Aberbach

Contemporary Israeli Haredi Society
Profiles, Trends, and Challenges
Edited by Kimmy Caplan and Nissim Leon

Jewish Hungarian Orthodoxy
Piety and Zealotry
Menachem Keren-Kratz

Jewish Women
Between Conformity and Agency
Katharina Galor

The Poetry and Essays of Uri Zvi Grinberg
Politics and Zionism
Tamar Wolf-Monzon

Hans Jonas
The Early Years
Edited by Daniel M. Herskowitz, Elad Lapidot and Christian Wiese

For more information about this series, please visit: https://www.routledge.com/Routledge-Jewish-Studies-Series/book-series/JEWISH

Hans Jonas
The Early Years

**Edited by Daniel M. Herskowitz,
Elad Lapidot and Christian Wiese**

LONDON AND NEW YORK

First published 2025
by Routledge
4 Park Square, Milton Park, Abingdon, Oxon, OX14 4RN

and by Routledge
605 Third Avenue, New York, NY 10158

Routledge is an imprint of the Taylor & Francis Group, an informa business

© 2025 selection and editorial matter, Daniel M. Herskowitz, Elad Lapidot and Christian Wiese; individual chapters, the contributors

The right of Daniel M. Herskowitz, Elad Lapidot and Christian Wiese to be identified as the authors of the editorial material, and of the authors for their individual chapters, has been asserted in accordance with sections 77 and 78 of the Copyright, Designs and Patents Act 1988.

All rights reserved. No part of this book may be reprinted or reproduced or utilised in any form or by any electronic, mechanical, or other means, now known or hereafter invented, including photocopying and recording, or in any information storage or retrieval system, without permission in writing from the publishers.

Trademark notice: Product or corporate names may be trademarks or registered trademarks, and are used only for identification and explanation without intent to infringe.

British Library Cataloguing-in-Publication Data
A catalogue record for this book is available from the British Library

Library of Congress Cataloging-in-Publication Data
Names: Zyzik, Eve C., author. | Bowles, Melissa A., author.
Title: The acquisition of Spanish: a research overview in multilingual learning contexts / Eve Zyzik and Melissa A. Bowles.
Description: New York, NY: Routledge, 2025. |
Series: Second language acquisition research series | Includes bibliographical references and index. |
Identifiers: LCCN 2024027293 (print) | LCCN 2024027294 (ebook) | ISBN 9781032214917 (hardback) | ISBN 9781032214900 (paperback) | ISBN 9781003268635 (ebook)
Subjects: LCSH: Spanish language–Study and teaching–Foreign speakers.
Classification: LCC PC4127.8 .Z99 2025 (print) | LCC PC4127.8 (ebook) | DDC 468.0071—dc23/eng/20240731
LC record available at https://lccn.loc.gov/2024027293
LC ebook record available at https://lccn.loc.gov/2024027294

ISBN: 978-1-032-57568-1 (hbk)
ISBN: 978-1-032-57569-8 (pbk)
ISBN: 978-1-003-43988-2 (ebk)

DOI: 10.4324/9781003439882

Typeset in Times New Roman
by codeMantra

Contents

List of Contributors vii
Preface xi

1. **From Husserl to Heidegger: Jonas' Double Memory** 1
   ELAD LAPIDOT

2. **Lessons in Interrogative Thinking: Jonas and Bultmann** 14
   ANDREAS GROSSMANN

3. **Hans Jonas' Contributions to Rudolf Bultmann's Demythologization** 28
   LUCA SETTIMO

4. **The Aporias of Human Freedom: An Early Letter and Its Long Impact** 54
   MICHAEL BONGARDT

5. **Hans Jonas' and Hannah Arendt's Variations on St. Augustine** 69
   YAEL ALMOG

6. **Hans Jonas on Gnosis and Late Antiquity: In Search of the Spirit of an Epoch** 84
   JOHANNES ZACHHUBER

7. **A Historical Transcendental at the Heart of Jonas' Research on Gnosticism** 102
   NATHALIE FROGNEUX

8. **The Gnostic Myth as a Gambit in German Intellectual Tradition** 123
   AMIR ENGEL

9. *Gnosis und spätantiker Geist. Teil II:* **The Forgotten Book** 141
   ELAD LAPIDOT

10 From *Gnosis und spätantiker Geist* to *The Gnostic Religion*:
   The Jerusalem Period in Hans Jonas' Intellectual Development   154
   DANIEL M. HERSKOWITZ

11 Once a Gnostic, Always a Gnostic: The Persistence
   of Gnosticism in Hans Jonas' Post-War Thought   178
   AGATA BIELIK-ROBSON

12 Resisting Nihilism: The Motif of *Entwurzelung* in Jonas'
   Early Writings   201
   LIBERA PISANO

Index   *219*

Contributors

Yael Almog is an Associate Professor of German at the School of Modern Languages and Cultures at Durham University. She previously held research positions in Berlin, Göttingen, and Frankfurt am Main. Her monograph *Secularism and Hermeneutics* (The University of Pennsylvania Press, 2019) examines exegesis as embedded in confessional belonging and challenges the modern presumption that interpretation is indifferent to religious concerns. Her research explores links between theology and literary theory; secularism and critical theory; and literature and political philosophy.

Agata Bielik-Robson is a Professor of Jewish Studies at the University of Nottingham and at the Institute of Philosophy and Sociology, Polish Academy of Science in Warsaw. Her research interests include modern Jewish thought, psychoanalysis, and philosophy of religion. She is co-editor of *Judaism in Contemporary Thought* (Routledge, 2014). She has published articles on philosophical aspects of psychoanalysis, romantic subjectivity, and the philosophy of religion (especially Judaism and its crossings with modern philosophical thought). Her publications include *The Saving Lie. Harold Bloom and Deconstruction* (in English, Northwestern University Press, May 2011), *Eros. Messianic Vitalism and Philosophy* (Cracow 2012), *In the Wilderness. Cryptotheologies of Late Modernity* (Cracow 2008), *Romanticism. An Unfinished Project* (Cracow 2008), *The Spirit of the Surface. Romantic Revision and Philosophy* (Cracow 2004), *Another Modernity* (Cracow 2000), and *On the Other Side of Nihilism* (Warsaw 1997).

Michael Bongardt is a German theologian and philosopher at the University of Siegen. Bongardt's field of research links the border areas of philosophy, theology, and cultural studies. He published monographs and numerous contributions to the philosophy of Sören Kierkegaard and Ernst Cassirer. As co-editor, he is involved in the editing of the works of the philosopher Hans Jonas and has published books on the influential German-language aphorist Elazar Benyoëtz. Further fields of activity of his work are questions of interreligious and intercultural dialogue, the transformation of religions under the conditions of secularization, as well as fundamental problems of philosophical ethics.

viii *Contributors*

Amir Engel is a Lecturer at the German department at the Hebrew University. He studied philosophy, literature, and culture-studies at the Hebrew University and completed his PhD at the German studies department at Stanford University, California. After that he taught and conducted research at the Goethe University in Frankfurt am Main. His main topics of interest include German Romanticism and German post-war literature and culture, theories of myth, literature, philosophy, and history of culture. He is also interested in intercultural transference, Jewish German culture, and German twentieth-century intellectual history. He has written a book about Gershom Scholem and has published essays about Hannah Arendt, Paul Celan, Martin Buber, Jacob Taubes, Salomon Maimon, and others in *New German Critique*, *German Studies Review*, *Modern Intellectual History*, and other high-profile venues.

Nathalie Frogneux is a Full Professor at the Catholic University of Louvain in Belgium, teacher of philosophy and in particular anthropological philosophy. She wrote *Hans Jonas ou la vie dans le monde*, De Boeck Université, Bruxelles, 2001, and several articles about Jonas. She was a Visiting Professor at the University of Rome, La Sapienza in May 2022. She also translated and introduced H. Jonas, *La Gnose et l'esprit de l'Antiquité tardive. Histoire et méthodologie de la recherche*, Milan, Mimesis, 2017; "Mito" and "Gnose" in Jelson Oliveira & Eric Pommier (org.), *Vocabolario Hans Jonas*, EDUS, 2019; "Cassandra: a voz do fim," in Nathalie Frogneux, Jelson de Oliveira, Thiago Vasconcelos, *Terra Nenhuma*, Educs: Curibita, 2020, 25–30, and "Frankophoner Sprachraum ausserhalb Frankreichs" and "Zwischen Nichts und Ewigkeit" in M. Bongardt, H. Burkhart, J.-S. Gordon, J. Nielsen-Sikora (Hg.), *Hans Jonas Handbuch. Leben-Werk-Wirkung*, J. B. Metzler, Berlin, 2021.

Andreas Grossmann studied philosophy and (protestant) theology. He received his doctorate in Philosophy at Ruhr University Bochum (*Spur zum Heiligen. Kunst und Geschichte im Widerstreit zwischen Hegel und Heidegger*, 1996). After positions held as research fellow and lecturer at the universities of Bochum, Hamburg, and Lüneburg, he has been academic director of the Forum of Interdisciplinary Research at Technical University of Darmstadt since 2015. He is the author of *Heidegger-Lektüren* (2005). He co-edited the correspondence between Rudolf Bultmann and Martin Heidegger (2009) and edited the correspondence between Rudolf Bultmann and Hans Jonas (2020).

Daniel M. Herskowitz is the Smart Family Associate Professor at the Department of Religious Studies at Duke University. Before this he taught at Trinity College and was the British Academy Postdoctoral Fellow at the Faculty of Theology and Religion University of Oxford. He was also a Research Fellow at Wolfson College, University of Oxford, and a postdoctoral fellow at the Religion Department at Columbia University, NY. His first book, *Heidegger and His Jewish Reception* (Cambridge University Press, 2021) was awarded the 2021 Salo W. and Jeannette M. Baron Young Scholars Award for Scholarly Excellence. His essay "Between Exclusion and Intersection: Heidegger's Philosophy and Jewish Volkism" was the winner of the Leo Baeck Year Book Essay Prize for 2020. His second book, *The Judeo-Christian Thought of Franz Rosenzweig*, is forthcoming with Oxford University Press.

Elad Lapidot is a Professor and Chair for Hebraic Studies at the University of Lille, France. Holding a PhD in Philosophy from the Paris Sorbonne University, he has taught philosophy, Jewish thought, and Talmud at many universities, such as the University of Bern, Switzerland, and the Humboldt Universität and Freie Univeristät in Berlin. His work is guided by questions concerning the relation between knowledge and politics. Among his publications: *Jews Out of the Question. A Critique of Anti-Anti-Semitism* (Albany: SUNY Press, 2020), Hebrew translation with introduction and commentary (with R. Bar) of Hegel's *Phänomenologie des Geistes*, Vol. 1 (Tel Aviv: Resling Publishing, 2020), *Heidegger and Jewish Thought. Difficult Others*, edited with M. Brumlik (London/ New York: Rowman & Littlefield, 2018), and *Etre sans mot dire: La logiqe de 'Sein und Zeit'* (Bucarest: Zeta Books, 2010).

Libera Pisano is currently Research Associate at IFILNOVA, Universidade Nova de Lisboa. She received her PhD in Theoretical Philosophy from La Sapienza (Rome) in 2014 with a dissertation entitled *Lo spirito manifesto. Percorsi linguistici nella filosofia hegeliana* (ETS 2016). She has been a Marie Sklodowska-Curie Fellow at the University Pompeu Fabra, Research Associate at the Exzellenzcluster "Understanding Written Artefacts" at the University of Hamburg, Research Fellow at the University of Calabria, at the Maimonides Centre for Advanced Studies, Visiting Research Fellow at the University of Haifa and at the Humboldt University of Berlin. She is the author of several essays on the role of language in Hegel's writings, Leopold Zunz, Moses Mendelssohn, Gustav Landauer, on contemporary German-Jewish philosophy and on the concept of diaspora. Her new book "The Exile of Language. German-Jewish Philosophical Challenges of Linguistic Autochthony" will soon be published by Brill.

Luca Settimo is a theologian and a scientist (with a background in pharmaceutical sciences). He obtained an MA in Systematic and Philosophical Theology in 2019, and then a PhD in Theology in 2022 (both at the University of Nottingham, UK). The title of his dissertation in Theology was: "Hans Jonas's reflections on cosmogony, theodicy and his argument for God's existence: a possible enrichment for Christian theology in dialogue with modern natural science." In this doctoral dissertation, he reflected on the philosophical–theological approach adopted by Hans Jonas in relation to Christian theology. Currently, he is an Honorary Postdoctoral Fellow (Theology) in the Department of Theology and Religious Studies at the University of Nottingham.

Christian Wiese holds the Martin-Buber-Chair in Modern Jewish Thought and Philosophy and is the Director of the Buber-Rosenzweig-Institute for Modern and Contemporary Jewish Thought and Philosophy at Goethe University Frankfurt, Germany. Holding a PhD from Goethe University, Frankfurt, he has held positions and visiting appointments in various universities, including University of Erfurt, McGill University, Montreal, Dartmouth College, New Hampshire,

Trinity College, Dublin, the University of Sussex, the University of Pennsylvania, and ETH Zurich. His research is devoted to Modern Jewish intellectual and cultural history, Jewish thought, the history of Jewish-Christian relations, and the history of anti-Semitism. His publications on Hans Jonas include the monograph *The Life and Thought of Hans Jonas: Jewish Dimensions* (Waltham, MA: Brandeis University Press, 2007), the collected volume *The Legacy of Hans Jonas: Judaism and the Phenomenon of Life*, edited with Hava Tirosh-Samuelson (Leiden/Boston: Brill, 2008). He has also widely published on the history of Jewish scholarship, for instance his monograph *Challenging Colonial Discourse: Jewish Studies and Protestant Theology in Wilhelmine Germany* (Leiden/Boston: Brill, 2005) or his edition of the correspondence of Markus Brann: *Zur Wissenschaft des Judentums: Aus der Gelehrtenkorrespondenz Markus Branns*, edited with Daniel Ristau (Göttingen: Vandenhoeck & Ruprecht, 2023).

Johannes Zachhuber is a Professor of Historical and Systematic Theology at the University of Oxford, UK. He is an historical and systematic theologian specializing in two main areas of research: the Eastern Patristic tradition of theology, its philosophical background, and its development up to John of Damascus; and modern theology from the Reformation to the present, with special interests related to nineteenth-century German theology. His published contributions to scholarship include two main works that correspond to these areas of research — *Human Nature in Gregory of Nyssa* (Brill, 1999; paperback 2014) and *Theology as Science in Nineteenth-Century Germany* (Oxford University Press, 2013) — along with many articles and edited books.

Preface

The work of Hans Jonas, the German-Jewish philosopher (1903–1993), is located at many crossroads: between theology and philosophy, neo-Kantianism and existentialism, antiquity and modernity, Judaism and Christianity, myth and rationalism, rootedness and exile, pre- and post-war intellectual world, and Europe and America. Appropriately, the scholarly attention granted to young Jonas has thus far been rich and multifaceted. However, the Holocaust has been a cesura not only in the lives of German-Jewish thinkers but also in scholarship on them, and Jonas research, especially in English, tends to focus on his later, post-Holocaust, English works.

We are currently in the midst of a new era in Jonas research. Half of the 14-volume critical edition of Jonas' work – the *Kritische Gesamtausgabe* – has been published over the last decade, and the remaining volumes are forthcoming in the next few years. Crucial aspects and significant texts that have so far received little attention, were less-known or practically unknown and unpublished, now come to light and offer new perspectives on Jonas' intellectual project in its systematic and genealogical configurations. One important milestone in the new scholarship on Jonas was the publication of the *Hans Jonas Handbuch. Leben – Werk – Wirkung*, edited by Michael Bongardt, Holger Burckhart, John-Stewart Gordon, and Jürgen Nielsen-Sikora in 2021.

One of the most important facets of Jonas' work that has so far been under-researched and now begins to draw growing attention are Jonas' early years of intellectual work. It is to this early period of Jonas' work that this volume is dedicated, offering new and surprising perspectives on Jonas through innovative studies of his German and Hebrew work in pre-war Germany and Palestine.

The early period of Jonas' work may be characterized thematically as preceding Jonas' focus on the phenomenon of life, nature, and environmental ethics, which belong to the later, more well-known and well-researched period of his work. The earlier period, as Jonas himself noted, was dedicated mostly to the deep intellectual history of Western thought and knowledge, namely its origins in philosophical and religious movements in late antiquity, which Jonas analyzed predominantly through the category of *Gnosis*. Major intellectual influence on Jonas in these years was exercised by his two doctoral advisors in Marburg, Martin Heidegger and Rudolf Bultmann, but also figures such as Edmund Husserl, Ernst Cassirer, and Oswald Spengler. During these years, Jonas developed his interest in Judaism and xii *Preface*

Zionism as well. Geographically, Jonas' early period is placed mostly in Germany and then in Palestine, before his move to North America. Politically and existentially, Jonas' early period ends with the Second World War.

As much as Jonas' early period consists in the most formative years of his thought, the challenges these years present to scholarship are considerable, due to the nature of the deep trauma that violently ended them. Jonas himself described his later work as an explicit break with his earlier interests and orientation, and his own autobiographical narrative in many ways presented and interpreted his early work already through the perspective of this traumatic break. Correspondingly, the existing research on some of the themes occupying his early work is not only limited in size but also often methodologically problematic, commonly interpreting the early in light of the late and as teleologically leading to it.

Jonas' early study on Gnosticism (in his dissertation and in the later published *Gnosis und spätantiker Geist I* and *II*) is a case in point: it is rarely read by scholars – even by those who reference it – and is usually understood and discussed in light of Jonas' post-war thought or through his later and much revised rendition of this work, the English book *The Gnostic Religion*. Moreover, many of Jonas' earlier texts, most significantly his dissertation, which are found at the Jonas Archive, have so far received either little or no scholarly attention, and many have never been published.

The present volume approaches Jonas' early period as an intellectual period worthy of sustained scholarly consideration on its own terms and within the context of its immediate historical, cultural, and political horizon. By introducing new materials and addressing new questions, it seeks to offer new perspectives on Jonas' intellectual project as a whole and to provide a historical and conceptual foundation for further scholarly explorations of his *oeuvre*.

This edited volume, which arises from an international conference that took place in Oxford in July 2022 – and which comes on the heels of the publication of the first critically edited volume of *Gnosis und spätantiker Geist* – brings together leading scholars of Jonas' early period to discuss the various aspects of its significance, the growing interest in it, and the challenges facing relevant scholarship. Contributors cover all facets of Jonas' early work, in their conceptual, historical, genealogical, and biographical contexts, in themselves as well as in relation to Jonas' later, more well-known oeuvre. Recent, innovative studies on early, pre-WWII Hannah Arendt and Leo Strauss have revolutionized the research on these thinkers. This volume aims to do the same in the scholarship on Hans Jonas.

The volume begins with a series of studies on Hans Jonas' relations to his teachers. In Chapter 1, "From Husserl to Heidegger: Jonas's Double Memory," Elad Lapidot reflects on Jonas' relation to his philosophy masters, Edmund Husserl and Martin Heidegger. The chapter contemplates the two opposite movements that Jonas accomplished: first, from Husserl to Heidegger; then, from Heidegger back to Husserl. The significance of these movements is studied through texts written by Jonas after he left Germany, mainly his obituaries to Husserl from 1938 and his post-war reminiscences. In contrast to a common narrative that portrays Jonas' shift from Husserl to Heidegger as a fall from ethics to nihilism that he later corrected, this chapter offers a more complex narrative, according to which the pursuit of ethical thought guided both Jonas' initial interest in Husserl as well as his turn to Heidegger.

The next three chapters are dedicated to Hans Jonas' intellectual relationship to the theologian Rudolf Bultmann. In Chapter 2, "Lessons in Interrogative Thinking: Jonas and Bultmann," Andreas Grossmann shows how the meeting of the young philosophy student with the great Protestant theologian in Marburg in the 1920s provided decisive impulses for Jonas' thought. The chapter studies these impulses as they are documented in the early works on Augustine and Paul as well as in the discussions on myth and demythologization. The chapter argues that these discussions are connected to the general philosophical problem of (self-)objectification and objectifying thought.

In Chapter 3, "Hans Jonas' Contributions to Rudolf Bultmann's Demythologization," Luca Settimo reverses the common perspective and studies Jonas' influence on Bultmann. The chapter studies how Jonas' reflections on myth and objectivation, concerning existential aspects of Paul's Romans 7 and of the hermeneutics of dogma, influenced Bultmann's existential interpretation of dogmas and biblical texts. The chapter focuses in particular on Bultmann's development of the notion and method of demythologization.

In Chapter 4, "The Aporias of Human Freedom: An Early Letter and its Long Impact," Michael Bongardt studies a letter that Jonas wrote to Bultmann in 1929, which was published several times in later decades. In this letter, Jonas provides an existential analysis that shows an inner structural obstacle of human freedom. Jonas' insistence that humans are able to overcome this obstacle places him in opposition to Paul, Augustine, and Bultmann, who consider such "redemption" possible through God alone. The chapter shows how this early reflection of Jonas on the aporias of human freedom continue to shape his later work, among others on Augustine.

Yael Almog's Chapter 5, "Hans Jonas and Hannah Arendt's Variations on St. Augustine," looks at Jonas' work on Augustine, which he published as his first book in 1930. The chapter centres on young Jonas' analysis in comparison to young Hannah Arendt's study of Augustine, both disciples of Heidegger. Confirming Michael Bongardt's study, Almog shows that young Jonas recognizes in Augustine's dogmas of the original sin and predestination the conundrum whereby freedom generates sin. The chapter demonstrates how later Arendt posits freedom as a central problem of political thought, in particular with respect to human agency. Arendt finds in Augustine not only, like Jonas, the aporias of freedom but also a possible solution to them.

The next six chapters are dedicated to exploring various facets of Jonas' central and most famous project in his early period – his studies of ancient Gnosticism. In Chapter 6, "Hans Jonas on Gnosis and Late Antiquity: In Search of the Spirit of an Epoch," Johannes Zachhuber inscribes Jonas' work of Gnosis into the history of interpretations of late antiquity. Since the eighteenth century, this period was often evoked in narratives of decline and seen in parallel with modernity, such as by Oswald Spengler. Zachhuber argues that Jonas' attempt to understand Gnosis as expressing the 'spirit of late antiquity' offers a novel interpretation of Gnosticism by building on these various historiographical traditions.

Chapter 7, "A Historical Transcendental at the Heart of Jonas' Research on Gnosticism," Nathalie Frogneux argues that Jonas' early work on Gnosticism, *Gnosis und spätantiker Geist*, was not confined to religious or philosophical history but laid the groundwork for an original philosophy of history. His research aimed to unveil the spirit of an era through historical phenomena. Examining Jonas' methodology as outlined in *Gnosis und spätantiker Geist I*, published 1934, Frogneux shows how Jonas, taking inspiration from Heidegger, developed the idea of a historical transcendental. Featuring the historical a priori of an era, Jonas' historical transcendental, however, at the same time preserves the role of human freedom, in contrast to the Heideggerian notion of destiny.

In Chapter 8, "The Gnostic Myth as a Gambit in German Intellectual Tradition," Amir Engel examines the role of the myth in Jonas' *Gnosticism and the Spirit of Late Antiquity, Part 1: Mythological Gnosticism*. The chapter suggests that Jonas' work should be considered in the context of the history of German thought, and more specifically as depicting a transition from German Romanticism to Existentialism. Engel argues that Jonas' innovation consists in his new use of two central terms of nineteenth-century German philosophy, the "symbol" and the "myth."

In Chapter 9, "*Gnosis und spätantiker Geist. Teil II*: The Forgotten Book," Elad Lapidot shifts the attention from the first to the second part of Jonas' early work on Gnosticism. He argues that this less-known book contains the most original version of Jonas' project. The chapter challenges common narratives, including Jonas' own post-war accounts of his pre-war work, which depict Gnosticism as nihilism. Lapidot argues that Jonas' initial project considered the late-antique Gnostic movement as heralding an ethics- and praxis-based conception of knowledge, in contrast to the theory-based conception of Greek epistemology. The chapter accordingly situates Jonas' project not only in the context of Husserlian and Heideggerian phenomenology, but also in the context of post–WWI German-Jewish thought.

Opening up a broader perspective on the relations between Jonas' earlier and later period, in Chapter 10, "From *Gnosis und spätantiker Geist* to *The Gnostic Religion*: The Jerusalem Period in Hans Jonas's Intellectual Development," Daniel M. Herskowitz details some aspects of the transformation of Jonas' Gnosis study from the work produces in the early German period to its later and better-known English adaptation. By examining the transcripts of lectures on Gnosticism delivered by Jonas in the Hebrew University in 1938, Herskowitz claims that the major shift in Jonas' approach to Gnosticism took place in his Jerusalem period in mandate Palestine of the 1930s.

In Chapter 11, "Once a Gnostic, Always a Gnostic: The Persistence of Gnosticism in Hans Jonas' Post-War Thought," Agata Bielik-Robson argues that, in contrast to a prevailing narrative of "overcoming Gnosticism" in favor of the natural cosmos, young Jonas' fascination with Gnosticism kept shaping also his later work. Complicating the story, Bielik-Robson depicts Jonas' development as shifting from the dualistic type of Gnosticism, which was the object of his early studies, to a dialectical type of Gnosticism, which in his later period he borrowed from the kabbalistic doctrine of Isaac Luria.

In the last Chapter 12, "Resisting Nihilism: The Motif of *Entwurzelung* in Jonas's Early Writings," Libera Pisano offers a broader look on Jonas' early period through the prism of uprootedness (*Entwurzelung*), as both a philosophical and a political concern. Pisano argues that Jonas responded to the philosophical and political rootlessness embodied in diasporic Judaism and Gnosticism by developing a position of deep belonging to this world. She shows how, based on a historical interpretation of the Prophets, Jonas adopted a stance of proactive Zionism as a strategy for combating the nihilism of ethical and political irresponsibility.

1 From Husserl to Heidegger

Jonas' Double Memory

Elad Lapidot

According to a common narrative, both biographical and autobiographical, Jonas' life-work is articulated by a fundamental turn from an early to a late period, around WWII: from a pre-WWII fascination with old texts of unworldly religion, inspired by the existential nihilism of the morally bankrupt Heidegger, to a post-WWII return to classical, Greek philosophy's commitment to the world, to life, to ethical responsibility.[1]

My scholarship of Jonas' early work reveals a different story. According to my assessment, it was precisely Jonas' concern for ethics that originally led him, as a thinker, from classic, Greek-inspired philosophy to the archives of Judeo-Christian traditions: from eidetics to hermeneutics. My chapter on *Gnosis und Spätantiker Geist II* demonstrates this counter-narrative in Jonas' early project on Gnosticism.[2] This chapter focuses on the even earlier genealogy of Jonas' intellectual project in his movement from Edmund Husserl to Martin Heidegger. The provocative claim of this chapter is that Jonas turned from Husserl to Heidegger because he perceived in Heidegger's philosophy a way to overcome the crisis of twentieth-century theory-based philosophy using the ethics-based knowledge of Judeo-Christian textual tradition.

A Student of Two Masters

Jonas' philosophical education was embodied by two major figures, Edmund Husserl and Martin Heidegger, whom Jonas regarded throughout his life as his two most important teachers of philosophy. In his lecture "Husserl and Heidegger" at the Leo-Baeck Institute in New York on March 13, 1963, he said: "Among living philosophers, these two figures exerted the strongest influence on my development."[3] These two names, Husserl and Heidegger, do not stand indifferently side by side in Jonas' self-description, but denote a development with a clear direction: "As the sequence shows, Heidegger's [influence] was finally the decisive one, as it was for so many Husserl students during the twenties."[4]

During the thirties, however, Jonas moved in the opposite direction – from Heidegger back to Husserl. This second movement determined Jonas' later, postwar development, as well as the common narrative about his earlier project, which tended to obliterate Jonas' original trajectory from Husserl to Heidegger.

DOI: 10.4324/9781003439882-1

2   Elad Lapidot

I will now reflect on the gap between the first narrative, from-Heidegger-to-Husserl, to the second narrative, from Husserl to Heidegger, by examining one specific historical moment in which the shift from the one narrative to the other became textually visible. This moment is situated at Jerusalem, in the spring of 1938. Daniel Herskowitz's chapter in this volume clearly indicates the significance of Jonas' time in mandatory Palestine of the late 1930s for the development of his intellectual orientation and more specifically for the turn from his earlier period to his later one.

My intervention focuses on one textual variation, albeit a significant one, featuring a shift between two versions of Jonas' obituary to his first teacher Husserl.[5] This variation between two obituaries of the deceased master, reveals Jonas' hesitation between two versions of the past, between two memories of his early years in Germany. More precisely, the two versions of the obituary tell two different, in fact contradicting stories about Jonas' initial interest in Husserl, and accordingly two contradicting accounts of his move from Husserl to Heidegger.

In a nutshell, one version presents Edmund Husserl as the master thinker who saved Hellenic philosophy of worldliness from the threat of Gnostic worldlessness.[6] This version corresponds to the more common narrative, whereby the young Jonas abandoned Husserl because he fell under the unworldly spell of Heidegger and the Gnostics, and then – through the wake-up call of National Socialism – sobered up, repented, and did *teshuva*, namely returned to his old master Husserl. In contrast, the second version – which is the original one – features Husserl as having saved pure, transcendental conscience from all too worldly immanence that is as having redeemed subjectivity from its fall into the objectified world. This second version, which is actually the first version that Jonas wrote, counters the common narrative, since it reports that what drew Jonas to Husserl was exactly the same thing that then drew him further to Heidegger and to ancient Gnosticism – and that there is at least one version of mandatory Jerusalem 1938 in which Jonas remained true to his initial project in German philosophy.

Two Obituaries to Husserl

In comparison to Heidegger's influence on Jonas, Husserl's influence on him has been scarcely discussed in the research literature.[7] As Jonas recounted in his memoirs, Husserl's reputation was his reason for choosing Freiburg as his first place of study.[8] Jonas paid tribute to this reputation in his oral obituary to Husserl, which he delivered in Hebrew in 1938 both at the Hebrew University and in the radio, and which was published in the journal *Turim*. I will refer here as the "original obituary" to the German version of the text, which seems to have served as the basis for the Hebrew obituary, and which is printed in the critical edition of Jonas' writings.[9] In Jonas' original obituary, he portrayed himself as "a student who sat at [Husserl's] feet years ago."[10]

What was Husserl's greatness? To this there are two answers, a double memory – or a split one. I begin with the second answer. It is found in Jonas' essay that was published in 1938 in Hebrew in the journal *Moznayim*. This text was inspired by the original obituary; however, it also deviated in some critical points from the original version, and produced a second narrative, which will become the common, standard one, also for Jonas himself.

In this version, Jonas described Husserl as "a supreme embodiment of Western conscience of reason [...], the last of that series of great figures that begins with Parmenides."[11] Husserl was the incarnation of the original ancient Greek world, which in late antiquity, as Jonas had described in his works on Gnosticism, was shaken by the Gnosis coming from the East. For Jonas, the principle of ancient Greece embodied in Husserl is the correlation between world and knowledge, between being and human reason. This correlation, he argued, is the precondition of the Hellenic mode of knowledge, the "*philosophia perennis* from its Greek foundation,"[12] that is the precondition of "philosophy as a science of the *archai*."[13] This formulation echoes Husserl's own conception of "philosophy as a rigorous science,"[14] which he still understood in 1936 as "the *telos* innate to European humanity with the birth of Greek philosophy."[15] Husserl's teleological, ethical understanding of scienticity continue to resonate in Jonas' description of reason in moral terms as "conscience of reason," *Vernunftsgewissen*. Jonas' obituary for Husserl in 1938, in the *Moznayim* version, thus affirmed Greek knowledge, that is, the knowledge of science and theory, as arising from ethics.

Just like Husserl himself in 1936, also Jonas two years later, in 1938, recognized an intellectual-historical crisis in the tradition of Greek philosophy. In a similar way to Husserl, Jonas too directed his gaze to the dawn of modernity. For Jonas, the modern crisis of philosophy consisted in the "gap" between reason and the world, opened above all by Descartes. The origin of this gap for Jonas, however, is not modernity but late antiquity. In Descartes' ego as *res cogitans* Jonas identified the principle of "the worldless (acosmic) ego," where he diagnosed the "influence of Christianity and its gnostic component," "in which the worldless ego had been discovered for the first time."[16] Gnosis stands here not for unity of knowledge and ethics, but for their falling apart, which in 1952 Jonas will designate as "nihilism."

In his *Moznayim* obituary to Husserl, however, Jonas discerned in modern philosophy, next to the problematic, nihilistic Gnostic heritage, also an antidote, namely the conception of the worldless I as nonetheless possessing knowledge of the world, that is to say as a "subject of knowledge." Modern epistemology thus offers a way to overcome Gnostic dualism: a "recovery of objectivity from the ground of the pure I."[17] Jonas asserted that this anti-Gnostic renaissance of the ancient conscience of reason, this restoration of the epistemic-ethical reunification of being and thinking, was accomplished by Husserl's philosophy. More specifically, Jonas emphasized the basic concept of "intentionality," which Husserl adopted from his own teacher Franz Brentano as pivotal for his own phenomenology. Husserl's characterization of human consciousness as "intentional," that is as consisting essentially in "consciousness of," as representational, ensure the existence of the ego's world, Jonas writes, as "objectivity that arises from subj[ective] performance," *Objektivität aus subj[ektiver] Leistung*.[18]

So far one version – the later, reworked version – of Jonas' obituary to Husserl, as published in *Moznayim*. This version articulated the basic structure of Jonas' later narrative that affirms Greek world-ethics, here represented by Husserl, against Gnostic nihilism, which Jonas will later identify with Heidegger. According to this version, Jonas' obituary to Husserl constitutes a sort of repentance, a sort of *teshuva*, the return to his original master from the misguided betrayal of worldly, ethical philosophy through the turn to unworldly, nihilistic Heidegger.

In the earlier, original version of the obituary of 1938, the version that he delivered orally, as well as in other texts, Jonas is more attuned to the ambivalences of the "subjective objectivity" that he suggested in the reworked version as the modern antidote to nihilism. After all, the difficulties with this notion already animated the thinking of Husserl, who consciously situated his phenomenology, for example in his *Cartesian Meditations*, in the legacy of Descartes. But the fragility of Jonas' intellectual-historical framing of Europe's crisis is already visible in the same reworked, *Moznayim* version of the obituary of 1938. The dissonance appears in a further, more peculiar characterization by Jonas of the excellence of Husserl's thought, to which young Jonas' veneration was, according to this narrative, initially directed, namely the explicitly, more directly ethical dimension of the deceased master's work.

In the original obituary, the one delivered orally, Jonas described Husserlian ethics, or Husserl's "creed," as an ethos of "serious work," *ernste[r] Arbeit*, as representing a "Prussian ascetic work ethic," characterized by "the strictness of the Prussian concept of duty."[19] In the *Moznayim* text, however, Jonas pointed to a deeper, more essential ethical motive in Husserl's philosophy, a "moral, even moralistic drive,"[20] which he no longer identified as Prussian, nor as Greek. In this text, Jonas sees in Husserl "the idea of absolute self-responsibility," which will become central for the author of *Das Prinzip Verantwortung*. As a principle, Husserl's idea of self-responsibility determines the essence of human cognition, which accordingly is no longer determined purely theoretically, no longer as reason for reason's sake, as philosophy, but in moral terms, that is as "self-justification through reason"[21]: "the Greek ideal of intuition becomes in Husserl the *duty* of intuition – for justifying thinking."[22] This "highest idea" of "duty of intuition" (related to "conscience of reason"), Prussia notwithstanding, Jonas considers "not itself philosophical," not Greek, but "an elementary impulse of Judeo-Christian origin."[23]

As noted, Jonas' alternative intellectual-historical narrative as to the ethical problem of knowledge shows itself more clearly in his original obituary for Husserl, the one he delivered orally, and which was published in *Turim*. The original obituary formulates an alternative historiography of the ethical-epistemological crisis of the West that is closer to Husserl's own historiographical ideas. This version situates the origin of the crisis in ancient Greece itself: in "H[usserl's] encounter with the philosophical skepticism, an ancient and symbolic situation in intellectual history repeated itself."[24] In this narrative, Husserl, in his struggle with psychologism, embodied not the struggle of philosophy against Gnosticism, but the constitutive struggle within the philosophical tradition itself: the struggle between knowledge and skepticism, between Socrates and the Sophists.

This struggle, as Jonas interpreted it in Husserl, is not about knowledge as such, it is not about the general relatedness of human consciousness to being and to the world, but about the exact nature of the objects of knowledge, the objects of "intuition," of *Anschauung*. In this context, and here lies the important point, Jonas does not characterize the anti-philosophical position as unworldliness, that is as akin to Gnosticism, but on the contrary, as empiricism, which is to say as the science of the real, positive, sensuous facts of the natural world, as worldliness. Real philosophical knowing and seeing, on the other hand, has a different direction. It is not empirically attached to the world, but "pure": "In his struggle with psychologism, H[usserl] rediscovered the Platonic idea. By rejecting psychology as mere factual science in its place, he showed the fundamental difference between factual science and knowledge of essence, between empirical and pure intuition."[25] Husserl's "pure intuition," *reine Anschauung*, has no facts, no world, as its objects, but essences, categories, ideas; this pure intuition is not natural but "eidetic" (from the Greek *eidos*). The paradigmatic *Ideen*, which were to be the objects of the philosophical science newly founded by Husserl, "phenomenology," do not belong to real being, to the world, but to the intentional, intuiting being itself, namely to consciousness, to subjectivity. "Pure" is the intuition that reflexively looks at itself, at its own act of looking, as self-consciousness.

Here, according to Husserl, lies the crisis of the European sciences. It does not consist in losing sight of the world, but on the contrary in understanding being exclusively as worldly,[26] and in failing to see that the natural world is a "correlate" of consciousness, namely that it is transcendentally constituted as an object only in perception. Accordingly, Husserl's answer to this crisis of science is phenomenology: an eidetic science that "brackets" the real world and turns to pure transcendental consciousness. Husserl's phenomenology turns away from the world to conscience, from the object to the subject.

In the divergence between the two versions of Jonas' obituary to Husserl in 1938, we can observe the gap between Jonas' two narratives. On the one hand, there is the narrative offered in the later, reworked version published in *Moznayim*, in which late antique, Gnostic, or Judeo-Christian, non-Greek thought features as a precursor of modern acosmic nihilism that undermines Greek commitment to the world, a narrative that will become dominant after the war. On the other hand, there is the narrative offered by the original obituary, which criticizes the ethical corruption in modern science as arising from its worldliness and against it, as epistemo-ethical corrective, asserts Judeo-Christian ethics combined with transcendental conscience.

This duality of versions features an exemplary moment in the formation of what I call the double – or split – memory of Jonas with regard to his early years. In the conclusion to this chapter, I will offer a more general reflection on this phenomenon. Before this, I now turn to Jonas' movement from Husserl to Heidegger.

From Husserl to Heidegger

Years later, Jonas will report, in his reminiscences from 1963 and again in 1989, about the critical reflections that led him from Husserl to Heidegger 40 years earlier. In contrast to the obituaries of 1938, which due to their genre and their timing required that Jonas expresses his devotion and commitment to Husserl, the distance of the later memories allowed Jonas to take a more critical perspective. This perspective allows us to understand his early turn from Husserl to Heidegger not as a deviation, but as a continuation of his initial attraction to Husserl's phenomenology, in accordance with the original version of the 1938 obituary.

In his already mentioned lecture "Husserl and Heidegger" from 1963, Jonas diagnosed in Husserl's notion of intentionality, which reunited world and reason, as Jonas had also argued in the *Moznayim* version of the 1938 obituary, also a counter-motive, namely an *alienation* from reality, a certain "naivety." What Jonas found to be detached from reality was Husserl's conception of the human being as a transcendental, purely observing consciousness, namely the notion

> that what is important for the human being is accessible specifically to intuition, *Anschauung*, which means intuition from the distance of the pure, neutral, transcendental consciousness. The premise or belief that the theoretical subject, for whom reality, as Husserl says, is bracketed or withdrawn, that this theoretical subject can stand for the human subject as a whole.[27]

In other words, according to this description, it was not Eastern Gnosticism, but the Hellenic heritage of knowledge as intuition and theory, which was to blame for Husserl's epistemological unworldliness.

In Jonas' later reminiscences, the problem of "naivity" also extends to the Husserlian ethos, that is to Husserl's existential posture as a thinker. In Jonas' memoirs of 1989, the moralizing dimension of Husserl, as a master-subject of knowledge, takes on a disconcerting character. Husserl was "unexciting, rather didactic."[28] "[T]he moral pathos, combined with belief in one's own truth," gave his thinking a "monological nature," "an almost solipsistic trait": "It was the naivety of complete security in one's own conviction, complete ignoring of everything else and complete unworldliness."[29] The intellectual-historical origins of this unworldliness as postulated by Jonas are particularly interesting. He alludes to the insidious political implications of Husserl's attitude to life – "[he] was completely conventional and of a naive, unreflective patriotism or German nationalism." In this context, Jonas traces back Husserl's unworldliness to the "innocence of the philosopher, even in political matters."[30] In other words, the root of Husserl's detachment from worldly reality was his fidelity to the Hellenic tradition of purely theoretical knowledge.[31]

According to older Jonas' memoirs, it was this tendency to philosophical, that is to *Greek* unworldliness in Husserl's philosophy, which made young Jonas turn from Husserl to Heidegger.[32]

"The strongest philosophical influence on my work was Heidegger," Jonas stated in his interview with Ioan Culianu in 1975.[33] In his memoirs, his enduring admiration for Husserl notwithstanding, Jonas acknowledged that Heidegger had a special place in intellectual history: "with respect to the originality of his thought, Heidegger is a powerful figure in intellectual history, a trailblazer who broke new ground."[34] Much has been written about Jonas' complex and multifaceted relationships with Heidegger.[35] In the following, I indicate only a few motifs that are of importance for Jonas' transition from Husserl to Heidegger.

The switch to Heidegger was clearly not politically motivated. Jonas described Heidegger as a man "out of touch with the reality of the twentieth century," who "in his own way again had that solipsistic hard-headedness that characterized Husserl in a much nobler and much more innocent way."[36] Just like Husserl, Heidegger too was "unworldly" and "apolitical," "basically a primitive person in matters of public life and politics."[37]

Rather, Jonas' shift from Husserl to Heidegger was motivated by criticism of Husserl's philosophical tendency to unworldliness and conceptually related to his early interest in late antiquity. In his Leo-Baeck lecture of 1963, Jonas described Heidegger as a counter-figure to the humanistic-Greek tradition, that is to say as a teacher who, quite differently from Husserl, was able to inspire him to a historiographical revolution:

> In Heidegger a challenge arose for the whole humanistic, rational tradition of Western thinking from the Greeks. He was an elementary event, not a continuator and innovator of the tradition like Husserl, but subverting this tradition, reaching into completely different depths than Husserl.[38]

In this narrative, as already noted, Greekness does not stand for epistemological and ethical worldliness, as in the *Moznayim* reworked obituary of 1938, but for unworldliness. In the 1963 lecture, the tradition of philosophy embodied by Husserl conceives of man as "the theoretical subject," as "the transcendental I of pure consciousness," that is, if not *weltlos*, then *weltfremd*. Heidegger, on the other hand, invoked "the mortal human," "the existential *Dasein*," the knowledge of which paradigmatically was not "the cool, objectifying, distant view, but determination, being engaged in situations of decision."[39]

From Eidetics to Hermeneutics

My claim is that exactly this criticism of Husserl as a representative of an objectifying epistemology of the philosophical tradition, in the name of an alternative, Heidegger-inspired existential, ethically engaged conception of knowledge, was Jonas' starting point for his intellectual-historical venture into the Judeo-Christian archives.[40]

This can already be seen in Jonas' earliest drafts for his studies in the history of religion in the 1920s, which are partly included in his dissertation and in *Gnosis und spätantiker Geist II*. Consider for example the fragment "Methodological Introduction," especially its second part, "On Hermeneutics of Religious Phenomena."[41] The text, which reads as a general methodological introduction to Jonas' philosophical investigations into the history of religion, repeatedly refers to Heidegger, whose "existential analysis [...], beyond and through the a priori knowledge of *Dasein* that it directly offers, at the same time made possible – and set the task for – a new type of a posteriori intellectual-historical undertaking."[42] More than *Being and Time*, however, this draft evokes Heidegger's early Freiburg lectures on the *Phenomenology of Religious Life*, above all the lecture on Paul in the winter semester 1920/1921, "Introduction to the Phenomenology of Religion," which is also preceded by a "Methodical Introduction."[43]

Heidegger, who was then Husserl's assistant and was supposed to apply the master's phenomenology to religious phenomena, decided in this lecture to introduce his students into the phenomenology of religion through a fundamental critique of Husserl's phenomenology. His central criticism against the "prejudice of philosophy as science"[44] unmistakably targeted Husserl's "philosophy as rigorous science"[45]: "There is a fundamental difference between science and philosophy."[46] Contrary to the purely theoretical attitude of science, Heidegger related philosophy to "factual life experience,"[47] "factual *Dasein*,"[48] as "the entire active and passive attitude of man to the world."[49] In factual life experience, I do not experience myself as a worldless "ego object," but "suffer in what I achieve, what I encounter, in my states of depression and exaltation," namely as a unity of self and world.[50]

In contrast, Heidegger argued, Husserl's phenomenology is afflicted with a scientific "prejudice" in that it methodologically prescribes for the philosophical relation to the phenomena "a theoretical type of reference," and thereby from the outset "conceals the performative aspect" [das *Vollzugs*mäßige], that is to say the existential event, the practice. Husserl's phenomenology also prejudices against what Heidegger calls the "core phenomenon" of philosophy and religion: "the historical." In this way, Husserl adheres to the "Platonic view" of the entire philosophical tradition, for which history, including his own, was always only a theoretical object and never the actual dimension of human action.[51] In other words, inasmuch as Husserl's transcendental conscience broke with the naturalistic, Hellenic world, it remained theoretical, intuition-based, objectifying, and therefore – still too Greek.

In a very similar way, Jonas' "Methodological Introduction. On the Hermeneutics of Religious Phenomena" speaks about science's "fundamental prejudice" against religion. By this, Jonas did not exactly mean the unworldly theorizing tendency of science, but almost the opposite, namely science's "principle of immanence," that is its worldliness, which excludes the transcendence that is essential to religion. For Jonas, the anti-religious prejudice of science takes on its "most radical form" in Husserl's phenomenology, namely "in the demand for unconditional identification, *Ausweisung*," which requires all its objects to be visible, intuitive – to be "phenomena."[52] This demand is contradicted by the main object of religion, which is perceived "διὰ πίστεως [...], οὐ διὰ εἴδους" (2 Cor. 5:7), that is "not in appearance" but by faith. In other words, as Jonas writes, religious phenomena are human experiences, "internal phenomena" that claim a transcendent, non-worldly origin. They claim to originate in God, be "of God," *von Gott*.[53]

The radical prejudice in Husserl's phenomenology against this claim – and here lies the main point – is not just that it is strictly committed to world immanence like all science, but that as "eidetic" it reduces all immanence to *theoretical*, pure consciousness. This reduction "brackets," by the phenomenological ἐποχή, not only the transcendence of God for the world, but also the transcendence of the world for consciousness. For Husserl's phenomenology, the question of God, the fundamental question of religion, is not answered negatively but is not asked at all, because for phenomenology, the question of the world does not arise either. In order for the world and for God to become a philosophical question, Husserl's "eidetic" phenomenology must transition into Heidegger's "hermeneutic" phenomenology.

Hermeneutic phenomenology does not regard human beings as a transcendental ego, but as "historical movement," as "being-in-the-world," with regard to which philosophy has the task of not only seeing but of *understanding*, as a basis for doing, for practice, for ethics.[54]

Jonas famously deployed the categories of Heidegger's existential analysis of Dasein for his reading in Gnostic texts from the late antiquity. More fundamentally, however, Jonas owes Heidegger the idea that human existence in its concrete, temporal, namely historical worldliness must be grasped, understood, and reinterpreted as arising from a specific conceptual constellation. The understanding of human consciousness, together with the world that it constitutes, not as purely theoretical and transcendental (Husserl), but as practical and historical performative existence (Heidegger), opened for Jonas the quest for ethical practice of philosophy by way of reading late antique texts of the non-Hellenic, Judeo-Christian religious tradition.

Conclusion

A comparative analysis of the two versions of Jonas' obituary to Husserl in 1938 showed that, in contrast to the more common narrative, the original version of the obituary reports that Jonas' original turn to Husserl was motivated not by the quest of worldly, Hellenic ethics against the nihilism of Eastern unworldliness, but on the contrary by the ethical quest of transcendental subjectivity against the worldly objectification of modern science.

A study of Jonas' later reminiscences indicated that the same quest drove Jonas further from Husserl to Heidegger. Criticizing Husserl's subjectivity as still too attached to the Greek forms of objectivity, theory, and intuition, to *eidos*, Jonas turned to Heidegger's existential categories of subjectivity which underlie not the abstract logos of Greek epistemology but the historical text of Judeo-Christian religion. It is this existential subjectivity, this ethical subject of knowledge, which Jonas will look for in the texts of Paul and Augustine, and then in the texts of late antique Gnosticism.

As a concluding reflection, I wish to contemplate briefly the phenomenon of what I called here a "double memory," which I indicated in the specific textual locus of Jonas' obituary to Husserl in 1938. At this textual and historical moment, a profound split emerged in Jonas' self-narration, and two versions of his past intellectual life in Germany appeared. This split, I believe, can be further traced in Jonas' later written autobiographical accounts.

The reason for this memory split is obvious: it arises from the trauma of National Socialism, which brutally ruptured Jonas' life. The retrospective gaze needed to identify a plot – both personal and intellectual – that was hidden from the original experience, which blindly led to its demise, to its failure. Two stories were thus generated: life as it was originally experienced and life as it was retroactively understood. Since the Nazi trauma was a generational one, the phenomenon of a split memory may be therefore suggested as a methodological hermeneutical tool for the study of German-Jewish authors after the Holocaust.

Notes

1 See for instance in Jürgen Nielsen-Sikora, *Hans Jonas. Für Freiheit und Verantwortung*, Darmstadt: WBG, 2017, 9–10: "Den Ausgangspunkt [von Jonas'] Denken bildet…die Kritik der Gnosis…Die Gnostiker waren weltfremd. Hans Jonas deutet diese Weltfremdheit vor der Folie der politischen und gesellschaftlichen Entwicklungen der 1920er und 1930er Jahre. Seine Kritik an der lebensfeindlichen Einstellung der Gnostiker ist nicht zuletzt auch eine Kritik an seinem Lehrer Martin Heidegger…Seine Kritik mündet in einer Philosophie des Lebens, die er als Antwort auf die weltabgewandte Haltung der Gnostiker formuliert."
2 See also Elad Lapidot, "Gnosis und Spätantiker Geist II. Hans Jonas' The Lost Book," in: *Hans Jonas- Handbook*, edited by Michael Bongardt, Holger Burckhart, John-Stewart Gordon und Jürgen Nielsen-Sikora, Stuttgart: J.B. Metzler Verlag, 2021, 88–95.
3 Hans Jonas, "Husserl und Heidegger," in *Herausforderungen und Profile. Jüdischdeutscher Geist in der Zeit – gegen die Zeit*, ed. Sebastian Lalla, Florian Preußger and Dietrich Böhler, KGA III/2, Freiburg i.Br./Berlin/Wien: Rombach Wissenschaft, 2013, 205–224, 205. See also in Dietrich Böhler und Jens Peter Brune (Hg.), *Orientierung und Verantwortung. Begegnungen und Auseinandersetzungen mit Hans Jonas*, Würzburg: Königshausen u. Neumann, 1994, S. 17–34.
4 Jonas, "Husserl und Heidegger," 205.
5 More precisely, two texts that Jonas wrote on the basis of his one single oral obituary.
6 For unworldliness as a guiding theme in early Jonas' thought, see Libera Pisano's chapter in this volume.
7 See Vittorio Hösle, "Hans Jonas 'Position in the History of German Philosophy," in: Hava Tirosh Samuelson & Christian Wiese (eds.), *The Legacy of Hans Jonas. Judaism and the Phenomenon of Life*, Leiden/Boston, MA, Brill, 2010, 19–38, S. 27–31; Udo Lenzig, *Das Wagnis der Freiheit: der Freiheitsbegriff im philosophischen Werk von Hans Jonas aus theologischer Perspektive*, Stuttgart, Kohlhammer, 2006, S. 47–50; Ian Alexander Moore, "Husserl and Heidegger," in: Bongard et al. *Hans Jonas-Handbuch*. See also Daniel M. Herskowitz, "The Husserl-Heidegger Relationship in the Jewish Imagination," *Jewish Quarterly Review* 110.3 (Sommer 2020): 491–522.
8 Hans Jonas, *Erinnerungen*, nach Gesprächen mit Rachel Salamander, Vorwort von Rachel Salamander, Geleitwort von Lore Jonas, Herausgegeben und mit einem Nachwort versehen von Christian Wiese, Frankfurt am Main 2003, 80.
9 Hans Jonas, "Edmund Husserl [Erste Fassung]," *KGA* III.2, 301–310, 301.
10 Hans Jonas, "Edmund Husserl [Erste Fassung]," *KGA* III.2, 301–310, 301.
11 Hans Jonas, "Husserl und die ontologische Frage," *KGA* III.2, 183–196, S. 183. This text, which was published in Hebrew in 1938 (*Moznayim* 7), is based on the radio speech from the same year. The critical edition of Jonas (KGA), contains the original German of the text, which was the basis for the Hebrew version.
12 Jonas, "Husserl und die ontologische Frage," 184.
13 Jonas, "Husserl und die ontologische Frage," 186.
14 Edmund Husserl, *Philosophie als strenge Wissenschaft* (1911), edited by Eduard Marach, Hamburg: Meiner Verlag, 2009.
15 Edmund Husserl, *Die Krisis der europäischen Wissenschaften und die transzendentale Phänomenologie. Eine Einleitung in die phänomenologische Philosophie* (1936), edited by Walter Biemel. Den Haag: Springer, 1976, Husserliana Band VI, 16.
16 Jonas, "Husserl und die ontologische Frage," 187.
17 Jonas, "Husserl und die ontologische Frage," 188.
18 Jonas, "Husserl und die ontologische Frage," 188.
19 Jonas, "Edmund Husserl," 303.
20 Jonas, "Husserl und die ontologische Frage," 193.
21 Jonas, "Husserl und die ontologische Frage," 189.
22 Jonas, "Husserl und die ontologische Frage," 195.

23 Jonas, "Husserl und die ontologische Frage," 189. This provenance raises questions about the relation of the two non-Greek principles, the Christian-Gnostic and the Judeo-Christian, and about their possible convergence in late antiquity. For texts of Hans Jonas concerning the Judeo-Christian, see Hans Jonas, *Herausforderungen und Profile. Jüdisch-deutscher Geist in der Zeit – gegen die Zeit*, ed. Sebastian Lalla, Florian Preußger and Dietrich Böhler, KGA III/2, Freiburg i.Br./Berlin/Wien: Rombach Wissenschaft, 2013, 3–160.
24 Jonas, "Edmund Husserl," 309.
25 Jonas, "Edmund Husserl," 309.
26 Edmund Husserl, *Ideen zu einer reinen Phänomenologie und phänomenologischen Philosophie. Erstes Buch: Allgemeine Einführung in die reine Phänomenologie*, 1. Halbband: Text der 1.-3. Auflage – Nachdruck, ed. Karl Schuhmann, Den Haag: Springer, 1977. Husserliana Band III, §1.
27 Jonas, "Husserl und Heidegger," 215.
28 Jonas, *Erinnerungen*, 82.
29 Jonas, *Erinnerungen*, 215–216.
30 Jonas, *Erinnerungen*, 217.
31 Interestingly, the two sources of Husserl's ethics, which were already rated positively in the obituary, are now mentioned rather negatively, but instead of being Prussian, Husserl is categorized as "a German professor," and the presumed "Judeo-Christian" provenance gives place to Jewish orthodoxy: "Certain traits that gave [Husserl] a kind of orthodoxy, something Jewish in its complete alienation from everything Jewish, were unmistakable. During his time in Goettingen, which preceded his time in Freiburg, his students called him 'the Rabbi from Goettigen'," see Jonas, *Erinnerungen*, 216.
32 Cf. Hösle, "Hans Jonas 'Position in the History of German Philosophy," 27, which contrasts Heidegger's "Dasein" with the "unworldliness of the Husserlian epoch."
33 Ioan Petru Culianu, "Interview with Hans Jonas," 54.
34 Jonas, *Erinnerungen*, 299.
35 See Benjamin Lazier, *God Interrupted. Heresy and the European Imagination Between the World Wars*, Princeton, NJ and Oxford: Princeton University Press, 2008, S. 34–36; Richard Wollin, *Heidegger's Children*, Princeton, NJ: Princeton University Press, 2001, S. 101–133; Eric Jakob, *Martin Heidegger und Hans Jonas. Die Metaphysik der Subjektivität und die Krise der technologischen Zivilisation*. Tübingen/Basel: Francke, 1996; Micha Brumlik, *Die Gnostiker. Der Traum von der Selbsterlösung des Menschen*, Frankfurt am Main: Fischer, 1992, S. 312–369; ders. "Ressentiment – Über einige Motive in Hans Jonas' frühem Gnosisbuch," in: C. Wiese/E. Jacobson (Hg.), *Weiterwohnlichkeit der Welt. Zur Aktualität von Hans Jonas*, Berlin: Philo Verlag, 2003, S. 127–144.
36 Jonas, "Husserl und Heidegger," 224.
37 Jonas, *Erinnerungen*, 85–86. Jonas perceived not only Husserl and Heidegger but his entire intellectual environment of the 1920s as "apolitical" and unworldly: "One cannot imagine how far from the world one could move in Marburg" (124). Referring to his fellow student at the time, Hannah Arendt, Jonas even makes "a comparison to the early Christians" who "turned away from the world or went into the desert in order to flee from the world and find their completion in direct exchange with God" (123). Curiously, to illustrate the particular unhealthy situation surrounding Heidegger, rabbinic figures again come to mind for Jonas: "What developed in Marburg at that time was in any case not a healthy atmosphere, but rather something like the relationship of the faithful to the Lubavitcher, as if Heidegger were a tzaddik, a miracle rabbi, or a guru" (109).
38 Jonas, "Husserl und Heidegger," 218.
39 Jonas, "Husserl und Heidegger," 218–219.
40 Cf. Daniel Herskowitz, *Heidegger and His Jewish Reception* (Cambridge: Cambridge University Press, 2021), 105, making a similar point concerning the similarity between Jonas' characterization of Judaism and of Heideggerian existentialism.

41 HJ 3-11-1. The catalogue of the Jonas-Archiv in Konstanz states: "Masch. Manuskript mit dem Titel 'Methodologische Einleitung. Zur Hermeneutik religiöser Phänomene.' Es handelt sich hierbei vermutlich um die Fassung eines Teils von Jonas' Diss."
42 "Methodologische Einleitung," Teil I, HJ 13-16-1, emphases in the original. In the archives's catalog it is stated: "'Methodologische Einleitung' titled part of an unspecified version of Hans Jonas' dissertation, possibly also a version produced between 1928 and the publication of Gnosis und spätantiker Geist. "Several indications, however, such as the centrality attributed to the "Pauline analysis," suggest that this text belongs rather to the drafts of Jonas' work concerning Paul's Epistle to the Romans (see KGA III.1, S. 23–58, and the editorial remarks, 510–511), possibly originating in the context of the Referat in the Augustine seminar with Heidegger in 1927 that led to Jonas' book on Augustine (see Jonas, Erinnerungen, 238; Culianu, "An Interview with Hans Jonas," 51).
43 Martin Heidegger, *Phänomenologie des Religiösen Lebens*, ed. Matthias Jung und Thomas Regehly, Frankfurt am Main: Vittorio Klostermann, 1995, GA 60, 3–67. Whether Jonas knew this lecture is unknown. He began his Freiburg studies only in the summer semester of 1921 and attended Heidegger's lecture "Augustinus und der Neuplatonismus" (Jonas, *Erinnerungen*, 82; siehe Heidegger, *Phänomenologie des Religiösen Lebens*, 160–299).
44 Heidegger, *Phänomenologie des Religiösen Lebens*, 4.
45 Edmund Husserl, *Philosophie als strenge Wissenschaft*, ed. Eduard Marbach, Hamburg: Meiner Verlag, 2009. Ursprünglich veröffentlichte in der Zeitschrift Logos 1 (1911), 289–341.
46 Heidegger, *Phänomenologie des Religiösen Lebens*, 3.
47 Heidegger, *Phänomenologie des Religiösen Lebens*, 8.
48 Heidegger, *Phänomenologie des Religiösen Lebens*, 54.
49 Heidegger, *Phänomenologie des Religiösen Lebens*, 11.
50 Heidegger, *Phänomenologie des Religiösen Lebens*, 13.
51 Heidegger, *Phänomenologie des Religiösen Lebens*, 46–48.
52 Jonas, "Methodologisch Einleitung. Zur Hermeneutik religiöser Phänomene," 22. Emphases in the original.
53 Jonas, "Methodologisch Einleitung," 23.
54 Jonas, "Methodologisch Einleitung," 25.

Bibliography

Böhler, Dietrich and Jens Peter Brune (eds.), *Orientierung und Verantwortung. Begegnungen und Auseinandersetzungen mit Hans Jonas*, Würzburg: Königshausen und Neumann, 1994.

Brumlik, Micha, *Die Gnostiker. Der Traum von der Selbsterlösung des Menschen*, Frankfurt am Main: Fischer, 1992.

Brumlik, Micha, "Ressentiment – Über einige Motive in Hans Jonas' frühem Gnosisbuch," *Weiterwohnlichkeit der Welt. Zur Aktualität von Hans Jonas*, edited by Christian Wiese and Eric Jacobson, Berlin: Philo Verlag, 2003, 127–144.

Heidegger, Martin, *Phänomenologie des Religiösen Lebens*, GA 60, edited by Matthias Jung und Thomas Regehly, Frankfurt am Main: Vittorio Klostermann, 1995.

Herskowitz, Daniel M., *Heidegger and His Jewish Reception*, Cambridge: Cambridge University Press, 2021.

Herskowitz, Daniel M., "The Husserl-Heidegger Relationship in the Jewish Imagination," *Jewish Quarterly Review* 110.3 (2020): 491–522.

Hösle, Vittorio, "Hans Jonas' Position in the History of German Philosophy," *The Legacy of Hans Jonas. Judaism and the Phenomenon of Life*, edited by Hava Tirosh-Samuelson and Christian Wiese, Leiden/Boston, MA: Brill, 2010, 19–38.

Husserl, Edmund, *Die Krisis der europäischen Wissenschaften und die transzendentale Phänomenologie. Eine Einleitung in die phänomenologische Philosophie*, Husserliana Band VI, edited by Walter Biemel, Den Haag: Springer, [1936] 1976.

Husserl, Edmund, *Ideen zu einer reinen Phänomenologie und phänomenologischen Philosophie. Erstes Buch: Allgemeine Einführung in die reine Phänomenologie*, 1. Halbband: Text der 1.-3. Auflage – Nachdruck, edited by Karl Schuhmann, Den Haag: Springer, 1977.

Husserl, Edmund, *Philosophie als strenge Wissenschaft*, edited by Eduard Marbach, Hamburg: Meiner Verlag, [1911] 2009.

Jakob, Eric, *Martin Heidegger und Hans Jonas. Die Metaphysik der Subjektivität und die Krise der technologischen Zivilisation*, Tübingen/Basel: Francke, 1996.

Jonas, Hans, "Edmund Husserl [Erste Fassung]," *KGA* III.2 (1938): 301–310.

Jonas, Hans, *Erinnerungen*, nach Gesprächen mit Rachel Salamander, Vorwort von Rachel Salamander, Geleitwort von Lore Jonas, Herausgegeben und mit einem Nachwort versehen von Christian Wiese, Frankfurt am Main: Insel Verlag, 2003.

Jonas, Hans, *Herausforderungen und Profile. Jüdisch-deutscher Geist in der Zeit – gegen die Zeit*, edited by Sebastian Lalla, Florian Preußger and Dietrich Böhler, KGA III.2, Freiburg i.Br./Berlin/Wien: Rombach Wissenschaft, 2013.

Jonas, Hans, "Husserl und die ontologische Frage," *KGA* III.2 (1938): 183–196.

Jonas, Hans, "Methodologische Einleitung," Teil I. HJ 13-16-1 (n.d.).

Lapidot, Elad, "Gnosis und Spätantiker Geist II. Hans Jonas' The Lost Book," *Hans Jonas-Handbook*, edited by Michael Bongardt, Holger Burckhart, John-Stewart Gordon and Jürgen Nielsen-Sikora, Stuttgart: J.B. Metzler Verlag, 2021, 88–95.

Lazier, Benjamin, *God Interrupted. Heresy and the European Imagination Between the World Wars*, Princeton, NJ and Oxford: Princeton University Press, 2008.

Lenzig, Udo, *Das Wagnis der Freiheit: der Freiheitsbegriff im philosophischen Werk von Hans Jonas aus theologischer Perspektive*, Stuttgart: Kohlhammer, 2006.

Moore, Ian Alexander, "Husserl and Heidegger," *Hans Jonas- Handbook*, edited by Michael Bongardt, Holger Burckhart, John-Stewart Gordon and Jürgen Nielsen-Sikora, Stuttgart: J.B. Metzler Verlag, 2021, 172–175.

Nielsen-Sikora, Jürgen, *Hans Jonas. Für Freiheit und Verantwortung*, Darmstadt: WBG, 2017.

Wollin, Richard, *Heidegger's Children*, Princeton, NJ: Princeton University Press, 2011.

2 Lessons in Interrogative Thinking
Jonas and Bultmann

Andreas Grossmann

In the memorial speech in honour of Rudolf Bultmann that he held at Marburg University on November 16, 1976, Hans Jonas looks back on more than fifty years of what turned out to be an extraordinary intellectual relationship and friendship between the Jewish philosopher and the Protestant theologian. Bultmann's seminar, which Jonas attended shortly after having moved from Freiburg to Marburg in 1924, was, as Jonas states, an "unforgettable school of interrogative thinking." Jonas experienced this kind of teaching as an expression of "Protestant freedom."[1]

The question of freedom itself also marks a crucial issue in Jonas' and Bultmann's thinking. The two scholars' "interrogative thinking" leads us back to early discussions on Augustine and Paul and the relationship between the respective understanding of freedom and humanity in ancient Greece and Christianity. Whereas Jonas and Bultmann are quite close to each other – I shall come back to this point shortly – Jonas' aforementioned memorial speech does not avoid points of difference with respect, in particular, to Bultmann's famous programme of "demythologizing" – a concept that Bultmann could find in the first appendix of Jonas' early study on *Augustin und das paulinische Freiheitsproblem* (1930); incidentally, it is worth mentioning that this book, like Jonas' investigations on *Gnosis und spätantiker Geist* (1934), could not have been published without Bultmann's decisive support.[2] The ways of thinking are indeed intertwined and call for a re-consideration.

In Jonas' correspondence with Bultmann, the issue of myth and demythologizing finds a remarkable echo in their debate about Jonas' lecture at Harvard on "Immortality and the Modern Temper" in 1961, where Jonas for the first time introduces his own myth of God, a notion that in later years became known as the "Concept of God after Auschwitz." The question is whether there is any connection between the issue of freedom in the early discussions on Augustine and Paul and Jonas' later occupation with the problem of myth – and Bultmann's role in these fields of "interrogative thinking." I shall refer here only to some aspects that seem to me crucial with respect to Jonas' intellectual relationship to Bultmann.[3]

Freedom and Its Failure

The idea of freedom is central to Christianity and Christian theology – "For freedom Christ has set us free," states Paul in his Epistle to the Galatians (Gal. 5:

DOI: 10.4324/9781003439882-2

13), and Martin Luther's treatise "De libertate Christiana" (1520) belongs to the founding documents of Protestant theology. In his early thinking about freedom, Hans Jonas does not refer to the tradition of Protestant theology, but he does refer to Paul and Augustine. According to Jonas, it was in Christianity, that is, the interpretation of Dasein found in the Jewish-Christian tradition that freedom was for the first time in history considered as a problem. Whereas in the late Stoa (Epicurus et al.), freedom was understood as man's independence and self-sufficiency, for Christianity exactly this "solution" becomes problematic as soon as man is seen as situated "before God" (*coram deo*).

Before elaborating this significant difference between Stoic and Christian thought in his investigation on *Augustin und das paulinische Freiheitsproblem*, Jonas examines the problem of freedom in ancient Greek thought and Augustine in Heidegger's Schelling seminar in January 1928. And in his seminar presentation, he already refers to the seventh chapter of Paul's Epistle to the Romans (Rom. 7: 7–25) as the *locus classicus* in the tradition of Christian thought. It is precisely there that Jonas finds the "most original account of the problem" of freedom in Christianity (*die ursprünglichste Darstellung des Problems im Christentum*).[4]

In his "epistolary monstrum," that is, his letter to Rudolf Bultmann of July 13, 1929, Jonas refers to Bultmann's article on the significance of the historical Jesus for Paul's theology ("Die Bedeutung des geschichtlichen Jesus für die Theologie des Paulus"), published in 1929.[5] Jonas declares that Bultmann's understanding of Paul, as elaborated in this text, speaks from the bottom of his heart, and that he could not conceive of anything more profound regarding the issue of freedom.[6] What Jonas himself tries to do in response to Bultmann is to *philosophically* explore why freedom, as articulated by the will, contains in itself the tendency to failure; in other words, to what extent the failure and "abyss" of freedom is ontologically rooted in the structure of Dasein.

Jonas' contribution many years later to the *Festschrift* for Bultmann on the occasion of his 80th birthday in 1964 was in a way a revised version of what he outlined in this letter to Bultmann. Moreover, Jonas integrated his philosophical meditations and reflexions on Paul into the second edition of his early study on *Augustin und das paulinische Freiheitsproblem* (edited by James M. Robinson in 1965).[7] The text indeed has a remarkable and intricate history.

But what precisely is the problem with freedom? The basic mode of Dasein, Jonas argues, is the will. Dasein cares about itself, that is, about its being (to put it in Heideggerian terms). Insofar as Dasein is concerned with itself, it exists in self-reflection – it is a "self" only in this original self-reflective relation to itself. "All phenomena of ethical life," Jonas declares, such as freedom, responsibility, conscience, and guilt, "are rooted in this original reflective relationship: and this is freedom."[8] But at the same time, the sphere of the will is also the sphere of bondage (*Unfreiheit*). And this, according to Jonas, is not by accident, but *necessary*. Why? Since the "reflexion of the will" (*Reflexion des Willens*) finds its counterpart "equiprimordially" (*gleichursprünglich*, as Jonas says, again using a Heideggerian concept familiar from *Sein und Zeit*) in what he calls self-objectivation (Selbstobjektivation). In this move – which is a move from willing to the consciousness of willing – a kind of self-alienation of freedom takes place.[9] Instead of acting, freedom becomes in a certain way its own observer or spectator, judging and questioning what it is doing and what its motives are.[10] This possibility belongs to freedom, and it is indeed a necessary relation to itself: the "deepest mystery of freedom," Jonas says, "concerns the relation of possibility and necessity in terms of freedom."[11]

What is going on in the self-objectivation of the will, that is, the move from *velle* to *cogito me velle*, is mediated by the law: the law or commandment brings freedom to its own by referring it to its "ought to" (*Sollen*), but simultaneously, it is this law or commandment that leads to man's distress (*Not*).[12] In other words, the law brings morality to its explicit form. When freedom is released to itself, however, this simultaneously has the consequence that freedom becomes entangled in itself. Freedom that has come to itself in the reflection of the will sees itself, as Jonas explains, exposed to the "tempting possibility of self-objectification."[13] Freedom "enjoys" itself,[14] as it were, "boasts" of its possibilities (the Paulinian καύχησις and καυχᾶσθαι; cf. Rom 3:27; 1 Cor 4:7): in this "superbia," as Jonas had already said at the end of his presentation in Heidegger's seminar, the will to be turns "into the objectifying will to have itself."[15] Thus, in realizing itself, freedom is or becomes ambiguous. Confronted with its autonomous possibilities, freedom finds itself in a state of dizziness or vertigo (*Schwindel*).[16] But the German word *Schwindel* can also mean fraud. Jonas uses the metaphor of "*Schwindel der Freiheit*" with obvious Kierkegaardian (and Schellingian?) overtones.[17] This "*Schwindel der Freiheit*" that seems to oscillate between dizziness and fraud marks for Jonas what in biblical language is considered to be "sin." For in self-objectivation, man is confronted with his conscience, the misery of spirit and morality,[18] and for the *homo religiosus* the situation before God is transformed into the situation before myself: one tries to look at oneself with God's eyes (and necessarily fails), and instead of the impeccability of God's view, the extreme mistrust of my own human view dominates the scene.[19] Thus, self-objectivation fosters freedom's self-alienation (Jonas speaks of *Entfremdung* [alienation] and *Enteignung* [dispossession]).[20] Seen this way, freedom indeed becomes problematic, for there is no way out of the "distress" that freedom gets itself into because of its own dialectic – unless it is the way of grace. In Jonas' elaboration of this problematic, there is no account of a move into the realm of grace (which would be the task of a theological exegesis). He leaves the message of grace, so to speak, to his teacher Bultmann.

The difference between ancient Greek thought and Christianity comes to the fore several times in Bultmann's writings. The crucial point in the relation between Greek antiquity and Christianity is for him, as well as for Jonas, the understanding of freedom. Thus, Bultmann contrasts the concept of freedom in the late Stoa, especially in Epictetus – freedom understood as inner independence – to the understanding of freedom in Paul. The decisive difference marked by Bultmann is that for Paul, the essence of man is recognized as historical (*geschichtlich*). Freedom comes to be understood as a possibility that is not in man's power. Freedom, in other words, is a historical *event* that becomes actual in making a decision for what Christ has offered – in faith. Freedom, therefore, is not to be grasped as man's inner quality, but as a gift given to man by God's grace. And as with freedom, so too with grace: "Grace is indisposable [*unverfügbar*, not subject to man's disposal, transcendent] and can only be received anew in faith in looking up to it in faith" (*Gnade ist unverfügbar und kann nur immer neu empfangen werden im glaubenden Aufblick zu ihr*).[21] The Christian freedom *from* the world, however, is at the same time to be understood as responsibility *for* the world.[22] In his essay on "The Concept of God and Modern Man" (1963) ("Der Gottesgedanke und der moderne Mensch"), Bultmann will explain this thought explicitly with reference to Luther's dialectic of Christian freedom, famously stated in his treatise "De libertate Christiana."[23] These are obviously thoughts that transcend Jonas' approach. They demonstrate the difference between the two scholars notwithstanding their shared conviction of the difference between ancient Greek and Christian thinking on freedom. While Jonas, in the later myth of God that he conceived himself, will admittedly even speak of man being responsible for the fate of the Godhead, for Bultmann, responsibility is only rightly understood and comprehended as responsibility *before* God (*coram deo*), but not as responsibility *for* God. In this sense, Bultmann repeatedly emphasized that "real freedom" only exists as freedom given by God, in the "encounter with the grace of God."[24] Freedom is thus "a freedom that is only ever achieved such that it becomes an event in responsibility and decision," as Bultmann maintains in his essay "Die Bedeutung des Gedankens der Freiheit für die abendländische Kultur" ("The Significance of the Idea of Freedom for Western Culture").[25] In the early 1925 essay "Welchen Sinn hat es, von Gott zu reden?" ("What is the sense of speaking of God?"), which will also occupy us as an important reference text in the next section, there is already talk of "concern and responsibility," so to speak, as existentials.[26] And in a sermon in Marburg on July 2, 1933, Bultmann took the opportunity to insist that in conscience, everyone stands in "solitude before God," and that in this solitude he has to assume "responsibility … for the right and wrong of his actions" – a responsibility that cannot be delegated, not even to what was called "national community" (*Volksgemeinschaft*, a common National Socialist ideological concept at the time[27])! Thus, out of the loneliness into which conscience calls, "the sense and the power of responsibility and the view for the claim of the other" grows.[28]

For Bultmann, the understanding of human freedom roughly outlined here is essentially connected to his understanding of human existence as such. And it is precisely in this context that Bultmann uses a concept that is characteristic of his understanding of theology (and, consequently, his self-understanding as a Christian theologian); this concept will also play a crucial role in his dispute with Jonas on myth and demythologization. I mean the concept (or, rather, the field of concepts) "objectivation," "objectifiable," and "non-objectifiable."

In his approach, Bultmann obviously follows decisive motifs of his teacher Wilhelm Herrmann (1846–1922) at Marburg University who maintained, following basic insights of Lutheran theology, that what is at stake in theology is (or, rather, should be) man's *experience* of God – and not philosophical speculation about God. As Martin Luther in his critical attitude towards scholastic theology proclaimed, "sola autem experientia facit theologum."[29] Bultmann picks up the

Lutheran heritage to which Herrmann once appealed with respect to Cohen's understanding of religion (which, in Herrmann's view, is conceptually graspable by scientific means),[30] and brings it to bear in the discussion with Jonas on objectivation, myth, and demythologization.[31] "But precisely because I studied with Herrmann," Bultmann explains, "I was prepared for Heidegger."[32] This dictum can be taken to refer to the Lutheran heritage adopted by Herrmann, which Bultmann in turn was to associate with the early Heidegger. This should not be underestimated as an element of the early Marburg "constellations" shaped by Heidegger and Bultmann, to which Jonas can also be counted (although in his Marburg period, he referred to Augustine and Paul, but not to Luther).[33] For the young Heidegger, however, it was Luther who avowedly became the "companion" in the exploration of a "hermeneutics of facticity,"[34] that is, the attempt to "explicate factual existence in terms of its origins, that is, to explicate it philosophically"[35] – and thus also, to a certain extent, a companion in the method of a hermeneutic-phenomenological "destruction" of tradition, which Jonas, for his part, followed in his Augustine studies in the transition from Augustine to Paul.[36]

Myth and Demythologization

Bultmann's concern with objectifying thought goes back to his famous essay of 1925, "What is the sense of speaking of God?" ("Welchen Sinn hat es, von Gott zu reden?").[37] It is actually a life-long concern that can be found in various texts of his, among others in the essay on *Wissenschaft und Existenz*, which first appeared in the *Festschrift* dedicated to Albert Schweitzer in 1955.[38] In a certain sense, objectifying thinking, according to Bultmann, is something like the "primal sin" in understanding human existence as well as God. For objectifying thinking tries to locate its "object" – be it human existence or God – within an order without taking into account that neither one's own existence nor God can be conceived adequately from the standpoint of a mere spectator. For God is no mere idea or thought. God is present in his call, in his word, which qualifies my reality in a new way. And the same is true of my existence. Insofar as it is what it is only in personal relations – in relation to other humans, but also in relation to God – my existence cannot be objectified. Nothing else is at stake when Bultmann speaks of one's existence as historical (*geschichtlich*). "Existence," he writes in his essay on *Wissenschaft and Existenz*, "is always a particular event in the decisions of the moment. It is not something that is present to hand, but always something that happens in the particular here and now (*Existenz ist jeweils Ereignis in den Entscheidungen des Augenblicks. Sie ist nichts Vorhandenes, sondern je und je Geschehendes*)."[39]

Therefore, one cannot adequately speak "about" (*über*), but only "from within" (*aus*) existence – just as one can adequately speak of God not by speaking "from outside" (*von außen*), but only from the perspective of one who is a participant of an encounter. Hence, to speak about God in an objectifying manner neglects the fact that "God encounters me only in his Word inasmuch as it affects my existence (*Ich kann nicht objektivierend über Gott reden, der mir nur je in seinem mich in meiner Existenz treffenden Wort begegnet*)."[40] And since this encounter is indisposable (*unverfügbar*) and not susceptible to my grasp, faith never permits man to claim anything like security: there is "certitudo" (*Gewißheit*), but no "securitas" (*Sicherheit*).[41] This is Bultmann's way to maintain God's eschatological presence. God is and remains the coming God who as such is ultimately never graspable in any concepts whatsoever.

For this reason, Bultmann differentiates several times in his early essay "Welchen Sinn hat es, von Gott zu reden?" between the perspectives "from inside" (*von innen*) and "from outside" (*von außen*). Objectifying thinking "on" or "about" instead of "from" God is inadequate since it neglects in what sense God affects my existence in and by his Word. God becomes an object within the rational order of a "whole." And then God is no longer experienced as the Other of faith, but rather seen without relation to the concrete situation of Dasein. Faith, for its part, has become a mere *Weltanschauung*.[42] And since mythical speech, according to Bultmann, is objectifying speech inasmuch as it treats something that is transcendent as immanent, demythologization is necessary.[43]

What Bultmann calls "existential interpretation" is just another expression for this programme, which has been often (mis)understood as if it was Bultmann's intention to eliminate myth. Demythologization means in fact the hermeneutical endeavour to interpret mythical speech for the sake of its *truth*.[44] "Demythologization is intended to assert the actual intention of myth," as Bultmann declares, "and that is to speak of the actual reality of man (*Die Entmythologisierung will ... die eigentliche Intention des Mythos zur Geltung bringen, nämlich die Intention, von der eigentlichen Wirklichkeit des Menschen zu reden*)."[45]

This has to be kept in mind when looking at the dispute between Bultmann and Jonas on myth and demythologization as it came up in Jonas' lecture at Harvard in 1961 on "Immortality and the Modern Temper." And it should also be called to mind that it was the young Jonas who directed his teacher's attention to this concept in the first appendix of his study on *Augustin und das paulinische Freiheitsproblem*,[46] though, to be sure, he did not invent the term.[47] This appendix deals with the hermeneutic structure of dogma. And what Jonas claims is that contrary to the objectification, rationalization, and abstraction of dogmatic speech, a "demythologized consciousness," as he calls it, is able to approach the "original phenomena" which are otherwise concealed and covered by dogmatic speech.[48]

When Jonas sent the manuscript of his lecture at Harvard to Bultmann, he was well aware that his attempt to come to grips with the actual reality of the universe by means of a self-conceived myth of God would contradict Bultmann's endeavours regarding myth and demythologization. To return to mythological or symbolic speech, Jonas had to admit that "it is a dangerous measure, this refuge to myth, and a matter of necessity, and one should not insouciantly make a virtue of it, but one must also be prepared to venture this one single time, in order not to have to remain completely mute."[49] Bultmann articulated his "doubting questions" regarding Jonas' re-mythologization in a long letter to Jonas dated July 31, 1962.[50]

On the one hand, Bultmann marks his agreement with Jonas with respect to man's responsibility to God: insofar as in the realm of immanence, transcendence remains a constant possibility and insofar as man has to be regarded as a free being, man is responsible to the transcendent authority.[51] Bultmann's "doubting questions," however, arise where Jonas defines this responsibility not only as a responsibility *to* God, but as one *for* God and his fate. Jonas' self-conceived myth tries in Bultmann's eyes to solve the problem of theodicy. But does this attempt, which is ultimately metaphysical, bring any comfort to those who suffer or have lost members of their families?[52] Does not Jonas view the world, the universe simply from the standpoint of a spectator – from outside, as it were?[53] According to the coordinates of Bultmann's thoughts it could be said: what Jonas offers is an objectifying world-view, a theoretical construct, a *Weltanschauung* that does not take into account the question of the meaning of being in the sense of *my* being (as Bultmann claims in Heideggerian terms).[54]

In his answer to Bultmann's objections, Jonas concedes that his myth indeed speaks of the human being in an objectifying manner, and that he tries to look at the "whole" from outside. However, Jonas claims that this attempt is due to the freedom of spirit (it is reminiscent of the ideas of pure reason which reason, according to Kant, cannot grasp, but which nonetheless impose themselves – "sich aufdrängen" – on it). Self-understanding, for Jonas, can therefore only be adequately understood within the horizon of an understanding of the whole, and this explicitly means: "from outside."[55] The "non-trinitarian myth of incarnation," as Jonas characterizes his myth, is in this sense intended to solve the riddle of being and to account for the ethical imperative as something that is founded ontologically.[56]

Bultmann and Jonas could not come to an agreement on these issues. Towards the end of his lecture on "Heidegger and Theology," held at Drew University in 1964 and repeated at Marburg University and several other German universities in the same year, Jonas once more comes back to the problem of objectivation and objectifying speech.[57] He claims that theology has to accept the "burden" of objective thinking, and he concedes that there are "degrees of objectivation" (*Grade der Objektivierung*).[58] But contrary to Bultmann, Jonas denies that Bultmann's existential interpretation (and demythologization) can be adequate where the question of God or the Divine is at stake. Existential concepts that Bultmann borrowed from Heidegger may elucidate Dasein, that is, the human being "sub lege," but not the human being "sub gratia," Jonas claims, referring once more to Augustine and Paul.[59] And he suggests again that with respect to the Divine and its "mystery," the speech of myth and symbols might be more adequate than the concepts of thinking.[60]

In response, it could be argued from a Bultmannian perspective that with his claim, Jonas neglects the basic conviction of Bultmann's understanding of theology, namely, as Bultmann articulated it since his essay "Welchen Sinn hat es, von Gott zu reden?," that one can speak of God only insofar as one speaks of man's understanding and faithful Dasein. As Bultmann declares in his *Theologische Enzyklopädie*: "it is not possible to understand what God is without understanding what faith is, and vice versa. Theology, therefore, is the science of God, insofar as it is the science of faith, and vice versa."[61] Theologians such as Karl Barth claimed that Bultmann reduced theology to anthropology.[62] It seems that Jonas' critique of Bultmann (which is, after all, a *theological* critique!) comes close to this position. Is this due to his anti-Heideggerian furore in this lecture?

Lessons in Interrogative Thinking: Jonas and Bultmann 21

In his memorial speech in honour of Bultmann, Jonas for the last time touches upon the crucial issues of myth and demythologization.[63] These issues were causes of disagreement and dispute – and remained so even after Bultmann's death. Yet despite all criticisms that Jonas felt compelled to raise, he demonstrated a deep sense of the integrity of his former teacher and friend. In all its complexity and with all its tensions, the dialogue between the Jewish philosopher and the Protestant theologian is a remarkable contribution to the intellectual history of the 20th century and in itself testimony of a unique "interrogative thinking" which cannot be adequately understood without considering its origins in the early Marburg constellations around Heidegger and Bultmann.[64]

Notes

1 Rudolf Bultmann/Hans Jonas, *Briefwechsel 1928–1976. Mit einem Anhang anderer Zeugnisse*, ed. Andreas Grossmann (Tübingen: Mohr Siebeck 2020), 123–143; 124.
2 Cf. my introductory remarks to the edition of the correspondence between Bultmann and Jonas, op. cit., XI–XXV; XIX–XX. See also Konrad Hammann, *Bultmann und seine Zeit. Biographische und theologische Konstellationen* (Tübingen: Mohr Siebeck 2016), 77–106.
3 For further perspectives of Jonas' reading of Augustine, see the contributions of Michael Bongardt and Yael Almog in this volume. A close reading of the role of Augustine in Jonas' thinking can be found in Udo Lenzig, *Das Wagnis der Freiheit. Der Freiheitsbegriff im philosophischen Werk von Hans Jonas aus theologischer Perspektive* (Stuttgart: Kohlhammer 2006).
4 Hans Jonas, *Das Freiheitsproblem bei Augustin* (Protokoll der Seminarsitzung vom January 21, 1928), University Library Tübingen (Nachlass Rudolf Bultmann, Mn 2/3357), 5–6. – The entire "Protokollheft" (minutes) of Heidegger's seminar on Schelling was made accessible in print by Lore Hühn and Jörg Jantzen (eds.), *Heideggers Schelling-Seminar (1927/28)* (Schellingiana, vol. 22) (Stuttgart-Bad Cannstatt: frommann-holzboog 2010), 331ff. For Jonas' seminar presentation (dated January 21, 1928), see pp. 373–402.
5 Rudolf Bultmann, "Die Bedeutung des geschichtlichen Jesus für die Theologie des Paulus," in *Bultmann: Glauben und Verstehen*, vol. 1 (Tübingen: Mohr Siebeck 1961), 188–213.
6 Rudolf Bultmann/Hans Jonas, *Briefwechsel*, 2.
7 Hans Jonas, *Augustin und das paulinische Freiheitsproblem. Eine philosophische Studie zum pelagianischen Streit*, second and revised edition, with an introduction by James M. Robinson (Göttingen: Vandenhoeck & Ruprecht 1965), 93–105. References in the present text are to this version.
8 Jonas, *Augustin und das paulinische Freiheitsproblem*, 96.
9 Jonas, *Augustin und das paulinische Freiheitsproblem*, 97.
10 Jonas, *Augustin und das paulinische Freiheitsproblem*, 99.
11 Jonas, *Augustin und das paulinische Freiheitsproblem*, 100.
12 Jonas, *Augustin und das paulinische Freiheitsproblem*, 102–103.
13 Jonas, *Augustin und das paulinische Freiheitsproblem*, 102. The reader of Heidegger will remember that he characterizes everyday existence as "tempting." See Martin Heidegger, *Sein und Zeit*, 16th ed. (Tübingen: Max Niemeyer Verlag 1986), 177: "das Dasein bereitet ihm selbst die ständige Versuchung zum Verfallen. Das In-der-Welt-sein ist an ihm selbst *versucherisch*." ("existence itself prepares for itself the constant temptation to decay. Being-in-the-world is in itself tempting").
14 Heidegger, *Sein und Zeit*, 100.

15 Jonas, *Das Freiheitsproblem bei Augustin*, 24; Hühn and Jantzen, eds., *Heideggers Schelling-Seminar (1927/28)*, 402. Cf. Jonas, *Augustin und das paulinische Freiheitsproblem*, 79.
16 Jonas, *Augustin und das paulinische Freiheitsproblem*, 100–101.
17 Kierkegaard's reflections on fear as the "vertigo of freedom" obviously owe much to his encounter with Schelling's *Treatise on Human Freedom*. Cf. Sören Kierkegaard, *Der Begriff Angst* (Collected Works, eds. Emanuel Hirsch and Hayo Gerdes, 2nd ed. (Gütersloh: Gütersloher Verlagshaus Mohn 1986), 60f.: "Fear can be compared to vertigo. He whose eye has to look down into a yawning depth becomes dizzy. But what is the cause? it is as much his eye as the abyss […]. In this way, fear is the dizziness of freedom that rises when the spirit wants to synthesize, and freedom now looks down into its own possibility, and then finitude grabs hold of it. In this vertigo freedom sinks down." An echo of this "vertigo of freedom" is also encountered in Heidegger's analysis of the "decay" of Dasein in *Being and Time*. Heidegger does not speak of "vertigo," but of "groundlessness" and the "mode of a groundless floating" that characterizes Dasein in its "inauthentic ordinariness." The "motility of decay" peculiar to Dasein can thus also be described by Heidegger as a "crash" and a "vortex." See Heidegger, *Sein und Zeit*, 177f. In a footnote to the following section 40 on the basic condition of anxiety, Heidegger explicitly refers to Kierkegaard's discussions in "The Concept of Anxiety" in addition to Augustine and Luther; Heidegger, *Sein und Zeit*, 190.
18 Jonas, *Augustin und das paulinische Freiheitsproblem*, 103. Jonas speaks of "distress" as "distress not of superficiality but of depth, not of the letter but of the spirit, not of legitimacy but of morality," because this distress in the relation of freedom to its own possibilities is, as he says, itself "a peculiar kind of necessity, namely of the necessary act of freedom" (Jonas, *Augustin und das paulinische Freiheitsproblem*, 100). It is thus the dialectic of freedom itself that leads it into this "distress" – as the "vertigo of freedom."
19 Jonas, *Augustin und das paulinische Freiheitsproblem*, 99–100.
20 A designation that again recalls Heidegger's characterization of the decay of Dasein in *Being and Time*. See Heidegger, *Sein und Zeit*, 178: "Die versuchend beruhigende Entfremdung des Verfallens führt in ihrer eigenen Bewegtheit dazu, daß sich das Dasein in ihm selbst *verfängt*." ("The tentative-reassuring alienation of decay leads, in its own agitation, to Dasein becoming entangled in itself.")
21 Rudolf Bultmann, *Freiheit nach antikem und christlichem Verständnis* (1959), in Bultmann, *Glauben und Verstehen*, vol. 4 (Tübingen: Mohr Siebeck 1975), 42–51; 49.
22 Bultmann, *Freiheit nach antikem und christlichem Verständnis*, 50.
23 Rudolf Bultmann, *Der Gottesgedanke und der moderne Mensch*, in Bultmann, *Glauben und Verstehen*, vol. 4, 113–127; 116.
24 Rudolf Bultmann, *Gnade und Freiheit* (1948), in *Bultmann: Glauben und Verstehen*, vol. 2 (Tübingen: Mohr Siebeck 1961), 149–161; 160f.
25 Rudolf Bultmann, *Die Bedeutung des Gedankens der Freiheit für die abendländische Kultur*, in Bultmann, *Glauben und Verstehen*, vol. 2 (Tübingen: Mohr Siebeck, 1961), 274–293; 282.
26 Rudolf Bultmann, *Welchen Sinn hat es, von Gott zu reden?* (1925), in Bultmann, *Glauben und Verstehen*, vol. 1 (Tübingen: Mohr Siebeck, 1961), 26–37; 33.
27 On this topic cf. Frank Bajohr and Michael Wildt (eds.), *Volksgemeinschaft: Neue Forschungen zur Gesellschaft des Nationalsozialismus* (Frankfurt am Main: S. Fischer 2012); Ian Kershaw, "Volksgemeinschaft. Potenzial und Grenzen eines neuen Forschungskonzepts," in *Vierteljahrshefte für Zeitgeschichte* 59.1 (2011), 1–17; Michael Wildt, "'Volksgemeinschaft.' Eine Antwort auf Ian Kershaw," in *Zeithistorische Forschungen/ Studies in Contemporary History* 8 (2011), 102–109.
28 Rudolf Bultmann, *Das verkündigte Wort. Predigten – Andachten – Ansprachen 1906– 1941*, edited, selected, and with an introduction by Erich Gräßer in collaboration with Martin Evang (Tübingen: Mohr Siebeck 1984), 257 and 259.

29 Martin Luther, WA TR 1, 16, 13 (Nr. 46). Luther therefore characterizes theology itself as a "scientia practica" (in opposition to a "scientia speculativa"). Cf. on this point, Gerhard Ebeling, *Luther. Einführung in sein Denken* (Tübingen: Mohr Siebeck, 1983), 59–81 ("Schrift und Erfahrung als Quelle als Quelle theologischer Aussagen").

30 See Wilhelm Herrmann, *Der Begriff der Religion nach Hermann Cohen*, in Helmut Holzhey (ed.), *Hermann Cohen* (Frankfurt am Main: Peter Lang Verlag 1994), 61–66; 65: "Aber die Gotteserkenntnis, die uns diese Befreiung verschaffen soll, stammt nicht aus der Logik und Ethik. Sie ist keine Schöpfung des Denkens, die sich als rein vor der kritischen Frage der Vernunft ausweisen könnte oder müßte. Sie ist nicht allgemeingültige oder beweisbare Erkenntnis, sondern der wehrlose Ausdruck des individuellen Erlebens." […] „Unser *Luther* hat zuerst in dem Bewußtsein der Wehrlosigkeit der religiösen Erkenntnis die Quelle ihrer befreienden Kraft und ihre Selbständigkeit neben Wissenschaft und Moral entdeckt. […] Ihr Grund ist niemals eine in Begriffen faßbare allgemeingültige Erkenntnis, sondern die Anschauung eines Erlebens, das kein anderer kennt als der Fromme selbst." – In English: "But the knowledge of God that is supposed to provide us with this liberation is not derived from logic and ethics. It is not a creature of thought that could or should prove itself to be pure before the critical questioning of reason. It is not a universally valid or provable knowledge, but rather the defenceless expression of individual experience." […] "Our *Luther* first discovered the source of the liberating power of religious knowledge and its independence alongside science and morality in the awareness of its defencelessness. […] Its ground is never a universally valid knowledge that can be grasped in concepts, but the intuitive-perceptual character of an experience that no one else knows but the pious person himself."

31 Bultmann's discussion with Luther's theology is scrutinized in Ulrich H. J. Körtner et al. (eds.), *Bultmann und Luther. Lutherrezeption in Exegese und Hermeneutik Rudolf Bultmanns* (Hannover: VELKD 2010). For an exploration of Jonas' notion of objectivation in his Gnosis studies, see the essay by Daniel M. Herskowitz, "From *Gnosis und spätantiker Geist* to *The Gnostic Religion*: The Jerusalem Period in Hans Jonas's Intellectual Development," in the present volume.

32 Karl Barth/Rudolf Bultmann, *Briefwechsel 1911–1966*, 2nd revised and extended edition, ed. Bernd Jaspert (Zürich: Theologischer Verlag Zürich 1994), 186. In the same context Bultmann notably adds that Heidegger had also "learned from Herrmann" and held him in "high esteem."

33 On this point cf. Andreas Grossmann and Malte Dominik Krüger (eds.), *Hans Jonas und die Marburger Hermeneutik* (Frankfurt am Main: Vittorio Klostermann Verlag 2023). The concept of intellectual "constellations" is associated with the work of Dieter Henrich, who has suggested that the Marburg affiliations around Heidegger and Bultmann and their students should also be seen and researched as a "constellation" (and decidedly not as a self-contained "school"). For him, Heidegger and Bultmann are the decisive "revolutionaries" in thought, from whose work common problem lines can be drawn in quite different directions – even in contradiction to the teachers. In this respect, Hans Jonas belongs to the "Marburg constellation," even though he goes his own way in relation to Heidegger and Bultmann. Cf. Dieter Henrich, "Was ist verlässlich im Leben?," in Matthias Bormuth and Ulrich von Bülow (eds.), *Marburger Hermeneutik zwischen Tradition und Krise* (Göttingen: Wallstein Verlag 2008), 13–64; 32; Grossmann and Krüger, "Hans Jonas und die Marburger Hermeneutik. Konstellationen, Probleme, Themen," in idem, *Hans Jonas und die Marburger Hermeneutik*, 9–21.

34 Martin Heidegger, *Ontologie (Hermeneutik der Faktizität), Gesamtausgabe* vol. 63, ed. Käte Bröcker-Oltmanns (Frankfurt am Main: Vittorio Klostermann Verlag 1988), 5: "The young Luther was my companion in searching, and Aristotle, whom he hated, was my role model. Kierkegaard gave me impulses, and Husserl implanted my eyes."

35 Martin Heidegger, *Phänomenologie des religiösen Lebens. Gesamtausgabe* vol. 60, ed. Matthias Jung, Thomas Regehly and Claudius Strube (Frankfurt am Main: Vittorio

24 Andreas Grossmann

Klostermann Verlag 1995), 54. For the broader context, see the chapter on Heidegger and Luther in my *Heidegger-Lektüren*. Andreas Grossmann, *Heidegger-Lektüren. Über Kunst, Religion und Politik* (Würzburg: Königshausen & Neumann 2005), 11–26.

36 Cf. Ian A. Moore, *Jonas's Augustine-Book: An Early Application of Hermeneutic-Phenomenological Destruktion*, in Grossmann and Krüger (eds.), *Hans Jonas und die Marburger Hermeneutik*, 131–154. On Jonas's reading of Paul cf. Christof Landmesser, Jonas' Paulus-Lektüre, Grossmann and Krüger (eds.), *Hans Jonas und die Marburger Hermeneutik*, 111–129.

37 Bultmann, *Glauben und Verstehen*, vol. 1, 26–37.

38 Rudolf Bultmann, *Glauben und Verstehen*, vol. 3 (Tübingen: Mohr Siebeck 1965), 107–121.

39 Bultmann, *Glauben und Verstehen*, 117. These classifications by Bultmann are tacitly associated with concepts that were developed in the existential analysis of *Being and Time* in order to distinguish the specificity of Dasein as being-in-the-world from what is present-at-hand (*vorhanden*) and ready-to hand (*zuhanden*). In a nutshell, "Dasein exists." See Heidegger, *Sein und Zeit*, 53.

40 Heidegger, *Sein und Zeit*, 120.

41 Heidegger, *Sein und Zeit*, 121.

42 Cf. Rudolf Bultmann, *Theologische Enzyklopädie*, ed. Eberhard Jüngel and Klaus W. Müller (Tübingen: Mohr Siebeck 1984), 195.

43 Bultmann's prominent description of the programme of "demythologizing" is found in his notorious 1941 lecture on "New Testament and Mythology." See Rudolf Bultmann, *Neues Testament und Mythologie. Das Problem der Entmythologisierung der neutestamentlichen Verkündigung*, reprint of the 1941 version, ed. Eberhard Jüngel (München: Kaiser 1988). On the controversies initiated by Bultmann's lecture, cf. the concise account in Konrad Hammann, *Rudolf Bultmann. Eine Biographie* (Tübingen: Mohr Siebeck 2009), 421–432.

44 Cf. Eberhard Jüngel, „Die Wahrheit des Mythos und die Notwendigkeit der Entmythologisierung," in Jüngel, *Indikative der Gnade – Imperative der Freiheit* (Tübingen: Mohr Siebeck 2000), 40–57.

45 Rudolf Bultmann, „Zum Problem der Entmythologisierung," in Bultmann, *Glauben und Verstehen*, vol. 4 (Tübingen: Mohr Siebeck 1975), 128–137; 134.

46 Jonas, *Augustin und das paulinische Freiheitsproblem*, 80–89. In a footnote in "Neues Testament und Mythologie," Bultmann remarks on the "important discussion of the hermeneutic structure of doctrine in *Hans Jonas*." See Bultmann, "Neues Testament und Mythologie," 25.

47 With regard to the coining of the neologism "demythologization," Konrad Hammann refers to Siegfried Kracauer, Julius Holtzmann, and Hermann Strathmann. Cf. Hammann, *Rudolf Bultmann und seine Zeit*, 86. Theodor Wiesengrund (Adorno) was probably aware of Jonas' work when he spoke of demythologization in 1931 as a "dialectic" process: the myth, he remarked, cannot "be simply eliminated," it comes up "again and again." See Paul Tillich, *Briefwechsel und Streitschriften. Theologische, philosophische und politische Stellungnahmen und Gespräche*, ed. Renate Albrecht and René Tautmann (Frankfurt am Main: Evangelisches Verlagswerk 1983), 314–369; 324. Jonas' influence on Bultmann, in particular, his programme of demythologization, is discussed in Luca Settimo's contribution to this volume.

48 Tillich, *Briefwechsel und Streitschriften*, 82. Cf. on Jonas' notion of objectification in his works on Augustine and Gnosis, the contribution by Elad Lapidot in this volume: "Gnosis und spätantiker Geist. Teil II: The Forgotten Book."

49 Rudolf Bultmann/Hans Jonas, *Briefwechsel*, 52.

50 Bultmann/Jonas, *Briefwechsel*, 57 (letter to Jonas from May 23, 1962); 57–62.

51 Bultmann/Jonas, *Briefwechsel*, 59.

52 Bultmann/Jonas, *Briefwechsel*, 60.

53 Bultmann/Jonas, *Briefwechsel*, 61.
54 Bultmann/Jonas, *Briefwechsel*, 61.
55 Bultmann/Jonas, *Briefwechsel*, 67.
56 Bultmann/Jonas, *Briefwechsel*.
57 For a detailed and, as far as the history of the reception of this lecture is concerned, highly informative study, see Daniel M. Herskowitz, "Hans Jonas's 'Heidegger and Theology' as Text and Event," in Grossmann and Krüger (eds.), *Hans Jonas und die Marburger Hermeneutik* (Frankfurt am Main: Vittorio Klostermann 2023), 83–109.
58 Hans Jonas, "Heidegger und die Theologie," in Gerhard Noller (ed.), *Heidegger und die Theologie* (München: Chr. Kaiser Verlag 1967), 316–340; 338.
59 Jonas, "Heidegger und die Theologie," 339.
60 Jonas, "Heidegger und die Theologie," 340.
61 Bultmann, *Theologische Enzyklopädie*, 34.
62 Based on this objection by Barth, I have discussed Bultmann's understanding of a "hermeneutic theology" and his determination of the relationship between theology and philosophy in the context of his dialogue with Heidegger. See Andreas Grossmann, "Was sich nicht von selbst versteht. Heidegger, Bultmann und die Frage einer hermeneutischen Theologie," in Ingolf U. Dalferth et al. (eds.), *Hermeneutische Theologie – heute?* (Hermeneutische Untersuchungen zur Theologie 60) (Tübingen: Mohr Siebeck 2013), 55–81.
63 Rudolf Bultmann/Hans Jonas, *Briefwechsel*, 123–143; 126ff.
64 I wish to thank Daniel Herskowitz and Elad Lapidot for their critical remarks on a previous version of this contribution and Donald Goodwin for his help in bringing the English text of a non-native speaker to a proper linguistic form.

Bibliography

Bajohr, Frank/Wildt, Michael (eds.), *Volksgemeinschaft: Neue Forschungen zur Gesellschaft des Nationalsozialismus*. Frankfurt am Main: S. Fischer, 2012.

Barth, Karl/Bultmann, Rudolf, *Briefwechsel 1911–1966*. 2nd revised and extended edition, ed. Bernd Jaspert. Zürich: Theologischer Verlag Zürich, 1994.

Bultmann, Rudolf, Das verkündigte Wort. Predigten – Andachten – Ansprachen 1906–1941, ed. Erich Gräßer in collaboration with Martin Evang. Tübingen: Mohr Siebeck, 1984.

Bultmann, Rudolf, Der Gottesgedanke und der moderne Mensch, in: Bultmann: *Glauben und Verstehen*, vol. 4. Tübingen: Mohr Siebeck, 1975, 113–127.

Bultmann, Rudolf, Die Bedeutung des geschichtlichen Jesus für die Theologie des Paulus, in: Bultmann: *Glauben und Verstehen*, vol. 1. Tübingen: Mohr Siebeck, 1961, 188–213.

Bultmann, Rudolf, Die Bedeutung des Gedankens der Freiheit für die abendländische Kultur, in: Bultmann: *Glauben und Verstehen*, vol. 2. Tübingen: Mohr Siebeck, 1961, 274–293.

Bultmann, Rudolf, Freiheit nach antikem und christlichem Verständnis (1959), in: Bultmann: *Glauben und Verstehen*, vol. 4. Tübingen: Mohr Siebeck, 1975, 42–51.

Bultmann, Rudolf, Gnade und Freiheit (1948), in: Bultmann: *Glauben und Verstehen*, vol. 2. Tübingen: Mohr Siebeck, 1961, 149–161.

Bultmann, Rudolf, *Neues Testament und Mythologie. Das Problem der Entmythologisierung der neutestamentlichen Verkündigung*. Reprint of the 1941 version, ed. Eberhard Jüngel. München: Kaiser, 1988.

Bultmann, Rudolf, *Theologische Enzyklopädie*, ed. Eberhard Jüngel and Klaus W. Müller. Tübingen: Mohr Siebeck, 1984.

Bultmann, Rudolf, Welchen Sinn hat es, von Gott zu reden? (1925), in: Bultmann: *Glauben und Verstehen*, vol. 1. Tübingen: Mohr Siebeck, 1961, 26–37.

Bultmann, Rudolf, Wissenschaft und Existenz, in: Bultmann: *Glauben und Verstehen*, vol. 3. Tübingen: Mohr Siebeck, 1965, 107–121.
Bultmann, Rudolf, Zum Problem der Entmythologisierung, in: Bultmann: *Glauben und Verstehen*, vol. 4. Tübingen: Mohr Siebeck, 1975, 128–137.
Bultmann, Rudolf/Jonas, Hans, *Briefwechsel 1928–1976. Mit einem Anhang anderer Zeugnisse*, ed. Andreas Grossmann. Tübingen: Mohr Siebeck, 2020.
Ebeling, Gerhard, *Luther. Einführung in sein Denken*. Tübingen: Mohr Siebeck, 1983.
Grossmann, Andreas, *Heidegger-Lektüren. Über Kunst, Religion und Politik*. Würzburg: Königshausen & Neumann, 2005.
Grossmann, Andreas, Was sich nicht von selbst versteht. Heidegger, Bultmann und die Frage einer hermeneutischen Theologie, in: Ingolf U. Dalferth et al. (eds.), *Hermeneutische Theologie – heute?* (Hermeneutische Untersuchungen zur Theologie 60). Tübingen: Mohr Siebeck, 2013, 55–81.
Grossmann, Andreas/Krüger, Malte Dominik (eds.), *Hans Jonas und die Marburger Hermeneutik*. Frankfurt am Main: Vittorio Klostermann, 2023.
Grossmann, Andreas/Krüger, Malte Dominik, Hans Jonas und die Marburger Hermeneutik. Konstellationen, Probleme, Themen, in: Andreas Grossmann/ Malte Dominik Krüger (eds.), *Hans Jonas und die Marburger Hermeneutik*. Frankfurt am Main: Vittorio Klostermann, 2023, 9–21.
Hammann, Konrad, Bultmann, Rudolf, *Eine Biographie*. Tübingen: Mohr Siebeck, 2009.
Hammann, Konrad, *Bultmann und seine Zeit. Biographische und theologische Konstellationen*. Tübingen: Mohr Siebeck, 2016.
Heidegger, Martin, *Ontologie (Hermeneutik der Faktizität)*. Gesamtausgabe vol. 63, ed. Käte Bröcker-Oltmanns. Frankfurt am Main: Vittorio Klostermann, 1988.
Heidegger, Martin, *Phänomenologie des religiösen Lebens*. Gesamtausgabe vol. 60, ed. Matthias Jung, Thomas Regehly and Claudius Strube. Frankfurt am Main: Vittorio Klostermann, 1995.
Heidegger, Martin, *Sein und Zeit*, 16th ed. Tübingen: Max Niemeyer, 1986.
Henrich, Dieter, "Was ist verlässlich im Leben?," in: Matthias Bormuth and Ulrich von Bülow (eds.), *Marburger Hermeneutik zwischen Tradition und Krise*. Göttingen: Wallstein Verlag, 2008, 13–64.
Herrmann, Wilhelm, Der Begriff der Religion nach Hermann Cohen, in: Helmut Holzhey (ed.), *Hermann Cohen*. Frankfurt am Main: Peter Lang, 1994, 61–66.
Herskowitz, Daniel M., Hans Jonas's 'Heidegger and Theology' as Text and Event, in: Andreas Grossmann and Malte Dominik Krüger (eds.), *Hans Jonas und die Marburger Hermeneutik*. Frankfurt am Main: Vittorio Klostermann, 2023, 83–109.
Hühn, Lore/Jantzen, Jörg (eds.), *Heideggers Schelling-Seminar (1927/28)* (Schellingiana, vol. 22). Stuttgart-Bad Cannstatt: Frommann-Holzboog, 2010.
Jonas, Hans, *Augustin und das paulinische Freiheitsproblem. Eine philosophische Studie zum pelagianischen Streit*. Second and revised edition, with an introduction by James M. Robinson. Göttingen: Vandenhoeck & Ruprecht, 1965.
Jonas, Hans, „Heidegger und die Theologie," in: Gerhard Noller (ed.), *Heidegger und die Theologie*. München: Chr. Kaiser 1967, 316–340.
Jüngel, Eberhard, Die Wahrheit des Mythos und die Notwendigkeit der Entmythologisierung, in: *Jüngel: Indikative der Gnade – Imperative der Freiheit*. Tübingen: Mohr Siebeck, 2000, 40–57.
Kershaw, Ian, Volksgemeinschaft. Potenzial und Grenzen eines neuen Forschungskonzepts, in: *Vierteljahrshefte für Zeitgeschichte* 59.1 (2011), 1–17.

Kierkegaard, Sören, *Der Begriff Angst* (Gesammelte Werke, ed. Emanuel Hirsch and Hayo Gerdes, 11. und 12. Abteilung). Gütersloh: Gütersloher Verlagshaus Mohn, 1986.

Körtner, Ulrich H. J. et al. (eds.), *Bultmann und Luther. Lutherrezeption in Exegese und Hermeneutik Rudolf Bultmanns*. Hannover: VELKD, 2010.

Landmesser, Christof, Jonas' Paulus-Lektüre, in: Andreas Grossmann and Malte Dominik Krüger (eds.), *Hans Jonas und die Marburger Hermeneutik* Frankfurt am Main: Vittorio Klostermann, 2023, 111–129.

Lenzig, Udo, *Das Wagnis der Freiheit. Der Freiheitsbegriff im philosophischen Werk von Hans Jonas aus theologischer Perspektive*. Stuttgart: Kohlhammer, 2006.

Luther, Martin, *Weimarer Ausgabe. Tischreden*. Vol. 1 (WA TR 1). Weimar: Hermann Böhlaus Nachfolger, 1912.

Moore, Ian A., Jonas's Augustine-Book: An Early Application of Hermeneutic-Phenomenological Destruktion, in: Andreas Grossmann and Malte Dominik Krüger (eds.), *Hans Jonas und die Marburger Hermeneutik*. Frankfurt am Main: Vittorio Klostermann, 2023, 131–154.

Tillich, Paul, *Briefwechsel und Streitschriften. Theologische, philosophische und politische Stellungnahmen und Gespräche*, eds. Renate Albrecht and René Tautmann. Frankfurt am Main: Evangelisches Verlagswerk, 1983.

Wildt, Michael, "Volksgemeinschaft". Eine Antwort auf Ian Kershaw, in: *Zeithistorische Forschungen/Studies in Contemporary History* 8 (2011), 102–109.

3 Hans Jonas' Contributions to Rudolf Bultmann's Demythologization

Luca Settimo

At the beginning of his career, Jonas produced some reflections on the notion of myth in religious discourse (including some writings on the origin and development of Gnostic myths),[1] and he reflected on the hermeneutics of dogma, drawing an important correlation between myth and objectivation.[2] He also sent a letter to Bultmann (dated July 13, 1929) containing some of his important thoughts on these issues; the text of this letter has been published in its entirety in 2020[3]; notably, only part of this letter was published by Jonas from the 1960s.[4] I will demonstrate that both the 1929 letter to Bultmann[5] and the reflections on the hermeneutics of dogma firstly published in 1930[6] had a significant impact on Bultmann's development of demythologization. Finally, I will also explore those thinkers – especially Wilhelm Dilthey (1833–1911) and Count Paul Yorck von Wartenburg (1835–1897) whose reflections Jonas learnt through the teachings of Heidegger – who most likely influenced him in his philosophical-theological perspectives on these issues during the 1920s and 1930s.

This chapter consists of five sections. I will first (i) provide a short description of the notion of demythologization; then (ii) I will present three scholars who have significantly engaged with Jonas' writings and recognized the key role that these played for Bultmann's own project of demythologization. I will then (iii) analyse the significance of Jonas' letter to Bultmann in 1929 and (iv) the key role played by the text on the hermeneutics of dogma (published in the appendix of Jonas' 1930s book) on St Augustine and the notion of freedom. Finally (v), I will explore how Jonas himself may have been influenced in his understanding of objectivation and the consequent need to deobjectify or demythologize.[7]

It is important to mention here the fact that Jonas was a philosopher (not a theologian); he in fact obtained his doctoral degree in philosophy at the University of Marburg in 1928 under the main supervision of Heidegger. Nevertheless, as we shall see in this chapter, at the end of the 1920s, Jonas also engaged significantly with the work of Bultmann and produced important philosophical-theological reflections on the notion of myth in religious discourse and the need to demythologize in order to better understand religious texts. In particular, we will analyse Jonas' philosophical-theological reflections on a Pauline text (Rom. 7) and on the dogma of original sin.

A Short Summary of the Notion of Demythologization

The notion of demythologization derives from the expression 'demythologizing' which is the literal translation of *Entmythologisierung*; this translation was firstly adopted by Schubert W. Ogden's (1928–2019) when he published in English the text of an important seminar of Bultmann discussing this topic.[8]

Demythologization is a hermeneutical procedure that seeks to examine and understand the existential meaning of a religious discourse (i.e. one relating to a biblical text or a dogmatic statement of the Church) that has been handed down using mythical-symbolic language. We shall in fact see that religious texts contain mythical-symbolic structures that convey truths to the faithful: some examples are the mythical story of Adam and Eve in the Garden of Eden, the Fall (cf. Gen. 2–3) and the resulting dogmatic interpretation of the doctrine of original sin. Demythologization aims to understand the true intentions of the author of the original religious text. It tries to separate factual claims (e.g. historical facts) from philosophical-theological or ethical teachings within a religious text and attempts to uncover the existential core found within the message conveyed by original religious texts – such as biblical texts or dogmatic formulations of the Church – given that these texts were initially inspired and motivated by an existential message that was essential for understanding and engaging with the Christian faith.[9]

In particular, demythologization also aims to preserve the difference between God and the world, since when we refer to a religious truth by means of mythological/symbolic language, there is a risk of losing the distinction between immanence and transcendence.[10] In other words, by referring to the divine through myths or symbols, there is a danger of describing the divine solely in immanent terms, thus demythologization helps to maintain and preserve divine transcendence in religious discourse. For this reason, "[m]yth objectifies the transcendent into the immanent."[11] This objectivation (also known as mythologization or mythization), which accompanies the presence of a mythical/symbolic language in religious writings, risks obscuring the true meaning that the original author of these texts wished to convey. In order to rediscover and reconnect with the original meaning conveyed by the mythologized/mythized/objectified text, it is therefore necessary to carry out demythologization or deobjectification. Thus, demythologization is an approach developed under the umbrella of existentialist philosophy, through which the original/existential message of a religious text expressed in mythical terms can be better understood.

Having briefly presented the notion of demythologization, I shall introduce three scholars who have actively engaged with Jonas' writings and recognize the critical significance that these played in Bultmann's own demythologizing endeavour.

Three Scholars Who Recognized the Importance of Jonas' Influence on Bultmann's Demythologization

Three English-speaking scholars – namely James M. Robinson (1924–2016), Roger A. Johnson (1930–2015), and David W. Congdon – have studied in detail how Bultmann came upon the notion of demythologization, and argued that Jonas' reflections had a key influence on Bultmann's contributions on this topic, especially in the development of his approach of demythologization applied to the hermeneutical study of the New Testament.[12] It is important therefore to summarize how these scholars have described the influence of Jonas on the development of Bultmann's demythologization.

Firstly, Robinson translated a key quotation from Jonas' reflections on the Gnostic myth (first published in 1934, but most likely written during the 1920s)[13] and claimed the importance of this for Bultmann's demythologization. In particular, Jonas writes:

[i]n the metaphysical emanation and deprivation schema we find gnostic myth in depersonalized (*entpersonalisiert*), logicized form, i.e., in a sense indeed demythed (*entmythisiert*), and yet, because of its nature as hypostasized, still mythical. We will run across these mythological, philosophical mediating forms in the metaphysics of Origen and Plotinus. But we first turn to an anthropological, ethical sphere of concepts, in which we would not in principle expect such mythographic analogies, and in which we too are primarily concerned with something else: to show how the assumed existential basic principle, the 'gnostic' principle, if it really is capable of separation from the mythological world of symbol and of treatment as a more general *arche*, is here in a quite distinctive way drawn back out of the outward mythical objectification and transposed into inner concepts of *Dasein* and into ethical practice, i.e., it appears as it were 'resubjectivized' – just as on the other hand also in this sphere the mythical element is not really overcome. Rather even in 'immanence' (i.e., even without mythological transcendence) the concepts of *Dasein*, with regard to their ontological structure, remain in a very broad sense 'mythical'—because of their pervasive origin in a basic objectification.[14]

It is very likely that this text in which Jonas uses the notions of myth, objectivation, and demythologization (which he also understood as deobjectivation) inspired Bultmann's research on these topics. For this reason, Robinson is not afraid to affirm that the notion of demythologization in Bultmann "was supplied already by Hans Jonas."[15]

Moreover, Robinson recognizes the importance of the following passage from Jonas' appendix on the hermeneutics of dogma for the birth of demythologization (as Bultmann would later understand it):

[there is] an inescapable fundamental structure of the spirit [*Geist*] as such. The fact that it [the spirit] interprets itself in objective formulae and symbols, that it is 'symbolistic,' is of the very essence of the spirit [*Geist*] – and the most dangerous thing about the spirit as well. In order to come to itself, it by its very nature enters in upon this detour via the symbol, in whose enticing jungle of problems it tends to lose itself, far from the origin preserved symbolically therein and taking absolutely what is only a substitute. Only by means of a long process of back-tracking, after an exhaustive traversal of that detour, is a demythologized (*entmythologisiert*) consciousness able to approach the original phenomena hidden in this camouflage also in a conceptually direct way (cf. the long road of the dogma of original sin up to Kierkegaard !).[16]

A few years after the publication of this translated text, also Johnson decided to translate the same (aforementioned) quotation in his book on the origins of demythologization,[17] noting also that the "hermeneutical possibility, of a conceptually direct recovery of the original existential phenomenon given initially in the objectivation of dogma, is a possibility that is ours because of the particular moment in the history of *Geist* in which we stand."[18] According to Johnson, for Jonas and Bultmann "[o]bjectivation, [is] the false interpretation of *Dasein* as thing, ... not an historically limited phenomenon – which is not yet a possibility for mythical *Dasein* – but an eternal possibility to which mythical and modern *Dasein* both fall victim."[19] Thus, for both Jonas and Bultmann, religious texts are rich in mythical/ symbolic structures also known as objectivations; therefore, there is the need to demythologize (or deobjectify) in order to reveal the existential 'core' within the message conveyed by the original text (i.e. a biblical text), which, in the first instance, inspired and motivated the writing of the sacred author.

In particular, Johnson notes a change in the interpretation of objectivation in Bultmann's writings after 1925, following the influence of Jonas:

> [a]fter 1925, 'objectifying' designates for Bultmann, not only an epistemological category, but also a false form of self-understanding or sin ... '[O]bjectifying' becomes [for Bultmann] a decisive category for the interpretation of mythology only after Hans Jonas adds a hermeneutical dimension to this concept.[20]

In particular, Johnson observes that during the years 1925 through to 1934, Bultmann developed an existentialist formulation of myth as a result of Jonas' studies on Gnosticism.[21] Johnson summarizes well the importance of Jonas' contribution during the 1930s and early 1940s for Bultmann's theology and his project of demythologization but also the fact that this influence has often been ignored in Bultmann's scholarship. He writes:

> [h]ad it not been for the political situation in Germany after 1934, there is no doubt that Jonas' contribution to the hermeneutical discussion should have been recognized much earlier. Because he was a Jewish emigré, Jonas' work was not given significant attention during the later thirties and early forties when the existentialist myth hermeneutic was disseminated and appropriated by a variety of thinkers. The one exception was Bultmann, who both dared and cared to continue to refer to Jonas' writings during this period of time. Bultmann consistently acknowledged his own debt to Jonas, both for

his understanding of Gnosticism and for his myth hermeneutic, and in his programmatic essay of 1941 cited the work of Jonas as a paradigm for his own project of demythologizing. Beyond the writings of Bultmann, however, the work of Jonas fell out of sight, and one can look in vain for references to his contribution in the literature relevant to the period or subject. This historical oversight is unfortunate, not only because it leaves clouded the historical origins of the existentialist hermeneutic, but also because it has made the substantive discussion of that hermeneutic go much more difficult. For the philosophical presuppositions of objectivation which are present in Jonas' writings tend to fall out of sight in Bultmann. They are still operative in Bultmann's thought, but not available for scrutiny. As a result, the neglect of Jonas' thought in the discussion of demythologizing has contributed significantly to the enigma of demythologizing.[22]

Additionally, Congdon emphasizes Jonas' influence on Bultmann during the 1920s, explaining the key role of Jonas' studies on Gnosticism in Bultmann's reflections on the Gospel of John already in 1927.[23] In particular, following Jonas' study of Gnostic myths, "Bultmann [already in 1927] sketches 'the newest approach to the Gospel of John,' which he calls 'mythological-historical' (*mythologiegeschichtliche*). Here he sets forth a programme for the existentialist interpretation of myth as the basis for understanding John."[24] Bultmann knew how Jonas interpreted the notion of freedom in his studies on St Augustine's theology during the dispute with Pelagianism (originally presented by Jonas in Heidegger's seminar in 1928).[25] Jonas' reflections on this topic were finally published, thanks to Bultmann's support in a book in 1930.[26] This influence continued also into the 1930s when Jonas' reflections on the topic of Gnosticism (*Gnosis und spätantiker Geist*) were published (thanks again to the help of Bultmann).[27] In particular, the reflections of Jonas on this topic were important for Bultmann given that they constituted "an exemplary model of the kind of existentialist interpretation he advocates for New Testament exegesis."[28] Congdon is also attentive in noting the gratitude expressed by Bultmann to Jonas in relation to his research in a quotation; Bultmann in fact wrote:

> I [Rudolf Bultmann, the author of this text] therefore would like to say that I, who have devoted for many years a large part of my work to the study of Gnosticism, have not learned as much from previous studies in this field – and we know they are quite excellent – regarding a real knowledge of the *geistesgeschichtliche* phenomenon of Gnosticism as I have from this one [Jonas's *Gnosis Und Spätantiker Geist* (1934)]; indeed, here the meaning of this phenomenon was first opened for me in its full scope. While this work stands entirely in continuity with that research, it nevertheless still appears to me that here for the first time the classification of Gnosticism within the history of late antiquity has been truly accomplished, and thus it is clear what Gnosticism means in the turn of world-understanding from antiquity to the Christianity of the West. Hence the question of the relation of Christianity and Gnosticism appears in a new light, since it does not remain limited to

individual phenomena of the New Testament and ancient Church history, but rather affects Christianity's entire understanding of the world and salvation. The method of the author [Jonas], which involves grasping the genuine meaning of a historical phenomenon through the principle of existentialist analysis [*Existenz-analyse*], appears to me to have brilliantly proved its fruitfulness here, and I am certain that this work will fructify *geistesgeschichtliche* research in many respects, not the least of which will even be the interpretation of the New Testament.[29]

Finally, Congdon also identifies another key quotation of Bultmann which shows the importance of Jonas' contributions for his research: "what I [Bultmann] have written in my commentaries on the Gospel of John and the epistles of John I could not have written without the instruction of your works and the exchange with you [Jonas]."[30]

Having presented the contributions of three scholars who significantly engaged with, and recognized the importance of Jonas' writings in relation to the important influence these played in Bultmann's development of demythologization, it should be noted that this influence is still neglected by modern scholars when discussing Bultmann's demythologization.[31] Thus, it is important to rediscover and reengage with Jonas' texts that have played such an important role for the development of Bultmann's demythologization. In this chapter, I focus on two texts: (i) Jonas' letter (dated July 13, 1929) to Bultmann[32] and (ii) Jonas' reflections on the hermeneutics of dogma originally published as an appendix in his 1930s book.[33] We will see that both writings relate to the issue of objectivation in religious texts; in the first, Jonas describes the objectivation of the will in the existential condition of Paul in Rom. 7; in the second, he focuses on the issue of objectivation in relation to the dogma of original sin (which, as we shall see, for him is closely linked to his interpretation of Rom. 7).[34]

The Key Role Played by Jonas' Letter to Bultmann in 1929

Jonas' 1929 letter is important because in this text, Jonas analyses phenomenologically the existential condition of Paul and the conflicted experience of Pauline will in Rom. 7 (where Paul faces the issue of obedience to and compliance of divine law).[35] In this letter, Jonas refers to the notion of objectivation, which, as we have seen in the section "A Short Summary of the Notion of Demythologization" (above), is closely related to the concept of mythologization and mythization. Thus, it is likely that Jonas' use of objectivation implicitly advocates for the theological need to demythologize Rom. 7.

On reading the beginning of Jonas' 1929 letter, it is evident that Bultmann previously sent Jonas an article that he had published that same year.[36] As the translation of the title of Bultmann's 1929 article suggests – "The significance of the historical Jesus for Paul's theology"[37] – Bultmann was still reflecting theologically on the paradigm of the historical Jesus who had been the old focus of liberal theology. According to the approach used by liberal theologians up until the 1920s, it was relevant and necessary to perform research on the historical Jesus in order to properly interpret the New Testament. However, in the aforementioned article (published in 1929), Bultmann shows that a study of the historical Jesus was not significant in the characterization of Paul's theology.[38] This is in agreement with the observation that after the 1920s, Bultmann is critical towards the use of the historical Jesus approach in the interpretation of the New Testament.[39] It is important to analyse carefully Jonas' response to Bultmann's article since this could help to understand the influence of Jonas' reflections on Bultmann's theological project after 1929.

Firstly, the fact that Bultmann sent his article on Paul's theology to Jonas implies that Bultmann sought and valued Jonas' opinion on this topic. We should not forget that Jonas, as already mentioned, was a philosopher (rather than a theologian). However, despite this fact, a biblical scholar and theologian such as Bultmann decided to bring to Jonas' attention his article on the significance of the historical Jesus in relation to Pauline theology; there is no doubt that Bultmann did this with the clear objective to obtain Jonas' reflections on this topic. We know that at that time Jonas was preparing his book on Augustine (which he published in the subsequent year as a part of a book series edited by Bultmann) and in it, Jonas included a section on the interpretation of Rom. 7.[40] We also know that in January 1928 (nearly a year and a half before his letter) Jonas presented his reflections on Rom. 7 in a seminar on Schelling organized by Heidegger,[41] and Bultmann was interested in what Jonas said on that occasion.[42]

It is interesting to read Jonas' response to Bultmann in July 1929 after the latter sent him his article on Paul:

> I read ... [the article entitled "The significance of the historical Jesus for Paul's theology"] with particular interest and felt that Paul's conception spoke so deeply from my heart that I couldn't really think of anything more striking on this subject.[43]

Jonas then explains that for this reason he wants to provide a reflection on the phenomenology of the existential condition of Paul in Rom. 7. In particular, Jonas paid attention to the dialectical structure of the movement of the will of Paul in this biblical text. Jonas explains that he wants to attempt a "structural analysis of the act itself [implied in the biblical story within Rom. 7], in which the human original sin is realized, and its demonstration as something dialectical in itself."[44]

However, in his reflections on Rom. 7, Jonas also explains that Paul experiences an objectivation of the will. In particular, for Jonas, the Fall (which he implicitly views as the myth of Adam and Eve eating from the tree of knowledge and thus disobeying God's commandment), represents the moment after which humanity experiences objectivation as the result of the "split which makes it possible for him [St Paul in Rom. 7/Adam in the garden of Eden/any human being facing the demands of the divine law] who can say 'I' to know about himself, and thereby generates freedom and its inescapable snare at the same time."[45]

In Jonas' view, the authentic reflection of the will is characterized by a dialectical relationship between *volo me velle* (or 'I will that I will') and *cogito me velle* (or 'I think that I will'). However, in the existential condition and experience of 'the Fall' (including the Pauline plight in Rom. 7) – which is characterized by human inadequacy when faced with the demands of divine law – the former type of will ("I will that I will") can 'switch' undialectically into the latter ("I think that I will"), and this 'undialectical switch' results in the objectivation of the will. Consequently:

> across this cleavage [the separation between man's ego and the rest of the objectified universe surrounding man] the ego confronts not only that objectified universe but also itself as one of whom it can say 'I' – and must say it because, with the isolation once happened (this 'once' is the imaginary past of the Fall), it thereafter must hold its own in this apartness for better or for worse. Thus, along with the objectivation of world, there is already inevitably given the possible, viewing objectivation of self (which is essentially distinct from the 'reflection of the will' [described above]).[46]

Thus, for Jonas, Paul in Rom. experiences an objectivation of the will when suffering his existential plight as a result of his inadequacy when facing the demands of the divine law.[47] Jonas thinks that there is a correlation between the existential condition of Paul in Rom. 7 and the story of Adam in the Garden of Eden facing the temptation to eat the forbidden fruit (Cf. Gen. 3.1–6).[48]

In 1932 (three years after Jonas' letter), Bultmann published his reflections on Rom. 7 as a chapter in a book on theological anthropology.[49] This text was translated into English by Schubert M. Ogden in 1961.[50] In particular, in this text, Bultmann comments on Rom. 7 and recognizes that some passages within this biblical text display an atypical Pauline attitude towards the understanding of divine law:

> I hold it to be completely impossible that in Rom. 7:14 ff. this basic idea [of Pauline understanding of the law from his Jewish tradition], which is the characteristically Pauline idea, is to be forgotten in favor of the reasonable insight: '*video meliora proboque, deteriora sequor.*' [I see the better course and approve it, but I follow the worse] But I believe that it may also be shown quite simply – at any rate, as soon as one recognizes that the anthropology presupposed by the usual interpretation is not that of Paul – that the meaning of Rom. 7:14 ff. is completely different.[51]

Given that Paul in Rom. 7.14 ff provides a different interpretation of the law (in comparison with other Pauline passages in which Paul has a much more positive vision of the law[52]), Bultmann suggests that this biblical text provides a "non-Pauline anthropology."[53] Bultmann was aware of Jonas' reflections on the possible influence of Gnosticism in relation to primitive Christianity and the consequent risk of dualisms in theology (i.e. between law and grace or between flesh and spirit); even if Bultmann never explicitly mentioned the possible influence of Gnostic writings in relation to Rom. 7, it is possible that he thought that such correlation existed since he affirmed, as we have seen, that some biblical passages within Rom. 7 were atypical for the theology of Paul in their description of the law.

This hypothesis seems to be strengthened by another writing of Bultmann in which he observes that occasionally Paul uses the term *sarx* (flesh) as a synonym for *soma* (body) and he thinks this is consonant with Gnostic dualism: "[Paul experiences] a tension between self and self, and so keenly feels the plight of the man who loses his grip upon himself and falls victim to outside powers, that he comes close to Gnostic dualism."[54]

Bultmann also recognizes that St Paul in Rom. 7 is divided in his interiority. In particular, he describes this situation using the German expression "*Zwiespalt* [split or inner conflict]."[55] Bultmann maintains that goodness is inherent with obedience to the divine law, but also recognizes that the latter can exacerbate the split between willing and doing in St Paul and, analogously, in every human being.[56]

A key passage of Bultmann reveals a strong similarity to Jonas' idea of objectivation of the will in Rom. 7:

> just because the will to be authentic is preserved in the false will to be oneself, even if only disguisedly and distortedly, it is possible so to speak of the split in man's existence that the authentic I is set over against the factual one.[57]

In the context of the interpretation of the notion of body in St Paul (most likely influenced by Jonas' phenomenological study on Rom. 7), Bultmann illustrates the risk of an inner psychological conflict, which could result in a perversion of the will:

> man is a being who has a relationship to himself, and that this relationship can be either an appropriate or a perverted one; that he can be at one with himself or at odds; that he can be under his own control or lose his grip on himself. In the latter case, a double possibility exists: that the power which comes to master him can make the estrangement within him determinative, and that would mean that it would destroy the man by entirely wresting him out of his own hands, or that this power gives him back to himself, that is, brings him to life.[58]

Arguably, also this language resembles Jonas' description of Paul in Rom. 7. In order to avoid a dualistic understanding of the notion of flesh and spirit in Paul, Bultmann implicitly advocates for the use of demythologization. In particular, in his reflections on Rom. 7 (originally published in 1932 as explained above) Bultmann writes:

> according to Paul's view... man wills and acts under the domination either of 'flesh' or of 'Spirit' (e.g., Rom. 8:5 ff., 8:12 ff; Gal. 5:16 ff.) and that *tertium non datur*. From the standpoint of a subjectivist anthropology, these 'powers' under which man stands can only be understood as mythological entities [thus, by using the approach of demythologization] or else interpreted in the sense of a naturalistic dualism. I [Bultmann] hope that the interpretation of Rom. 7 will show that these 'powers' in truth designate the possibilities of historical existence.[59]

Even if in this specific writing Bultmann does not acknowledge Jonas' contributions – namely the reflections in Jonas' letter (from 1929) on the existential condition of Paul in Rom. 7 and/or Jonas' reflections on myth and the concept of demythologization – the influence of Jonas on Bultmann's anthropological reflections on Rom. 7 in undeniable, given his reference (in the above passage) to "mythological entities" in relation to the flesh and spirit in the Pauline text[60] and the desire to achieve an interpretation of "historical existence." Arguably, the fact that Bultmann uses these expressions shows that at the beginning of the 1930s, he started to abandon the *Religionsgeschichtliche* formulation of myth and moves towards an existential interpretation of biblical texts.[61] It was most likely Jonas who sowed the seed for Bultmann's *existential* interpretation of Paul, given that, as we already seen, Jonas linked objectivation with mythization/mythologization and advocated for a "demythologized (*entmythologisiert*) consciousness able to approach the original [religious] phenomena."[62] As already mentioned, for Bultmann, the notion of objectivation (thus of mythization/mythologization) changed in the second half of the 1920s after Jonas had added a hermeneutical dimension to this concept.[63]

Another key sentence from the same text which also arguably demonstrates Bultmann's turn towards an existentialist approach is the following:

> [b]ecause man is a self who is concerned with his authenticity and can find it (as that of a creature) only when he surrenders himself to the claim of God, there is the possibility of sin [which could be correlated to the objectivation of the Pauline will in Rom. 7 as demonstrated by Jonas]. Because from the beginning the claim of God has to do with man's *authentic existence*, there is the possibility of misunderstanding: the man who is called to authenticity falsely wills to be himself.[64]

Bultmann's interpretation of Rom. 7 is that "man is 'of the flesh' precisely because he is characterized by the split between willing and doing. In him, in his 'flesh,' dwell both things, his willing as his doing."[65] It is interesting to note that Bultmann wrote this sentence after having recognized that flesh and spirit needed to be interpreted as "mythological entities."[66] It is as if the implied teaching which he wishes to convey is that by using the approach of demythologization, the notion of human flesh in Rom. 7 (initially perceived as a mythological entity) can be redefined and reinterpreted in existential terms, so that the relation between flesh and spirit can be understood in dialectic (rather than dualistic) terms. Thus, similarly to Jonas, Bultmann seems to endorse a dialectic (rather than dualistic) view of the relation between flesh and spirit, or between law and grace for an authentic life of religious faith.

In summary, in this section I have suggested that the exchange of philosophical-theological ideas between Jonas and Bultmann at the end of the 1920s could represent an important event in their careers in relation to their own understanding of objectivation/mythization and the development of the demythologization project. Thus, the genealogy of demythologization in relation to existentialist philosophy/

theology needs to be framed within the fruitful dialectical exchange of ideas and theoretical impulses between Bultmann (as teacher) and Jonas (as student) at the end of the 1920s at the University of Marburg.

Having summarized the key role played by the 1929 letter to Bultmann, we can now analyse the second writing of Jonas which arguably also played an important role in Bultmann's demythologization work. This text consists of Jonas' reflections on the hermeneutics of dogma contained in an appendix of his first book (originally published in 1930).[67] A common thread between Robinson, Johnson, and Congdon is that all these scholars recognize the importance of this text for Bultmann's research on demythologization.[68] Their assumption is correct because Bultmann himself (as biblical scholar and theologian) appreciated and invited the study of Jonas' philosophical-theological reflections on the notion of deobjectivation/demythologization in relation to the hermeneutics of dogma.[69] Given the importance of Jonas' contributions on the hermeneutics of dogma for Bultmann's theological project, it is important to analyse this text in more detail. This task is particularly important, given that this writing has never yet been translated into English.

The Key Role Played by Jonas' Reflections on the Hermeneutics of Dogma

For Jonas, the distortion of authentic freedom and the objectivation which he describes in the experience of the will of St Paul (in Rom. 7) – which was briefly presented in the previous section – have also affected the formulation of dogmas in Western society. Concerning this point, Jonas explains that:

> dogma is often the answer to intimidating/tormenting rationalist antinomies, which in turn have themselves arisen from the attempt to construct a metaphysics [in which being is described objectively] as a consequence of mundane objectivation (i.e. the dogma of original sin). It has been the destiny of the question of freedom in Western society that its existential elements from the beginning were handed over to this ontological transformation and discussion, thus leading to a hopeless and unproductive enterprise.[70]

According to Jonas, the fundamental act that allows for the formation of dogma is objectivation through symbolic language which points towards transcendence: "this objectivation pushes towards a transcendentalization into the metaphysical or mythological, i.e. into a symbolic sphere that transcends existence."[71]

Jonas explains that dogma's objectivation goes hand-in-hand with its rationalization, and the result of this process is that dogma becomes an abstraction.[72] The final result is that dogma is completely disconnected from the lived experience of an individual who is supposed to encounter and embrace the truthfulness of a dogma. Thus, at the end of the 1920s, Jonas believes that objectivation takes place through the symbolic language used in religious discourse[73]; however, when this happens, the original meaning of the existential experience (e.g. behind a biblical text or a dogmatic statement of the Church) is lost.[74]

It should be noted that Jonas focuses his attention on original sin, a dogma strictly linked with the story in Rom. 7 in which Paul's struggle with sin represents the universal human predicament resulting from the Fall of Adam. In other words, Paul repeats the existential condition of Adam (and of every human being) when faced with the issue of obedience to divine law, and this situation results in the phenomenon of objectivation of Pauline will in Rom. 7 (as described in the previous section).

In particular, Jonas referred to the problematic attitude of St Augustine, who, in his view, seemed to rationalize the dogma of original sin in light of the controversy against the Pelagians. Notably, Augustine is so forceful in stressing the need for baptism of infants (underlining its role in delivering individuals from original sin inherited in the flesh from Adam) because he is in a dispute with Julian of Eclanum (c. 386–c. 455) – a well-known leader of the Pelagians – who argued that baptism, instead of purifying one from original sin, is only "endow[ing] infants with various divine gifts such as spiritual enlightenment, their adoption as children of God, and ultimately to ensure their transformation into members of the body of Christ through the liturgy."[75] It is clear that for Augustine the dogmatic formulations of original sin played a highly relevant role as reasoning tools for his arguments and demonstrations.[76]

A dogma (such as the doctrine of original sin) can also be used in order to rationalize incompatibilities. For example, it helps to rationalize the fact that God creates everything perfectly; however, as a consequence of Adam's sin, the true freedom of all humanity is lost, but this can be restored again through the action of grace. For Jonas, these are clear examples of objectivation and rationalization being employed when the dogma of original sin has lost the ability to convey the original authentic experience of the Fall of Adam (the event which originally gave birth to this dogma). Jonas seems to suggest that a faithful will only be able to 'apprehend' and 'go beyond' the dogma of original sin when they are able to somehow 'repeat' the existential condition of Adam (in the Garden of Eden), and thus feel what Adam felt after his act of disobedience, transgression, and rebellion against God.

Augustine explains that as a consequence of the sinful act of Adam, freedom to do evil remains in him. As a result, we can observe the desperate feeling of human powerlessness before God, and man's necessity for grace (which is also the experience of Paul in Rom. 7. Cf. Rom. 7.24–25). For Jonas, the mythological formation of the dogma of original sin starts with the original phenomena of Adam's existential experience of the Fall. To 're-connect' to the existential condition of Adam (which led to the birth of the dogma of original sin), one should feel his inadequacy in front of God when facing the demands of the divine law, as Adam did in the story of after the Fall.[77] A dogma therefore should be able to elicit an authentic experience that can be repeated by an individual in his interiority today. Instead, when dogma is already objectified, an authentic re-experience of the original phenomena, which lies behind the dogma, is hindered in the faithful. Thus, the objectivation of dogma is, for Jonas, an ontological transformation of the original experience that led to the formation of the dogma into a metaphysical symbolic structure (a myth), which is expected, but often fails, to represent the original event.

For Jonas, this process of objectivation also leads to the realization of the *Geist* (spirit) in history: "[o]bjectivation is thus the ontological concepts which designates being in the mode of expression or manifestation of historical actualization."[78] It is within this philosophical-theological framework that Jonas interprets the process of demythologization (which, for him, is clearly a synonym of deobjectivation) in order to rediscover the original individual experience that led to the spiritual event. This process enables the perception of the existential-ontological realm behind a dogma, which otherwise would be perceived inauthentically (in an objectified/mythical way).[79]

In other words, Jonas believes that deobjectivation/demythologization is needed in order that the faithful can reconnect existentially to a dogma in the present moment of their life; he does not want to understand dogma as something relegated to the past (i.e. understanding original sin as a mere event of the past) or in the future (predestination). Jonas observes how the demythologization of the dogma of original sin (which refers to the existential past) and the dogma of predestination (which refers to the existential future), help to understand the existential condition of the faithful. For him, both of these dogmas complement each other since both relate to the temporality of being given that the original sin – by referring to the 'corruption of human nature' – points to the eternal past, whereas predestination – with its determination – points to the eternal future. For Jonas, the present moment in which faith is explicated takes place between the two temporal and existential horizons (past and future) outlined by these two dogmas.[80]

Returning to Bultmann, he knew well these reflections of Jonas on the hermeneutics of dogma since they were published in the 1930s book series that he himself edited.[81] Thus, it is very likely that he apprehended from Jonas the existentialist interpretation of religious myth in relation to the hermeneutics of dogma (i.e. the story of Adam in the Garden of Eden and his disobedience – reflected also in the story of Paul in Rom. 7 – in relation to the understanding of the dogma of original sin).

Thus, what has been presented so far in relation to the notion of objectivation in Rom. 7 (as described above in the section entitled "The Key Role Played by Jonas' Letter to Bultmann in 1929"), and in some additional considerations of Jonas' reflections on the hermeneutics of dogma (this section), consolidate the fact that Jonas' philosophical-theological perspective played an important role for Bultmann's own theology and his development of demythologization.

In the last section of this chapter, I will expand how Jonas was influenced in his understanding of objectivation and the consequent need to deobjectify.[82]

How Jonas Was Influenced in His Understanding of Objectivation and the Consequent Need to Deobjectify/Demythologize

An important influence on Jonas' perspective was undoubtedly played by the teachings of Martin Heidegger, who, during the 1920s, was Jonas' doctoral supervisor. There is no doubt that Heidegger's perspective on objectivation[83] influenced Jonas. Heidegger, in turn, was most likely influenced by the writings of Dilthey and Count

Paul Yorck von Wartenburg, who both reflected on this notion.[84] Most probably, Jonas knew, through the 1920/1921 lectures of Heidegger, that Dilthey developed a concept of "the Objecthood of God"[85] and identified the use of an "objectifying, Greek-metaphysical manner [in the religious discourse concerning God]."[86]

The influence of Heidegger's teachings on Jonas' own understanding of objectivation is evident already in January 21, 1928 when Jonas delivered his paper in the seminar on Schelling, organized by Heidegger. On this occasion, Jonas explained that when Augustine refers to love as *caritas*, through which one desires to see and enjoy an object, the result is the description of God as an object.[87] For Jonas, this is testified by the existence in Augustinian theology of the "fundamental ontological principle of God as *summum bonum* [as 'the highest good'] and thus as *res – qua fruendum est* (de doctr. christ. lib. I°) [thus God is intended as an object, as 'something to enjoy.']"[88]

Thus, in this text, Jonas thinks that Augustine risks depicting God as an object of human desire. Heidegger also taught his students:

> Dilthey ... shows how Christianity becomes a doctrine and a philosophy under the influence of ancient science. – What is Augustine's significance in this process? In the face of ancient skepticism, Augustine ascertained the absolute reality of internal experience (in the form of a precursor to the Cartesian "*cogito, ergo sum*").[89]

Heidegger refers to Dilthey in order to reinterpret the division found within a thinking individual between *res cogitans* as subject and *res extensa* as object in a process not too dissimilar to the objectivation of the Pauline will in Rom. 7. It seems that Jonas embraces this Dilthean view (through the teaching of Heidegger) by underlining the issues of objectivation.[90]

Count Yorck (also mentioned in the lectures by Heidegger, as we shall see) identifies within the psychology of one's life the presence of a polarity between inwardness and outwardness, feeling and cognition, affectivity and volition; the common denominator in these is a dialectical relation between objectlessness and objectified representation.[91] Yorck underlines that both aspects are present in one's life and are not independent of each other.[92] This is similar to Jonas' understanding of the dialectical relationship between *volo me velle* and *cogito me velle* (described previously), or between the two interpretations of action: 'how to act' and the 'whatness of the action' (the representation of the action). Arguably, in this Count Yorck expresses the concept of objectivation with the word representation (*Vorstellungsinhalt*),[93] suggesting that he could be the first philosopher to inspire the idea of demythologization (understood in existential terms) since he recognizes the risk of objectifying representation in history. Farin comments on the writings of Yorck:

> [a]t the limit, feeling is object-less and an immersion in subjective life. As Yorck explains, feelings are only secondarily attached to objects. Pain or pleasure, for instance, has no 'representational content' ... the center of feeling or affectivity is the sphere of one's own, pure interiority, not as representation, but as something felt. Therefore, it is the actual seat of 'all things

personal', the innermost centre of personal life. It is the 'central' and immediate pulse of life, antecedent to the objectifications by cognition and volition.[94]

For Yorck, the inner aspect of an individual is not cognitive but is characterized by feelings; it does not provide knowledge or objectified representation since it is not "something thought or represented and projected outwards."[95] In fact, Yorck writes that "the relation of self to feeling is more immediate [than the subject's relation to representation]."[96]

Heidegger taught his students (including Jonas) that the historicity of *Dasein* can be positioned in relation to the research of Dilthey.[97] In particular, Heidegger explains that Count Yorck influenced Dilthey in his development of a particular hermeneutical philosophy of history:

[t]he analysis of the problem of history ... has arisen in the process of appropriating the labors of Dilthey. It has been corroborated and at the same time strengthened, by the theses of Count Yorck, which are found scattered through his letters to him.[98]

The Heideggerian *Dasein* resonates with the writings of Count Yorck, through the work of Dilthey. Heidegger in fact writes that the "preparatory existential-temporal analytic of *Dasein* is resolved to foster the spirit of Count Yorck in the service of Dilthey's work."[99]

Notably, Jonas uses the concept of 'representation' (originally proposed many years before by Count Yorck with the German word *Vorstellungsinhalt*)[100] to speak of objectivation or myth formation. Yorck is critical of objectified views of history which use the concept of representation: 'to grasp natural and historical communities by means of representation' [is an incorrect approach] because it misses the felt personal attachment, which alone lends reality to the historical connectivity and relation."[101] This view influenced Heidegger and therefore may arguably have also influenced Jonas who applies the same reasoning to the interpretation of dogma.

Remarkably, Count Yorck wrote about his vision of dogma in a letter to Dilthey in 1892 explaining that dogmatics helps to formulate an ontology of history.[102] Dilthey agreed with this point when he explains that:

all dogmas need to be translated so as to bring out their universal validity for all human life. They are cramped by their connection with the situation in the past in which they arose. Once they have been freed from this limitation they become ... the consciousness of the supra-sensual and supra-intelligible nature of historicity pure and simple ... [O]nce they [Christian dogmas] are re-interpreted as statements of universal validity they express the highest living form of all history.[103]

In other words, it appears that both Yorck and Dilthey already proposed (many years before Jonas) a reinterpretation of dogma through a reengagement with the original historical event. Jonas fully embraces their view in his writings on the hermeneutical structure of dogma. Jonas – similarly to Dilthey and Yorck[104] – tries to provide an antidote to the Kantian separation between subjectivity and objectivity, and between the theoretical and the practical in historical sciences, but extends this scope significantly to provide a new hermeneutics of dogma; their common objective consists of re-engaging with history and dogma so that these events can be 're-lived' once again.

Heidegger's teachings (which strongly affected Jonas) echoed Dilthey and Yorck and recognized the risk of losing authenticity when an objectifying language is used by historians in the description of past events. For this reason, Heidegger develops the concept of 'appropriation' (*Ereignis*) as a corrective to interpreting and reengaging with an historical event:

> appropriation is the hermeneutical event by which ontology is reinfused into a reading of historical sources ... [H]istoricity is the self-reflexive historical involvement by which we become aware of what contemporary, philosophical conditions necessitate this reengagement... allow[ing] for reinterpretation at a revivified ontological level constantly in view of the question of being.[105]

It is clear that Jonas adopts and further develops this method (proposed by Heidegger) in his idea to deobjectify (or demythologize) existentially religious texts and to propose a new understanding of dogma.

Heidegger's 1920–1921 lecture notes (which Jonas most likely read) were in fact critical of the objectivation of dogma:

> [t]he dogma as detached content of doctrine in an objective, epistemological emphasis could never have been guiding for Christian religiosity. On the contrary, the genesis of dogma can only be understood from out of the enactment of Christian life experience.[106]

Jonas, however, has the merit of expounding Heidegger's view on the objectivation of dogmas by considering the impact of symbolic language on the hermeneutics of dogma. He contemplates that objectivation could take place also through the use of symbolic language.[107]

It is not surprising therefore that already in 1930 Jonas used the expression "demythologized (*entmythologisiert*) consciousness" in his reflections on the hermeneutics of dogma.[108] In relation to this fact, Congdon has further suggested that Jonas may have inherited the notion of demythologization from the theologians Hermann Strathmann (1882–1966) and Wilhelm Caspari (1876–1947):

> the word *Entmythologisierung* first entered German literature in 1914 in a review of Wilhelm Herrmann's *Ethik* by Hermann Strathmann, in which he praised Herrmann for his 'energetic work in the demythologizing of Christianity.' The word *Entmythisierung* was then used in the title of an article by Wilhelm Caspari in 1928, before Hans Jonas picked up the word (*entmythologisierte*) in his study of Augustine in 1930.[109]

44 Luca Settimo

Given what has been presented in this section, it is very likely that the idea that led to the birth of demythologization/deobjectivation was planted before 1914, especially through the reflections of Dilthey and Yorck. Although both of these scholars did not specifically use the expression 'demythologization,' their idea must have influenced both Strathmann and Caspari, who, as explained by Congdon, in the period 1914–1928 were the first theologians to refer to the notion of demythologization. However, as already mentioned, during this period, German theologians were still using the *Religionsgeschichtliche* formulation of myth. As I have shown, it is through the reflections of Jonas – as a doctoral student in philosophy under the supervision of Heidegger (whose teachings refer also to Dilthey's and Yorck's philosophical-theological perspective on objectivation) – that religious myths (including Gnostic myths) began to be reinterpreted in existentialist terms. We have seen how these ideas developed by Jonas, influenced Bultmann especially since 1929 and also how these contributed to a new understanding of religious myth and thus the development of demythologization in religious discourse. In particular, we have seen how the story of Adam in the Garden of Eden, reflected also in the story of Paul in Rom. 7, make use of a mythical/objectified language, thus showing the importance to demythologize/deobjectify religious discourse (i.e. for a proper hermeneutics of the dogma of original sin in relation to these biblical texts).[110]

In conclusion, within this chapter I have outlined the key role of Jonas' reflections (matured at the end of the 1920s) in relation to Bultmann's theology and the development of his demythologization. In order to achieve this, I have focused on two of Jonas' writings, namely (i) a phenomenological study of the existential condition of Paul in Rom. 7 contained in a letter that he sent to Bultmann in July 1929 (whose entire text has recently been published) and (ii) some reflections on the hermeneutics of dogma that he published in 1930. We have seen that for Jonas the risk of objectivation of the Pauline will in Rom. 7 is concomitant with the risk of the objectification of the dogma of original sin. For Jonas (and consequently also for Bultmann), objectivation is a synonym of mythization or mythologization within the religious text; thus, implying the need to deobjectify or demythologize religious writings in order to uncover the existential truths and universal insights that may be found within these texts.[111] I have argued that these reflections played an important role for Bultmann's development of his theological approach of demythologization. Finally, I have analysed how Jonas may have been influenced in his own philosophical-theological reflections on these topics.

Notes

1 In particular the text of Jonas' dissertation – mainly supervised by Martin Heidegger (1889–1976) and partly also by Rudolf Bultmann (1884–1976) – was published in H. Jonas, *Der Begriff Der Gnosis. Inugural-Disertation Zur Erlangung Der Doktorwürde Der Hohen Philosophischen Fakultät Der Philipps-Universität Zu Marburg* (Göttingen: Hubert & Co., 1930). Another writing discussing these topics was: Hans Jonas, *Gnosis und Spätantiker Geist*, Forschungen Zur Religion Und Literatur Des Alten Und Neuen

Testaments (Göttingen: Vandenhoeck & Ruprecht, 1934); Hans Jonas, *Gnosis Und Spätantiker Geist*, 2, Forschungen Zur Religion Und Literatur Des Alten Und Neuen Testaments (Göttingen: Vandenhoeck & Ruprecht, 1954).

2 Jonas' reflections on the relation between myth and objectivation (with a particular focus on the dogma of original sin) were firstly published in an appendix of his 1930s book: Hans Jonas, "Zur hermeneutischen Struktur des Dogmas" in Hans Jonas, *Augustin Und Das Paulinische Freiheitsproblem: Ein Philosophischer Beitrag Zur Genesis Der Christlich-Abendländischen Freiheitsidee*. Forschungen Zur Religion Und Literatur Des Alten Und Neuen Testaments (Göttingen: Vandenhoeck & Ruprecht, 1930), 66–76. Jonas republished this text later in the second edition of the same book: Hans Jonas, *Augustin Und Das Paulinische Freiheitsproblem: Eine Philosophische Studie Zum Pelagianischen Streit*, 2nd Ed., Forschungen Zur Religion Und Literatur Des Alten Und Neuen Testaments (Göttingen: Vandenhoeck & Ruprecht, 1965), 80–89. This text will be analysed later within this book chapter.

3 Hans Jonas, "1. Paulus-Entwurf (Brief an Bultmann vom 13.7.1929)." The entire text of this letter has been published recently: Hans Jonas, "Hans Jonas an Rudolf Bultmann [letter] – Freiburg d. 13.7.29" in Andreas Großmann (Ed.), *Rudolf Bultmann, Hans Jonas: Briefwechsel 1928–1976. Mit Einem Anhang Anderer Zeugnisse* (Tübingen: Mohr Siebeck, 2020), 2–11.

4 Part of this letter was adapted for the following publications: (i) H. Jonas, "Philosophische Meditation über Paulus, Römerbrief, Kapitel 7" in E. Dinkler und T. Hartwig (Eds.), *Zeit und Geschichte: Dankesgabe an Rudolf Bultmann zum 80. Geburtstag* (Tübingen: Mohr, 1964), 557–570; (ii) Jonas, *Augustin* [1965], 93–105 – notably, this appendix was not present in the first edition of this book [1930]; (iii) Hans Jonas, "Philosophical Meditation on the Seventh Chapter of Paul's Epistle to the Romans" in J. M. Robinson (Ed.), *The Future of Our Religious Past: Essays in Honour of Rudolf Bultmann* (London: SCM Press, 1971), 333–350; (iv) Hans Jonas, "The Abyss of the Will: Philosophical Meditation on the Seventh Chapter of Paul's Epistle to the Romans" in Hans Jonas, *Philosophical Essays: From Ancient Creed to Technological Man* (Englewood Cliffs, NJ: Prentice-Hall, 1974), 335–348.

5 See note 3.

6 See note 2.

7 The meanings of these expressions will all be expounded later in this chapter.

8 Rudolf Bultmann, "New Testament and Mythology: the Problem of Demythologizing the New Testament Proclamation [1941]" in Rudolf Bultmann, *New Testament and Mythology and Other Basic Writings*. Translated by Schubert M. Ogden (Philadelphia: Fortress Press SCM, 1984), 1–43. In this chapter, for grammatical reasons, I prefer to use the expression "demythologization" rather than the gerund form "demythologizing."

9 For an overview of Bultmann's perspective on demythologization, see: David Fergusson, *Bultmann*, Outstanding Christian Thinkers (London, England: G. Chapman, 1992), 107–125.

10 Ernst Cassirer, *Philosophie Der Symbolischen Formen* (Darmstadt Wissenschaftliche Buchgesellschaft, 1923 [1973]), Zweiter Teil, Das Mythische Denken, 59–77.

11 Bultmann, *New Testament and Mythology*, 99.

12 James M. Robinson, "Hermeneutic since Barth" in James M. Robinson and John B. Cobb (Eds.), *The New Hermeneutic*. New Frontiers in Theology (New York: Harper and Row, 1964), 34–36; James M. Robinson, "Interpretation in Contemporary Theology – viii. The Pre-History of Demythologization," *Union Seminary Magazine* 20, 1 (1966), 69–70; Roger A. Johnson, *The Origins of Demythologizing: Philosophy and Historiography in the Theology of Rudolf Bultmann*. Studies in the History of Religions (Leiden: Brill, 1974), 31, 170, 207–231, 234ff; David W. Congdon, *The Mission of Demythologizing: Rudolf Bultmann's Dialectical Theology* (Minneapolis, MN: Fortress Press, 2015), 163ff, 570, 592, 612, 649, 767. Notably, however, Bultmann, already in

the early 1920s – thus, before his encounter with Jonas when he was a doctoral student in Marburg – was using the notion of myth following the *Religionsgeschichtliche* formulation of myth. Cf. Johnson, *The Origins of Demythologizing*, 30, 87–126; see Johannes Zachhuber's contribution to this volume. Notably Bultmann reinterpreted his notion of myth by using an existential approach which was inspired by Jonas' philosophical-theological reflections. Nevertheless, "[Bultmann's use of the 'slogan' of demythologization, after his encounter with Jonas remained] fully compatible with his earlier hermeneutical and theological convictions." Fergusson, *Bultmann*, 109, and references therein.

13 The doctoral studies of Jonas during the 1920s dealt in fact with the topic of Gnosticism. Cf. H. Jonas, *Der Begriff Der Gnosis*. Bultmann (who was also Jonas' supervisor for his doctoral thesis during the 1920s) knew well Jonas' research during this time: this is testified by the fact that Bultmann helped in the publication of Jonas' work on Gnosticism in a book series which he edited (*Forschungen zur Religion und Literatur des Alten und Neuen Testaments*) firstly in 1934 and then in 1954. Hans Jonas, *Gnosis und Spätantiker Geist* [1934]; Hans Jonas, *Gnosis Und Spätantiker Geist*, [1954].

14 Jonas, *Gnosis und Spätantiker Geist* [1934], 3 f. as translated in Robinson, "Hermeneutic since Barth," 37.

15 Robinson, "Interpretation," 69.

16 Jonas, *Augustin* [1930], 68 as translated and quoted in Robinson, "Hermeneutic since Barth," 36 and also in Robinson, "Interpretation," 69–70. In the second edition of Jonas' book, the notion of demythologized consciousness appears on page 82: Jonas, "Zur hermeneutischen Struktur des Dogmas," 82.

17 Johnson, *The Origins of Demythologizing*, 220.

18 Johnson, *The Origins of Demythologizing*, 220.

19 Johnson, *The Origins of Demythologizing*, 212.

20 Johnson, *The Origins of Demythologizing*, 202.

21 Johnson, *The Origins of Demythologizing*, 30, 31, 169–231. For Johnson, this is concomitant with the fact that Jonas joins Heidegger's ontology with Hegelian dialectic: "[t]he hermeneutical concept of 'objectifying' was born of this union of Hegel and Heidegger, first developed by Jonas in his study of Gnosticism and later appropriated by Bultmann for demythologizing the New Testament." Johnson, *The Origins of Demythologizing*, 31.

22 Johnson, *The Origins of Demythologizing*, 230–231 and references therein. Already in 1974 Johnson explained that very few scholars had commented before him on Jonas' reflections in relation to Bultmann's theology (one of these scholars is Robinson whom I have presented above). Cf. footnote 3 in Johnson, *The Origins of Demythologizing*, 230 and references therein.

23 Congdon, *The Mission of Demythologizing*, 164–166.

24 Congdon, *The Mission of Demythologizing*, 164, 166 and references therein.

25 The text of Jonas' paper delivered in Heidegger's seminar on Schelling has been published in H. Jonas, "Das Freiheitsproblem bei Augustin" in Lore Hühn and Jörg Jantzen (Eds.), *Heideggers Schelling-Seminar (1927/28)* (Stuttgart-Bad Canstatt: Frommann-Holzboog, 2010), 373–402 and 439–457. At that time, Bultmann asked to see the text of this paper and suggested it for publication. Christian Wiese (Ed.) *Memoirs – Hans Jonas*. Translated by Krishna Winston (Waltham, MA: Brandeis University Press, 2008), 146.

26 Jonas, *Augustin*, [1930].

27 Jonas, *Gnosis und Spätantiker Geist* [1934]; Jonas, *Gnosis Und Spätantiker Geist* [1954]. Similarly, both these books were published in *Forschungen zur Religion und Literatur des Alten und Neuen Testaments* (the book series edited by Bultmann).

28 Congdon, *The Mission of Demythologizing*, 167; Bultmann, *Neues Testament und Mythologie – das Problem der Entmythologisierung der neutestamentlichen Verkündigung*. Ed. Eberhard Jüngel, (München: Chr. Kaiser, 1985), 26–29.

29 Bultmann, "Vorwort" in Jonas, *Gnosis Und Spätantiker Geist* [1934], vi, as quoted and translated in Congdon, *The Mission of Demythologizing*, 165–166. Here Congdon agrees with Robinson, who also translated the same quotation. Robinson, "Hermeneutic since Barth," 34–35.
30 Rudolf Bultmann, "Grußwort," in Barbara Aland (Ed.), *Gnosis: Festschrift für Hans Jonas* (Göttingen: Vandenhoeck & Ruprecht, 1978), 13 as translated by Congdon, *The Mission of Demythologizing*, 167.
31 In particular, a search of the digital library JSTOR https://www.jstor.org/ of the terms: [demythologiation OR demythologization] AND "Rudolf Bultmann" as keywords in 'all fields' in the writings of this database (published in the last ten years) provided 84 results. However, out of these 84 writings, only 7 mention the name of Hans Jonas (there are in fact only 7 entries in JSTOR which fulfil the following search criteria over the last 10 years: [demythologisation OR demythologization] AND ["Rudolf Bultmann" AND "Hans Jonas"]). This means that approximately 8% of those authors who recently discussed demythologization and Bultmann mention Hans Jonas. Last search performed in August 2023.
32 See note 3.
33 See note 2. Notably, this text has never been translated into English.
34 For a further analysis of how Jonas interpreted the writings of St Paul, the reader is invited to engage with the contributions offered by Bongardt and Großmann in this volume. A further analysis of Jonas' perspective in relation to Gnosticism, myth, and the issue of objectivation can be found in Elad Lapidot, "Gnosis und spätantiker Geist II. Von der Mythologie zur mystischen Philosophie (1954)" in M. Bongardt, H. Burckhart, J. S. Gordon, and J. Nielsen-Sikora (Eds.), *Hans Jonas-Handbuch* (Stuttgart: J.B. Metzler, 2021), 88–95 and references therein.
35 It is beyond the scope of this chapter to offer an interpretation and exegesis of Rom. 7. For an overview cf. J. C. O'Neill, *Paul's Letter to the Romans*, Pelican Books (Harmondsworth: Penguin, 1975), 118–133; Robert Jewett, *Romans – a Commentary*, Ed. Eldon J. Epp. Hermeneia – a Critical and Historical Commentary on the Bible (Minneapolis, MN: Fortress Press, 2007), 428–473 and references therein. In this book chapter I will mainly focus on specific comments offered by Jonas and Bultmann on this biblical text.
36 This article is: Rudolf Bultmann, "Die Bedeutung des geschichtlichen Jesus für die Theologie des Paulus" [The significance of the historical Jesus for Paul's theology (my translation)] *Theologische Blätter* 8 (1929), 137–151. This was later published in Rudolf Bultmann, *Glauben und Verstehen*. Bd. 1. (Tübingen: Mohr, 1933 [1961]), 188–213. Notably, Jonas in his letter cites Bultmann, *Glauben und Verstehen*, 194 f., 195 and 196. Cf. Jonas, "Hans Jonas an Rudolf Bultmann," 2.
37 See note 36.
38 Bultmann, *Glauben und Verstehen*, 188–213.
39 Johnson, *The Origins of Demythologizing*, 63, 105, 106, 112, and references therein.
40 In particular, Jonas explains how the interpretation of Rom. 7 had an impact on both Augustine's and Pelagius' interpretation of the human attitude towards obedience to divine laws. Jonas, *Augustin* [1965], 39–63.
41 Jonas, "Das Freiheitsproblem bei Augustin," 379 ff.
42 In particular, Jonas explains that: "[a]t that time Heidegger had been so impressed that he'd told Bultmann about the paper [*Das Freiheitsproblem bei Augustin* delivered in Jan 1928]. Bultmann asked to see the manuscript and suggested to his publisher, Wilhelm Ruprecht, that he publish it in his series Studies of the Religious and Literary Aspects on the Old and New Testament." Wiese, *Memoirs*, 146. Thus, it is unsurprising that in 1929, Bultmann sent his article on Pauline theology to Jonas, given that he knew that Jonas had reflected on Rom. 7 in the previous year.
43 Jonas, "Hans Jonas an Rudolf Bultmann," 2. My own translation from German. I have translated all the following quotations from this writing except where these have been translated by Jonas himself in Jonas, "Philosophical Meditation."

44 Jonas, "Philosophical Meditation."
45 Jonas, "Philosophical Meditation," 346.
46 Jonas, "Philosophical Meditation," 339.
47 Cf. Jonas, "Philosophical Meditation," 337–340.
48 Jonas, "Philosophical Meditation," 346. Interestingly, some biblical scholars have noted the parallel between Rom. 7 and the story of the Fall of Adam in the Garden of Eden. In particular, O'Neill explains that Rom. 7 was influenced by Gnostic literature which provides "allegorical readings of the story of Adam and Eve in the garden, and how they were deceived with the serpent." O'Neill, *Paul's Letter to the Romans*, 123–124 and references therein. It is therefore possible that Jonas, after his studies of Gnosticism, had an intuition for the possible effect of Gnostic myths on the biblical stories in Gen. 3.1–6 and Rom. 7.
49 Rudolf Bultmann, "Römer 7 und die Anthropologie des Paulus" in Heinrich Bornkamm (Ed.), *Imago Dei: Beiträge zur theologischen Anthropologie* (Giessen: A. Töpelmann, 1932), 53–62.
50 Rudolf Bultmann, "Romans 7 and the Anthropology of Paul" in Schubert M. Ogden (Ed.), *Existence and Faith: Shorter Writings of Rudolf Bultmann* (London: Hodder & Stoughton, 1961), 147–157.
51 Bultmann, "Romans 7 and the Anthropology of Paul," 150. The Latin text mentioned in this quotation is from the text of the "Medea" in *The Metamorphoses of Ovid* (VII, 19 f.) also translated in O'Neill, *Paul's Letter to the Romans*, 130 and references therein.
52 See e.g. Gal. 1.14–15 or Phil. 3.6b in which Paul explains his extreme zealousness for the Jewish tradition in which he was raised and the resulting righteousness under this law. In particular, Bultmann also underlines that Paul repented (of the great sin of persecuting the Church) but never renounced the law. Bultmann, "Romans 7," 148.
53 Bultmann, "Romans 7," 150.
54 Rudolf Bultmann, *Theology of the New Testament* (New York: Scribner, 1951), Vol. I, 199.
55 Bultmann, "*Römer 7*," 53.
56 Bultmann, "Romans 7," 147–157.
57 Bultmann, "Romans 7," 156.
58 Bultmann, *Theology of the New Testament*, (vol. I), 16–17.
59 Bultmann, "Romans 7," 150.
60 However, it should be noted that Bultmann's understanding of *sarx* and *pneuma* in Paul is complex and there are some ambiguities when comparing his different writings. For example, in other writings, he explains that these two notions "have been divested by Paul of their original mythological meaning and become expressive of the 'Christian understanding of being.'" Johnson, *The Origins of Demythologizing*, 205 and references therein. Nevertheless, it seems that after receiving Jonas' letter, Bultmann starts to adopt a hermeneutical approach that aims to reveal the existential condition conveyed by the original author of the biblical text (in this case the existential condition of Paul in Rom. 7).
61 According to Johnson, Bultmann adopts the *Religionsgescichtliche* formulation of myth predominantly "during the years 1920–1933." Johnson, *The Origins of Demythologizing*, 87. Thus, according to this scholar, after 1933 (approximately) Bultmann starts to use an existential approach to understand religious myths. However, the influence of letter exchanges with Jonas in 1929 (discussed in this chapter) suggests that Bultmann was seeking to recover the existential meaning of biblical texts already at the end of the 1920s. We shall analyse in the section entitled "How Jonas Was Influenced in His Understanding of Objectivation and the Consequent Need to Deobjectify/Demythologize" (in this book chapter) the perspective of those thinkers (firstly Heidegger) who influenced Jonas in his existential interpretation of religious texts.
62 Jonas, *Augustin* [1930], 68. When Jonas wrote this sentence, he had in mind the dogma of original sin, which, as we have seen, is closely related to the story of Paul in Rom. 7.

63 Johnson, *The Origins of Demythologizing*, 202. However, Johnson does not discuss the content of the 1929 letter to Bultmann in order to account for this effect. For this reason, it is important to study the text of this letter.
64 Bultmann, "Romans 7," 157. My emphasis in italics.
65 Bultmann, "Romans 7," 151. Here Bultmann refers to Rom. 7.18 as the passage which supports his argument.
66 Bultmann, "Romans 7," 150.
67 See note 2.
68 Robinson, "Interpretation," 69–70; Johnson, *The Origins of Demythologizing*, 176, 207–234; Congdon, *The Mission of Demythologizing*, 167.
69 Bultmann in fact explains: "[f]or a critical interpretation of myth, see the important remarks on the hermeneutical structure of the dogma in Hans Jonas, *Augustine and the problem of Pauline freedom* 1930, 66–76 [which are the pages referring to the appendix in Jonas's book in which he reflects on the hermeneutics of dogma]." Bultmann, *Neues Testament und Mythologie*, 24 (my translation). Bultmann recognized the value of Jonas' appendix on the hermeneutical structure of dogma as an "important accomplishment" in the "critical interpretation of myth." Bultmann, *Neues Testament und Mythologie*, 25n1 as quoted and translated in Congdon, *The Mission of Demythologizing*, 167. Moreover, "[Bultmann's] understanding of human existence which the New Testament itself enshrines… [takes place through a] critical re-interpretation of myth [as illustrated by Jonas's reflections on the hermeneutics of dogma within] … *Augustine und das paulinische Freiheitsproblempublished* [published in] 1930." Rudolf Bultmann (and five critics), *Kerygma and Myth: a Theological Debate*, Ed. by Hans Werner Bartsch (London: S.P.C.K., 1972), 12. The specific bibliographical reference in relation to this reinterpretation of myth illustrated by Jonas (mentioned in this page of *Kerygma and Myth*) is Jonas, *Augustin* [1930], 66–76, thus Jonas' appendix on the hermeneutics of dogma. Finally, this appendix was published in the book series "Forschungen zur Religion und Literatur des Alten und Neuen Testaments" edited by Bultmann.
70 Jonas, "Zur hermeneutischen Struktur des Dogmas," 82 (my translation).
71 Jonas, "Zur hermeneutischen Struktur des Dogmas," 81 (my translation).
72 Jonas, "Zur hermeneutischen Struktur des Dogmas," 81–82.
73 Jonas, "Zur hermeneutischen Struktur des Dogmas," 81–82.
74 Jonas, "Zur hermeneutischen Struktur des Dogmas," 82. Jonas' perspective on this topic will evolve later in his career. This is particularly evident in Jonas' paper "Heidegger and Theology" (originally presented in April 1964 at a conference at Drew University in USA) where he criticizes the excessive use of deobjectivation in theology by Heidegger and some of his followers. Cf. Hans Jonas, *The Phenomenon of Life: Toward a Philosophical Biology*, Northwestern University Studies in Phenomenology & Existential Philosophy (Evanston, IL: Northwestern University Press, 2001), 235–261. It is outside the scope of this chapter to analyse the changes in Jonas' understanding of myth during the 1960s.
75 Nozomu Yamada, "Rhetorical, Political, and Ecclesiastical Perspectives of Augustine's and Julian of Eclanum's Theological Response in the Pelagian Controversy," *Scrinium* 14, 1 (2018), 184.
76 Jonas, "Zur hermeneutischen Struktur des Dogmas," 87–88. In addition, the following two dogmatic statements support this view which was first defined at the Council of Carthage in 418 (a Church Council that dealt with some Pelagian issues and at which Augustine participated): (i) "[Grace] heals nature vitiated by original sin and restores the liberty (of the sons of God)" Heinrich Denzinger, *The Sources of Catholic Dogma* (St. Louis: Herder, 1957), 26; (ii) "[whoever affirms that] even if grace … [was] not given, we could nevertheless fulfil the divine commands without it [without grace], though not indeed easily, let him be anathema." Denzinger, *The Sources of Catholic Dogma*, DS105.
77 Jonas, "Zur hermeneutischen Struktur des Dogmas," 84–85.

78 Johnson, *The Origins of Demythologizing*, 216.
79 Jonas, "Zur hermeneutischen Struktur des Dogmas," 82. We have already seen in the first section of this book chapter (entitled "A Short Summary of the Notion of Demythologization") that objectivation is a synonym of mythologization or mythization and that deobjectivation/demythologization is needed to re-connect "existentially" with the original meaning of the religious text.
80 Jonas, "Zur hermeneutischen Struktur des Dogmas," 89.
81 See note 2.
82 We have already seen that objectivation is a synonym of mythologization/mythization and that deobjectivation is a synonym of demythologization.
83 Notably, on different occasions, Heidegger refers to the concept of objectivation in his famous writing *magnum opus Being and Time* (*Sein und Zeit* originally published in 1927). Heidegger, *Being and Time*, 73, 113, 414, 417, 430, 433, 471. There is no doubt that Jonas was very familiar with this notion that he learnt from the teachings of his doctoral supervisor during 1920s.
84 My claim is consonant with the suggestion by Claudio Bonaldi who also notes the key influence of Dilthey on Jonas' notion of objectivation through Heidegger's teachings. C. Bonaldi, "Introduzione," in H. Jonas, *Agostino e il Problema Paolino della Libertà*, translated by C. Bonaldi (Brescia: Morcelliana, 2007), 10. Cf. Wilhelm Dilthey, "*Einleitung in die Geisteswissenschaften I*," in K. Gründer and F. Rodi (Eds.), *Gesammelte Schriften* (Göttingen: Vandenhoeck & Ruprecht, 1961[1966]). Additionally, Yorck Von Wartenburg played a key role in this influence. Concerning the existential approach of the latter, cf. Hans Ruin, "Yorck Von Wartenburg and the Problem of Historical Existence," *Journal of the British Society for Phenomenology* 25, 2 (1994), 111–130.
85 Martin Heidegger, *The Phenomenology of Religious Life*, Studies in Continental Thought (Bloomington: Indiana University Press, 2004), 130. Notably, this book contains Heidegger's 1920–1921 lectures on religion including some reflections on Pauline texts. It is very likely that Jonas knew well this material given the fact that Heidegger was his doctoral supervisor.
86 Heidegger, *The Phenomenology of Religious Life*, 131.
87 Jonas, "Das Freiheitsproblem bei Augustin," 399.
88 Jonas, "Das Freiheitsproblem bei Augustin," 399 (my translation); the same sentence is used in Jonas, Augustin [1965], 77.
89 Heidegger, *The Phenomenology of Religious Life*, 118.
90 Moreover, in Marburg, there was an important discussion on the notion of objectivation in the neo-Kantian school founded by Hermann Cohen (1842–1918), including the teachings of the Lutheran neo-Kantian theologian Wilhelm Herrmann (1846–1922). Cf. Johnson, *The Origins of Demythologizing*, 32, 39–48, 191; see also Großmann's contribution to this volume.
91 Ingo Farin, "Count Paul Yorck Von Wartenburg" in *The Stanford Encyclopedia of Philosophy* (Ed. Edward N. Zalta) (2016), https://plato.stanford.edu/entries/yorck/ (Last accessed on September 4, 2024).
92 Paul Yorck von Wartenburg, *Bewusstseinsstellung Und Geschichte: Ein Fragment Aus Dem Philosophischen Nachlass* (Tübingen: M. Niemeyer, 1956), 72.
93 Wartenburg, *Bewusstseinsstellung Und Geschichte*, 71–72.
94 Farin, "Count Paul Yorck Von Wartenburg."
95 Farin, "Count Paul Yorck Von Wartenburg."
96 Yorck von Wartenburg, *Bewusstseinsstellung und Geschichte*, 99 as cited and translated in Farin, "Count Paul Yorck Von Wartenburg."
97 Martin Heidegger, *Being and Time* (Oxford: Blackwell, 1967), 449–455.
98 Heidegger, *Being and Time*, 449.
99 Heidegger, *Being and Time*, 455.
100 Yorck von Wartenburg, *Bewusstseinsstellung und Geschichte*, 71–72.

101 Yorck von Wartenburg, *Bewusstseinsstellung und Geschichte*, 72 as cited and translated in Farin, "Count Paul Yorck Von Wartenburg."
102 Wilhelm Dilthey, *Briefwechsel Zwischen Wilhelm Dilthey Und Dem Grafen Paul Yorck V. Wartenburg, 1877–1897* (M. Niemeyer, 1923), 154.
103 Dilthey, *Briefwechsel Zwischen Wilhelm Dilthey*, 158.
104 Notably, also Kantian philosophy dealt both with the issue of objectivation (resulting from a split between subjectivity and objectivity) and in particular with the separation of theoretical and practical reason. Arguably, this separation has led to the view that historical research has become a theoretical discipline, without practical implications. Ruin, "Yorck Von Wartenburg," 116.
105 Todd S. Mei, "Heidegger and the Appropriation of Metaphysics," *The Heythrop Journal* 50, 2 (2009), 257.
106 Heidegger, *The Phenomenology of Religious Life*, 79.
107 Notably, Jonas knew the writings of Ernest Cassirer (1874–1945), a Jewish philosopher belonging to the neo-Kantian movement of the Marburg school, who discussed the key role of symbolic language in relation to the human encounter with the divine. Luca Settimo, "Hans Jonas's Reflections on the Human Soul and the Notion of Imago Dei: An Explanation of Their Role in Ethics and Some Possible Historical Influences on Their Development," *History of European Ideas* 49, 5 (2023), 876 and references therein.
108 See note 16.
109 Congdon, *The Mission of Demythologizing*, 570 and references therein.
110 We recall that Jonas refers to the "Fall [in relation] to the eating from the tree of knowledge." Jonas, "Philosophical Meditation," 346; he also uses the expression "the imaginary past of the Fall." Jonas, "Philosophical Meditation," 339.
111 It is important to underline again that given that this book focuses on Jonas' work up until 1945, in this chapter I have not explored the change in the philosophical-theological perspective of (the later) Jonas in relation to myth and objectivation.

Bibliography

Aland, Barbara (Ed.). *Gnosis: Festschrift für Hans Jonas*, Gottingen: Vandenhoeck und Ruprecht, 1978.
Bongardt, M., H. Burckhart, J.S. Gordon, J. Nielsen-Sikora (Eds.). *Hans Jonas-Handbuch*, Stuttgart: J.B. Metzler, 2021.
Bornkamm, Heinrich (Ed.). *Imago Dei: Beiträge zur theologischen Anthropologie*, Giessen: A. Töpelmann, 1932.
Bultmann, Rudolf. „Die Bedeutung Des Geschichtlichen Jesus Für Die Theologie Des Paulus," *Theologische Blätter* 8 (1929): 137–151.
Bultmann, Rudolf. *Glauben Und Verstehen*, Tübingen: Mohr, 1933.
Bultmann, Rudolf. *Kerygma and Myth: A Theological Debate*, edited by Hans Werner Bartsch, London: S.P.C.K., 1972.
Bultmann, Rudolf. *Neues Testament und Mythologie – das Problem der Entmythologisierung der neutestamentlichen Verkündigung*, edited by Eberhard Jüngel, München: Chr. Kaiser, 1985.
Bultmann, Rudolf. *New Testament and Mythology and Other Basic Writings*, translated by Schubert M. Ogden, London, PA: Fortress Press SCM, 1984.
Bultmann, Rudolf. *Theology of the New Testament,* 2 vols., New York: Scribner, 1951.
Cassirer, Ernst. *Die Philosophie Der Symbolischen Formen*, 3 vols., Das Mythische Denken. Darmstadt Wissenschaftliche Buchgesellschaft, Berlin: Bruno Cassirer Verlag, 1923 [1973].

Congdon, David W. *The Mission of Demythologizing: Rudolf Bultmann's Dialectical Theology*, Minneapolis, MN: Fortress Press, 2015.
Denzinger, Heinrich. *The Sources of Catholic Dogma*, St. Louis, MO: Herder, 1957.
Dilthey, Wilhelm. *Briefwechsel zwischen Wilhelm Dilthey Und Dem Grafen Paul Yorck V. Wartenburg, 1877–1897*, Halle (Saale): Verlag M. Niemeyer, 1923.
Dinkler, E. und Hartwig, T. (Eds.), *Zeit und Geschichte: Dankesgabe an Rudolf Bultmann zum 80. Geburtstag*, Tübingen: Mohr, 1964.
Farin, Ingo. "Count Paul Yorck Von Wartenburg," *The Stanford Encyclopedia of Philosophy*, ed. Edward N. Zalta, (2016). https://plato.stanford.edu/entries/yorck/ (last accessed on September 4, 2024).
Fergusson, David. *Bultmann*. Outstanding Christian Thinkers, London, England: G. Chapman, 1992.
Großmann, Andreas (Ed.). *Bultmann, Rudolf. Briefwechsel 1928–1976. Mit Einem Anhang Anderer Zeugnisse*, Tübingen: Mohr Siebeck, 2020.
Gründer, Karlfried and Rodi, Frithjof (Eds.). *Gesammelte Schriften*, vol. 1–12, Göttingen: Vandenhoeck & Ruprecht, 1961 [1966].
Heidegger, Martin. *Being and Time*, Oxford: Blackwell, 1967.
Heidegger, Martin. *The Phenomenology of Religious Life*, Studies in Continental Thought, Bloomington: Indiana University Press, 2004.
Hühn, Lore and Jantzen, Jörg (Eds.). *Heideggers Schelling-Seminar (1927/28)*, Stuttgart-Bad Canstatt: Frommann-Holzboog, 2010.
Jewett, Robert. *Romans – a Commentary. Hermeneia – a Critical and Historical Commentary on the Bible*, Minneapolis, MN: Fortress Press, 2007.
Johnson, Roger A. *The Origins of Demythologizing: Philosophy and Historiography in the Theology of Rudolf Bultmann*, Studies in the History of Religions, Leiden: Brill, 1974.
Jonas, Hans. *Agostino e il problema Paolino della Libertà*, translated by Claudio Bonaldi, Brescia: Morcelliana, 2007.
Jonas, Hans. *Augustin Und Das Paulinische Freiheitsproblem: Ein Philosophischer Beitrag Zur Genesis Der Christlich-Abendländischen Freiheitsidee*, Forschungen Zur Religion Und Literatur Des Alten Und Neuen Testaments, Göttingen: Vandenhoeck & Ruprecht, 1930.
Jonas, Hans. *Augustin Und Das Paulinische Freiheitsproblem: Eine Philosophische Studie Zum Pelagianischen Streit*, Forschungen Zur Religion Und Literatur Des Alten Und Neuen Testaments, 2nd ed., Göttingen: Vandenhoeck & Ruprecht, 1965.
Jonas, Hans. *Der Begriff Der Gnosis. Inugural-Disertation Zur Erlangung Der Doktorwürde Der Hohen Philosophischen Fakultät Der Philipps-Universität Zu Marburg*, Göttingen: Hubert & Co., 1930.
Jonas, Hans. *Gnosis Und Spätantiker Geist*. Forschungen Zur Religion Und Literatur Des Alten Und Neuen Testaments, Göttingen: Vandenhoeck & Ruprecht, 1934.
Jonas, Hans. *Gnosis Und Spätantiker Geist*. Forschungen Zur Religion Und Literatur Des Alten Und Neuen Testaments, 2 vols., Göttingen: Vandenhoeck & Ruprecht, 1954.
Jonas, Hans. *Philosophical Essays: From Ancient Creed to Technological Man*, Englewood Cliffs, NJ: Prentice-Hall, 1974.
Jonas, Hans. *The Phenomenon of Life: Toward a Philosophical Biology*, Northwestern University Studies in Phenomenology & Existential Philosophy, Evanston, IL: Northwestern University Press, 2001.
Mei, Todd S. "Heidegger and the Appropriation of Metaphysics," *The Heythrop Journal* 50, 2 (2009): 257–270.
Ogden, Schubert M. (Ed.). *Existence and Faith: Shorter Writings of Rudolf Bultmann*, London: Hodder & Stoughton, 1961.

O'Neill, J. C. *Paul's Letter to the Romans*, Pelican Books. Harmondsworth: Penguin, 1975.
Robinson, James M. (Ed.). *The Future of Our Religious Past: Essays in Honour of Rudolf Bultmann*, translated by Charles E. Carlston and Robert P. Scharlemann, London: SCM Press, 1971.
Robinson, James M. "Interpretation in Contemporary Theology – viii. The Pre-History of Demythologization," *Union Seminary Magazine* 20, 1 (1966): 65–77.
Robinson, James M. and John B. Cobb (Eds.). *The New Hermeneutic*, New Frontiers in Theology, New York: Harper & Row, 1964.
Ruin, Hans. "Yorck Von Wartenburg and the Problem of Historical Existence," *Journal of the British Society for Phenomenology* 25, 2 (1994): 111–130.
Settimo, Luca. "Hans Jonas's Reflections on the Human Soul and the Notion of Imago Dei: An Explanation of Their Role in Ethics and Some Possible Historical Influences on Their Development," *History of European Ideas* 49, 5 (2023): 870–884.
Wiese, Christian (Ed.). *Memoirs – Hans Jonas*, translated by Krishna Winston, Waltham, MA: Brandeis University Press, 2008.
Yamada, Nozomu. "Rhetorical, Political, and Ecclesiastical Perspectives of Augustine's and Julian of Eclanum's Theological Response in the Pelagian Controversy," *Scrinium* 14, 1 (2018): 161.
Yorck von Wartenburg, Paul. *Bewusstseinsstellung Und Geschichte: Ein Fragment Aus Dem Philosophischen Nachlass*, Tübingen: M. Niemeyer, 1956.

4 The Aporias of Human Freedom

An Early Letter and Its Long Impact

Michael Bongardt

On July 13, 1929, Jonas wrote a letter to his teacher Rudolf Bultmann.[1] His successful doctoral viva on his dissertation on gnosis was a few months ago. The freshly graduated Jonas presumably writes the letter from Heidelberg, where he moved after his doctorate – if not from Paris, where he also regularly stays during this time.[2]

The letter is a response to an essay by Rudolf Bultmann, which the latter had sent to Jonas a little earlier: "Die Bedeutung des geschichtlichen Jesus für die Theologie des Paulus (The Significance of the Historical Jesus for Paul's Theology)."[3] Jonas apparently wrote this letter in feverish concentration. In the preserved original, after eight handwritten pages, he apologizes for now resorting to the typewriter. Seven more pages follow, until it is said what was to be said for Jonas.

Thirty-five years later – after the book on Augustine, the first volume on gnosis, Jonas' time as soldier in Second World War, the draft of a "philosophical biology" – Jonas takes up this old letter again. He publishes it in 1964, supplemented by an introduction and two sections still to be considered, almost word for word in the Festschrift for Bultmann's 80th birthday.[4] One year later, he included this text as "Appendix III" in the second edition of his book on Augustine.[5] Finally, the text appears in an English-language version edited by Jonas in 1971,[6] then again in 1980 under the title "The Abyss of the Will: Philosophical Meditation on the Seventh Chapter of Paul's Epistle to the Romans."[7] Even if it is not unusual for Jonas to reuse texts largely unchanged even after a long period of time, the repeated publication of the early letter over a period of more than 50 years speaks to the special importance Jonas himself attached to this text.

It is this significance, not least for Jonas' own thinking, that I will attempt to demonstrate in the following text. To do this, it is first necessary to introduce Bultmann's text, which was the occasion for the letter of 1929 (1.). Only then will it be possible to work out the basic theses of Jonas' letter (2.). In a concluding part, I will point out the further developments of these theses in Jonas' complete works (3.).

Jesus and Paul

The juxtaposition of Jesus and Paul serves Bultmann in his aforementioned essay to present the Pauline or Christian doctrine of grace and salvation. In doing so, he remains true to his profession, the exegesis of the New Testament. However, his efforts to interpret the texts in a form that is accessible and acceptable to his contemporaries are unmistakable. In his collaboration with Jonas, he will increasingly place this effort at the centre of his exegetical work by the method of "demythologization."[8]

That Jesus and Paul never met; that in the few places where Paul refers to the authority of Jesus' words, he rather draws on a congregational tradition than using it to legitimize his preaching; that for Paul the life and deeds of Jesus were of secondary importance theologically; that the scandal of the death on the cross and the belief in the abiding presence of Christ are central to Paul's Christology: all this is unquestionable and self-evident for Bultmann.[9]

If, therefore, historical encounters as well as content-related receptions fail to determine the relationship between Jesus and Paul, one must, according to Bultmann, take a look at the message and practice of both and search for similarities and differences therein. Contrary to the first impression of biblical texts and a widespread exegetical opinion, Bultmann sees "a far-reaching factual agreement of Paul's theology with Jesus' preaching […] in the *teaching of law*."[10] Both, according to Bultmann, assume that the law expresses the will of God; that "*the commandment of love* is *the basic content of the law*"[11]; that the law reveals man's sin. "*Man's real sin* is that he himself takes his will, his life, into his own hands, secures himself, and thus has his self-confidence, his 'glory'."[12] This "original sin"[13] leads to man no longer being able to follow the divine law adequately. For, from his basic attitude, he will take it as a commandment, the observance of which will give him new glory and a legal claim against God. For Paul's theology as well as for Jesus' preaching and practice, according to Bultmann's exegesis, it is certain that man needs God's mercy and grace in order to be freed from captivity in his sin.

Against the background of this common ground, Bultmann can also make clear what he sees as the decisive difference between Jesus and Paul: for Jesus, God's liberating action lies in the future, in the approaching kingdom of God, which has already dawned in Jesus' healing attention to sinners. Paul's perspective is different. He never met Jesus. After joining the Christian community, he becomes probably its most influential theologian. At the centre of his theology are the "scandalon" of death of Jesus on the cross and his resurrection. In them, Paul sees – in retrospect – the decisive event through which God redeemed humanity. For Paul, the access to salvation is faith in the redemptive effect of Jesus' death. For him, the gracious justification of the sinner "has already taken place and become accessible to faith by virtue of the work of salvation ["Heilswerk"] that has taken place in Jesus."[14] Bultmann also emphasizes that faith is only possible for those who accept the "scandalon" that only through Jesus' death was salvation possible.[15] This message – and thus Christ himself – meets the people of all future generations through the preaching of those who believe in him. "Only through the kerygma is Christ accessible, and only in faith is new aeon seen."[16]

Philosophy and Judaism

The letter in which Hans Jonas deals with Rudolf Bultmann's contribution, which has just been briefly described, is concerned with two, at best loosely connected, questions. On the one hand, he is concerned with a "*philosophical approach*"[17] to the sinfulness of all people presupposed by Paul and Bultmann. The other is a critique of the Christian dogma that only baptism in the name of Jesus can free people from sin.

Original Sin

Like Bultmann, Jonas uses the term "original sin," which according to church doctrine refers to Adam's sin, which is passed on to all those on earth coming after Adam.[18] For Jonas, the reference to church dogma cannot, of course, be a philosophical argument. Therefore, he sets himself the goal of opening up the meaning of this Christian dogma philosophically. Methodologically, he chooses the path of a "structural analysis," which is supposed to reveal the "existential ground" for the sinfulness of all human beings.[19] In terms of content, any philosophical reflection on original sin immediately faces a serious problem: the talk of a "necessary sin" is a contradictio in adjectu. For sins or culpable deeds are those for which a person has decided willingly, i.e. freely. Therefore, there can be no sin without freedom.[20] This excludes a "necessary" sin in the strict sense of the word. Jonas therefore sees it as his duty to elucidate the existential reason for the necessity of sin that "is *nevertheless precisely* that of a deed for one's own account and thus the self-doom of freedom surrendered to itself."[21]

At this point in his text and probably earlier, the assumption suggests itself that Jonas is borrowing from Kierkegaard's examination of the dogma of original sin. For Kierkegaard also begins his analysis of human freedom and fear – which he characterizes as a "psychological approach" – with a reference to the inner contradiction of the dogma of a necessary sinfulness (transmitted through procreation). He succinctly formulates: "Innocence is lost through guilt alone, every human being loses innocence essentially in the same way as Adam did."[22]

For Jonas, the starting point of his structural analysis is the human capacity for reflexivity and self-consciousness. Man directs his attention not only to the world around him, but also to himself. He can – and always will – think of himself as a thinking individual. According to Jonas, this basic structure – called the "dreaming mind" by Kierkegaard[23] – is initially a "harmless[…] iteration."[24] If man thinks of himself merely as a thinker, it may become as meaningless as in the Glass Bead Game. But another quality and reality arises when the will awakens, which wills itself as freedom. This will is not "some individual psychic act", but "it is always already there 'a priori'."[25] However, it is not initially directed at any object alien to it – but "it is concerned with itself."[26] Heidegger, to whom Jonas explicitly refers here, called this orientation of the willing human being towards himself "care" [Sorge].[27] Only through the (self-)reflection of the will does the human being become a self, "the continual self-constitution of the moral person" takes place.[28] Man understands himself as freedom and becomes free in this.[29]

This self-constitution of freedom, however, is not yet self-entanglement. Jonas explains its emergence in a further step: as a subject, the human being, freely orienting himself towards the world, turns the world surrounding him (and other human beings) into an object. Since, however, in objectifying the world, man always also relates to himself, he – looking at himself – becomes an object to himself. Fixating entirely on himself as his object, man steps out of the "'original' unity with the totality of being,"[30] and isolates himself in his arrogance. Freedom, according to Jonas, expropriates itself when it only thinks of itself as willing – and does not move towards the world as humble freedom. Such freedom, which is only directed towards itself and is only interested in itself, is described by Jonas with the metaphor of "entanglement in itself." Such freedom is no longer able to relate to other beings, even to other people. Already in his letter of 1929, Jonas connects this isolation of the self with the biblical myth of the Fall.[31] In the later version of his text, he adds: "Shouldn't this be at least one meaning, the minimal as well as the fundamental meaning, of the Pauline 'self-glorying' in one's work?"[32]

Jonas is aware that he has not yet reached his goal with this existential analysis of human self-consciousness. He has indeed shown the possibility inherent in freedom that this freedom cancels itself out, that man thus fails using his freedom and in this sense becomes guilty or sinful. He has also made clear why and how freedom itself becomes entangled in itself. But why, as presupposed by the original sin dogma and Bultmann, should every human being "necessarily" commit or have committed this sin? Once again, the answer is close to Kierkegaard: like Kierkegaard, Jonas speaks of a "giddiness" that grips man when he sees the open possibility of his freedom. In this giddiness, man seeks a foothold. That is why he decides to stand on his own, to hold on to himself – or to the objectivation of his self. In this step, he freely loses his freedom.[33] And all efforts to follow ethics, or the "law," are marked by this self-assertion and are thus doomed to failure.

It is not readily apparent why the self-objectifying, entangled freedom – i.e., the human being who is entirely self-referential – fails, ties itself down, loses its freedom. The numerous metaphors found in Jonas, but also in Kierkegaard and Heidegger, sometimes seem to obscure rather than reveal what is described. However, there are hints of the phenomena discussed here in the text: for example, it has already been mentioned that Jonas sees the danger that a person who focuses entirely on himself loses contact with the world, with other people – contact that can certainly be understood as the purpose of freedom. For Kierkegaard, the talk of freedom caught up in itself has above all a religious dimension: the failing – desperate – human being is the one who does not see or does not accept, that his self is connected to God, to whom man owes his being and his freedom. Last but not least, Jonas himself builds a bridge to Kant's understanding of freedom: for Kant, a deed is only good if it is carried out because it is good. If, on the other hand, the motive for doing it is the praise or merit to be expected for this deed, it has lost the basis for its goodness.[34]

Jonas' existential analysis of the dogma of original sin, which ends with these thoughts, can confidently be called a "demythologisation avant la letter." In the context of the 1929 letter, however, the analysis serves primarily to support Bultmann's theology of human sinfulness, which is oriented towards Jesus and Paul.

"Solus Christus"

This unity breaks down in the second part of the letter. The disagreement is already indicated when Jonas writes within his analysis of universal sinfulness:

> However, with the turn from [...] the reflection of the will to self-objectification the matter does not rest. A freedom that is in earnest about itself will not stop here. [...] The will in his living reflection *will* catch itself in the self-abnegation it has just undertaken in objectivation [...] – and dissolve it again in a new decision that already embraces it.[35]

The thrust of this thesis is obvious: it is directed against the Christian conviction that only the "salvific work of Christ" and faith in it can free the sinner from his self-entanglement in sin. Bultmann's exegesis of Pauline theology also rests on this foundation of Christian soteriology, as already mentioned above.[36] Aware of the radical nature of his objection, Jonas writes almost appeasingly: "About this possibility [of divine intervention in dialectically unfolding freedom, M.B.] philosophy has nothing to say."

But he does not drop his critical concern. However, he changes the level of argumentation and deals with the theological and historical question of the interpretation of the Pharisees, an authoritative Jewish movement at the time of Jesus. Jonas criticizes the understanding of Pharisaism that Bultmann and Paul develop. For both, the Pharisees are protagonists of a particularly strict and consistent Judaism. According to Bultmann, they seek to fulfil the "law" in every detail in order to be able to boast about their correct behaviour and be rewarded by God.[37] In this way, according to Paul, they represent the prototype of entangled freedom, which in fact affects all people and from which only faith in Christ can liberate. Jonas, on the other hand, sees Jesus' relationship to the Pharisees differently: Jesus confronts them as well as other Jewish groups of his time by focusing the divine law on the commandment of love. He presents God's love and readiness to forgive in his preaching as well as in his deeds. Jesus invites the Pharisees as well as all others who listen to him to the redeeming faith in God's readiness to forgive and to the freedom regained through this. Many aspects of Jesus' message are found precisely in the Pharisaic tradition, to which Jesus was obviously much closer than the reports in the Gospels suggest. Thus, according to Jonas, the same applies to the Pharisees as to Jesus:

> And so in his [Jesus', M.B.] proclamation [...] a redemption of constant sinful humanity through the death of a saviour on the cross and his resurrection would have no place at all, because people have direct access to God and to real being before him.[38]

It is not without reason that I have devoted much attention to the early letter Jonas wrote to his teacher Bultmann. For in this letter, which at first glance has as its theme the relationship of Paul to Jesus examined by Bultmann, Jonas is concerned with a philosophical reflection on human freedom, its possibilities and dangers, its success and failures – in short: with the aporias of freedom, which can lose itself but also be saved.

This short text marks the beginning of a path of thought by Jonas that starts in his studies on the history of religion and the philosophy of existence, but will go far beyond this field of research. The question of the peculiar constitution of human freedom runs as a core idea through Jonas' Augustine book, his philosophy of life up to his late work on human responsibility. I would like to present this core idea succinctly in the following pages.

Continuations

At the beginning, I put forward the thesis that the existential-ontological and anthropological questions developed in his early letter to Bultmann are significant for Jonas' entire work: he pursued them in different directions and found new answers. For the research on gnosis, which is rightly regarded as Jonas' early work, its significance for the later Jonas is presented in many facets by numerous contributions in this volume. In the following, I will limit myself to tracing the analysis and the concept of human freedom found in the aforementioned letter in Jonas' further work.

Augustine

At first glance, it is surprising that in the later publications of his long letter to Bultmann, Jonas gives it the title "Philosophical Meditation on Paul, Epistle to the Romans, Chapter 7." It is true that in these publications he placed the text of Rom 7: 7–25 first,[39] but the Epistle of Paul plays no discernible role in the "existential analysis" that follows. The concluding critique of Paul's characterization of Pharisees is only indirectly connected to Chapter 7 of the Letter to the Romans. Bultmann, too, in his text commented on by Jonas, refers much more to the second rather than the seventh chapter of the Letter to the Romans.

The "late" title only becomes comprehensible when one takes into account the book on Augustine and its first appendix. As the subtitle suggests ("A Philosophical Study of the Pelagian Controversy"), this book is first of all a theological-historical reconstruction of the dispute between Augustine and Pelagius. The core of the dispute was the question of the scope of human freedom – in relation to the world, to oneself, and above all to God.[40] Pelagius sees human beings as fundamentally able, with faith in God, to shape the aforementioned relationships, to orient themselves towards the good and, in the case of sin, to hope for forgiveness. Already in his early writings, Augustine wrestled with the question of how to explain the power of evil that can be experienced again and again and how human freedom relates to this power.[41] In his debate with Pelagius, Augustine shows – according to Jonas – an increasing tendency to "extend more and more the sphere of action of grace and to restrict more and more that of man's own capacity."[42] Therefore, he argues that sinful man can neither know, will, nor do the good.[43] There are above all three motives that pushed Augustine to this argumentation: the already mentioned power of evil, which people see themselves at the mercy of again and again, and which prevents them from doing the good; the Christological conviction that the death of Jesus is necessary for the redemption of mankind;[44] finally, the eschatological motif that is only understandable under the widespread conviction in Augustine's time that most people will be damned in the Last Judgement and only a few will be saved: according to Augustine, this is only compatible with God's justice if it is just that God condemns all people because they all are sinners – but it does not contradict this justice if he saves individuals out of grace by working the good in them. To think of the sinfulness of all human beings, Augustine developed the idea of inherited sin, that is, sin transmitted through procreation.

With his book on Augustine, Jonas does not intervene in this dispute – which continues to this day – as a theologian, which in fact he is not. It is again a "philosophical study."[45] To this end, he resorts on the one hand to the argumentation of his letter of 1929 and on the other hand refers at length to Chapter 7 of the Letter to the Romans.[46] At the centre of this text, Paul describes the inner conflict he experiences again and again:

> I do not do the good I want, but the evil I do not want is what I keep on doing. Now if I do what I do not want, it is no longer I who do it, but sin that dwells within me.[47]

Jonas reads this text as a phenomenology of human freedom, drawing on key insights from his 1929 letter to Bultmann. This freedom is always in danger of becoming entangled in itself and of dissolving in this entanglement – and at the same time it is painfully aware of what it is doing and tries to escape its own dynamics. The disruption of will and action described by Paul in this text Jonas reads as a phenomenology of human freedom. This freedom is always in danger of becoming entangled in itself – and at the same time is painfully aware of what it is doing and tries to escape its own dynamics. Jonas is able to illuminate all this on the basis of his existential analysis without sharing Paul's theological presuppositions. However, it should be noted here that he only succeeds in doing so by ignoring the Christological point of Paul's description, which sees salvation from brokenness as guaranteed by Christ alone.[48] The consequence of this Pauline exegesis is that Jonas sharply criticizes the Augustinian theology of (inherited) sin and salvation. He sees in it a one-sided resolution of the dialectic of freedom and bondage by which human existence is determined. Paul, on the other hand, according to Jonas, is able to endure this tension.[49]

According to Jonas, such one-sidedness is a specific characteristic of dogmas (and myths). They have the tendency to solidify in the course of history until finally the questions behind them are no longer recognized. For Jonas, the task of philosophical, or more precisely existential, analysis of dogmatic and mythical texts is to uncover these primary questions.[50] For him, it is a "retranslation" from the rational, dogmatic to the existential sphere:

> In the existential sphere, 'contradiction' means something essentially different than in the rational thing-sphere. While here, according to the *principium contradictionis*, only one *or* the other can be – referring to the corresponding propositions: one must be true and the other must be false – human life [Dasein] is the livingly unified *consummation of* the incommensurable; in this

consummation of itself, it is in each case the one and the other antithesis as the most intrinsic and tragically indissoluble, structurally conditioned movability of being – this very movability is its existing.[51]

The universal and formative reception of Augustine's theology in the churches of the West may be seen as an indication that the doctrine of original sin was for a long time an apparently plausible explanation of the aporias of freedom experienced by human beings. The evidence of this "myth" has declined ever faster since the 18th century – although the inner conflict of his will and freedom is still experienced by every reflecting human being today. The loss of credibility of this Christian dogma can be read as an illustration of the "historical transcendental" described by Nathalie Frogneux in this volume.[52]

Whether and to what extent Jonas had Chapter 7 of the Letter to the Romans in mind when he wrote his letter to Bultmann cannot be established. But this text played a central role in the debate with Augustine. It turned out that his early analysis was ideally suited to open up this Pauline text, even if it was not originally intended to do so. Thus, the late title of the early letter is justified in terms of content.

Organism and Freedom

Modern biology, especially the theory of evolution, challenged Jonas to reflect on man and his place in nature. From the war years onwards, this subject becomes more and more the focus of his interest. The new question also confronts him with polarities, dualisms, and one-sided monisms. Again, he starts from a phenomenon: the polar unity of body and soul, matter and spirit, and in particular necessity and freedom,[53] as that which man experiences himself. Jonas opposes the dualistic conception of man in the tradition of Descartes, but also the monistic concepts of the idealistic fading out of materiality and the exclusive claim to explanation by the natural sciences. Once again, he is concerned with doing justice to the directly experienced polar unity in an ontological reflection.[54] The "young Jonas" is easily recognizable in the task: his struggle with the phenomenon of man's simultaneous experience of freedom and lack of freedom in relation to God as well as to himself; his critique of Gnostic dualism, which grows with his insights into the history of religion and which not only contradicts Greek cosmic thinking and the biblical faith in creation, but, according to Jonas, inevitably leads to nihilism;[55] his critique of Pelagius' (focusing on human freedom) and Augustine's (focusing on the bondage of sin experienced by men) one-sided understandings of freedom, which he overcomes with the help of Pauline anthropology.

This time Jonas goes much further than in his earlier works. He focuses his gaze not only on human beings, but on the phenomenon of living organisms as a whole.[56] Life, according to Jonas, is defined as metabolism. Every metabolizing being, however, stands in the dialectic of freedom and necessity: as long as it lives, it is faced with the alternative of continuing the metabolism or ending it. But this "freedom," which Jonas attributes to even the simplest organisms, is necessarily dependent on the continuation of metabolism. For him, "inwardness," which arises through the clear demarcation of the living being from the environment, and "transcendence," which is realized in every metabolic transgression of one's own limits, are also part of every form of life. In all these aspects, man is a living being like any other. And yet, he is different from all these others: only he can become conscious of himself, only he can choose freely, only he can take responsibility for his actions and his thinking beyond his death. But all this is only possible for him because and as long as he is a living being.[57]

In later years, Jonas took up these questions again, now in a determined confrontation with brain research. This research denies man's freedom with new intensity and claims to be able to explain all his thinking and acting as causally determined and thus necessary. In his answer, Jonas remains true to his unique structure of thought: "Diversity does not cancel out unity; the unified being [of brain and mind, M.B.] is not yet exhausted by the predominant physical aspect, as the voice of our own self has always told us.[58] Can we think of oppositeness and connectedness, freedom and determination as a polar unity? Jonas already discovered such an attempt in Paul, who described himself in this way in Romans 7; in his philosophical biology, Jonas transferred this structure of thought to an ontology of the living.

Responsibility

As is well known, in the last phase of his life and thought, Jonas once again confronts a new task. In view of the threat of military or ecological catastrophe due to human action, he searches for an appropriate ethics for today. He is concerned with the justification and description of human responsibility for the future possibility of "genuine human life."[59] Jonas has in mind the ever-developing technology, which extends the consequences of human action beyond every conceivable spatial and temporal boundary. In the application, man experiences himself as a being capable of action who can decide to develop and apply technology. According to Jonas, "homo faber" has taken the fate of the earth into his own hands.

Now he seems to have left the reflections of his early letter behind. There is no longer any talk of the self-entanglement of freedom, of the polarity of necessity and freedom, of the relationship between brain and mind.[60] Admittedly, the multiple conditionality of human freedom of decision and action is a recurring theme, not only with regard to the consequences of technical interventions, which can no longer be controlled. But at the centre is the experience of unimagined ability. In a remarkable reversal of Kant's argumentation, which concluded from the moral ought that there is a moral ability, Jonas emphasizes: "The ability carries with it the ought."[61] Man's responsibility for his actions and their consequences follows from his ability – even if he can no longer control them. Responsibility grows with power. And it has long been foreseeable that man will have to forego some of his abilities so that future generations can still survive.

Such thoughts are not found in the 1929 letter. But they can be read as a filling of a void that remained in the existential analysis of the dialectic of human freedom. Focusing entirely on the "demythologization" of the Christian dogma of original sin, the letter doesn't consider the alternative. Nevertheless, Jonas emphasizes – against the Christian dogma – the ability of freedom to escape its entanglement. How a successful realization of freedom, i.e. not fixated on isolated self-assertion, can look, is only hinted at: on the one hand, with the summary of the divine (and ethical) law in the commandment of love, for the fulfilment of which Jonas referred to the example of Jesus; on the other hand, with the reference to a possible "immediate humility of the simply creaturely."[62] "The Imperative of Responsibility" translates this possibility of non-failing freedom into the radical threat to every possible freedom in our present. Jonas demonstrates that the assumption of this responsibility is possible through parental care for the infant, but also through the image of the responsible politician.

Thus, at the beginning and end of Jonas' path of thought, a reflection on the abysses and an appeal to the positive possibilities of human freedom confront each other. Thus here is another polarity whose tension must be endured. In the best case, it can lead to a realistic picture of human freedom of decision and action through mutual criticism and enrichment.[63]

Notes

1 The original draft can be found in the Jonas Archive at the University of Konstanz under the shelfmark HJ 7-12-27. A transcription of the original is published under the title "Erster Paulus-Entwurf. Brief an Rudolf Bultmann vom 13. Juli 1929," in Hans Jonas, *Kritische Gesamtausgabe (KGA)*, ed. by D. Böhler et al., Freiburg i.Br./Berlin/Wien 2010 ff, vol. III/1, 23–33 (cited as Jonas, "Erster Paulus-Entwurf"); the authentic version of the letter by Jonas can be found in: Rudolf Bultmann/Hans Jonas, *Briefwechsel 1928–1976* (Tübingen: Mohr, 2020), ed. by Andreas Großmann, 2–11.
2 Cf. editorial remarks in: *KGA III/1*: 510f.
3 Rudolf Bultmann, "Die Bedeutung des geschichtlichen Jesus für die Theologie des Paulus," in *Theologische Blätter* VIII (1929): 137–151; reprint: Rudolf Bultmann. "Glauben und Verstehen," in *Gesammelte Aufsätze*, vol. 1 (Tübingen: Mohr, 1954), 188–213 (cited as: Bultmann, "Die Bedeutung des geschichtlichen Jesus").
4 Hans Jonas, "Philosophische Meditation über Paulus, Römerbrief, Kapitel 7," in *Zeit und Geschichte. Dankesgabe an Rudolf Bultmann* (Tübingen: Mohr, 1965), ed. by E. Dinkler, 557–570.
5 Hans Jonas, *Augustin und das paulinische Freiheitsproblem* (Göttingen: Vandenhoeck & Ruprecht, 1965), 93–105; reprinted in: *KGA III/1*, 35–55 (cited as Jonas, *Augustin*).
6 In *The Future of Our Religious Past* (New York/London: Harper & Row, 1971), ed. by J. E. Robinson, Chapter 15.
7 In Hans Jonas, *Philosophical Essays* (Chicago, IL: Chicago University Press, 1980), 335–348.
8 On the significance of Jonas' philosophical reflection for Bultmann's theology, I gladly refer to the detailed contribution by Luca Settimo in this volume (xxx).
9 Cf. Bultmann, "Die Bedeutung des geschichtlichen Jesus," 188–191.
10 Bultmann, "Die Bedeutung des geschichtlichen Jesus," 191. All quotations from German-language sources have been translated into English by the author of this text.
11 Bultmann "Die Bedeutung des geschichtlichen Jesus," 195.
12 Bultmann "Die Bedeutung des geschichtlichen Jesus," 196.
13 Bultmann "Die Bedeutung des geschichtlichen Jesus," 196.
14 Bultmann, "Die Bedeutung des geschichtlichen Jesus," 200.
15 Cf. Bultmann, "Die Bedeutung des geschichtlichen Jesus," 206–208.
16 Bultmann, "Die Bedeutung des geschichtlichen Jesus," 212f. Two things are particularly striking about this final thought of the text from today's perspective: On the one hand, the emphasis on the kerygma as the place of Christ's presence points to Bultmann's later

"demythologising" interpretation of Jesus' resurrection, while, for example, the preceding talk of Christ's "work of salvation" is still couched entirely in traditional dogmatic language; on the other hand, Bultmann – like the broad consensus of Christian theology of his time – evidently presupposes without question that for Jews too, the only possibility of salvation is faith in Christ.
17 Jonas, "Erster Paulus-Entwurf," 23.
18 Both do not use the term "inherited sin (Erbsünde)" (lat. peccatum hereditarium), which expresses more clearly than the term "original sin" the ecclesiastical dogma that original sin is transmitted "not by imitation but by procreation" (cf. DH 231 et al.).
19 Both quotations from Jonas, "Erster Paulus-Entwurf," 23.
20 In his letter to Bultmann, Jonas presupposes that man has will and freedom. In his later works, he defends this conviction against manifold objections from contemporary philosophy.
21 Jonas, "Erster Paulus-Entwurf," 23.
22 Sören Kierkegaard, *Der Begriff Angst*, in *Gesammelte Werke* (Gütersloh: Gütersloher Verlagshaus, 1983), ed. by E. Hirsch u. H. Gerdes, 11th vol., 2nd ed., 34 (cited as Kierkegaard, *Angst*). In his text "On the Hermeneutical Structure of Dogma", Appendix I of his book on Augustin, which appeared with this appendix a year after the letter, Jonas explicitly refers to Kierkegaard: "Cf. the long path of the dogma of original sin up to Kierkegaard" (Jonas, *Augustin*, 152).
23 Kierkegaard, *Angst*, 39.
24 Jonas, "Erster Paulus-Entwurf," 24.
25 Jonas, "Erster Paulus-Entwurf," 24.
26 Jonas, "Erster Paulus-Entwurf," 25.
27 Jonas, "Erster Paulus-Entwurf," 25; on this Martin Heidegger: Sein und Zeit. 16th ed. (Tübingen: Mohr, 1986), esp. 316–323.
28 Jonas, "Erster Paulus-Entwurf," 25.
29 Cf. Sören Kierkegaard, "Entweder/Oder," in *Gesammelte Werke* (Gütersloh: Gütersloher Verlagshaus, 1987), ed. by E. Hirsch and H. Gerdes, 2nd vol., 2nd ed., 227–230.
30 Jonas, "Erster Paulus-Entwurf," 26.
31 Jonas, "Erster Paulus-Entwurf," 26.
32 Jonas, *Augustin*, 44.
33 Cf. Jonas, "Erster Paulus-Entwurf," 28, and on this Kierkegaard, *Angst*, 60f. It is striking that Jonas takes up Kierkegaard's image of the "giddiness" of freedom, but not the analysis of the anxiety associated with freedom that also resonates in Heidegger's "Sorge". It is not necessary to go into this in detail here.
34 Cf. Jonas, *Augustin*, 45–48.
35 Jonas, "Erster Paulus-Entwurf," 27.
36 Cf. endnote 14 above.
37 This polemical view of the Pharisees certainly has its points of reference in the New Testament writings. From the early twentieth century onwards, Jewish scholars who studied Christianity worked out that the group of Pharisees, who played a major role in detaching the religion of Israel from its attachment to the temple and its priesthood, by no means corresponded to the distorted picture painted in the Gospels. In today's Christian exegesis of the New Testament, it is undisputed that Jesus himself was quite close to the Pharisees and that no anti-Judaism based on the classical Pharisee image can refer to Jesus. Among the important pioneers of this correction in the history of religion is Joseph Klausner with his work: Jesus von Nazareth, *His Time, His Life and His Teachings [1922]* (Jerusalem: The Jewish Publishing House, 1952), 3rd ed., 506–512.
38 Jonas, "Erster Paulus-Entwurf," 32.
39 Cf. Jonas, *Augustin*, 39f.
40 At this point I would like to refer to two contributions in this volume: Yaël Amog goes into detail on Augustine's concept of love – this mainly in connection with Hannah Arendt's dissertation. She also traces Jonas' reception of Augustine and his focus on the

The Aporias of Human Freedom   65

concept of freedom. Here, too, there are a number of very inspiring references (cf. in this volume p. xxx). My own contribution attempts to go beyond Amog in two directions: firstly, by focusing on the critique Jonas makes of Augustine; secondly, by emphasising freedom as the fundamental condition of the possibility of love.

Andreas Großmann's contribution is very close to my thoughts in terms of content. However, it is thematically much broader: Thankfully, he reconstructs Jonas' distinction between the Stoic and the Christian concept of freedom. He also deals with the topic of "demythologisation" in desirable detail. In essence, Großmann is concerned, as I am, with the determination of freedom in man's relationship to himself, to the world, and to God. It is left to the reader to detect the differences between our interpretations – which are probably rooted not least in our different denominational backgrounds (Protestant and Catholic) and prove once again how important it is to interweave these perspectives.

41 Cf. Jonas, *Augustin*, 91f.
42 Cf. Jonas, *Augustin*, 112.
43 Cf. Jonas, *Augustin*, 112–128.
44 Cf. Jonas, *Augustin* 92: "The question, then, in brief, is: What can man do in the face of God without God? – Equally briefly, the Pauline answer is: Nothing. There is no sufficiency of man with regard to the demands of God – and from this there results for him the necessity of grace (which has become available to him in a certain sense through the redeeming death of Christ)". On the current Christian theological and philosophical debate on the doctrine of original sin and Augustine's understanding of freedom, see Kurt Flasch, *Augustin. Introduction to His Thought* (Stuttgart: Reclam, 1980), 172–226; Karl-Heinz Menke, *Das Kriterium des Christseins. Grundriss der Gnadenlehre* (Regensburg: Pustet, 2003), 24–76.
45 Cf. Jonas, *Augustin*, 80.
46 Cf. Jonas, *Augustin*, 97–128.
47 Rom 7:19–21.
48 Cf. Rom 7, 25.
49 Cf. Jonas, *Augustin*, 129–149.
50 Cf. the precise description of the methodology (and its changes) in which Jonas sought to make religious and mythical texts existentially accessible in the very precise contribution by Daniel M. Herskowitz in this volume. What seems particularly important to me is the proof that myths are understood by Jonas as "objectivisations" of "Dasein" – which can be observed particularly vividly in Augustine's doctrine of original sin. On myth-making as objectification, see also Luca Settimo's chapter in this volume.
51 Jonas, *Augustin*, 153f.
52 Cf. the third chapter in Frogneux's chapter in this volume.
53 Cf. Hans Jonas, *Organismus und Freiheit. Ansätze zu einer philosophischen Biologie* (Göttingen: Vandenhoeck & Ruprecht, 1973); reprinted in in: *KGA I/1*, 1–359 (cited as Jonas, *Organismus*), esp. 277–323; Hans Jonas: "Evolution und Freiheit" (cited as Jonas, "Evolution"), in *KGA III/1*, 209–226.
54 Cf. Jonas, *Organismus*, here: 36–47.
55 Cf. Hans Jonas, "Gnosis, Existentialismus und Nihilismus," in *Zwischen Nichts und Ewigkeit. Zur Lehre vom Menschen* (Göttingen: Vandenhoeck & Ruprecht, 1987), 2nd ed., 5–25.
56 Cf. on the following Jonas, *Augustin*, 152–168; Jonas, "Evolution," 218–221.
57 On the differentiation of man and animal, cf: Hans Jonas, "Werkzeug, Bild und Grab," in *Scheidewege* 15 (1985/1986), 47–58; reprinted in: *KGA III/1*, 227–239.
58 Hans Jonas, *Macht oder Ohnmacht der Subjektivität* (Frankfurt: Suhrkamp, 1981), reprinted in: *KGA I/2.1*, 421–509, here: 477.
59 Hans Jonas, *Das Prinzip Verantwortung* (Frankfurt: Suhrkamp, 1979): reprinted in: *KGA I/2.1*, 1–420 (cited as Jonas, *Verantwortung*), here: 40.

The justification of an ethical ought in general as well as the responsibility for the future possibility of human life in particular is not easy to ascertain from Jonas' work and is the subject of highly controversial debates. There is no question in my mind that for Jonas the argument of self-affirmation, which every living organism carries out in metabolism, carries great ontological weight (cf. Jonas, "Evolution"). The consciousness of freedom that characterises human beings makes ethically relevant decisions possible in the first place, and makes human beings responsible for the continuation of life.

In the search for a non-ontological justification of responsibility, Dietrich Böhler – supported by Hans Lenk, Vittorio Hösle, and others – has presented a draft to justify the demands highlighted by Hans Jonas in terms of discourse ethics. Cf. e.g.: Dietrich Böhler, "Ethik der Zukunfts- und Lebensverantwortung. Erster Teil: Begründung. Zwischen Metaphysik und Reflexion im Dialog," in *Orientierung und Verantwortung. Begegnungen mit Hans Jonas* (Würzburg: Königshausen & Neumann, 2004), ed. by Dietrich Böhler and Jens Peter Brune, 97–159.

Elad Lapidot reads Jonas "against the grain" and suggests that Jonas' understanding of ethics is closely linked to Heidegger's philosophy (cf. his contributions in this volume). This remains worthy of consideration. But in view of Jonas' explicit distancing from his teacher's philosophy, which he describes as incapable of developing an ethics, this interpretation is also problematic. Cf. Hans Jonas, *Husserl und Heidegger*, Lecture from 1962, typescript: Jonas Archive, University of Konstanz HJ 17-3-1; reprinted in *KGA III/1*, 205–224, here: 220f. On the central concept of "nihilism" in this debate, see the illuminating contribution by Libera Pisano in this volume, in which she discusses the political background and interventions of Jonas' philosophical thought.

Also relevant – as briefly presented by Lapidot in this volume – is Jonas' concept of human responsibility not only *towards* but *for* God: a God who cannot be comprehended and is a "becoming God" whose future depends on human action. It seems likely to me that this motif was particularly important to Jonas – while he knew about the limited persuasive power of religious or even metaphysical reasons. Cf. Hans Jonas, "Gottesbegriff nach Auschwitz. Eine jüdische Stimme," in *Reflexionen finsterer Zeit. Zwei Vorträge von Fritz Stern und Hans Jonas* (Tübingen: Mohr, 1984), ed. by O. Hofius; reprinted in *KGA III/1*, 407–426; Hans Jonas, "Wie kann wir unsere Pflicht gegen die Nachwelt und die Erde unabhängig vom Glauben begründen?" in *Dem Leben trauen, weil Gott es mit uns lebt. 88. Deutscher Katholikentag München 4.–8. Juli 1984* (Paderborn: Verlag Bonifacius-Druckerei, 1984); reprinted in *KGA I/2.1*, 515–528.

60 However, the study on "Macht oder Ohnmacht der Subjektivität" (cf. endnote 46) was written during this period. It was supposed to be part of "Das Prinzip Verantwortung", but was – in the German edition – published separately and was received only to a very limited extent.

61 Hans Jonas, "Prinzip Verantwortung – Zur Grundlegung einer Zukunftsethik," in *Zukunftsethik und Industriegesellschaft* (München: Piper, 1986), ed. by Th. Meyer and S. Miller, 3–14; reprinted in: *KGA I/2.1*, 529–544, here: 531. In contrast to this Kant, KprV, A 54: Man "thus judges that he can do something, therefore, as he is aware that he ought to, and recognises in himself the freedom that would otherwise have remained unknown to him without the moral law". Directly related to this, see Jonas, *Verantwortung*, 249–251.

62 Jonas, "Erster Paulus-Entwurf," 26.

63 Last but not least: many thanks to James Pankhurst and Jens Ole Beckers for their valuable help in translating and formatting this text.

Bibliography

Böhler, Dietrich. "Ethik der Zukunfts- und Lebensverantwortung. Erster Teil: Begründung. Zwischen Metaphysik und Reflexion im Dialog." In *Orientierung und Verantwortung*, edited by Dietrich Böhler and Jens Peter Brune. Würzburg: Könighausen & Neumann, 2004, 97–159.

Bultmann, Rudolf. "Die Bedeutung des geschichtlichen Jesus für die Theologie des Paulus," *Theologische Blätter VIII* (1929): 137–151; reprinted in: Bultmann, Rudolf. *Glauben und Verstehen. Gesammelte Aufsätze*. Vol. 1. Tübingen: Mohr, 1954, 188–213.

Bultmann, Rudolf and Hans Jonas. *Briefwechsel 1928–1976*, edited by Andreas Großmann. Tübingen: Mohr, 2020.

Flasch, Kurt. *Augustin. Einführung in sein Denken*. Stuttgart: Reclam, 1980.

Heidegger, Martin. *Sein und Zeit*. 16th ed. Tübingen: Mohr, 1986.

Jonas, Hans. „Erster Paulus-Entwurf. Brief an Rudolf Bultmann vom 13. Juli 1929." *KGA III/1*, 23–33.

Jonas, Hans. *Husserl und Heidegger*, Lecture from 1962, typescript: Jonas Archive, University of Konstanz HJ 17-3-1, reprinted in: *KGA III/1*, 205–224.

Jonas, Hans. "Philosophische Meditation über Paulus, Römerbrief, Kapitel 7." In *Zeit und Geschichte. Dankesgabe an Rudolf Bultmann*, edited by E. Dinkler. Tübingen: Mohr, 1964, 557–570.

Jonas, Hans. *Augustin und das paulinische Freiheitsproblem. Eine philosophische Studie zum pelagianischen Streit*. Rev. 2nd ed., edited by J. M. Robinson. Göttingen: Vandenhoeck & Ruprecht, 1965, 93–105; reprinted in: *KGA III/1*: 35–55.

Jonas, Hans. "Philosophical Meditation on the Seventh Chapter of Paul's Epistle to the Romans." In *The Future of Our Religious Past: Essays in Honour of Rudolf Bultmann*, edited by J. M. Robinson, Chapter 15. New York/London: Harper & Row, 1971.

Jonas, Hans. *Organismus und Freiheit. Ansätze zu einer philosophischen Biologie*. Göttingen: Vandenhoeck & Ruprecht, 1973; reprinted in: *KGA I/1*, 1–359.

Jonas, Hans. *Das Prinzip Verantwortung. Versuch einer Ethik für das technologische Zeitalter*. Frankfurt: Insel Verlag, 1979; reprinted in: *KGA I/2.1*, 1–420.

Jonas, Hans. "The Abyss of the Will: Philosophical Meditation on the Seventh Chapter of Paul's Epistle to the Romans." In *Philosophical Essays: From Ancient Creed to Technological Man*. Chicago, IL: Chicago University Press, 1980, 335–348.

Jonas, Hans. *Philosophical Essays. From Ancient Creed to Technological Man*. Chicago, IL: Chicago University Press, 1980.

Jonas, Hans. *Macht oder Ohnmacht der Subjektivität? Das Leib-Seele-Problem im Vorfeld des Prinzip Verantwortung*. Frankfurt: Suhrkamp, 1981; reprinted in: *KGA I/2.1*, 421–509.

Jonas, Hans. "Evolution und Freiheit." *Scheidewege 13* (1983/84): 85–102; reprinted in: *KGA III/1*, 209–226.

Jonas, Hans. "Gottesbegriff nach Auschwitz. Eine jüdische Stimme." In *Reflexionen finsterer Zeit. Zwei Vorträge von Fritz Stern und Hans Jonas*, edited by O. Hofius. Tübingen: Mohr, 1984; reprinted in: *KGA III/1*, 407–426.

Jonas, Hans. „Wie kann wir unsere Pflicht gegen die Nachwelt und die Erde unabhängig vom Glauben begründen?" In *Dem Leben trauen, weil Gott es mit uns lebt. 88. Deutscher Katholikentag München 4.–8. Juli 1984, Dokumentation*. Paderborn: Verlag Bonifacius-Druckerei, 1984, 934–945; reprinted in: *KGA I/2.1*, 515–528.

Jonas, Hans. "Werkzeug, Bild und Grab." *Scheidewege 15* (1985/1986): 47–58; reprinted in: *KGA III/1*, 227–239.

Jonas, Hans. "Gnosis, Existentialismus und Nihilismus." In *Zwischen Nichts und Ewigkeit. Zur Lehre vom Menschen*. 2nd ed. Göttingen: Vandenhoeck & Ruprecht, 1987.

Jonas, Hans. "Prinzip Verantwortung – Zur Grundlegung einer Zukunftsethik." In *Zukunftsethik und Industriegesellschaft*, edited by Th. Meyer and S. Miller. München: Piper, 1986, 3–14; reprinted in: *KGA I/2.1*, 529–544.

Jonas, Hans. *Organismus und Freiheit. Philosophie des Lebens und Ethik der Lebenswissenschaft*, vol. 1 of *Kritische Gesamtausgabe der Werke von Hans Jonas*, edited by Horst Gronke. Freiburg i. Br./Berlin/Wien: Rombach, 2010 (KGA I/1).

Jonas, Hans. *Metaphysische, religions- und kulturphilosophische Schriften*, vol. III/1 of *Kritische Gesamtausgabe der Werke von Hans Jonas;* edited by Michael Bongardt, Udo Lenzig, and Walther Ch. Zimmerli. Freiburg i. Br./Berlin/Wien: Rombach, 2014 (KGA III/1).

Jonas, Hans. *Das Prinzip Verantwortung. Erster Teilband: Grundlegung*, vol. I/2.1 of *Kritische Gesamtausgabe der Werke von Hans Jonas;* edited by Dietrich Böhler and Bernadette Herrmann. Freiburg i. Br./Berlin/Wien: Rombach, 2015 (KGA I/2.1).

Kant, *Kritik der praktischen Vernunft* (KprV).

Kierkegaard, Sören. "Der Begriff Angst." In *Gesammelte Werke*, edited by E. Hirsch and H. Gerdes, 11th vol., 2nd ed. Gütersloh: Gütersloher Verlagshaus, 1983.

Kierkegaard, Sören. "Entweder/Oder." In *Gesammelte Werke*, edited by E. Hirsch and H. Gerdes, 2nd vol., 2nd ed. Gütersloh: Gütersloher Verlagshaus, 1987.

Klausner, Joseph. *Jesus von Nazareth. His Time, His Life and His Teachings* [1922], 3rd ed. Jerusalem: The Jewish Publishing House, 1952.

Menke, Karl-Heinz. *Das Kriterium des Christseins. Grundriss der Gnadenlehre*. Regensburg: Pustet, 2003.

5 Hans Jonas' and Hannah Arendt's Variations on St. Augustine

Yael Almog

Hans Jonas' and Hannah Arendt's Variations on St. Augustine

Intellectual interlocutors since their early training, Arendt and Jonas were both enthusiastic recipients of the principles of Heidegger's philosophy – while their respective innovations in their early writings hint at their original thinking. Both thinkers have famously become disillusioned with Heidegger's endorsement of German fascism and questioned, consequently, the ethical valence of his philosophy. In this vein, both Jonas and Arendt have ultimately traced a Faustian-nihilistic transition that implicated Western philosophy. In their respective late works both Arendt and Jonas engage with the loss of proportion or limit that pushed the modern age to a moral abyss.[1]

Arendt's most famous engagement with ethics resulted in a world-spanning controversy. Her *Eichmann in Jerusalem: A Report on the Banality of Evil* (1963) investigates the fallacies of political action in modern times.[2] With the example of Eichmann's evading of moral accountability for the crimes against humanity that he has facilitated, Arendt advances a historiographical thesis that sketches the shortcomings of political participation in modernity. Surprisingly, she traces the roots of European fascism in the Enlightenment, a philosophical movement that promoted, in her mind, the observation of the world through an instrumental lens – a trend resulting in the automatization of human conduct. In a similar vein, Jonas pronounced the problems inherent to the newly overwhelming reliance of human society on technology. In his foremost work on ethics, *The Imperative of Responsibility: In Search of an Ethics for the Technological Age* (1979, *Das Prinzip Verantwortung. Versuch einer Ethik für die technologische Zivilisation*), Jonas calls for a renewal of the human connection to nature, a position that he substantializes through the description of morality as inherent to the human essence.[3]

The Eichmann book can be said to revisit Jonas' understanding of human will. According to Arendt's main thesis, one can be implicated in evil without the intention to commit evil. Eichmann exhibited, she writes, "such remoteness from reality and such thoughtlessness."[4] Evil is thus possible without the corruption of the will. Eichmann's conduct shows that he committed crimes without thinking, i.e., without self-reflection. It follows that he was able to silence his consciousness, which would normally be the side effect of thinking.[5] In a sense, therefore, Arendt takes

Eichmann's exemplary crime-without-thinking as a historical transition point that revokes the constitutive human capacity described in Jonas' thesis.

However, there are evident differences between Jonas and Arendt. Jonas' early focus on theology, particularly on gnosis, became a trademark of his career notwithstanding his turn in his postwar work to engage with the phenomenon of life. In comparison, it is only in recent decades that Arendt's reliance on ancient theology has been recognized as a main thread of her reflections on civic ethics. As scholars have recently noted, Arendt's approach to institutional religion contrasts some common expectations from her political philosophy.[6] In this way, her affirmative statements on religion as an empowering social force seem at odds with her reception as a proponent of political secularism.

Notwithstanding the differing reception of their engagements with theology, St. Augustine should be recognized as a longstanding influence on both Arendt and Jonas. Arendt dedicated her doctoral thesis to the notion of love in Augustine's works. Her 1929 doctoral thesis is a phenomenological enquiry of Augustine's understanding of love. In this framework, Arendt understands Augustine's notion of the *caritas* as a route for self-constitution that aspires to overcome human finitude. As we shall see, Arendt returns to Augustine in her late writings while reflecting on the correlation between human will and the (im)morality of political actions.

In his own early thesis on Augustine (published in 1930), Jonas presents a historiographical assessment of Augustine's thought on the background of the ancient world. Jonas focuses on the human proclivity to sin as the major stress of Augustine's thought (a position enhanced by Augustine's reaction to the Pelagian heresy that rejects the predominance of the original sin). This focus delineates Jonas' original contribution: an epistemological investigation of self-reflection. Jonas describes an inner conflict that ensues from the Augustinian idea of the freedom of choice. What one 'can' do, in Jonas' interpretation of Augustine, does not necessarily lead to a virtuous choice. For Jonas, freedom is at the heart of human existence. Freedom reiterates the constant possibility of sinfulness.

Throughout her career, Arendt revisited terms developed in this early study. Her attention to Augustine was modulated in tandem with her inquiries into political affairs and amended by them.[7] As will be shown henceforth, it is in her late writings that Arendt expands Jonas' perspective on Augustine. The detachment between aptitude and will, which Jonas presents as Augustine's historical legacy, resonates with Arendt's late reflections on cultural association of sovereignty with oppression.

Jonas' Augustine

During the time of Arendt's and Jonas' participation in his seminars, Heidegger was occupied with Augustine himself. His 1921 lecture course on Augustine, titled "Augustine and Neo-Platonism," positioned Augustine's teachings as a historical milestone. This is due to their prompting of attention to self-reflection: "In the face of ancient skepticism, Augustine ascertained the absolute reality of internal experience (in the form of a precursor to the Cartesian 'Cogito, ergo sum')."[8]

The lecture course attends to Augustine's confession as an act of accountability "before God and the people."[9] This setting draws attention to self-knowledge, or its lack. For Heidegger, Augustine's legacy is embodied in his promotion of the notion of care. The broad connotations of this term encompass the intensive occupation with one's culpability (Heidegger often uses the German term 'Bekümmerung,' which can be translated as concerning oneself with a certain matter). In sum, Heidegger's lectures thus advanced his turn away from Husserl towards the focus on the existential human experience featured in his magnum opus *Being and Time* (*Sein und Zeit*, 1927).[10]

Augustin und das paulinische Freiheitsproblem was Jonas' first published book. He dedicated the work to his teacher Rudolf Bultmann, who was instrumental in encouraging the publishing house to include the book in the series for which he served as the editor.[11] This decision has become controversial, when the work provoked blunt critiques of its Heideggerian language.[12] The work originated in a presentation given in Heidegger's seminar and it reflects Jonas' introduction to philosophy through Heidegger's compelling if yet enigmatic lectures.[13] Heidegger often discussed early theological texts in his seminars, presenting them as prolific grounds for philosophical investigation even though he conspicuously did not approach those texts with conventional philological apparatus. His students were thus encouraged to follow his steps and engage early theology in inventive examinations into Western civilization.

Jonas' thesis on Augustine reflects his influence by Heidegger, while pushing further the view of Augustine as promoting a new mode of self-reflection on the background of his time. The thesis' secondary title – "a philosophical contribution to the genesis of the Western Christian idea of freedom" (ein philosophischer Beitrag zur Genesis der christlich-abendländischen Freiheitsidee) – hints at the central intervention at the core of this effort. Jonas' appeal to Augustine is meant to unpack a conflict pertinent to Western civilization. In sum, Augustine's philosophy demarcates an epistemological split at the core of human introspection.

The thesis remains a close analysis of Augustine against the backdrop of this time. Jonas overviews several streams of thought which infuse Augustine's theology. The first is his dispute with Pelagianism: the belief that sinfulness is not inherent to human character from birth. Counteracting this trend, Augustine insists that the original sin is constitutive to man's relationship to God. In Jonas' reading, therefore, sinfulness peremptorily pervades human self-reflection. The second influence is Manichaeism, a group that constituted a dualistic presentation of the constant struggle between darkness and light, and its interrelated promise to award adherents esoteric knowledge (or gnosis). Jonas stresses Augustine's emphasis on the original sin as the constitutive aspect of his legacy that contrast this group's venture for redemption.[14]

Thirdly, Jonas juxtaposes Augustine to Stoicism, whose philosophy accentuates human will, presenting it as a means to consolidate the self and isolate it from the world. In contrast, early Christian theology introduced, in Jonas' reading, a conflicted notion of the self. The problem of freedom is exemplary of the human inner conflict: humans are responsible for their acts, but their freedom of choice presupposes their inherent incapacity or proclivity to sin.[15] Jonas grants that Stoicism has yielded the examination of the power of will, leading to the interrogation of human freedom.[16] He reads Augustine as exacerbating the scrutiny of freedom with his view of freedom as intertwined with an inner human proclivity to act against one's own good. This emphasis opens a new venture in relating to humans as trapped in inner distress. In this scheme of things, the Christian's 'freedom' prompts the constant consideration of sin, with the attempt – of the will – to avoid it.

Beyond this contextualization on the background of competing theologies, one should alert to Jonas' differentiation between Augustine's and Paul's teaching as the driving force of his thesis. As opposed to the above-mentioned competing sectorial ideas, Paul was an important proponent of Augustine's notion of freedom. Paul has underpinned the identification of man with law, which leads to the striving for virtue. What Augustine borrows from Paul is this human internalization of law, which drives self-scrutiny.[17]

Jonas takes Augustine to presume that the human attempt to evade sin is not centered predominantly in the fear of penalty.[18] The choice of good corresponds with an immanent human inclination. In this way, the state of *timor poenae* signifies a situation in which human cannot perceive themselves as potential sinners.[19] This position contrasts, however, the ongoing human existence – human beings experience their will power through the constant potential to sin. The work's point of departure is that the principle of freedom haunts human existence. The predominance of the freedom of choice, according to Jonas' reading of Augustine, prompts the view of an inherent inaptitude that is revealed by sin – namely the human inclination to jeopardize one's well-being and best interest. In comparison with Stoic adherents, who sought to leave this world behind them, early Christianity engaged with the risks embodied in the self.[20]

Jonas stresses, along these lines, the human accountability to God (or 'in front of God'– a theological terminology that Jonas presents in several languages, including biblical Hebrew).[21] The possibility of choosing evil, of committing sin, forestalls the human total exposure in front of God. Humans thus anticipate their moral scrutiny by Him.[22] The relationship to God is essentially dialectic, therefore, because it is defined through human being's changing level of virtue or sinfulness.

Augustine does propose a viable solution for the inability to concur with God's virtue due to the human proneness to sin. The notion of the *caritas* disrupts these dynamics. As we have seen, the term could be translated as 'love' (while signifying one among other appearances of 'love' in Augustine). *Caritas* pertains to human beings' relationship to fellow beings. Through compassionate relationships to others, humans are able to experience the divine presence.

Overall, human beings witness conflicting affects: will (*Wollen*) and the deriving efforts to comply with the inclination for the good stand in contrast to an underlying feeling that pervades human actions: the sense of not being able to adhere to virtue, despite one's endeavors. This underlying inaptitude is crucial to the human orientation in the world. Central to humans' relation to God, the predestination dogma leads to a temporal understanding of sinfulness. As Augustine established after the Pelagian polemics, committing sin *in the present* corresponds to a mythical past demarcated by man's original sin. At the same time, this dogma also alerts to an eternal future (by means of defining man's *Betsimmung*). These two horizons define human beings' present by alerting them to their moral accountability.[23] This constant reminder wears in Jonas' early reflections on theology the form of an existential conflict between man's inclination to the good and his awareness of sin as an impending necessity – an imperative emanating from the dogma of the original sin.

The interest in Augustine may be said to forestall Jonas' later pairing of existentialism with theology. Augustine reveals awareness of how introspection guides human orientation in the world via the perception of time. This orientation is guided by the awareness to sinfulness and how sin may shape one's accountability to God. In later works, Jonas will conceptualize human action as engrained in human beings' somatic grasp of their environment. Human beings' "existential attributes" are shared, according to his view, with other living organisms.[24] On a last account, whereas Jonas' early theological writings command existentialism for explicating human tormenting dilemmas, his later writings do not only characterize nihilist existentialism but also refer in similar, critical terms to the ancient theological sources that forestalled this modern philosophy. As scholars have shown, in his later works on science, Jonas rejected existentialism on both moral and logical grounds.

In his memoir, Jonas reflects on what brought Arendt and him together: "What brought us together," Jonas writes, "was that we were the only Jews in Rudolf Bultmann's seminar on the New Testament. The seminar was packed, of course, with Protestant theologians and certified goyim, while we two, who to begin with were philosophers, not theologians, but above all Jews, not Christians, really didn't belong there."[25] A fellow outsider to this environment, Arendt was a "defiant Jew," who expressed adamantly her dismay at the anti-Semitic remarks that she had experienced.[26] Jonas recalls the topic of Arendt's doctoral dissertation – the concept of love in Augustine – as manifesting her astonishing detachment from politics during her early training. He notes that his own doctoral dissertation's topic, gnosticism, "was potentially a thousand times more political."[27] In this way, while he was already engaging in the 1920s in Zionist activism, Arendt was oblivious, in his mind, to political interests, particularly a political interest in Judaism.[28]

Against this judgment, however, Arendt's early thesis on Augustine may be deemed political if its conclusion is observed as an ethical imperative that will continue to inform her thinking about politics. At the end of her doctoral thesis, Arendt relates to Augustine's theological vision as sustaining an earthly political order that informs human cohabitation.[29] Arendt considers Augustine as a thinker of civil order, focused on creaturely mutability as an equalizing measure: men are equal in their facing of death as well as in their ultimate accountability in facing God.[30] The view of cohabitation as ingrained in the awareness of creaturely differentiality on earth has informed, as we shall now see, Arendt's main works, including her famous *Eichmann in Jerusalem: A Report on the Banality of Evil*, a work that is exemplary of her engagement with political affairs as an ongoing influence on her thinking. It is, interestingly, at the very end of her career that she focused on Augustine in a manner close to Jonas' early thesis, reading Augustine as a theoretician of the human conflicted self.

74 Yael Almog

Arendt's Augustine: Love of the Eternal

As we have seen, Jonas' essay on Augustine furthers Heidegger's emphasis on self-reflection as a main thread of Augustine. In comparison, Arendt's occupation with Augustine demarcates a different trajectory: her discussion is ultimately occupied with cohabitation – with the grounds for collective political life – more than it is with the inner struggles of the individual.

Arendt's emphasis on love animates this emphasis. Arendt's attention to the different words that Augustine uses for 'love' prompts an inquiry of three modes of relationality: of man to himself; of neighborly love; and of man to God. From the point of view of amor, e.g., of earthly love, the 'good' and the 'bad' are two poles that are defined by life and death. On the backdrop of this binary opposition, a third notion, the *beata vita*, signals a kind of life that is not threatened by death. This venture signals the ceasing of fear, which in Arendt's mind is provoked by the incessant possibility of impending death. Arendt explicates *caritas* through a juxtaposition to *amor* – this form of love targets the earthly world. Neighborly love, in contrast, is a mode of turning towards the transcendental.

Arendt reads Augustine as a theoretician of human existence. For both Arendt and Jonas, this approach to early Christian theology was informed by her occupation with existentialism as it manifested in Heidegger's, Jaspers', and Bultmann's respective oeuvres. Arendt's doctoral thesis on Augustine centers on a distinction between forms of love. Each defines a different mode of relationality of human beings to their earthly surroundings. Arendt thus cites craving as the form of desire (*amor*); the relationship between creatures and the Creator and neighborly love (*caritas*). Among the different notions of love, it is only *caritas* that enables one to transcend the confines of the earthly realm and reach a transcendental standing. Interpersonal accountability translates, therefore, into a channel for overcoming the finitude of human existence.

Arendt notes Augustine's description of emotions as corresponding to moral inclinations. In this way, whereas human desire (*Begehren*) resonates with 'the good' (*bonum*), fear is connoted with evil (*malum*).[31] Desire materializes into *amor* – the notion of love that presides in the earthly realm. The object of desire for *amor* is life. This notion of earthly life is defined by its limited scope, that is, by death. *Amor* is thus guided by the conflicting operation of two affects: desire and fear. Fearlessness is only possible in a state of peace that cannot be disturbed by a future event.[32]

Arendt sees *caritas* as a foremost notion in resolving certain existential conflicts. The human love to God emanates from the recognition that unlike humans, God is eternal. She defines *caritas* as love that is grounded in eternity (*absoluten Zukunft*.)[33] This form of love is engrained in a rejection of this world, which appears like wasteland to those who engage with it. *Caritas* is a path for moving beyond oneself. It is thus a way to transcend one's belonging to this world.[34] Arendt stresses the human liability to God: man stands in front of Him. Man strives to exceed his limits to connect to the divine. The striving for the Creator amounts to self-love. This is because this striving is a turn towards man's origins, his *Ursprung*.[35]

In this context, Arendt insists on the radical difference of each individual – both from God and from other individuals. As opposed to God, the objects of His creation are malleable and perishable. The aspiration to connect with God is grounded in the preliminary separation of the Creator from the creatures He created. God generated a great multiplicity, which is manifested in the uniqueness of creatures. At the same time, He remains both distinct and unchanged by their existence: "The Creator remains exactly the same, regardless of what he creates" ("*Der Creator bleibt als identisch derselbe, unabhängig von dem, was er schafft*").[36] It is the explorative search after one's own essence that ultimately leads one to the Creator.[37] In this vein, the human aptitude for spontaneous creation powerfully resonates with God even when the human constitution of the world through creation is faulty.[38]

Arendt contends that for Augustine, the moment of creation distinguishes the organism from the Creator. In her mind, creation signifies the independence of the organism from others' actions. Separated from God, the beings that He created share, in a sense, the capacity of spontaneous creation.[39] This quality alerts to a leading principle of Arendt's thesis: Augustine is positioned as a theoretician of human equality. For her, since all humans have sinned, they are held accountable in an equal manner. This accountability confirms their equal membership in civil society by perpetuating their social belonging:

> The cohabitation (*Miteinander*) of men in society turns necessarily and naturally [to be] freely apprehended and binding for the individual. Binding still due to the shared situation, which in its manifestation transforms into a shared being-in-the-sin.[40]

The longstanding influence of Augustine's thought on Arendt lies in this depiction of human society through equal membership. In a similar way, Arendt's examination of the *caritas* presumes the discomfort or hurdles associated with life in a collective. This presumption informs Arendt's reading of Augustine as a thinker who conceptualized interpersonal ethics. According to Arendt, in coining this notion, Augustine wishes to reconcile the neo-Platonic striving for transcendence with humans' earthly life. One's love for one's neighbor is always uneasy – it is an ethical demand which ultimately facilitates this reconciliation. Arendt establishes that *caritas* is grounded in free will. Employing the will through the *caritas* references both the future and the past of the individual's existence.[41]

The indeterminacy of political action and, more generally, the ethical dimension of Augustine's thought constitute a central notion of human existence: individuals' constant awareness of other individuals who cohabit the earth. This awareness entails recognizing the unpredictability of the potential actions of others.

Importantly, throughout her *oeuvre*, Arendt argues that certain historical transformations have shaped this premise for cohabitation. She approaches critically some tendencies of Enlightenment philosophy, which, in her mind, have instituted the conviction that the world should be investigated rather than lived-in; science and notions of progress, particularly those connoted with modern technology, entailed an instrumental approach to the world. A crucial cesura is the rise of fascism.

76 *Yael Almog*

According to Arendt, as will be discussed henceforth, totalitarian regimes bring the openness of human actions to a halt.

In her *Life of the Mind*, Arendt thus writes: "not Man but men inhabit this planet. Plurality is the law of the earth."[42] As we shall see, this late work, which was left uncompleted and published posthumously, attaches the vision of plurality in politics to a theological vision that Arendt traces in early Christianity. This vision builds on Arendt's presentation of Augustine as a constitutive voice in Western philosophy. An occupation with Augustine as a theoretician of an inner conflict at the core of human will guides Arendt's late engagement with him, echoing, thereby, Jonas' early work on Augustine.

Arendt's Late Reflections on Politics

Arendt conceptualizes a parallel between human action and the divine creation of man. In *The Human Condition* (1958), she declares in connection with what she names Augustine's political philosophy that "With the creation of man, the principle of beginning came into the world, which, of course, is only another way of saying that the principle of freedom was created when man was created but not before."[43] Through Augustine's conception of human freedom, Arendt develops a notion of political agency that views the world as a sphere open to transformation. Political action is spontaneous. Its outcomes are necessarily unexpected – a quality that in Arendt's mind is integral to human existence. Arendt conceives the uncontrollability of political action by referring miracles, particularly those performed by Jesus, as they were conceived in early Christianity.[44]

Arendt contends that early Christianity held a notion of free will that was starkly different from its conception in modernity, particularly in its liberal adaptation. Her lecture "What is Freedom?" (1961) argues that in contrast to modern individuals, for early Christian theologians, freedom of choice was conceived in separation from the public realm. Taking a similar position to Jonas in his early thesis on Augustine, Arendt argues that these thinkers were intimidated by an exposure to the outside world. They viewed sin as a constant threat that is integral to one's freedom of action.

This leads Arendt to establish that early Christian theology viewed will as entangled with an inner struggle. This predicate has therefore disengaged the predicate "I will" from "I can." In a formulation that echoes Nietzsche's historiography of Western culture, she writes:

> In the deadly conflict with worldly desires and intentions from which will-power was supposed to liberate the self, the most willing seemed able to achieve was oppression. Because of the will's impotence, its incapacity to generate genuine power, its constant defeat in the struggle with the self, in which the power of the I-can exhausted itself, the will-to-power turned at once into a will-to oppression. I can only hint here at the fatal consequences for political theory of this equation of freedom with the human capacity to will; it was one of the causes why even today we almost automatically equate power with oppression or, at least, with rule over others.[45]

Whereas Jonas' early thesis is descriptive, Arendt claims for the need to amend the cultural and philosophical heritage of early Christianity in the West. For her, power is a potentially positive force that emanates from the will. Will is incapable of controlling positively and proactively in the state of human sinfulness; all it can do is oppress. Power is linked to the power of will. Power is thus conceived, still in modern political thought, as a force of restraint and oppression. This conception leads, in Arendt's mind, to a major problem that is at the core of politics up until modernity: the association of sovereignty (of an individual or of a group of people) with freedom. Modern political institutions advocate sovereignty as the means to grant citizens political freedom, but they enforce their sovereignty as a means that harm individuals' personal freedom, and eliminate, therefore, the basic notion of politics. This problem dates back to the early Christian discovery of the will as a quality that conflicts with self-governance. Arendt contends that,

> Where men wish to be sovereign, as individuals or as organized groups, they must submit to the oppression of the will, be this the individual will with which I force myself, or the 'general will' of an organized group. If men wish to be free, it is precisely sovereignty they must renounce.[46]

In her mind, while Augustine disseminated the early Christian notion of will – which confines free will to entangled, inner conflict of the will against itself – he also managed to rescue a view of freedom that entertains the veracity of human action. What Arendt names "the gift of action" corresponds to Augustine's notion of birth as signifying beginning, openness, and therefore, radical potential. Beginning implies the awareness that all creatures are able of spontaneous creation.

One can mention Arendt's seminal work, *Eichmann in Jerusalem* (1963) as centering on the decline of the appreciation and respect for societal accountability: the theological vision that Arendt infers from Augustine's notion of beginning. Arendt's well-known account of Eichmann's compliance with Nazi ideology takes him to represent a reality that affected civilization since the Enlightenment. In Arendt's mind, the sweeping success of progress as a social ideal led to an instrumental vision of participatory politics. Reason is instrumentalized for a predetermined goal – a model that became stronger with the prevalence of modern technology. The rise of European fascism was a radical derivation of the instrumentality of political action. Fascist ideology both builds on and brings to extreme the automatization of human actions. In Eichmann's actions and in his legal defense, Arendt finds a radical expression of the decline of spontaneity: fascism demarcates an epoch in which miracles cease to exist. The famous conclusion to her Eichmann book may thus be seen as reverting to Augustinian ideals. Close to the end of her report, she reflects on the reasoning for punishing Eichmann – reasoning that should inform, in her mind, his appropriate punishment. Arendt articulates how Israeli court should have explained the capital punishment:

> We are concerned here only with what you did, and not with the possible noncriminal nature of your inner life and of your motives or with the criminal

potentialities of those around you. [...] Let us assume, for the sake of argument, that it was nothing more than misfortune that made you a willing instrument in the organization of mass murder; there still remains the fact that you have carried out, and therefore actively supported, a policy of mass murder. [...] in politics obedience and Support are the same. And just as you supported and carried out a policy of not wanting to share the earth with the Jewish people and the people of a number of other nations – as though you and your superiors had any right to determine who should and who should not inhabit the world – we find that no one, that is, no member of the human race, can be expected to want to share the earth with you. This is the reason, and the only reason, you must hang.[47]

Eichmann's deeds violated the universal commitment to human coexistence – the grounds of politics, as Arendt establishes in her readings of Augustine. Her Augustine thesis was constitutive to her premise that the realm of politics necessitates accepting the presence of other humans even as – or especially as – this presence encompasses incessant discomfort emanating from the unpredictability of the agency of other humans. It follows that the State of Israel should have correlated the capital punishment not to violence against an ethnic and religious minority but to Eichmann's ostensible threat to the underlying imperative of Augustinian ethics – an ethics that, throughout Arendt's oeuvre, supplies a vision for a reflective human action.

An investigation of Jonas' early writings, in particular of his thesis on Augustine, exemplifies the intellectual influences on Arendt's longstanding occupation with Augustine's legacy. Jonas described Augustine as developing Paul's conviction that human existence features an inherent epistemological split between will and aptitude. According to Jonas, Augustine connoted this split with the dogma of the original sin, grounding human accountability in self-reflection. Though Arendt does not refer to his thesis directly, Jonas' contextualization of Augustine on the background of ancient theology sheds light on Arendt's late comments on ancient Christian theology as a catalyst of passivity. Her understanding of will as inherently conflicted, primarily in her late writings, reveals strong similarities to Jonas' conceptualization of the problem of freedom in Augustine. The outset of Jonas' theological inquiries of the problem of freedom prompts another novel venture: the examination of gnosis as an ongoing influence on Arendt's political thought.

At the end of *The Human Condition*, Arendt reflects on forms of human activity that diverge from productivity, putting it at risk. A quote from Cato the Elder serves this focus on activity that is the counteraction to will and on the internal dilemmas that this activity elicits: *Numquam se plus agere quam nihil cum ageret, numquam minus solum esse quam cum solus esset* (in English: Never is he more active than when he does nothing, never is he less alone than when he is by himself).[48] That same quote appears at the beginning of her *The Life of the Mind*, signaling, thereby, the philosophical project that links her later works together.[49] Commenting on this quote, Arendt asks, "Assuming Cato was right, the questions are obvious: What are we 'doing' when we do nothing but think? Where are we when we, normally always surrounded by our fellow-men, are together with no one but ourselves?[50] *The Life of the Mind* could thus be said to mark a transition that makes Arendt's elaborated return to Augustine in this work much closer to Jonas' early interest in him. Rather than interpreting Augustine as a theoretician of societal coexistence, which instructs her 1929 thesis on Augustine and her later references to him, *The Life of the Mind*'s examination of Augustine is much closer to Jonas' thesis decades earlier. Like young Jonas, in her last work, Arendt turns to Augustine to explore humans as inherently conflicted, torn by competing strands of the self.

Thus, in a section titled "Augustine, the first philosopher of the Will," *The Life of the Mind* explores Augustine's distinction between will and ability. For Augustine, Arendt writes, "there is only one law, and the first insight therefore is the most obvious but also the most startling one: 'Non hoc est velle quod posse,' 'to will and to be able are not the same.'"[51] The separation between them has in her mind longstanding ramifications that pervaded Western civilization. *The Life of the Mind* takes Augustine to be a pillar of Western philosophy, based on this principle of inner conflict. Augustine's originality lies in his contention that the inner struggle occupying the self is not between the soul and the flesh, but between two faculties that exist within the soul. Arendt crowns him as a predecessor to Kant and Hegel, eminent voices who pursued the inquiry of human faculties as existing in a constant dynamic and conflicting relation to one another. Underpinning Augustine's constitutive status in this tradition, Arendt turns to the terms *velle* and *nolle*. In Arendt's reading, *nolle* is not merely a contradiction of *velle* (or will): it is not the materialization of not-to-will, or the mode of passivity. Rather, like *velle*, *nolle* is an active force existing in the soul.[52]

Arendt's last engagement with Augustine in *The Life of the Mind* is curious considering the role that Augustine has played in her earlier works. A shift to Jonas' early existentialist focus appears apolitical in that it marks the human inner conflict as an ongoing strain on active engagement with the outside world. The curious aspect of this move lies in Arendt's engagement with politics in the previous decades via an Augustinian prism on cohabitation: a theological vision that bore an ethical imperative. Corresponding to Augustine's accentuation of creation, Arendt focused much of her political thought on beginnings. This focus crowned spontaneous political action as an open-ended miracle: a description that borrowed its ferocity from the early Christian understanding of grace. What is more, as we have seen, Arendt has reflected on ways to revise the notion of oppression permeated in Western politics by the ongoing influence of early Christianity. Revisiting Augustine in *The Life of the Mind* seems to exchange these reflections with Jonas' early existentialist focus, one that, in its debt to a notion of the tormented self, eliminates the efficacy of human freedom.

In sum, one could locate three key notions as mapping the intellectual exchange on Augustine between Heidegger, Jonas, and Arendt. Albeit reductively, the following keywords capture each of these thinkers' intervention in turning to early Christianity as part of an existentialist quest. Heidegger found in Augustine the pertinence of 'care,' understood in connection to concern and self-reflection. Developing the epistemological ramifications of self-reflection, Jonas works to describe 'freedom' as synonymous with human existence. Self-reflection centers on the possibility of sin, which, in turn, makes human agents aware of their incessant liability due to their prior internalization of the law. For Arendt, 'birth' marks a life-long engagement with natality as a boon for political action. In Augustine, she finds a proponent of civil freedom. Her early thesis is perhaps the most pro-active of these three interpretations of St. Augustine. Through it, she seeks to define affirmative principles for political participation. Albeit in implicit ways, these elements continued to inform her political thinking throughout.

Notes

1 For a description of this transition as entrenched in their disappointment at Heidegger, see Richard Wolin, *Heidegger's Children: Hannah Arendt, Karl Löwith, Hans Jonas, and Herbert Marcuse* (Princeton, NJ/Oxford: Princeton University Press, 2001), 13.
2 Dana Villa argues that Arendt employed Heidegger's version of existentialism to establish her concept of social plurality while ultimately both using his notion of authentic worldly presence and distancing herself from it. Villa writes: "Worldliness" as Arendt uses the term has a certain philosophical affiliation with Heidegger's notion of being-in-the-world, an existential category of *Dasein* that took direct aim at the disembodied and atomistic Cartesian subject. But 'worldliness' for Arendt has a broader cultural context. It is intended to fight not just the distortions of the modern epistemological traditions […] rather, it is intended to reveal the antiworldly, antipolitical bias of Western culture from the fall of Rome to the present." Villa, "Arendt and Heidegger, Again," in Samuel Fleischacker (ed.), *Heidegger's Jewish Followers: Essays on Hannah Arendt, Leo Strauss, Hans Jonas, and Emmanuel Levinas* (Pittsburgh, PA: Duquesne University Press, 2008), 77–78.
3 On Jonas' longstanding ethical quest, see Elad Lapidot's "Jonas from Husserl to Heidegger: In Search of Judeo-Christian Ethics" in this volume.
4 Hannah Arendt, *Eichmann in Jerusalem: A Report of the Banality of Evil* (New York: Penguin Books, 1977), 288.
5 I thank Liesbeth Schoonheim for elucidating this point for me.
6 See Peter E. Gordon, "The Concept of the Apolitical: German Jewish Thought and Weimar Political Theology," *Social Research* 74.3, Hannah Arendt's Centenary: Political and Philosophical Perspectives, Part I (Fall 2007): 855–878; Samuel Moyn, "Hannah Arendt on the Secular," *New German Critique* 105 (Fall 2008): 71–96.
7 On Arendt's consideration of political events as an ongoing impact on her thinking, see Margaret Canovan, *Hannah Arendt: A Reinterpretation of Her Political Thought* (Cambridge: Cambridge University Press, 2011), 3–7. Canovan takes Arendt's early thesis on Augustine as marking a certain unpolitical debut to Arendt's career, in its early years. Canovan, *Hannah Arendt*, 8.
8 Martin Heidegger, "Augustine and Neo-Platonism," in *The Phenomenology of Religious Life*, trans. by Matthias Fritsch and Jennifer Anna Gosetti-Ferencei (Bloomington/Indianapolis: Indiana University Press, 2010), 118. Heidegger's discussion of this point is anchored in a critique of Dilthey. Heidegger objects Dilthey's focus on the truth value of metaphysical claims, which illustrates a scrutiny of the origins of the social sciences. This approach presumes, in Heidegger's reading of Dilthey, the probability of unearthing an objective historical truth (Heidegger, "Augustine and Neo-Platonism," especially 121–122).
9 Heidegger, "Augustine and Neo-Platonism," 129.
10 See Chad Engelland, "Augustinian Elements in Heidegger's Philosophical Anthropology: A Study of the Early Lecture Course on Augustine," *Proceedings of the American Catholic Philosophical Association* 78 (2004): 263–275.

Hans Jonas' and Hannah Arendt's Variations on St. Augustine 81

11 On the longstanding intellectual influence of Bultmann on Jonas, see Andreas Grossmann's contribution to this volume "Lessons in Interrogative Thinking: Jonas and Bultmann."
12 In his autobiography, Jonas cites his use of the existential term 'thrownness' (Geworfenheit) as an instance of such vocabulary. Hans Jonas, *Memoirs: Hans Jonas* (Waltham, MA: Brandeis University Press, 2008), 147. For an account of the controversy, see Benjamin Lazier, "Pauline Theology in the Weimar Republic: Hans Jonas, Karl Barth, and Martin Heidegger," in Hava Tirosh-Samuelson and Christian Wiese (eds.), *The Legacy of Hans Jonas: Judaism and the Phenomenon of Life* (Leiden: Brill, 2008), 107.
13 See Jonas, *Memoirs*, 41.
14 Hans Jonas, *Augustin und das paulinische Freiheitsproblem. Ein philosophischer Beitrag zur Genesis der christlich-abendländischen Freiheitsidee* (Göttingen: Vandenhoeck & Ruprecht, 1930), 76–77.
15 For a contextualization of this juxtaposition in Jonas' polemical reception of Heidegger, see Lazier, "Pauline Theology in the Weimar Republic" 113.
16 See Udo Lenzig, *Das Wagnis der Freiheit. Der Freiheitsbegriff im philosophischen Werk von Hans Jonas aus theologischer Perspektive* (Stuttgart: Kohlhammer, 2006), 22. Lazier helpfully summarizes Jonas' argument: "Freedom for the Stoic self therefore consists of self-restriction to its "most-own." Yet for the Christian, the problem of freedom begins precisely there. Like the Stoic, the Christian finds salvation in a turn away from the world, if in a different way. For the Stoic, the world unsettles. For the Christian, that disquiet merely distracts the self from its true and deeper distress." Lazier, "Pauline Theology in the Weimar Republic," 113.
17 Michael Bongardt's contribution to this volume "The Aporias of Human Freedom: An Early Letter and its Long Impact" establishes that Jonas engaged with Paul through his correspondence with Bultmann. Bongardt understands the correspondence with Bultmann as a milestone in Jonas' development of his strong emphasis on self-reflection as necessarily entangled. In this context, Jonas defines the isolation of the self in connection with Paul's notion of self-glorying in one's works.
18 Jonas, *Augustin und das paulinische Freiheitsproblem*, 30.
19 Jonas, *Augustin und das paulinische Freiheitsproblem*, 32.
20 Jonas, *Augustin und das paulinische Freiheitsproblem*, 13.
21 Jonas, *Augustin und das paulinische Freiheitsproblem*, 17.
22 Jonas, *Augustin und das paulinische Freiheitsproblem*, 16.
23 Jonas, *Augustin und das paulinische Freiheitsproblem*, 76.
24 Especially in Hans Jonas, *The Phenomenon of Life: Toward a Philosophical Biology* (New York: Harper and Row, 1966).
25 Jonas, *Memoirs*, 61.
26 Jonas, *Memoirs*, 61.
27 Jonas, *Memoirs*, 70.
28 Jonas, *Memoirs*, 70.
29 Arendt, *Der Liebesbegriff bei Augustin*, 88.
30 Arendt, *Der Liebesbegriff bei Augustin*, 78–79.
31 Hannah Arendt, *Der Liebesbegriff bei Augustin. Versuch einer philosophischen Interpretation* (Berlin: Springer, 1929), 8.
32 Arendt, *Der Liebesbegriff bei Augustin*, 11.
33 Arendt, *Der Liebesbegriff bei Augustin*, 13.
34 Arendt, *Der Liebesbegriff bei Augustin*, 22.
35 Arendt, *Der Liebesbegriff bei Augustin*, 34.
36 Arendt, *Der Liebesbegriff bei Augustin*, 37.
37 Arendt, *Der Liebesbegriff bei Augustin*, 46.
38 Arendt, *Der Liebesbegriff bei Augustin*, 51.
39 It appears unclear whether Arendt alerts in her early thesis to the possibility that this capacity is also owned by non-human creatures. In some parts of her thesis, she does

refer to the "human life on earth" as exhibiting the constant fear of death (Arendt, *Der Liebesbegriff bei Augustin*, 23–24). Some other engagements with the topic describe the "creatureliness" that is the property of all beings in their relationship to the Creator (Arendt, *Der Liebesbegriff bei Augustin*, 66).
40 Arendt, *Der Liebesbegriff bei Augustin*, 80.
41 Arendt, *Der Liebesbegriff bei Augustin*, 59.
42 Hannah Arendt, *Life of the Mind* (New York: Harcourt Brace Jovanovich, 1978), 19.
43 Hannah Arendt, *The Human Condition* (Chicago, IL/London: The University of Chicago Press, 1998 [1958]), 177.
44 See her "What Is Freedom?" in Arendt, *Between Past and Future* (New York: Pinguin, 2006 [1961]), 168.
45 Arendt, "What Is Freedom?," 162.
46 Arendt, "What Is Freedom?," 164–165.
47 Hannah Arendt, *Eichmann in Jerusalem: A Report on the Banality of Evil* (New York: Pinguin, 1977 [1963]), 278.
48 Arendt, *The Human Condition*, 325.
49 Arendt, *The Life of the Mind*, 7–8.
50 Arendt, *The Life of the Mind*, 8.
51 Arendt, *The Life of the Mind*, 87.
52 Arendt, *The Life of the Mind*, 89.

Bibliography

Arendt, Hannah. *Der Liebesbegriff bei Augustin. Versuch einer philosophischen Interpretation*, Berlin: Springer, 1929.
Arendt, Hannah. *Eichmann in Jerusalem: A Report of the Banality of Evil*, New York: Penguin Books, 1977.
Arendt, Hannah. *The Human Condition*, Chicago, IL/London: The University of Chicago Press, 1998 [1958].
Arendt, Hannah. *Life of the Mind*, New York: Harcourt Brace Jovanovich, 1978.
Arendt, Hannah. "What Is Freedom?," in *Between Past and Future*, edited by Hannah Arendt, New York: Pinguin, 2006 [1961], 143–171.
Canovan, Margaret. *Hannah Arendt: A Reinterpretation of her Political Thought*, Cambridge: Cambridge University Press, 2011.
Engelland, Chad. "Augustinian Elements in Heidegger's Philosophical Anthropology: A Study of the Early Lecture Course on Augustine," *Proceedings of the American Catholic Philosophical Association* 78 (2004): 263–275.
Gordon, Peter E. "The Concept of the Apolitical: German Jewish Thought and Weimar Political Theology," *Social Research* 74, Hannah Arendt's Centenary: Political and Philosophical Perspectives, Part I (2007): 855–878.
Heidegger, Martin. "Augustine and Neo-Platonism," in *The Phenomenology of Religious Life*, trans. Matthias Fritsch and Jennifer Anna Gosetti-Ferencei, Bloomington/Indianapolis: Indiana University Press, 2010, 115–184.
Jonas, Hans. *Augustin und das paulinische Freiheitsproblem. Ein philosophischer Beitrag zur Genesis der christlich-abendländischen Freiheitsidee*, Göttingen: Vandenhoeck & Ruprecht, 1930.
Jonas, Hans. *Memoirs: Hans Jonas,* Waltham, MA: Brandeis University Press, 2008.
Jonas, Hans. *The Phenomenon of Life: Toward a Philosophical Biology*, New York: Harper and Row, 1966.

Lazier, Benjamin. "Pauline Theology in the Weimar Republic: Hans Jonas, Karl Barth, and Martin Heidegger," in *The Legacy of Hans Jonas: Judaism and the Phenomenon of Life*, edited by Hava Tirosh-Samuelson and Christian Wiese, Leiden: Brill, 2008, 107–130.

Lenzig, Udo. *Das Wagnis der Freiheit. Der Freiheitsbegriff im philosophischen Werk von Hans Jonas aus theologischer Perspektive*, Stuttgart: Kohlhammer, 2006.

Moyn, Samuel. "Hannah Arendt on the Secular," *New German Critique* 105 (2008): 71–96.

Villa, Dana. "Arendt and Heidegger, Again," in *Heidegger's Jewish Followers: Essays on Hannah Arendt, Leo Strauss, Hans Jonas, and Emmanuel Levinas*, edited by Samuel Fleischacker, Pittsburgh: Duquesne University Press, 2008, 43–82.

Wolin, Richard. *Heidegger's Children: Hannah Arendt, Karl Löwith, Hans Jonas, and Herbert Marcuse*, Princeton, NJ/Oxford: Princeton University Press, 2001.

6 Hans Jonas on Gnosis and Late Antiquity

In Search of the Spirit of an Epoch

Johannes Zachhuber

Introduction

In 1934, Hans Jonas brought out his first, major monograph, entitled *Gnosis und spätantiker Geist*.[1] The volume was billed as the first of two; the second volume was announced together with the publication of the first. Yet history intervened. By the time of the book's appearance in print, Jonas had already left Germany. His initial hope to complete the second volume in London, his first place of exile, proved unrealistic. After relocating to Palestine in 1935, other needs and duties kept him occupied and 'soon what happened in Germany' made him disinclined 'to continue publishing there.'[2]

Only in 1945, Jonas re-entered Germany and immediately contacted former teachers and colleagues, including the philosopher, Karl Jaspers, and the theologian, Rudolf Bultmann. In Göttingen, Jonas also paid a visit to his publisher, Vandenhoeck & Ruprecht.[3] For obvious reasons, however, he nevertheless resisted the request to prioritize the completion of the second volume of his work on Gnosis. It was only a decade later, in 1954, that the first volume was reprinted and a first part of the second volume published. A planned second part of that volume was never completed. Instead, in 1958, Jonas brought out an English version of the work, *The Gnostic Religion: The Message of the Alien God and the Beginnings of Christianity*, which, while using his earlier research, was far from a simple translation of the German book.[4] As my concern here is primarily with the early Jonas, I will refer to the original text of *Gnosis* throughout and leave to one side his motivation in reworking the material into an English publication as well as the details of this process.

The present chapter is based on the observation that Jonas' book, whatever else it may be, is primarily a study in the history of late antiquity and, specifically, late ancient religion. As such, it needs to be understood in the context of research on late antiquity more broadly. Yet such an approach is rarely chosen. The reasons for this are easy to understand. Jonas is primarily remembered today as a philosopher whose intellectual journey from Heideggerian existentialism to philosopher of environmental responsibility is as fascinating as it remains relevant in our own time. His historical interests, by contrast, are meaningful at best for a small group of experts. Jonas himself observed in 1954 that Gnosticism 'lies off the main road

DOI: 10.4324/9781003439882-6

of historical knowledge, and philosophers do not usually come across it.'[5] Those interested in Jonas today can therefore be forgiven if they would rather bypass the historical questions with which the thinker occupied himself and instead approach directly his properly philosophical ideas.

In what follows, I will argue that closer attention to the historiographical context of Jonas' work does not have to be a distraction from his more properly philosophical ideas but can help put them into relief. The centuries after the birth of Christ have long fascinated scholars, despite their relative obscurity for the educated public more broadly. Often, late antiquity has appeared to modern Europeans as a period of time similar to their own. The precise sentiments underlying this assessment have, however, varied. Late antiquity could appear as a time of crisis, a time of transition, or a time of new beginnings. These interpretations applied specifically to the one dimension of late antiquity that has, arguably, always been most familiar to the general public, namely, its significance for the history of religions. To Westerners, whether Christian or Jewish, late antiquity inevitably evokes memories of religious transition and transformation, the end of paganism, the origin of Christianity and (later) Islam, and the emergence of Rabbinic Judaism.

As is clear already from its title, Jonas' book inscribes itself into this larger quest for an understanding of the character or even the 'spirit' of an epoch of transition. By focusing on Gnosis,[6] Jonas chose a religious movement which to many students of late ancient history of religions has seemed emblematic of the strange and unstable religious signature of the age, a mix of old and new, speculative and fantastical, absorbing various elements from surrounding cultures without a clear identity of its own.[7] Jonas' argument is pitched against this notion of Gnosticism as syncretism, seeking instead to establish the movement as a novel departure in Mediterranean culture with a considerable legacy which ultimately reaches into the modern world. This does not mean, however, that Gnosis for Jonas was free from ambiguities. On the contrary, in his interpretation, Gnosis for all its innovation is deeply problematic. But its problems are, the reader realizes, problems well known to the citizens of the modern world; they are a harbinger to some deep-seated issues that continue to plague the twentieth century and may be said to be responsible for some of its worst tragedies.

In what follows, I will begin with some comments on scholarly attempts to understand and interpret late antiquity as an epoch. I will specifically focus on the enduring fascination to finding in these centuries a parallel with Western modernity. In a second step, I will move on to religion in late antiquity and consider specifically interpretations of Gnosticism prior to Jonas. From there, I shall proceed in a third section to an analysis of Jonas' own understanding as both indebted to earlier approaches and strikingly innovative. I will close with a few reflections on the place of Jonas' study of Gnosticism in his broader oeuvre.

Interpretations of Late Antiquity: Decline or Transformation?

Many people, including those with some historical knowledge, may struggle when asked to identify events or individuals associated with late antiquity.

Our historical canon continues to be focused on the classical period, Athenian democracy, and the Roman Republic, including their philosophical, literary, and cultural achievements. To many, it must therefore appear counterintuitive that this particular epoch could appear a fascinating object of study, let alone invite comparisons with our own modern world. In fact, Jonas was far from the only one who would beg to differ.

To begin with, a word is needed on periodization, as Jonas' usage is somewhat idiosyncratic. Despite the reference to late antiquity in the title of his book, he nowhere clarifies how exactly he understands this historiographical designation. It is nevertheless evident that the 'spirit' he is interested in is located above all in the early centuries after Jesus Christ. At the center of his study stand the first three centuries of the Common Era; only a few documents that are clearly of a later date are investigated and discussed by him.[8]

Delimiting late antiquity in this way was, however, somewhat unusual even in Jonas' own time. Historians have mostly understood late antiquity as beginning in the third century and stretching into the sixth, seventh or even eighth century.[9] The difficulties in defining the end of late antiquity are of no relevance to the topic of this chapter. With a view to the history of religions, it is, however, clear that for most historians, late antiquity is the period within the ancient world characterized by the increasing dominance of Christianity or, put differently, by the Christianization of the Mediterranean during these centuries. If, by contrast, one considers Gnosis as characteristic for the 'spirit' of late antiquity, the point of reference is an earlier period during which the traditional religions of Greece and Rome were in decline while it was as yet unclear what would take their place in the long run. Such a view of 'late ancient' religion, however, mirrors the broader perception historians have of 'late antiquity' and so may be a good fit despite the superficial incongruity of the proposed periodization.

This broader perception conceives of late antiquity as an epoch of crisis in which old institutions and traditions lost their sway while new ones were slow to emerge. Sometimes, this has led scholars to adopt narratives of decline when interpreting the period. This is paradigmatically evident from the earliest full account of the epoch, at the same time one of the most important works of Western historiography ever, *The Decline and Fall of the Roman Empire*. Written between 1776 and 1788 by the Enlightenment historian Edward Gibbon, the multi-volume work offers a narrative from the time of Emperor Trajan (late first century) to the fall of Constantinople in 1453 (and beyond).[10] Its overall tendency is aptly captured by the book's title. For Gibbon, the unifying character of this entire era is the gradual decline of the ancient civilization from its heights in the classical period to its eventual demise. It is this development, the dynamic of the gradual slide of a once-mighty empire to its eventual disappearance which Gibbon seeks to document and explain by way of his uniquely extensive research.

Around a century later, the same question animated Otto Seeck, who wrote *Die Geschichte des Untergangs der antiken Welt*, published, like Gibbon's monumental opus, in six volumes.[11] Seeck's work has remained the most expansive presentation of the history of late antiquity in German. In characterizing the period he studied,

Seeck, a long-term correspondent of Thomas Mann's, does not shy away from strong and unequivocal language. Late antiquity, the historian wrote, was "weak and morally degenerate"; endowed with "flaccid mental powers"; and characterized by "intellectual laziness lacking independence."[12]

Both Gibbon and Seeck were arguably inspired by events of their own time to study late antiquity, a period they perceived in such unflattering terms. In Gibbon's case, it was the crisis of the British Empire caused by the American War of Independence and the ensuing loss of the important North American colonies, while for Seeck, the context of the *fin de siècle* was decisive. Both were arguably attracted to the study of late antiquity by a more immediate concern for the potential termination of empires and civilizations in their own times.[13]

While both Gibbon and Seeck thus reduced the centuries of late antiquity to a period of decline, an author closer to Jonas' own present argued for a more nuanced perception of the period. For Oswald Spengler, dilettante historian and philosopher of history, late antiquity was a mix of old and new; it featured crisis and decline intertwined with the birth of a novel culture. This assessment is to be found in his two-volume work, *Der Untergang des Abendlandes* (*The Decline of the West*), a book rarely remembered let alone studied today except for the occasional reference to its evocative title. In the decade after its first publication, however, *The Decline of the West* proved a highly stimulating contribution to a range of discussions about culture, history, and the fate of nations.

It is in some ways inevitable that Spengler's work is considered in the context of the Weimar years, as it was during this period of cultural and political crises that it made its impact on the German public. It should nevertheless not be forgotten that, while Spengler did indeed publish the first volume in 1918, he had, according to his own testimony, nearly completed the work before the outbreak of the Great War.[14] Its main goal was not to find reasons in history to explain the West's – or indeed Germany's – current state of catastrophic conflagration, although such an association must have come naturally to many of his early readers. Rather, Spengler aimed at the highly speculative idea of understanding world history as a whole, beyond its parochial reduction to a teleology of the modern West. To accomplish this aim, he proposed what he called (in Goethian language) a morphological approach, revealing world history as a succession of cultures each of which had a limited life span and, within this time, underwent a series of regular transitions and transformations.[15] Such analysis, he claimed, would establish laws of history as reliable as the laws of nature albeit of a radically different character.[16] Locating any given historical moment within this cyclical scheme would even permit a certain prediction of future developments.[17]

Within this broader scheme, Spengler drew especially close parallels between the early centuries of the Common Era and the modern West:

A comparative study reveals the 'contemporaneity' of [our historical] period with the time of Hellenism, and especially the [contemporaneity] of its current climax – indicated by the [First] World War – with the transition from the Hellenistic to the Roman era.[18]

By contrast, he explicitly and emphatically rejects the idea of a special bond between the modern West and classical antiquity:

> The entire work of the nineteenth century in philosophy of religion, history of art, and social criticism was needed not to finally make us understand the plays of Aeschylus, the doctrine of Plato, Apollo and Dionysus, the Athenian state and Caesarism – from this we are far removed, but to make us feel how immeasurably strange and distant all this is from our inner selves, stranger perhaps than the Mexican gods or Indic architecture.[19]

Compared with Gibbon and Seeck, a few observations are pertinent. Firstly, Spengler much more directly and explicitly emphasizes the significance of the historical parallel between 'late antiquity' (a term he does not, however, use) and his own present. In fact, he uses the term *Gleichzeitigkeit*, contemporaneity, to make this point in an almost paradoxically strong manner. Secondly, the period he is interested in is not so much the 'end' of antiquity but the transition from the Hellenistic to the Imperial age and thus precisely the time Jonas calls *Spätantike*. Thirdly, it is therefore clear that, despite the book's title, Spengler's interest in emphasizing the "contemporaneity" of the early centuries after Christ and the twentieth century was less driven by the notion of impending civilizational breakdown in his own time but rather by the idea that the West was undergoing a deep and unsettling transition from one phase within its existence, culture, to another which he called "civilization."[20] Cultures become civilizations, according to Spengler, when they have surpassed the apex of their evolutions and, having run out of creativity and novel ideas, expend their energies on the administration of established ones. In this sense, Spengler saw his own time as an "evening," the transition from Western 'culture' to Western "civilization," but not yet its demise.

Yet Spengler's view of late antiquity differed from the perspective often adopted in the wake of Gibbon's famous work in yet another, more fundamental regard. For him, the early centuries of the Common Era did not only mark the transition to the final phase of classical civilization; they also saw the beginnings of another culture which would eventually come to dominance with the rise of Islam and the Arabic conquest. To explain this coincidence, Spengler introduced one of his most influential ideas. According to his analysis, late antiquity witnessed the birth of radically novel ideas which were, however, hidden under lingering cultural forms that were still being retained from classical civilization. This mismatch between content and form, so to speak, Spengler called pseudomorphosis. He defines it as follows:

> Historical pseudomorphoses I call cases in which an old culture lies so heavily on the land that a young one, which is at home there, cannot breathe. Not only does the latter fail to come to the formation of pure, genuine expressions of its character, it does not even achieve the full development of its self-consciousness.[21]

When historians of late antiquity complained about its degenerate character or, like Seeck, spoke of its "flaccid mental powers," they often had in mind the intermingling of different cultural forms and ideas during this period. While traditionally Greek or Roman practices and ideas were outwardly continued, they apparently changed their character under the influence of extraneous influences, often summarily referred to as 'Eastern.' Judged from the ideal of cultural purity, this had to appear as a sign of decadence. Spengler's pseudomorphosis, however, offered a fascinatingly different interpretation. Rather than indicating a world in decline, a culture no longer capable of reproducing its characteristic ideas and practices in their pure form, this coincidence of different influences in late ancient culture pointed to the emergence of a novel culture that was forced into the Procrustean bed of an older civilization from whose strangling modes of expression it was unable to escape.

Looked at from today's perspective, Spengler's interpretation of late antiquity still smacks perhaps too much of the narrative of decline and fall which more recent historians, in the wake of Peter Brown, have decisively rejected in favor of a much more upbeat account of centuries of multicultural flourishing.[22] Characteristic of the current paradigm are, for example, the following lines from Peter Frankopan's bestselling *The Silk Road*:

> Two millennia ago, silks made by hand in China were being worn by the rich and powerful in Carthage and other cities in the Mediterranean, while pottery manufactured in the southern France could be found in England and in the Persian Gulf. Spices and condiments grown in India were being used in kitchens in Xinjiang, as they were in those of Rome. Buildings in northern Afghanistan carried inscriptions in Greek, while horses from Central Asia were being ridden proudly thousands of miles away to the east.[23]

Hans Jonas, as we shall see, was far from such effusive affirmation of either late antiquity or the modern age. Yet he was not drawn to the narrative of decline and fall either. The 'spirit' of late antiquity was, above all, radically *different* from that prevalent in classical antiquity. In fact, it was much closer to the character of the modern West than it was to that of the earlier Hellenistic world. Yet it found expression under the guise of older Greek symbols and formulas. It was, in other words, *pseudomorphosis* in Spengler's sense. For that reason, its true character was so easily misunderstood.

Before turning to Jonas' own analysis, however, a few words need to be said about the specific role played by religions in the narrative of late antiquity as a period of transition and interruption. After all, Jonas' own work concerns the history of religion as it is in Gnosticism that he seeks to identify the spirit of the age.

Gnosis and the History of Religions in Late Antiquity

It is arguable that a perception of late antiquity emphasizing transition and innovation more than decline was attractive to Jonas simply because his primary interest was in the history of religions. After all, it is hard to deny that the early centuries of the Common Era, while witnessing the end of religious practices and rituals that had previously shaped the Mediterranean region for at least a millennium, also saw the emergence of the great so-called Abrahamic religions in the form in which we know them to this day: rabbinic Judaism, Christianity, and Islam. Those who know little about this epoch will at least be aware that it set the course for the following two millennia of Western religious history.

This in turn has fed into the broader tendency, observed above, to speculate about parallels between those centuries and developments in Western modernity. By their very nature, religions are designed to last; they therefore also usually legitimize themselves through traditions that have passed the test of time. The large-scale death of certain religions and the emergence of others has not happened all that often in the history of humankind. It is for this very reason that the weakening of Christianity in Europe, which has been felt more and more strongly since the nineteenth century, has often seemed so worrying to contemporaries wondering in which direction a society may be heading that is losing its religious foundation.[24]

Due to the paucity of historical analogies that could provide answers to this question, the caesura that presents itself to us in the centuries after the birth of Christ was bound to attract considerable attention. It is therefore hardly coincidence that research into the religious transformations of that period has increased dramatically over the past century. The radicality of this change makes the era a fascinating reflection of our own time. Back then, too, many had to wonder where developments would lead. Then as now, there were gloomy fantasies of doom, and political upheavals, such as the sack of Rome by the Goths in 410, were quickly blamed on the betrayal of the traditional gods – an accusation that St. Augustine tried to reject comprehensively in *The City of God* (*De civitate dei*; completed in 426).[25]

That said, any attempt to discover in the religious upheavals of late antiquity insights explaining the identity crises of today is confronted with the irreducible alterity of the period, its cultural distance from the present which makes it extremely difficult even to define what was at issue back then. Notably, any understanding of what counted as religious in late antiquity is fraught with methodological difficulties. In his classical study, *Conversion: The old and the new in religion from Alexander the Great to Augustine of Hippo*, Arthur Derby Nock asserted that it was philosophy which in Greek antiquity came closest to what we understand by religion, implying that not only the meaning of religion but also that of philosophy had changed fundamentally during the Christian era.[26] Ancient philosophy, as Pierre Hadot later emphasized, was 'a way of life' and as such directly concerned with what we would call 'religious' questions, such as happiness, self-knowledge, and the spiritual dimension of life. To be a philosopher therefore meant more than possessing theoretical knowledge of these ideals but involved practicing them in one's own life as well.[27]

Difficulties in grasping the essence of religious transformation in late antiquity are not, of course, limited to problems of terminology and categorizations. The religious changes of the period evidently touched the lives of large parts of the population. Yet our sources are largely silent when it comes to the question of individual beliefs and motivations. As early as the third century – and thus *before* the official Christianization of the empire – we hear complaints, for example, about people's declining willingness to participate in traditional sacrificial rituals. The extent to which this was the case, however, is mostly hard to quantify, and when it comes to the question of reasons, modern research largely depends on conjecture.[28]

Researchers studying religious transformation in late antiquity often follow one of two guiding questions. Many ask primarily about the emergence and growth of Christianity in a pagan environment. In that case, the *telos* of their studies is the Christianization of the Roman Empire whose genesis is deemed in need of an explanation. Others, however, forego the teleological perspective seeking instead to understand religious history in late antiquity in its plurality and diversity as in principle open-ended.

For both approaches, Gnosis is highly significant, but the way its importance is understood differs rather starkly between them. To explain why this is the case, we may begin by observing that Gnosis was a religious movement whose ideas were sharply rejected by the authoritative Christian, Jewish, and Platonic writers known to us. I use the word 'movement' deliberately because the further specification of Gnosis as either a religion in its own right or as a mere variation of existing traditions is already controversial.

Polemic against the Gnostics was certainly rife. For a long time, in fact, scholars knew about Gnosis exclusively from texts written by its detractors.[29] It is fair to say that the sharpness of anti-Gnostic polemics was at least partly due to the fact that Gnostic texts contain elements of Christian, Jewish, and pagan ideas, as well as obvious parallels to the philosophies of the time. In this way, Gnosis was somehow both at odds with major contemporaneous religions and philosophies and remarkably similar to all of them. Gnosis could thus appear as a microcosm of late ancient religion and a melting pot of its diverse currents and trends. This in turn made it attractive to modern scholars interested in the historical evolution of religion of the time. An analysis of Gnosis, it seemed, could provide the key to a fuller understanding of the historical process which dislodged traditional religions from their position in society and culture while leading to the emergence of a new crop of belief systems destined to remain dominant for the subsequent two millennia.

In what precise way the study of Gnosis illuminates this process depends on which of the two above approaches one chooses. For a researcher principally interested in the study of late ancient religion on its own terms, Gnosis appears as *pars pro toto* of the irreducibly pluralistic religious culture of the first centuries of our era. Contemporaneous testimonies often characterize Gnosis as a confused mixture of diverse and heterogeneous religious and philosophical ideas. As such, it would be paradigmatic for a religious culture resembling an alchemist's kitchen in whose cauldron a multitude of ideas, symbols, and rituals of Jewish, Greek, Roman, Egyptian, and Persian origin, as well as Hellenistic philosophy were mixed together before finally Christianity asserted itself as the dominant faith of the region. Until then, however, people could apparently 'patch together' their own religious options, not unlike what many do today. For a long time, scholars called this patchwork of late antique religious culture 'syncretism,' a term that was meant pejoratively.[30] From today's perspective, of course, the same phenomenon can also be seen in a more positive light.

The significance of Gnosis appears in a very different light to those whose principal interest is in the emergence and growth of Christianity. Considered from this angle, Gnosis comes into view as the other of mainstream, orthodox Christianity, the first decisive Christian heresy. The confrontation with Gnosis appears as an early junction in church history, the assertion of one form of the religion over against a powerful rival. The decision of the early Church to reject Gnostic ideas, in this perspective, was an important step on the way toward the ecclesial form of Christianity which subsequently came to dominance.[31] From today's vantage point, this outcome permits, once again, positive as well as negative assessments, and evidence for both can be found in older and more recent literature.[32]

A preliminary summary at this point will serve to put into relief the fascination of Gnosis as well as lasting difficulties in understanding and interpreting this phenomenon in late ancient religious history. Late antiquity, I have argued, has long appeared as a period of crisis which often was understood as decline but sometimes also as a transition. Since it was first studied, it has invited comparison with contemporaneous Western developments. Religions, in particular, underwent dramatic changes during those centuries. In many ways, Gnosis can be seen as standing at the center of these complex transformations and therefore as uniquely attractive for the study of the period. But its interpretation is also ridden with difficulties; to scholars it has frequently seemed to lack a character of its own and merely reflect the heterogeneous mixture of religious interests in a period of change. In considering now Jonas' interpretation of Gnosis, it will become clear how all these aspects fed into his own approach to the topic and ensured the remarkable success of his early publication.

Hans Jonas on Gnosis: An Alien Spirit Intrudes into the Greek World

When Hans Jonas first investigated Gnosis in the early 1930s, it was clear to him that it was a religious movement that extended beyond Christianity and had its historical origin in the pre-Christian period.[33] For this view, which today has largely lost currency, Jonas relied not least on the influential work of his theological teacher Rudolf Bultmann, who also contributed a preface to the first volume of *Gnosis und spätantiker Geist*.[34] This *status quaestionis* led Jonas to ask how Gnosis should be conceptualized if it was *not* simply or primarily a Christian heresy. Was there a concern that stood at its center and could explain what made it attractive? How could the essence of Gnosis be defined in such a way that made its enormous success, albeit for a limited time, understandable?

To tackle these questions, Jonas had no access to newly discovered sources or to texts that had been unknown to previous researchers. Rather, he used the same materials that had been the basis of previous scholarship before him. These sources suggested that at the center of Gnosis there was a myth.[35] This myth, whose concrete form varies and often takes on fantastic features, tells the story of the origin of the world as a cosmic fall; through unfortunate circumstances, seduction, or deceit, a bad, material cosmos was created alongside an original, spiritual world ruled by a good God. This evil world is the world we inhabit, the world of our experience. Spiritual or pneumatic beings are trapped in this world, and the Gnostic myth is ultimately a narrative of the liberation of these beings. To bring about this liberation, a redeemer, himself part of the upper spirit world, voluntarily enters the dark cosmos to show those spirits who are lost and trapped there the way back to their original home.

Redemption for the Gnostics was thus a return of pneumatic beings to the world to which they belonged and from which they were evicted at some point in the past. There was not, by contrast, a salvation of the fallen world as such, which, as fundamentally evil, is literally irredeemable. Decisive for the redemptive potential of an individual is their capacity for knowledge – hence the name of the movement (gnosis, γνῶσις = knowledge). This ability drives the process of redemption, but it also determines who can be redeemed in the first place. Not all people possess the prerequisites for this, but only those who originally belonged to the spirit world. In this sense, then, Gnosis also means self-knowledge, the insight that one's own self is ultimately not part of the physical cosmos, but belongs to another, better world to which it can and should return.

Jonas took for granted that a religious movement based on this intellectual foundation had existed in the Eastern Mediterranean since Hellenistic times. What was missing, in his opinion, was a plausible interpretation of the ideas expressed in the Gnostic myth. Jonas was deeply dissatisfied by the existent literature which for the most part characterized Gnosis by its tendency toward syncretism.[36] The Gnostics, in other words, did not really have original ideas, but merely drew on concepts and symbols they encountered elsewhere in the Hellenistic world integrating Eastern and Western religions as well as philosophical ideas from different schools. By appropriating these resources, the Gnostics produced an admittedly colorful but parasitic synthesis which, since it lacked any true originality, could not develop any lasting stability.

One might argue that the interpretation of Gnosis as a hotchpotch of heterogeneous ideas and conceptions suggests itself to anyone who deals with Gnostic texts due to its abundant and evocative use of various sources. From Jonas' point of view, however, the reason for the syncretism thesis was not quite so innocent. Rather, this interpretation itself relied fundamentally on a more general intuition about the character of late antiquity as a time of decline and decay. Once this view has been adopted, it becomes intuitively plausible that the major religion of late antiquity, Gnosis, is likewise nothing but an unoriginal play with various inherited theological and philosophical motifs.

This understanding of Gnosis is the primary target against which Jonas' account is aimed. If Gnosis to its students primarily appears as syncretism, he argues, this is because they have not recognized its inner kernel, its own fundamental character. The task he set for himself, accordingly, was to identify a vanishing point from which the confusing diversity of Gnostic ideas could be understood in their unity. For Jonas, the key to this solution was to be found in a certain understanding of existence (*Existenzverständnis*) that lies at the center of all Gnostic systems. Jonas here used the terminology of his philosophical teacher, Martin Heidegger, even though he later sharply criticized him as a person and a thinker.[37] By focusing on the Gnostic *Existenzverständnis*, according to Jonas, the modern researcher is enabled to perceive Gnosis in its essential incompatibility with the Greek tradition. In this religious movement, an attitude to self and world comes to the fore that is radically different from and alien to Hellenism, something "radically un-Greek [albeit expressed] in the Greek language and the conceptual garb of the time."[38] An analysis that merely considers the terminology of Gnostic texts, Jonas suggests, may be led astray by the fact that properly Gnostic ideas are expressed in Hellenistic language, whereas the existential approach permits to pierce "the Greek, often pseudo-philosophical conceptual garb [... opening up] behind it a view of a foreign world still on the mythical level of consciousness."[39]

Specifically, according to Jonas, the Gnostic longing for redemption from the evil, material world is radically different from the Platonic idea of an intelligible soul as the core of true humanity.[40] Plato may well adopt the Pythagorean quip of the body (σῶμα) as the tomb (σῆμα) of the soul, but like the entire Greek tradition, he ultimately holds to a deep belief in the goodness of the cosmos: "Hellenism was a grandiose expression of being-at-home-in-the-world (*Weltheimischkeit*) and everything in its 'theory' served to secure [this existential attitude] by firmly integrating existence into the objective world of perception and work (*Anschauungs- und Werkwelt*)."[41] For this reason, Gnosis with its profoundly dualistic opposition to this cosmic piety of the Greeks seemed so offensive and ultimately blasphemous to it contemporaries: "The great equation 'world = darkness' (*kosmos = skotos*) emerges as a concise expression of this new experience of the world."[42]

It is precisely from this antithesis, however, that, according to Jonas' thesis, the radically new and different understanding of existence characteristic of Gnosis must be understood. The Gnostics know themselves to be strangers in the world into which they were born. In the place of a continuity of non-human and human nature, they adopt a radical juxtaposition:

> In Gnosis [is discovered] for the first time (and for all subsequent time) the radical difference of human and non-human-worldly being [...], which is not bridged by any intermediate stages and transitions but is ontological. The world is what is alien to human beings (*das Weltfremde*), the other ...[43]

In place of the traditional Greek interconnectedness of human beings with the world around them, Gnosis postulates an antithetical relationship between the two. Jonas describes this novel idea in the strongest terms: "Whereas the Greeks encountered in [their environment] deep familiarity and self-appropriateness (*Ihmgemäßheit*), [...] – the Asiatic people of those days were confronted [in it] by terrible hostility and strangeness." The consequences were a tremendous "insecurity of existence, human world-fear, fear of the world and of themselves."[44]

The goal of Gnostic existence, therefore, was redemption understood as the overcoming of the sensible world by returning to the spirit world to which in truth they had always belonged.

This fundamental sense of being estranged from the world around them, according to Jonas, also explains why the Gnostics did not feel bound by conventional ethical rules. In his analysis, Gnosis introduced a revolutionary concept of freedom.[45] By realizing that they ultimately formed no part of their *seemingly* powerful environment, the Gnostics gained an unprecedented sense of independence. From this, they derived the legitimacy to suspend all social and moral conventions to the point of 'frenzy' (*Raserei*), a Jonas puts it, a sense of superiority over "any norms"[46] and a "resentment against the previous statutes of life."[47] Therefore, Jonas considers accurate the (controversial) reports about the Gnostics' sexual excesses to be found in the writings of their Patristic opponents. Precisely in the area of sexuality, so strictly regulated by conventional morality, the Gnostics demonstrated their independence from the standards that applied to a world from which they knew themselves liberated. According to Jonas, libertinism sits right "at the center of the Gnostic turn"[48] even though its opposite, the ascetic denial of socially mandated relationships, was equally possible and, in fact, became over time "the permanent form (*Dauerform*) of the anticosmic [...] attitude."[49]

At this point, it is worth recalling the title of Jonas' book: *Gnosis und spätantiker Geist*. Ultimately, his thesis is not limited to the interpretation of Gnosis as a religious movement. Rather, Jonas considers Gnosis as paradigmatic for the 'spirit' of an entire epoch. In the first part of this chapter, I showed that the historiography of late antiquity for a long time was dominated by the paradigm of decline but that from the early twentieth century, it began to be associated more with notions of transition and new beginnings. We can now see that Jonas was part of this paradigm shift. His protest against the interpretation of Gnosis as a mere syncretism of older ideas and symbols is at the same time a plea for the perception of late antiquity as a genuinely novel and different cultural epoch. His direct predecessor in this respect, as he himself explicitly acknowledged, was Oswald Spengler, who, like Jonas, saw in late antiquity the beginning of what he called 'Arab civilization,' the identification of which was complicated by its initial development under the guise of Greek forms of expression foreign to its nature ('pseudomorphosis'). There is no doubt that Jonas' idea that the nature of Gnosis needs to be found underneath its superficial use of Hellenistic language and concepts is principally owed to Spengler's *pseudomorphosis*, a term Jonas himself adopts in his analysis even though his own methodology, as we have seen, owes more the Heideggerian existential analysis than Goethean morphology.[50]

We saw earlier that Spengler explicitly postulated a 'simultaneity' between the first centuries of our era and the early twentieth century. In Jonas' original book of 1934, such considerations can at best be guessed at. Only in the years after the Second World War did he make such parallels explicit. Now he would analyze the fate of the modern world since the seventeenth century as the increasing alienation of human beings from their environment. The scientific view of the world, which no longer allowed for teleology, led to a new, existential loneliness. Already for Blaise Pascal, according to Jonas, the human being is 'lost' "in this remote corner of nature [...], the universe."[51] The contingency of humanity's physical existence undermines any attempt to derive the meaning of life from a connection with the world.

This alienation reaches its climax in existentialism, which as a whole is sustained by the sense of a radical opposition between the self and the world surrounding it. For modern, atheistic existentialism, as Jonas saw it before him above all in Sartre and Heidegger, this opposition results from specifically modern developments such as the triumph of natural science and modern technology, the death of God, as Nietzsche called it, and the loss of plausibility of the Christian tradition. However, behind these specifically modern aspects, fascinating parallels with Jonas' analysis of ancient Gnosis are readily apparent.

In fact, Jonas in 1952 explicitly endorses the view that there are far-reaching parallels between the world of late antiquity and Western modernity.[52] Even if he shows a certain reserve vis-à-vis Spengler's more speculative ideas,[53] it can hardly be doubted that in comparing Gnosis and existentialism, he thinks of more than an accidental, isolated parallel. We have already seen that, for Jonas, Gnosis with its postulate of the subject's radical alienation from its surrounding universe was paradigmatic for a major cultural transformation in late antiquity. At this point, it becomes furthermore clear that something very similar can be said for the modern era. Here, too, an understanding of existence prevails that combines world negation, existential despair, and a radical revaluation of values. In other words, Jonas' proposed understanding of Gnosis not only helps understand late antiquity correctly, but it is just as significant for comprehending the nature of the modern world.

In drawing this kind of parallel in the post-war period, Jonas was far from advancing a purely theoretical observation. Unlike Spengler, he was not primarily interested in speculating about the laws of world history. Rather, by establishing the Gnostic character of modernity, Jonas sought to expose a deeply uncomfortable and problematic truth about our own world. This very awareness of the modern world as untethered from its bond with nature continued to animate his subsequent work and can be seen as underlying not least his famous *Das Prinzip Verantwortung*.[54] With its radical dichotomy of self and world, Gnosis provided no sustainable spiritual basis for late ancient culture. Modern existentialism, based on the same existential foundation, is similarly unsuitable as the intellectual and spiritual basis of modern Western societies.

Conclusion

It has been the task of this chapter to consider Hans Jonas' early book on Gnosis in the context of the historiography of late antiquity and especially of late ancient religion. My purpose was not to offer a detailed *Forschungsgeschichte* but rather to indicate some broad trajectories that could help situate Jonas' own work and explain the effect it had on its field. Influential scholarly works are often distinguished by two tensional features: on the one hand, they continue earlier traditions and can therefore be appreciated by their readers as sequels, so to speak, to a conversation that is already familiar. On the other hand, however, they offer a break with this tradition by means of a novel configuration of a well-worn narrative, the establishment of a new vantage point from which to perceive the material, or the application of a new methodology.

Jonas' *Gnosis und spätantiker Geist* fits this mold excellently. The book appeals to ideas that for a long time were associated with late antiquity, such as the notion of crisis and the increase of non-Greek influences in the Hellenistic world. He also, undoubtedly, adopts some rather essentialist tropes about Greek and Asian cultures that must have seemed plausible at the time but appear problematic from today's point of view. Then there is the realignment that Jonas undertakes in the wake of recent scholarly reevaluations, notably his acceptance of key concepts from Spengler's *Untergang des Abendlandes*. With Spengler, Jonas shifts a narrative of decline to a narrative of transformation, while also crucially accepting the notion of pseudomorphosis to explain the existence of radically novel ideas in an alien conceptual framework. As far as Gnosis is concerned, Jonas likewise does not pretend to rewrite the rulebook completely. He follows the (now discarded) consensus of the *Religionsgeschichtliche Schule* of accepting a pre-Christian origin of Gnosis and thus the imperative to explain the movement independently of its confrontation with the early church fathers.

Based on all these pre-existent scholarly conceptions, however, Jonas advances his own set of strikingly original, simple, and powerful theses establishing Gnosis as based on a novel understanding of existence (*Existenzverständnis*) according to which the individual self exists in radical confrontation with a hostile cosmos. This idea, Jonas urged, was new and represented an 'Asian' culture incompatible with traditional Hellenism. Gnosis thus lost its status as a mere mixture of various influences and appeared as a historical phenomenon in its own right with paradigmatic significance for the period during which it emerged.

All this makes it easy to understand why Jonas' work was enthusiastically welcomed by specialists in various disciplines and how it developed over the decades into a classic study of late ancient Gnosis. And yet, this is not the whole story that deserves to be told about *Gnosis und spätantiker Geist*. For in the midst of Jonas' research in late ancient religious history, key philosophical ideas can be made out that were of importance to him beyond their historical application to the study of Gnosis. In particular, the juxtaposition between the 'Greek' notion of the self as embedded in the cosmos and the 'Gnostic' idea of the self's radical alienation from the world prepares crucial insights underlying Jonas' later work. In fact, the historical scholar may well suspect that Jonas' preoccupation with these questions ultimately made him turn ancient Gnosis into a merely negative foil despite his claim of understanding it on its own terms. That said, it would be wrong to discard his historical work as a mere garb permitting him to articulate his more proper ideas. Rather, the early Jonas is a good example of the potential of historical and religious study to engender original philosophical reflection as well.

Notes

1 Hans Jonas, *Gnosis und spätantiker Geist. Erster Teil: Die mythologische Gnosis. Mit einer Einleitung zur Geschichte und Methodologie der Forschung*, 4th edn. (Göttingen: Vanhoeck & Ruprecht, 1980). The present text draws on my "Die Gnosis als das faszinierende Fremde: Hans Jonas und die moderne Leidenschaft für eine geheimnisvolle Facette der spätantiken Religionsgeschichte" which is forthcoming in: Andris

Breitling and Roman Seidel (eds.), *Identität und Verantwortung in der Welt von heute: Kritische Reflexionen des Eigenen und Fremden im Anschluss an Hans Jonas* (Berlin: Logos Verlag).
2 Jonas, *Gnosis*, vii.
3 Jonas, *Gnosis*, vii.
4 Hans Jonas, *The Gnostic Religion: Message of the Alien God and the Beginnings of Christianity* (Boston, MA: Beacon Press, 1958). On the relationship between this book and the earlier German original, see the contribution by Daniel M. Herskowitz in this volume.
5 Hans Jonas, "Gnosticism and Nihilism," *Social Research* 19 (1952), 430–452. Here: 434.
6 For the purposes of this essay, I will use Jonas' term Gnosis in the place of the more common Gnosticism. On the debate about the use of the two terms, see Christoph Markschies, *Gnosis: An Introduction*, trans. John Bowden (London: T&T Clark, 2003), 13–16.
7 For this approach, see Karen L. King, "The Politics of Syncretism and the Problem of Defining Gnosticism," *Historical Reflections/Réflexions Historiques* 27/3 (2001), 461–479.
8 He does discuss texts that cannot be dated with certainty and *might* in theory be of a later time. If so, however, this would, if anything, be detrimental to Jonas' broader point.
9 The extensive *Oxford Handbook of Late Antiquity*, ed. Scott Fitzgerald Johnson (Oxford: OUP, 2012) only begins with the reign of Constantine the Great. For a wide-ranging discussion of the concepts of late antiquity that have been employed by scholarship, see the helpful first chapter of this book: Hervé Inglebert, "Introduction: Late Antique Conceptions of Late Antiquity," in Scott Fitzgerald Johnson (ed.), *Oxford Handbook of Late Antiquity* (Oxford: OUP, 2012), 3–28.
10 Edward Gibbon, *The History of the Decline and Fall of the Roman Empire*, ed. David Womersley. 3 vols. (London: Penguin, 1996).
11 Otto Seeck, *Geschichte des Untergangs der antiken Welt*, 6 vols. (Stuttgart: Metzler, 1895–1920. Reprint of the 4th edn.: Darmstadt: WBG, 2000). On Seeck and his work, see also: Stephan Lorenz, "Otto Seeck und die Spätantike," *Historia: Zeitschrift für Alte Geschichte* 55 (2006), 228–243.
12 Quoted from Lorenz, "Otto Seeck," 228 (translation my own).
13 See Arnaldo Momigliano, "Declines and Falls," *The American Scholar* 49 (1980), 37–50.
14 Oswald Spengler, *Der Untergang des Abendlandes: Umrisse einer Morphologie der Weltgeschichte* (Munich: Beck, 1923; Reprint 1990), ix. Spengler's work whose first volume first appeared in 1918 with Braumüller in Vienna, was published with Beck in many editions from 1922. I have been unable to ascertain which edition Jonas used in *Gnosis* but assume that it was one of the slightly modified prints of the 1920s.
15 Spengler, *Der Untergang des Abendlandes*, 35.
16 Spengler, *Der Untergang des Abendlandes*, 7.
17 Spengler, *Der Untergang des Abendlandes*, 3.
18 Spengler, *Der Untergang des Abendlandes*, 36 (my own translation).
19 Spengler, *Der Untergang des Abendlandes*, 37.
20 Spengler, *Der Untergang des Abendlandes*, 43–45.
21 Spengler, *Der Untergang des Abendlandes*, 581.
22 Peter Brown, *The World of Late Antiquity. AD 150–750* (London: Thames and Hudson, 1971). Cf. however the revisionist account in Bryan Ward-Perkins, *The Fall of Rome and the End of Civilization* (Oxford: OUP, 2005). See also Henri-Irenée Marrou, *Decadence romaine ou Antiquité tardive? IIIe-IVe siècle* (Paris: Seuil, 1977).
23 Peter Frankopan, *Silk Roads: A New History of the World* (London: Bloomsbury, 2015), 25.

24 Cf. the famous lines at the end of Emile Durkheim's *The Elementary Forms of the Religious Life*, trans. Joseph Ward Swain (Mineola, NY: Dover, 2008), 546, culminating in the claim that "old gods are growing old and already dead, and others are not yet born."
25 Augustine, *De civitate dei* I, 1 (ed. B. Dombart/A. Kalb. Corpus Christianorum. Series Latina 2 vols, Turnhout: Brepols, 1955). English translation: Augustine, *The City of God*, trans. William Babcock, vol. 1 (Hyde Park, NY: New City Press, 1952).
26 Arthur Darby Nock, *Conversion. The Old and the New in Religion from Alexander the Great to Augustine of Hippo* (Oxford: Clarendon Press, 1933), 164 ff.
27 Pierre Hadot, *Philosophy as a Way of Life: Spiritual Exercises from Socrates to Foucault*, ed. Arnold I. Davidson, trans. M. Chase (Oxford: Blackwell, 1995).
28 Cf. on this point the cautious analysis by Jan Bremmer, "Transformations and Decline of Sacrifice in Imperial Rome and Late Antiquity," in Michael Blömer and Benedikt Eckhardt (eds.), *Transformationen paganer Religion in der römischen Kaiserzeit* (Berlin: de Gruyter, 2018), 215–256.
29 Christoph Markschies, *Gnosis*, 29–39.
30 King, "Syncretism."
31 This is often referred to as the 'Gnostic crisis.'
32 For a nuanced assessment of recent debates, see David Brakke, *The Gnostics: Myth, Ritual, and Diversity in Early Christianity* (Cambridge, MA: Harvard University Press, 2012).
33 Jonas, *Gnosis*, 1.
34 Jonas, *Gnosis*, vi. Behind Bultmann stood the earlier work of the so-called *religionsgeschichtliche Schule*, represented by scholars such as Wilhelm Bousset and Richard Reitzenstein. Cf. Bousset's, *Hauptprobleme der Gnosis* (Göttingen: Vandenhoeck & Ruprecht, 1907. Reprint 2011), 323–326. And the articles by Grossman, Bongardt, and Settimo in the present volume.
35 Bousset, *Hauptprobleme der Gnosis*, 5.
36 Bousset, *Hauptprobleme der Gnosis*, 11–12.
37 For Jonas' reliance on Heidegger's philosophy, see Micha Brumlik, '*Ressentiment*. A Few Motifs in Hans Jonas' Early Book on Gnosticism', in Hava Timosh-Samuelson/Christian Wiese (eds.), *The Legacy of Hans Jonas: Judaism and the Phenomenon of Life* (Leiden: Brill, 2008), 73–90 and Elad Lapidot's chapter in the present volume.
38 Jonas, *Gnosis*, 3.
39 Jonas, *Gnosis*, 3.
40 Jonas, *Gnosis*, 144. See e.g. Plato, *Phaedo* 82e.
41 Jonas, *Gnosis*, 141.
42 Jonas, *Gnosis*, 144.
43 Jonas, *Gnosis*, 170.
44 Jonas, *Gnosis*, 143–144.
45 Jonas, *Gnosis*, 215.
46 Jonas, *Gnosis*, 215.
47 Jonas, *Gnosis*, 234.
48 Jonas, *Gnosis*, 234.
49 Jonas, *Gnosis*, 236.
50 Jonas, *Gnosis*, 74.
51 Jonas, "Gnosticism," 431. On Jonas' critique of existentialism and of Heidegger in particular, see Jonathan Cahana, "A Gnostic Critic of Modernity. Hans Jonas from Existentialism to Science," *Journal of the American Academy of Religion* 86 (2018), 158–180; Daniel M. Herskowitz, "Reading Heidegger against the Grain: Hans Jonas on Existentialism, Gnosticism, and Modern Science," *Modern Intellectual History* 18 (2021), 1–24. For a fine-grained analysis of this development, see Elad Lapidot, "*Gnosis und spätantiker Geist. Teil II*: The Forgotten Book," in the present volume.
52 Jonas, "Gnosticism," 433–434.

53 Jonas, "Gnosticism," 433–434.
54 Hans Jonas, *Das Prinzip Verantwortung: Versuch einer Ethik für die technologische Zivilisation* (Frankfurt: Suhrkamp, 1979).

Bibliography

Bousset, Wilhelm, *Hauptprobleme der Gnosis*. Göttingen: Vandenhoeck & Ruprecht, 1907.
Brakke, David, *The Gnostics: Myth, Ritual, and Diversity in Early Christianity*. Cambridge, MA: Harvard University Press, 2012.
Bremmer, Jan, "Transformations and Decline of Sacrifice in Imperial Rome and Late Antiquity." Michael Blömer and Benedikt Eckhardt (eds.), *Transformationen paganer Religion in der römischen Kaiserzeit*. Berlin: de Gruyter, 2018, 215–256.
Brown, Peter, *The World of Late Antiquity. AD 150–750*. London: Thames and Hudson, 1971.
Brumlik, Micha, "*Ressentiment*. A Few Motifs in Hans Jonas' Early Book on Gnosticism." Hava Timosh-Samuelson and Christian Wiese (eds.), *The Legacy of Hans Jonas: Judaism and the Phenomenon of Life*. Leiden: Brill, 2008, 73–90.
Cahana, Jonathan, "A Gnostic Critic of Modernity. Hans Jonas from Existentialism to Science." *Journal of the American Academy of Religion* 86 (2018), 158–180.
Durkheim, Emile, *The Elementary Forms of the Religious Life*, trans. Joseph Ward Swain. Mineola, NY: Dover, 2008.
Frankopan, Peter, *Silk Roads: A New History of the World*. London: Bloomsbury, 2015.
Gibbon, Edward, *The History of the Decline and Fall of the Roman Empire*, ed. David Womersley. 3 vols. London: Penguin, 1996.
Hadot, Pierre, *Philosophy as a Way of Life: Spiritual Exercises from Socrates to Foucault*, ed. Arnold I. Davidson; trans. M. Chase. Oxford: Blackwell, 1995.
Herskowitz, Daniel M., "Reading Heidegger against the Grain: Hans Jonas on Existentialism, Gnosticism, and Modern Science." *Modern Intellectual History* 18 (2021), 1–24.
Inglebert, Hervé, "Introduction: Late Antique Conceptions of Late Antiquity." Scott Fitzgerald Johnson (ed.), *Oxford Handbook of Late Antiquity*. Oxford: OUP, 2012, 3–28.
Johnson, Scott Fitzgerald, *Oxford Handbook of Late Antiquity*. Oxford: OUP, 2012.
Jonas, Hans, "Gnosticism and Nihilism." *Social Research* 19 (1952), 430–452.
Jonas, Hans, *The Gnostic Religion: Message of the Alien God and the Beginnings of Christianity*, Boston, MA: Beacon Press, 1958.
Jonas, Hans, *Das Prinzip Verantwortung: Versuch einer Ethik für die technologische Zivilisation*. Frankfurt: Suhrkamp, 1979.
Jonas, Hans, *Gnosis und spätantiker Geist. Erster Teil: Die mythologische Gnosis. Mit einer Einleitung zur Geschichte und Methodologie der Forschung*, 4th ed. Göttingen: Vanhoeck & Ruprecht, 1980.
King, Karen L., "The Politics of Syncretism and the Problem of Defining Gnosticism." *Historical Reflections/Réflexions Historiques* 27/3 (2001), 461–479.
Lapidot, Elad, "*Gnosis und spätantiker Geist. Teil II*: The Forgotten Book," in the present volume.
Lorenz, Stephan, "Otto Seeck und die Spätantike." *Historia: Zeitschrift für Alte Geschichte* 55 (2006), 228–243.
Markschies, Christoph, *Gnosis: An Introduction*, trans. John Bowden. London: T&T Clark, 2003.
Marrou, Henri-Irenée, *Decadence romaine ou Antiquité tardive? IIIe-IVe siècle*. Paris: Seuil, 1977.

Momigliano, Arnaldo, "Declines and Falls." *The American Scholar* 49 (1980), 37–50.
Nock, Arthur Darby, *Conversion. The Old and the New in Religion from Alexander the Great to Augustine of Hippo.* Oxford: Clarendon Press, 1933.
Seeck, Otto, *Geschichte des Untergangs der antiken Welt*, 6 vols. Stuttgart: Metzler, 1895–1920. Reprint of the 4th ed.: Darmstadt: WBG, 2000.
Spengler, Oswald, *Der Untergang des Abendlandes: Umrisse einer Morphologie der Weltgeschichte*. Munich: Beck, 1923; Reprint 1990.
Ward-Perkins, Bryan, *The Fall of Rome and the End of Civilization*. Oxford: OUP, 2005.

7 A Historical Transcendental at the Heart of Jonas' Research on Gnosticism

Nathalie Frogneux

Introduction

We would like to address two paradoxes in Jonas' relationship to Gnostic studies. These are in fact two ambiguities: his own and that of his interpreters. On the one hand, the importance of his studies and their poor reception; on the other hand, the fact that he minimizes their importance in the *Memoirs* whereas they circumscribe the double focus of his philosophy. Thereafter, Jonas will not cease, on the one hand, to reply to the cosmological and anthropological dualisms that make the history of man in the world futile, a world where human action doesn't matter; on the other hand, he develops an evolution of the living and, within it, a human history. The initial misunderstandings are undoubtedly at the basis of the contrasting reception of his work *Gnosis und spätantiker Geist*.[1] It is on the question of "enigmatic" history that we will focus our attention.[2]

By adopting the Heideggerian hermeneutics to study the Gnostic phenomenon, Jonas immediately posits history as the place where individual and collective human freedom is played out in the world. This makes him from the outset a dissident disciple of Heidegger, as will become clear in the lecture he gave at Drew in 1964. Indeed, there are two conceptions of history that confront each other: the Heideggerian one of the Fate of Being and the Jonasian one of human history. This distinction supposes that of a historical and anhistorical transcendental.

At the Threshold of the History of Religions and Philosophy, an Innovative Hermeneutic

The publication of GSG I in 1934 seems to have marked a turning point for historians of religion.[3] Rudolf Bultmann underlines the importance of Jonas' research on Gnosis, as he writes in his foreword to GSG.

> For having devoted a large part of my work for years to the study of gnosis, I have never, in any of the research devoted up to now to this field – and it is known that there are excellent ones – learned as much as in this one for a true knowledge of the phenomenon of gnosis in *the history of ideas*; in fact, it is only here that the significance of the phenomenon has emerged for me in all its magnitude.[4]

DOI: 10.4324/9781003439882-7

Similarly, in Heidegger's recently published evaluation of Jonas' dissertation, one can read his appreciation for this research work: "Compared to the common, merely lexicographic listing of the various meanings of philosophical terms, the present work represents a considerable progress both with respect to the results of the content and especially with respect to the method."[5]

From then on, his synthesis allowed the history of religions to take a decisive step, thanks to a new hermeneutical framework elaborated in the wake of Bultmann and Barth. James Robinson shows how much Jonas contributed not only to the foundation of a philosophy of language for the hermeneutics of religions, but also to the formation of the concept of demythologization itself, thus inscribing himself in the "pre-history of demythologization,"[6] whose history and development have nevertheless remained linked to the name of Bultmann. His influence on the history of religion was therefore major. In an interview with Culianu, Jonas declared that Bultmann "became fascinated by [his] works."[7] In 1993, Kurt Rudolph, a specialist in Gnosticism and Manichaeism, did not hesitate to qualify Jonas' work as a "masterpiece"[8] in the third completed edition of the second volume of GSG that he published and prefaced. And he insisted again in 2008: "Without a doubt, in 1934 *Gnosis und spätantiker Geist* constituted an important advance in the landscape of research, *which is still relevant today.*"[9]

Although Jaspers revealed to him the muted reception of GSG when they met in Germany during the 1944–1945[10] campaign, in 1954, in the second edition of *Gnosis und spätantiker Geist I*, Jonas explicitly deplores the lack of interest of philosophers for this phenomenological–existential research, of which he had hoped for more reaction than from historians of religions.

This disappointing reception by both historians of religion and philosophers can no doubt be explained in part by the hybrid character of his research, which stood, so to speak, on the border and thus on the threshold of disciplines.

On the one hand, it had to be very well informed on the historical level in order to bring out the spirit of an epoch from the most manifest phenomena of this moment. On the other hand, Jonas probably seemed too preoccupied with questions usually dealt with by historians of religion for philosophers to understand his philosophical stakes, namely to bring out the spirit of the age and thus to develop a philosophy of history. And this is in addition to a difficulty of language that some have not failed to point out.

However, GSG presents a historical research based on philosophy and which includes a philosophical scope. To understand what is at stake, we need to return to the methodology of his research. Indeed, Jonas is inspired by Heideggerian hermeneutics to explore the vital and self-generating unity of a historical phenomenon of late antiquity without being limited to the sects and Gnostic religion which are, however, the focus of his research. To be able to grasp the spirit of the time, he must, however, endeavor to describe its relatively explicit or central manifestations. In this case, the focus of this Gnostic period would be found in the Mandean sectarian system, which explained the coherence of Gnostic thought almost without veil.

It is by starting from this composite unity – to be determined – that the spirit of an era opened up to Jonas' reading and that he was able to describe its extension in return (even going so far as to speak of Plotinus' Gnosticism and a root within primitive Christianity): "This root must be freed from the given diversity of expressions provided by literature: this is the true hermeneutical exercise."[11]

Without ever really losing interest in this initial research, Jonas will continue his dialogue with the historians of religions when they will have access to new material sources with the discoveries of Nag Hammadi in 1945. He will thus follow the publications and translations.

In his letter to Bultmann of December 11, 1952, he confessed that even though he was completely absorbed by his book on the philosophy of the organism, he felt "the call of gnosis."[12] He will still attempt to describe the dualistic root that primitive Christianity shared with Gnosticism in the text that he offers to Bultmann in 1964. In 1965, he also wrote a new text dedicated to the "Hymn to the Pearl", which was particularly dear to his heart.[13]

In contrast, in the *Memoirs*, he minimizes the importance of his work on Gnosticism by reducing it to a work of formation.[14] Even though he continued his research well beyond his formative years. And when he was the object of criticism at the Messina colloquium in 1967, which led to a stabilization of the distinction between Gnosis and Gnosticism, he nevertheless published his contribution under the title "The Gnostic Syndrome" in the important collection of *Philosophical Essays*, using the adjective "gnostic" rather than choosing between the nouns Gnosis and Gnosticism, and the term "syndrome" to designate this historical phenomenon of great magnitude with vague contours but with an identifiable focus for those who manage to liberate the mind from forms (pseudomorphosis). Jonas will thus maintain his thesis from the 1930s until the 1990s and his reply to an apolitical and ethical thought.[15]

Moreover, the debates continue around the main theses, characterizing Gnosticism and they are five in number: (1) the possibility of unifying the diversity of sectarian movements of the time under the term "Gnosticism";[16] (2) the relevance of the category of anticosmic dualism to characterize such a movement; (3) the possibility of understanding the Gnostic attitude as a rebellion, even revolutionary; (4) the extension of a "Gnostic" period from the Diadochi to Manichaeism, that is to say half a millennium and (5) the possibility of releasing "a new total form of the mind (*Gestalt des Geistes*),"[17] that is to say a specific Dasein, thanks to the hermeneutic method.

A New Total Spiritual Form

It is this last point that we would like to underline; less for the question of its cultural extension, than for the question of its historical form insofar as it supposes a circular hermeneutical process. Here is a long quotation that allows us to identify Jonas' position:

> We understand [...] the productive factor as that which is transcendentally constitutive, as that which is rooted each time in a fundamental factual historical situation of "Dasein". From it, the whole interpretation of the world, from the coarsest mythical forms to the most refined philosophical ones, is determined

in a historical field that draws its unification and its essential unity from it, that is to say that it forges a domain from this ground and thanks to it. It is the universal all in itself, the central unity of its principle. This principle is, by nature, historical – perhaps we do not even have the right to say historically "conditioned". Whether this central principle of meaning-giving is itself also a function of the causal processes internal to history, or rather whether it is an unrelated, original, independent birth, which bursts into time, unfolds, and after exhausting its possibilities disappears again (as Spengler asserts), is a question that must remain open. – In any case, it is necessary to postulate a priori such an existential root as the homogeneous and unifying principle for each set of testimonies of contemporary history, as long as there is an active production in it. It is each time a Dasein that has constructed this system of statements that attests itself in this world of testimonies and objectifies in it its being – so that it is also from there that a go to line of elements of testimonies receives its cohesion. This fundamental presupposition, founded in the essence of Dasein, becomes a practical-methodological principle for proceeding in the history of ideas: this presupposition authorizes and compels one to interrogate the given phenomena with reference to this root, to hear them, as it were, from this root, in order to grasp, with this root, the central principle of their interpretation. That such a principle must really be at the base is the a priori of the history of ideas and consequently, as we said, to be postulated from the outset in each case.[18]

Insofar as human language is objectifying, interpretations are always themselves somehow objectifying, demythologization will have to work at de-objectifying certain excessively mythological discourses, in order to bring it back into line with the subjective experience that gives it life, even if it is never reached as such.[19] The particular universal that emerges in this way appears as the ground of an epoch, its focus or most explicit version. Rather than Dilthey,[20] for example, who nevertheless thematized the historical transcendental, Jonas prefers to quote the "maverick"[21] Oswald Spengler, from whom he borrows, on the one hand, the notion of "*Kulturseele*" that he translates by "*Daseinshaltung*," and on the other hand, the notion of pseudomorphosis to understand how the new Gnostic spirit could hide in old notions.

This hermeneutic thus allows him to understand the change of period within the history of ideas, which are neither separated nor determined by material achievements. If late antiquity was not a period of decline or decadence, it is because it sees the emergence of a new being-in-the-world as the horizon of the thought of time (*Zeitalter*). Now, the spirit of time, the spirit of a period which is the product of this time, its objectivation, is also its producing factor which emerges also from a subjective experience.[22]

A Historical Transcendental Ground

It is a question of understanding by this hermeneutical method "the transcendental Ground and its historicity,"[23] that is to say this underlying principle of objectivation, by carrying out the inverse movement of subjectivation. Through texts and debates of late antiquity, which he names the finished products, Jonas thus seeks to seize a unity and an underlying existential coherence capable of these realizations and these testimonies.

> When we spoke of 'finished products' as the object of objective historical research, we were already alluding to an underlying factor of production. But we do not understand it here as subjects each time empirical (individual, collective, ethnological, etc....) themselves, indeed, points of intersection of innumerable causal chains external to them, but as the fundamental attitude of the Dasein at this original level of the imaginative perception of the being, from which is temporalized, as a historical act, the encompassing constitution of the 'world' and of the relation of the Dasein to the world valid for a whole epoch in the following way: this original constitution is the necessary a priori horizon of the understanding of the world and of oneself for the epoch concerned and the empirical subjects of it, within which each of the respective attempts, differences and modifications of explicit interpretation, which are otherwise, as empirical realities, subject to worldly causes, must be accomplished.[24]

This transcendental foundation thus appears as an a priori of the finished products which present only diversity and juxtaposition as long as it is not revealed and understood.

> The aim is to bring the structure of the conception of Dasein in question to this philosophical intelligibility, which then itself, as a source of intelligibility, makes it possible to illuminate the periphery of the objective field of expression. But for this, such an intelligibility, which is principle of itself, must already be given at the beginning: the starting point must be taken from an already available philosophical knowledge of Dasein, even if this does not provide the results of content, but essentially the mode of questioning Dasein from its logos. The structures of being derived from the pure analysis of Dasein become concrete perspectives of interrogation with respect to the historical forms of Dasein.[25]

Thus, the real stake of his research on Gnosticism was undoubtedly more on the side of his philosophy of history, since in the line of Heidegger, he highlights a historical level (*geschichtlich*) of an epoch that will be a historical transcendental.

In order to establish this thesis of a historical transcendental in the field of research, Jonas criticizes two positions that he considers excessive: On the one hand, the radical autonomy of ideas defended by the syncretist thesis and on the other hand, the determinism of the historical circumstances of the supporters of psychologism and sociologism.

In fact, syncretism, which grants too much autonomy to the sphere of thought and leaves too much room to the ideal level, presupposes that ideas are able to recombine themselves independently of the experience of concrete people. The syncretist understanding of the Gnostic movement is therefore "an amalgam of morphological elements, which, considered individually, unrelated and alien to each other, only came together by chance; but which, when brought together in a network of forces, inevitably also formed something new."[26] He thus ironizes on the possibility of understanding, as Wilhelm Bousset proposed, the Gnostic dualism as a recombination of the Zoroastrian and Platonic dualisms, i.e. as a pure resultant, whereas it is precisely a question of understanding how a dualism of a new type was able to emerge in its spontaneity and its specificity.[27]

For all that, psychologism and sociologism do not satisfy Jonas either, because they presuppose, on the contrary, that the history of ideas is dependent on the concrete conditions of existence and therefore leave no autonomy to historical freedom. However, history cannot be a list of facts independently of the meaning given to them. Psychological–causal research intends to explain the ideal level by an empirical level, by "an original subjective reality and thus it understands Gnosticism above all as a fact of life,"[28] an existential situation, which Jonas agrees with. However, the psycho-sociological perspective remains too superficial in that it dispenses with a transcendental ground and claims to explain what, without it, remains incomprehensible. They make the concrete situation of the persons the unilateral cause of history and of its great historical changes. Indeed, in the psychologist hypothesis, the real *Dasein*, that is to say the attitude or the vision of the world, receives too little space and the historical novelty remains unthinkable in its coherence. In the sociologist explanation, no autonomy of thought remains in front of the empirical conditionings. Yet, it is precisely freedom within history that we have to understand.

History has indeed largely shown that no strict causality can be established in this way, since, however cruel they may be, the destinies of particular peoples or communities did not systematically lead to a fundamentally hostile attitude to the world – nor, a fortiori, to the elaboration of a radically dualistic metaphysics, to an idea of an extra-mundane God, to an acosmic conception of "life," or to an anti-cosmism as radical as that of the Gnostics. Faced with concrete situations comparable to those experienced by the Gnostics of late antiquity, the times and peoples reacted very differently. Moreover, late Hellenism was not a particularly horrible period for the East, as the Syrian opulence testifies. Men respond collectively to situations and are therefore responsible, collectively and individually, because they have accepted or refused the spirit of their time.

In the same way, in spite of his admiration for the work of Max Weber, Jonas recognizes that the psychological–sociological hypotheses and explanations are too hasty when they want to understand Gnosis from the political situation or from the concrete feeling of being on the margins of the Roman Empire, although this could indeed have provoked a feeling of fracture in relation to God, as was undoubtedly the case at the time of the destruction of the Temple in 70. This is why Jonas affirms "we pose the subjective basis in a less 'psychological' and more 'transcendental' way than psychologism and sociologism do."[29]

Without rejecting the link of ideas to the empirical situation of those who produced them or to the experience that motivated them, Jonas thus posits, behind the facts of life and below the ideal motives, a historical transcendental moment that he names the *Dasein* (Gnostic in this case).

> The psychological motivation always enters already in play on the basis of a more elementary and always previously decided relation to being, which is not constituted only by the psychological factor, but also contains its own "transcendental" moment. This one, understood however as historical and not as timeless, is principally situated "before" the psychological as such (*proteron psychei*, or *chrono*) and transforms this one in a continuous way in *its* truth.[30]

A more elementary relationship to being and always already decided is a free relationship, even if it is not absolutely devoid of determination, since it is linked to concrete historical conditions. Indeed, Jonas seems to take literally and according to the etymology the term of decision of which English and German have kept the trace: *Ent-scheiden*, decide (from "to cut off"). Coming from both thought and freedom, the decision is what allows one to distinguish oneself, to separate oneself and to take distance.

> At the heart of its *possibilities* of meaning, which encompass a pre-empirical judgment of *Dasein*, all psychological, sociological and also natural causalities act. What consequences are drawn from experiences, what experiences are actually 'made,' is what is decided from there. Thus, the psychological motivation, insofar as the circumstances push it, can provide a tone and a tendency, a matter and an attraction, but it cannot found an ontology by itself, that is to say the material *a priori* of a whole constitution of being, which collects much more the occasion which arises from the transcendental ground of the *Dasein* – and *exceeds* it at once (as it can also refuse itself to similar psychological occasions or answer them quite differently). In its *determination*, it is that which overcomes circumstantial reactions by a new foundation and a donation of categorical images ('schematization'), survives validly and, no longer needing external confirmation and additional motives, and determines in its turn, from what is unconditioned, the most remote form of experience, the fundamental mode of apprehension of external and internal reality, and thus the form of action. What in this way exceeds the pure vital reaction – as it is designated in the concepts that signal an 'optimism-pessimism,' 'affirmation of life-negation of life' tone – and by unifying it, still overflows the exchange of such impressionistic modes of affection, it is therefore what constitutes the authentic truth and strength of a historical and even history-creating 'worldview.' All psychological experience, henceforth thus sustained and regulated, must then be the confirmation of the only fundamental experience in which total being is anticipated. However, the transcendental center that is effective here must

also be influenced beforehand by the fundamental temporality and reactive receptivity of man, – and this affection is produced precisely by the factual history without which man and his ability to create cannot be, and whose coincidences between the event and the disposition that corresponds to it depend on fate. (Precisely for this reason, every worldview is 'only historical,' but yet at the same time also an essential truth of the spirit, which in evolution can only be 'exceeded.')[31]

This circularity between the transcendental level of historical Dasein and individual and collective experiences distinguishes Jonas from both deterministic explanations (psychologism and sociologism) and a totally indifferent freedom. In this case, freedom can be understood as both creative and receptive, as both an extraction from and an adherence to its epoch, since this transcendental level is both the fruit of its possibilities and what conditions it.
Of what nature is this anticipation then?
For the historian of ideas, it is thus a question of releasing a new, spontaneous, and autogenous root.

We aim at something that exceeds principally all the systems of causes, something that encompasses them integrally, as what would be 'triggered' by them, without that they do not cover it or do not exhaust the sense of it (although they are indispensable to its becoming).[32]

Exceeding the realities that can be explained causally, this principle which is the true object of historical research is, so to speak, caused by them without ever being reduced to them.

This meaning does not anticipate that of the existential consideration, but fundamentally requires it on the contrary – already in a very preventive way, in order not to reduce its own meaning too much from this examination, just as the transcendental ('spirit') of an epoch is ultimately always already contained as a constituent factor in the so-called 'real conditions' themselves, for example in the social basis of facts. (For this reason, the explanatory sociology of the spirit always comes up against a fundamental circle). And we believe that one can speak of a Gnostic epoch.[33]

The fundamental circle thus designates at the same time the production and the product of an epoch in its unity and its coherence.
Since Jonas was trying to understand the disparity of the Gnostic forms through a unique Gnostic principle which would be the primitive focus, he had to discover it at work in the concrete testimonies.

Thus this direction of research fits into the type of genetic *explicative* science; which, of course, is not explicative by a return to *actual* factors underlying such ideal events and thus by a return to the general empirical life circumstances of the groups that were their concrete representatives – for this, a break from the ideal level would be precisely required.[34]

For this reason, Jonas neither minimized nor neglected the texts resulting from archaeological discoveries in 1945. Impatient for the library to open up to manifest all its richness, he wrote in the preface to the third edition of The Gnostic Religion in 1970: "It is the Coptologists' day. Everyone else is holding his breath and, if wise, his hand."[35] Finally, we should note his great prudence and modesty in the face of the new texts that were gradually being edited and translated, since he did not exclude the possibility that they might invalidate his work, and this was undoubtedly due to the rigor he had shown from the outset with regard to the sources available to him, i.e. those of the heresiologists. However, Jonas has always been clear about his interests:

> What interests us in the end in the historical deductions of motives [...], is not what remains constant, but the characteristic variants. Now, in order to be able to identify them as such and to evaluate their degrees of difference, we must first have at our disposal what is constant as that from which they diverge.[36]

This spirit of time, or *Zeitgeist*, is thematized in a footnote of major importance on pages 62 and 63 of GSG I. Jonas indeed describes there what he understands by historical transcendental and its relation to the history of the spirit and of humanity.

> The level on which the positive consideration distinguishes the "ideal" and the "factual," the "subjective" and the "objective," the "theoretical" and the "practical," and other groups of phenomena (such as political, economic phenomena, etc.) and delimits them regionally from each other, this level of reality is in total "after" the one in which we establish the ground of the total attitude towards the being and delimits them regionally in relation to each other, this level of reality is in total 'after' the one in which we establish the ground of the total attitude towards being and by which it is already constituted with its polarities – only to refer back from the ground and determine it in turn.[37]

The ontological or existential foundation sought is then itself historical and essentially dynamic, rather than metaphysical, and is constituted in a polarization between subjectivity and objectivity.

> This constitutive ground is thus itself nothing static, but is essentially historical; and, on the other hand, it is nothing purely intellectual, no more than purely emotional: one could speak of a transcendental function of the *will*, if one does not take this one as a part or a particular act of the soul, but as a total mode of being of the human Dasein.[38]

This collective and anonymous ground makes history as much as it is constituted by it. It is the fact of a creative humanity of what Jonas calls elsewhere the human image, always linked to an era. Its freedom cannot be reduced to the causal or deterministic forces of its positive products or of the concrete circumstances of existence. The history, in the sense in which it is understood here, is that of a freedom or a will at work through particular historical productions:

> the ground receives its determination from human history, to which it belongs, and, indeed, from all its levels – from the biological to the spiritual levels – in each of which it is subject-object, active-passive: originating in history, even accomplishing the latter, it is affected by history, as much by what breaks into it as by what it itself produces, moreover it is affected by its own acting to become something new also in its fundamental position.[39]

The history of this transcendent will or freedom with respect to individual freedoms thus acquires a determining character for the spirit of the age.

> History is thus continuously, apart from the drift due to external forces, *immanent self-affection of its own spontaneity*. If this does not, no longer or not yet take place, then we are in the anhistorical – for not every being of man belongs equally to history.[40]

This immanent self-affection of freedom, that is to say this reflexivity, characterizes history and thus the possibility of a memory; it can thus establish a continuity within ruptures and determine itself in the face of external forces that condition it but do not determine it.

The Historical *Dasein* as a Free Cultural Form

The hermeneutic circularity follows the circularity of the spirit and of freedom in a continuous process of objectification and subjectivation by which meaning emerges and can be understood.[41] The *Dasein* (Gnostic in this case) as a historical transcendental that would be a free response to a given epoch: a collective response conditioned – and not determined – by the concrete historical context, not being determined by it, it conditions in its turn the practices and the reactions of a given epoch.

Jonas underlines in parentheses the *enigmatic* character of the freedom of choice thus engaged. It is self-justifying and can therefore only resist any causal explanation or reduction to the past.

> (The vagueness of this answer to the question of provenance, which asserts only the totality of the contexts of becoming, consciously leaves the enigma unresolved, for each particular condition is made obligatory by itself, *eo ipso* a deformation; and the question which, in so doing, always arises about the mind: Is it a representative or a factor, or to what extent is it not rather one and the other, – always a false alternative – it is in the end a sterile trap question of science (just as insoluble as the Kantian antinomies, a character which as for them can be proved by a transcendental philosophical analysis)).[42]

Freedom is thus manifested by contrast, opposition, detachment, or resistance to the spirit of the age and sometimes contributes to the appearance of a new ground. From then on, lucidity often imposes a struggle against the prejudices and the accepted options of an era. This is how he describes his own critique of the contemporary definition of death.[43]

Freedom seems identical to the spirit: The history of human freedom is indeed that of the meaning that it can give individually and collectively to the external circumstances to which it responds.

Thus, the foundation cannot be reduced to its historical manifestations:

> The ground as a process has its before and after, its irreversibility and non-repeatability (for its self-affection is a memory of itself), its breaks and its totally new beginnings, without coming with them from nothingness, – and whatever its provenance each time as a totality; for each determined phase of its real history, it is already an a priori.[44]

Underlying the production of the meaning of an epoch, this a priori is the point of arrival of a hermeneutical research that illuminates from its center the peripheral zones. The contours are not very well defined.

Thus, such a ground of the spiritual-subjective level can only manifest itself through objectivities, which are derived from it and from which it will derive:

> As such, it [the ground] also asserts itself with respect to purely external constellations: there are no 'merely objective' facts and events here. Insofar as they are not already co-instituted by it, they are affections of the historical subject in accordance with the form of its receptivity. By the fact that he allows himself to be approached and his response, they are 'constituted' into objectivities for this subject, into his objects.[45]

Human freedom and its history must therefore be understood together, as well as the necessity that unfolds on the objective level.

> In this lies a moment of freedom (but not of free will), which, as a transcendentally projecting factor, is the complement of all necessity. Even in the most unilateral causality of the "relations", there is still the let-occur of those who are touched "passively" by it. The subject of the history "chooses" in this relation his not chosen destiny, gives him the "plus-value", because of which he must now answer for the totality, for the not-wanted. *The subject thus becomes in return responsible for what he has of objective, what is affected by what affects him. Thus, he becomes his personal destiny.* Despite the indecipherable character of chance and heteronomous necessity, history is in essence the history of freedom.[46]

Freedom thus understood is ontological or existential and cannot be limited to the level of an individual or existential free will, this one being always already situated on a level derived from this original freedom understood as a *dynamic of freedom*. In the same way, responsibility is posed at a transcendent level.

This is Jonas' succinct presentation of his reworking of Heidegger, i.e. of the presupposition he formulates at the threshold of his analysis of Gnostic *Dasein*. Beyond the regional or ontic distinctions, it is the ontological foundation of *Dasein* that is targeted by his analysis. Even though Jonas claims to be a Heideggerian, he nevertheless confers, in his interpretation, quasi-Hegelian[47] accents to being understood as freedom constituting itself historically in existential situations that are always particular – a freedom and a will that are not to be understood as human faculties, but as the foundation of the existence of an epoch that conditions our way of responding to it. It is from this ontological level that the positive (subject–object) and regional polarities are drawn, in a derived way.

This historical *Dasein* is thus at the same time the condition of the reactions of the concrete people to their time and it conditions the concrete answers of a time. However, each epoch is at equal distance from its foundation.

Consequently, Jonas describes thereafter this ideal level of the historical *Dasein* in the modern era, in the contemporary era and shows how this collective imaginary can be worked on by individuals or anonymous collective currents by adopting the vocabulary of the image that results from a moment of decision, i.e. a movement of freedom of thought in its relation to the given.

Resumption of This Scheme in Later Works

Let us extend some of the issues of this historical transcendental in the rest of Jonas' work. Jonas will not depart from this philosophy of history, of human history.

Thus he writes in the 1957 preface to *The Gnostic Religion* that the Gnostic option was taken in the middle of possible crossroads, and that it is indeed a free choice. He understands it as the fruit of a "decision made long ago"[48] that has conditioned the history of the West. However, he has considerably evolved on one point: The biological level to which he referred in the second note on page 62 of GSG I: Jonas counted the biological levels (up to the spiritual levels) among the levels of human history, whereas afterward, that is to say from "Didactic Letters to Lore Jonas 1944–1945"[49] onward, the biological dimension will be explicitly excluded to become an *anhistorical transcendental*. The hermeneutical process of objectivation and subjectivation, which is at once the fact of freedom in history and of the mind capable of grasping its meaning, is based on a more fundamental objectivity. In 1934, Jonas did not seem to be very concerned with the distinction between the meaning conferred on the biological level and the biological level itself (which is only said negatively as resisting and conditioning the historical foundation).

In his introduction to philosophy, he explains in fact that history is neither that of the being, nor that of the nature, but that of the historical meanings unceasingly to be taken again.

> Rather do these [Philosophical] problems pose themselves afresh at each succeeding age, in the light of their whole antecedent history, which is

the history of their successive statements as problems, of their successive elaborations & of the successively attempted answers to them.[50]

The history of philosophy, the history of culture, and the history of ideas is thus at the same time a continuous history and a history marked by distinct epochs that appear then as a preponderant hermeneutical framework. Now, these historical prisms, these historical transcendentals, can be more or less correct attempts according to their compatibility with the anhistorical transcendental that Jonas calls the human condition.

> His own being forms a part of it, & this being is essentially historical; i.e., man's being is the outcome of his past doings. The past meant here is the cultural past of the race as retained in historical memory, and only insofar as this past is really remembered, is man truly aware of what his present being is & what therefore is now the true meaning of his problems with regard to existence.[51]

The Human History and Not the Destiny of Being

Meanwhile, this attention to the stakes of a biological transcendental that conditions the historical ground appears to him essential to understand freedom as decision and thus as responsibility. For Jonas, history is indeed that of individual and collective human choices and not that of being.

We can measure the gap between history as the destiny of being for Heidegger and that of human history in the world according to Jonas. In this very famous conference given at Drew in 1964 within the framework of a colloquium entitled "Non-Objectifying Thinking and Speaking in Contemporary Theology," Jonas virulently opposes the later Heidegger who makes man the shepherd of being and thus cancels out his capacity for action by offering an absolute priority to the call of being to which man can only obey.[52] In "Heidegger and Theology," Jonas intends to denounce the dangers of the Heideggerian posture for the Protestant theologians who think of recovering the Neo-Testamental link between the call and the faith[53]. History is then reduced to the "divine comedy of being" (to allude to the title of Dante that Jonas takes up about Origen).[54]

Indeed, after the *Kehre*, Heidegger does not put the emphasis anymore on *Dasein*, but on being and its self-disclosure, thus developing an immanentist way of thinking that would enslave man to the permanent revelation of Being.

Having perfectly understood the oscillation between two opposed philosophies of the call, one extremely transcendent "from outside" in *Sein und Zeit* and the other purely immanent and without separation, of the later Heidegger, Jonas underlines that neither one nor the other gives right to freedom and to human action in the world.[55] Paradoxically, this ontic historicity is ultimately reduced either to eternity, or to the flux of Being which is not distinguished from its moments: And the result is, and should be according to the Heideggerian perspective, a submission of human thought to the history of Being, "the fate-laden character of thinking as self-unveiling history of being it-self."[56] What to do when this human history, the history of the world, gets out of hand? Is it really impossible to resist and oppose the march of Being? The question is obviously not academic. "Most of all, [we – as the theologian] must resist the idea of fate itself."[57] And as he criticized the Gnostic fate (*heimarmenè*), Jonas criticizes the fate of Being, since in both cases, the absence of freedom of action makes history vain and the only stake would be to adapt one's own inner attitude to that of the universal rule. "The universal necessity which rules all things and make them conform to the interest of the whole is called *heimarmenè*."[58]

Paradoxically then, after *letter in Humanism* (1946), this thought of Heidegger is entirely understood in this world, the *saeculum*, below the transcendence to which it claims, because it reduces the difference between the initial thought and the human thought (depending on the revelation), that is to say of the distance that is the fact of our humanity: "since Heidegger, too, speaks of revelation, or what sounds suspiciously like it, viz, the self-unveiling of being (*Entbergung*), these two – "revelation-dependent and 'primal' thinking – seem to be compatible, even identical."[59] In this way, human history in the world is reduced to nothing, that is to say, the meaning that humans give to it through their freedom to think and act.

By denying the polarity of subjectivation and objectivation in history, Heidegger would thus have simply rendered human thought and action, that is, human life in the world, unthinkable and futile. Indeed, the dual subject–object relationship is not based on a philosophical error or on a cultural decline, but on the heavy prerogative that humanity receives as a duty. "Not Plato is responsible for it but human condition, its limit and nobility under the order of *creation*."[60] The term of creation being used to designate the separation and therefore required mediation that is at the heart of the human condition: "the basic human condition, that of being at a distance to things that we must bridge by the reaching-out of our mind, the so called subject-object split."[61] And this bridge must unceasingly be crossed, again and again, in each epoch, collectively and individually.

The Historical Transcendental to the Proof of the Anhistorical Transcendental

Human history is thus the fact of collective and individual choices, giving place to *autogenous* historical moments (i.e. not justifiable or explicable by the past) by which the image of the man reveals its possibilities, from the most moderate to the most extreme. Each epoch poses its own choices at a transcendental level that becomes transcendental for it and the historical *Dasein* that follow one another thus form the history of humanity through successive circumstantial decisions. Jonas will insist on this transcendental character of the history of collective human freedom by seeing in it the image of God.[62] If a constellation of objective and subjective meanings is progressively put in place to produce a new epoch by crossing a threshold.

If Gnosticism allows for a better understanding of the human being, it is because it constitutes one of the most radical reactions of man in front of the situation that is made for him, "one of the more radical answers of man to his predicament."[63] In the same way, Jonas will keep this idea of a freedom of resistance or reaction to a presupposed spirit. Thus, Jonas notes that a subversion by the "gnostic world of ideas"[64] has taken place in the face of the "classical mind"[65] that gave it its form. The vocabulary by which he designates the ethos as *Zeitgeist* can vary, it will be sometimes a civilization, a spirit, or a mind, but in all cases, it is a presupposition within which the free will is determined. Let's take another example. Foreseeing what we named since then "the anthropocene," he speaks about an "era of 'enormous consequences' of human action,"[66] or of the *Technological Age* in the subtitle of his *Imperative Responsibility*.[67]

Fruit of the opacity of the Will, the history of the ontological freedom does not coincide with the aggregation of the individual liberties and the free will, which is the reason why it is so difficult to bring about historical change deliberately. Indeed, individual freedoms and criticisms remain marked by the historical a priori on whose background they stand out. Thus, the "contemporary mind"[68] is that of abstraction and hyperspecialization, while the "Modern Temper"[69] is inhospitable to the question of immortality.

Thus in *Dem Böse Ende näher*, Jonas explains that discussions of Peter Singer's theses are trapped in Germany because "the past casts frightening shadows on this subject" of euthanasia.[70] Similarly, this is how Jonas describes our contemporary time: "Living now constantly in the shadow of unwanted, built-in, automatic utopianism."[71] And he also designates our time as that of "dark times."[72] This spirit of the times thus creates a coherent set of meanings that it is difficult to resist, because each resistance implies questioning presuppositions, even prejudices, and then trying to win the support of one's interlocutors by a rational argument. This is what Jonas does when he argues against the contemporary thought against the definition of death by the cessation of cerebral activity or when he pleads in favor of a transcendence whereas our contemporary mentality has opted for an immanent monism.

Thus, Jonas knows that the will is opaque and that the mind can err in its interpretations.

Indeed, the historical transcendental is distinguished from an anhistorical transcendental which sets its condition of possibility: a body, an ambivalent freedom that is exercised in the world and the belonging to a natural community of living species within the biosphere, that is to say the shared organic base. Any historical interpretation that denies this is untenable.

In his text "Change and Permanence," Jonas in fact identifies the historical dimension of a subhistorical transcendental, which is none other than our biological condition: "It is well to start with the biological dimension which we tacitly presuppose as a matter of course; although subhistorical itself, it pervades everything historical and cannot be left out of our account."[73] This transcendental is not only what makes global historical meanings possible, but also what allows it to judge past times and acts in terms of creation. "The reality is that we are not the subjects who can create man, because we have already been created: we are creatures, certainly not creators."[74]

It is in the name of this anhistorical transcendental, that is to say our human nature and the entire biosphere, that Jonas will take most of his ethical positions. If he sees in the responses of an era, even the most radical ones, an explicitation of our historical human condition by the creation of new meanings, on the other hand, he is opposed to interpretations and technological options that would materially transform our biological condition in a unilateral way, thus confusing the two transcendental levels. What is given to us is a condition in which the freedom-spirit is ambiguous and that must be maintained with the amplitude of the risk and the richness that this entails.

Notes

1 H. Jonas, *Gnosis und spätantiker Geist, I, Die mythologische Gnosis*, with an introduction entitled "Zur Geschichte und Methodologie der Forschung," (Vandenhoeck & Ruprecht, Göttingen, 1934) (from now on: GSG I).
2 R. Kampling, "Gnosis und spätantiker Geist I: Die mythologische Gnosis (1934)," in M. Bongardt, H. Burkhart, J.-S. Gordon, J. Nielsen-Sikora (Hg.), *Hans Jonas Handbhuch. Leben- Werk-Wirkung* (J. B. Metzler, Berlin, 2021), 86. See also Elad Lapidot's chapter on GSG II in this volume, and Elad Lapidot, "Hans Jonas' Work on Gnosticism as Counterhistory", in *Philosophical Readings*, IX/1, (2017): 61–68.
3 We refer to the introduction of our French translation, "Présentation", in H. Jonas, *La Gnose et l'esprit de l'Antiquité tardive. Histoire et méthodologie de la recherche*, traduit et présenté par N. Frogneux (Mimesis, Milano, 2017), 9–152.
4 R. Bultmann, "Vorwort", in GSG I, VI. (The emphases are mine).
5 Rudolf Bultmann, Hans Jonas, *Briefwechsel 1928–1976*, A. Grossmann (hrsg) (Mohr Siebeck, 2020), 112 (our translation.)
6 J. M. Robinson, "Einleitung", in *Augustin und das paulinische Freiheitsproblem. Eine philosophische Studie zum pelagianischen Streit* (Göttingen, Vandenhoeck & Ruprecht, 1965 [1930]), 14. (Henceforth APFP) This text was translated into English J. M. Robinson, "The Pre-History of Demythologization," *Interpretation*, 20 (1966), 65–77.
7 H. Jonas, "From Gnosticism to the Dangers of Technology," I, in I. P. Culianu, *Gnosticismo e pensiero moderno: Hans Jonas* ("L'Erma" di Bretschneider, Roma, 1985), 144 (from now GDT).
8 Jonas, *Gnosis und spätantiker Geist, II, Von der mythologie zur mystischen Philosophie* (Vandenhoeck & Ruprecht, Göttingen, 1954), 225. Unfortunately, Jonas, who died a few months earlier, did not know of this volume. See "A Retrospectiv View," éd. G. Widengren, *Proceedings of the International Colloqium on Gnosticism, Stockholm, août 20-25, 1973* (E. J. Brill, Leyden, 1977).
9 K. Rudolph, "Hans Jonas and Research on Gnosticism from a Contemporary Perspective," in H. Tirosh-Samuelson and Chr. Wiese, *The Legacy of Hans Jonas. Judaism and the Phenomenon of Life* (Brill, Leiden, 2008), 96. See also Blumenberg's interest in his work: Hans Blumenberg, Hans Jonas, Correspondence 1954–1978 and Further *Material / Briefwechsel 1954–1978 und weitere Materialien*, H. Bajohr (hrsg), (Suhrkamp, Frankfurt am Main, 2022).
10 Jonas, GDT, 144. Rudolf Bultmann subsequently relied on Jonas' work in his own research, for example in *Das Urchristentum* (1949), 137–138.
11 Jonas, GSG I, 14.
12 A. Grossmann, "'Und die Gnosis ruft mich immer noch…' Hans Jonas's Denkwege im Lichte seines Briefwechsels mit Rudolf Bultmann," *Journal Phänomenologie*, 20 (2003), 23; Rudolf Bultmann, Hans Jonas, *Briefwechsel 1928–1976*, A. Grossmann (hg), (Mohr Siebeck, 2020).

13 See H. Jonas, "'The 'Hymn of the Pearl': Case Study of a Symbol, and the Claims for a Jewish Origin of Gnosticism," in *Philosophical Essays from Ancient Creed to Technological Man* (University of Chicago Press, Chicago, IL, Midway reprints, 1980), 277–290.
14 H. Jonas, *Memoirs*, trad. K. Winston, ed. Christian Wiese (Brandeis University Press, Walham, MA, 2008).
15 On this topic, see Agata Bielik-Robson's contribution in this volume.
16 See K. King, *What Is Gnosticism?* (Harvard University Press, Cambridge, MA/London, 2003). In particular Chapter 5, "Gnosticism Reconsidered" which she dedicates almost exclusively to the critique of Jonas; Antti Marjanen, *Was There a Gnostic Religion ?* (Finnish Exegetical Society, Helsinki, / Vendenhoeck & Ruprecht, Göttingen, 2005). See Roelof van den Broek, *Gnostic Religion in Antiquity* (University Press, New York, 2015).
17 Jonas, GSG I, 19. In *The Gnostic Religion*, he reiterates his refusal of partial or partially true explanations and intends to be at the height "to the total and integral phenomenon" (GR, xvi) by discovering his "unifying character" (GR, xvi). He writes: "My aim […] was a philosophic one: to understand the spirit speaking through this voices and its light to restore an intelligible unity to the baffling multiplicity of its expressions" (GR, xvii).
18 Jonas, GSG I, 13.
19 Bultmann and Jonas agree on a hermeneutic of demythologization, but they diverge as to the possibility that it is carried out to its end.
20 See W. Dilthey, *Grundlegung der Wissenschaften vom Menschen, der Gesellschaft und der Geschichte* (Vandenhoeck and Ruprecht, Göttingen, 1982); J.-Cl. Gens, *La Pensée herméneutique de Dilthey. Entre néokantisme et phénoménologie* (Presses universitaires du Septentrion, Villeneuve d'Ascq, 2002); J. Grondin, "La solution de Dilthey au problème du relativisme historique", in *Revue internationale de Philosophie* 4, 226 (2003/2004), 467–476 ; S. Camilleri, "Dilthey et l'historicisation du transcendantal," in A. Feneuil, Y. Meessen, Ch. Bouriau, *Le transcendantal. Réceptions et mutations d'une notion* kantienne (Presses universitaires de Lorraine, Nancy, 2018), 75–86.
21 Jonas, GDT, 145.
22 In 1975, in his interview with I. P. Culianu, Jonas summarizes the circularity between objectivity and subjectivity already presented in GSG: "The content of the theoretical information is dependent on a feedback from an experiential ground, while this also is exposed to a feedback from the theoretical pole. The circle modifies both sides." Jonas, GDT, 143.
23 Jonas, GSG I, 12.
24 Jonas, GSG I, 12–13. Because of the importance of these excerpts and the absence of an English translation of GSG so far, we take the liberty of quoting them extensively. An Italian translation of the two volumes has been published by Claudio Bonaldi: H. Jonas, *Gnosi e spirito tardoantico*, introduzione, traduzione, note e apparati di Claudio Bonaldi (Bompiani, Milano, 2010).
25 Jonas, GSG I, 14. The two decisive texts for his hermeneutical options are very early, since they are, on the one hand, the text of his doctoral dissertation of 1928, *Der Begriff der Gnosis*, published in 1930, and, on the other hand, *Über die hermeneutische Struktur des Dogmas, the appendix to Augustin und das paulinische Freiheitsproblem,* also published in 1930, and which will know a better fortune than the text it accompanied. Moreover, we know from the archives of Constance and the remarkable work of Claudio Bonaldi that two texts dating from the years 1927–1930 presented his methodology. See H. Jonas, *Conoscere Dio. Una sfida al pensiero*, a cura di Claudio Bonaldi (Albo versorio, Milano, 2006).
26 Jonas, GSG I, 11.
27 See W. Bousset, *Hauptprobleme der Gnosis* (Vandenhoeck & Ruprecht, Göttingen, 1907).
28 Jonas, GSG I, 59.
29 Jonas, GSG I, 59.

30 Jonas, GSG I, 60.
31 Jonas, GSG I, 60–61.
32 Jonas, GSG I, 61–62.
33 Jonas, GSG I, 64.
34 Jonas, GSG I, 10.
35 Jonas, GSG I, XX.
36 Jonas, GSG I, 84 n. 1.
37 Jonas, GSG I, 63 n. 2.
38 Jonas, GSG I, 63 n. 2. Jonas' emphasis.
39 Jonas, GSG I, 63 n. 2.
40 Jonas, GSG I, 62 n. 2. Emphasis added.
41 See N. Frogneux, "La figure d'Ouroboros ou le schème du sens selon Hans Jonas", in *Revue Philosophique de Louvain*, 117, 2 (2019): 375–398.
42 Jonas, GSG I, 62 n. 2.
43 See Jonas, "Against the Stream: Comments on the Definition and Redefinition of Death," *Philosophical Essays from Ancient Creed to Technological Man* (University of Chicago Press, Chicago, IL, Midway reprints, 1980), 132–140 (from now PhE).
44 Jonas, GSG I, 63 n. 2.
45 Jonas, GSG I, 63 n. 2.
46 Jonas, GSG I, 63 n. 2. Emphasis added.
47 To establish the genealogy of this notion of the historicization of the transcendental, it would undoubtedly be necessary to study its relation to Heidegger, but also to Dilthey and Cassirer: which goes far beyond the framework of this article. See R. dos Santos, M. Bongardt, and J. Nielsen-Sikora, "Kant/Neukantismus ", in Bongardt, M., Burkhart, H., Gordon, J.-S., Nielsen-Sikora, J. (Hg.), *Hans Jonas Handbuch. Leben- Werk-Wirkung* (J. B. Metzler, Berlin, 2021), 24–27.
48 Jonas, GR, xiv.
49 "Didactic Letters to Lore Jonas 1944–1945", trans. A. Allred, in H. Jonas, *Memoirs*, trans. K. Winston, ed. Ch. Wiese, (Brandeis University Press, Walham, MA, 2008), 220–245.
50 H. Jonas, "Introduzione alla filosofia (1949–1950)," in H. Jonas, *Sulle cause e gli usi della Filosofia*, a cura di Fabio Fossa (Edizioni ETS, Pisa, 2017), 53. We thank Fabio Fossa, the Italian editor and translator of these texts, for giving us the original English version [HJ 4-9-9], in order to avoid a retranslation into English. (Henceforth SCU).
51 Jonas, SCU, 54.
52 H. Jonas, "Heidegger and Theology," in *The Phenomenon of Life* (University of Chicago Press: Phoenix Books, Chicago, IL, 1982), 235–262 (from now PhL). This lecture was given at the opening session of the Second Consultation on Hermeneutics at Drew (Graduate School, Drew University, Madison, NJ) in April 1964. For a critique of this interpretation that misses the ontological difference. See R. Wolin, *Heidegger's Children: Hannah Arendt, Karl Löwith, Hans Jonas, and Herbert Marcuse* (Princeton University Press, Princeton, NJ, 2001), 101–104); for a direct account, see R. W. Funk, "Colloquium on Hermeneutics," *Theology Today* (31 (3), October 1964), 287–306. See also D. Herskowitz, "Hans Jonas's "Heidegger and Theology" as Text and Event", in Andreas Grossmann und Malte Dominik Krüger (hrsg.) *Hans Jonas und die Marburger Hermeneutik*, Vittorio Klostermann, Frankfurt am Main, 2023, 83–109.
53 For a critique of the harshness of his position, see E. Brito, *Heidegger et l'hymne du sacré* (Peeters, Leuven, 1999), 301–303 and K. Harries, "Heidegger's Conception of the Holy", *The Personalist*, 2 (XLVII, 1966): 169–175. Jonas' critique would be external and is violently contested by Richardson, who accuses him of "simply" missing the issue of ontological difference. See W. J. Richardson, "Heidegger and God – and Professor Jonas," *Thought: Fordham University Quarterly* (40(1), 1965): 13–40.
54 We are referring here to the title given by Jonas to his 1949 article on Origen in the *Philosophical Essays*, "Origen's Metaphysics of Free Will, Fall and Redemption: A 'Divine Comedy' of the Universe," in *Philosophical Essays: From Ancient Creed to*

Technological Man (The University of Chicago Press, Chicago, IL, Midway reprints, 1980), 305–323.
55 On this philosophy of the Gnostic call, see Jonas, GR, "The Call from Without," 75. When he distanced himself from Heidegger, Jonas seemed to "reply" to him more than he managed to completely free himself from his influence, to use Jacques Taminiaux's expression. He thus suffers the shadow of a thought in spite of himself. See on this subject: J. Taminiaux, "Les enjeux de la lecture gnostique de Sein und Zeit," *Etudes phénoménologiques*, XVII, 33–34 (2001): 91–109 ; J. Taminiaux, *Sillages phénoménologiques : Auditeurs et lecteurs de Heidegger*, Editions Ousia, Bruxelles, 2002; F. Fossa, "Existentialism, Nihilism—and Gnosticism? Reassessing the Role of the Gnostic Religion in Hans Jonas' Thought," *Philosophy and Social Criticism*, 46, 1, (2019): 64–90.
56 Jonas, PhL, 244.
57 Jonas, PhL, 244.
58 H. Jonas, *Problemi di libertà*, a cura di E. Spinelli, trad. di A. Michelis (Aragno, Torino, 2010), 302.
59 Jonas, PhL, 241–242.
60 Jonas, PhL, 258 emphasis added.
61 Jonas, PhL, 257.
62 H. Jonas, "The Concept of God After Auschwitz: A Jewish Voice," trans. by L. Vogel, in *Mortality and Morality*, edited by L. Vogel (Northwestern University Press, Evanston, IL, 1996), 131–143.
63 Jonas, GR, xvii.
64 Jonas, GR, 239.
65 Jonas, GR, 239.
66 Jonas, PhE, 177–178.
67 H. Jonas, "Immortality and the Modern Temper," in *The Phenomenon of Life: Toward a Philosophical Biology* (Harper & Row, New York, 1966), 262–281.
68 Jonas, PhL, 263.
69 Jonas, PhL, 262.
70 See H. Jonas, *Dem bösen Ende näher. Gespräche über das Verhältnis des Menschen zur Natur* (Frankfurt am Main, Suhrkamp, 1993), 63–64.
71 Jonas, IR, 21. H. Jonas, *The Imperative of Responsibility. In Search of an Ethics for the Technological Age*, trans. H. Jonas with the collaboration of D. Herr (University of Chicago Press, Chicago, IL, 1984), 21.
72 Jonas, IR, 151.
73 Jonas, PhE, 251. Emphasis added.
74 Jonas, "Anima e corpo. Conversazione di Vittorio Hösle con Hans Jonas," in P. Becchi, *Hans Jonas. Un profilo*, (Morcelliana, Brescia, 2010), 126 (our translation).

Bibliography

Michael Bongardt, Holger Burkhart, J.-S. Gordon, Jürgen Nielsen-Sikora, (Hg.), *Hans Jonas Handbuch. Leben- Werk-Wirkung.* J. B. Metzler, Berlin, 2021.

Emilio Brito, *Heidegger et l'hymne du sacré*, Peeters, Leuven, 1999.

Rudolf Bultmann, Hans Jonas, *Briefwechsel 1928–1976,* Andreas Grossmann (hrsg.), Mohr Siebeck, 2020.

Sylvain Camilleri, "Dilthey et l'historicisation du transcendantal," Anthony Feneuil, Yves Meessen, Christoph Bouriau, *Le transcendantal. Réceptions et mutations d'une notion kantienne*, Presses universitaires de Lorraine, Nancy, 2018, 75–86.

Wilhelm Dilthey, *Grundlegung der Wissenschaften vom Menschen, der Gesellschaft und der Geschichte*, Vandenhoeck and Ruprecht, Göttingen, 1982.

Fabio Fossa, "Existentialism, Nihilism – and Gnosticism? Reassessing the Role of the Gnostic Religion in Hans Jonas' Thought," *Philosophy and Social Criticism*, 46(1), 2019, 64–90.

Nathalie Frogneux, "La figure d'Ouroboros ou le schème du sens selon Hans Jonas," *Revue Philosophique de Louvain*, 117(2), 2019, 375–398.

Robert W. Funk, "Colloquium on Hermeneutics," *Theology Today*, 21(3), October 1964, 287–306.

Jean-Claude Gens, *La Pensée herméneutique de Dilthey. Entre néokantisme et phénoménologie*, Presses universitaires du Septentrion, Villeneuve d'Ascq, 2002.

Jean Grondin, "La Solution de Dilthey au Problème du Relativisme Historique," *Revue internationale de Philosophie*, 226, 2003/2004, 467–476.

Andreas Grossmann, "'Und die Gnosis ruft mich immer noch...' Hans Jonas's Denkwege im Lichte seines Briefwechsels mit Rudolf Bultmann," *Journal Phänomenologie*, 20, 2003, 18–32.

Karsten Harries, "Heidegger's Conception of the Holy," *The Personalist*, 2 (XLVII), 1966, 169–175.

Daniel M. Herskowitz, "Hans Jonas's "Heidegger and Theology" as Text and Event", in Andreas Grossmann und Malte Dominik Krüger (hrsg.) *Hans Jonas und die Marburger Hermeneutik,* Vittorio Klostermann, Frankfurt am Main, 2023, 83–109.

Hans Jonas, *Augustin und das paulinische Freiheitsproblem. Eine philosophische Studie zum pelagianischen Streit*, Vandenhoeck & Ruprecht, Göttingen, 1965 [1930].

Hans Jonas, *Gnosis und spätantiker Geist, I, Die mythologische Gnosis*, with an introduction entitled "Zur Geschichte und Methodologie der Forschung," Vandenhoeck & Ruprecht, Göttingen, 1934.

Hans Jonas, *Gnosis und spätantiker Geist*, II, *Von der mythologie zur mystischen* Philosophie, Vandenhoeck & Ruprecht, Göttingen, 1954.

Hans Jonas, "A Retrospective View," ed. Geo Widengren, *Proceedings of the International Colloqium on Gnosticism, Stockholm, August 20–25, 1973*, E. J. Brill, Leiden, 1977.

Hans Jonas, *Philosophical Essays from Ancient Creed to Technological Man*, University of Chicago Press, Chicago, IL, Midway reprints, 1980.

Hans Jonas, "Heidegger and Theology," *The Phenomenon of Life*, University of Chicago Press; Phoenix Books, Chicago, IL, 1982, 235–262.

Hans Jonas, *The Imperative of Responsibility. In Search of an Ethics for the Technological Age*, University of Chicago Press, Chicago, IL, 1984.

Hans Jonas, "From Gnosticism to the Dangers of Technology," I. P. Culianu, *Gnosticismo e pensiero moderno: Hans Jonas*, "L'Erma" di Bretschneider, Roma, 1985, 133–153.

Hans Jonas, *Dem bösen Ende näher. Gespräche über das Verhältnis des Menschen zur Natur*, Suhrkamp, Frankfurt am Main, 1993.

Hans Jonas, *Mortality and Morality*, edited by Lawrence Vogel, Northwestern University Press, Evanston, IL, 1996.

Hans Jonas, *Conoscere Dio. Una sfida al pensiero*, a cura di Claudio Bonaldi, Albo versorio, Milano, 2006.

Hans Jonas, *Memoirs,* trans. K. Winston, ed. Christian Wiese, Brandeis University Press, Walham, MA, 2008.

Hans Jonas, "Anima e corpo. Conversazione di Vittorio Hösle con Hans Jonas," in Paolo Becchi, *Hans Jonas. Un profilo,* Morcelliana, Brescia, 2010.

Hans Jonas, *Gnosi e spirito tardoantico*, introduzione, traduzione, note e apparati di Claudio Bonaldi, Bompiani, Milano, 2010.

Hans Jonas, *Problemi di libertà,* a cura di E. Spinelli, trad. di A. Michelis, Aragno, Torino, 2010. Hans Jonas, *La Gnose et l'esprit de l'Antiquité tardive. Histoire et méthodologie de la recherche,* traduit et présenté par Nathalie Frogneux, Mimesis, Milano, 2017.

Rainer Kampling, "Gnosis und spätantiker Geist I: Die mythologische Gnosis (1934)," Michael Bongardt, Holger Burkhart, John-Stewart Gordon, J. Nielsen-Sikora (Hg.), *Hans Jonas Handbhuch. Leben- Werk-Wirkung,* J. B. Metzler, Berlin, 2021, 83–87.

Karen King, *What Is Gnosticism?* Harvard University Press, Cambridge, MA/London, 2003.

Antii Marjanen, *Was There a Gnostic Religion?* Finnish Exegetical Society, Helsinki; Vendenhoeck & Ruprecht, Göttingen, 2005.

William J. Richardson, "Heidegger and God – and Professor Jonas," *Thought. Fordham University Quarterly,* 40(1), 1965, 13–40.

Kurt Rudolph, "Hans Jonas and Research on Gnosticism from a Contemporary Perspective," Hava Tirosh-Samuelson and Christian Wiese (eds.), *The Legacy of Hans Jonas. Judaism and the Phenomenon of Life,* Leiden, Brill, 2008, 91–106.

Jacques Taminiaux, "Les enjeux de la lecture gnostique de Sein und Zeit," *Etudes phénoménologiques,* XVII, 33–34, 2001, 91–109.

Jacques Taminiaux, *Sillages phénoménologiques: Auditeurs et lecteurs de Heidegger,* Editions Ousia, Bruxelles, 2002.

Roelf van den Broek, *Gnostic Religion in Antiquity,* New York University Press, New York, 2015.

Richard Wolin, *Heidegger's Children: Hannah Arendt, Karl Löwith, Hans Jonas, and Herbert Marcuse,* Princeton University Press, Princeton, NJ, 2001.

8 The Gnostic Myth as a Gambit in German Intellectual Tradition

Amir Engel

Hans Jonas' first major project, his 1920s analysis of the spiritual underpinning of Gnosticism,[1] occupies an unusual position in the annals of Modern thought. It is both phenomenally influential and relatively unknown. As Jonathan Cahana-Blum shows, it shaped Modern scholarship on Gnosticism but received relatively limited scholarly attention.[2] Existing scholarship mostly mentions this work in passing, presenting it as an opening gambit in a life-long struggle, that is, as part of a debate with Martin Heidegger's Existentialism, as the beginning of a career in philosophy, or in the context of the Modern study of Gnosticism.[3] The purpose of the present essay is, conversely, to concentrate on Jonas' early work originally titled, *Gnosis und spätantiker Geist, Teil 1: Die mythologische Gnosis* (Gnosticism and the Spirit of Late Antiquity, part 1: mythological Gnosticism) by emphasizing its engagement with a persistent cultural and philosophical debate that came before it, namely the debate about the myth, central to German nineteenth-century thought.

The rediscovery of the myth by German thinkers in the late eighteenth century became a defining feature of German philosophical, literary, academic, and cultural debates during the nineteenth century. Thomas Mann even sought to define Germanness along these lines, stating that "between the social instinct of the French and the mythical primitive poetic spirit of the German ... the intricate old question of 'what is German' perhaps finds its answer."[4] For Thomas Mann, in other words, nothing was more German that the fascination with the myth.

The notion of myth serves in this essay as a cipher for gaining a historical perspective onto several key ideas in the history of Modern German philosophy from nineteenth-century Romanticism to twentieth century Existentialism. Not less importantly, this historical perspective allows for a new appreciation of Jonas' early work, which, as noted, was rarely understood on the background of earlier philosophical developments.

The discussion of myth in the nineteenth century is complex and multifaceted. For the sake of simplicity, this discourse will be subsumed here under the title of "romantic myth." The romantic myth is made up by works of figures as different from each other as Georg Friedrich Creuzer is from Johann Wolfgang Goethe and Friedrich Hölderlin from Friedrich Nietzsche. Nevertheless, a recurring theme for these nineteenth-century German thinkers – like those mentioned above – is the hope that the myth can somehow help reimagine the relationship between

DOI: 10.4324/9781003439882-8

the material world, human consciousness, freedom, and morality. This hope was deemed necessary in an age that underwent rapid *Entzauberung* (demystification), brought about by urbanization, industrialization, and the rationalization of human relations. As George Williamson noted, the term myth "became a means of expressing just what has been lost in the transition to modernity, as well as a means for imagining the eventual reintegration of aesthetics, religious, and public life in some future society."[5] The romantic myth, in short, was a figure for imagining a new kind of grounding in the world, and possibly even a long-lost harmony with nature and God.

Jonas' reconstruction of the Gnostic sources in the shape of the myth takes a completely different approach to the problems of disenchantment and belonging. Written after World War One, the Gnostic myth projects an unflinching view of the horrors of being spiritually abandoned, in exile in the world. As Michael Waldstein writes: "gnostic *Entweltlichung* is a radical and revolutionary attitude of anticosmism; it is an attitude which negates, ultimately, all definite and ordered being and all definite moral norms."[6] The Gnostic myth of *Entweltlichung* can be thus construed as a harsh reply to the romantic solution for the disenchantment of the world (*Entzauberung*), namely, the romantic myth. And yet, even as the Gnostic myth forgoes harmony, it still offers some horizon of spiritual salvation. Here, hope is the result of awakening by the myth to truth about the real nature of the universe. Understanding the desolate reality of being is thus also the first step in recovering spirituality. The myth, in other words, is a call for spiritual awakening. As we shall see, the kind of salvation offered by the Gnostic myth is essentially similar to the one offered by Heidegger's Existentialism. As such, it is a fleeting and hard-earned salvation but one that may nevertheless appear meaningful, especially in a world where the promises of Romanticism proved unattainable.

The comparative reading of the romantic and the Gnostic myth aims to represent, as noted, a central development within German philosophical history from the early nineteen century philosophy to the beginning of the twentieth. At the same time, however, it offers also several insights about Modern German philosophical tradition, most importantly, its continuous search for the meaning of existence in an immanent world and its immediate proximity to esoteric thinking. Regardless of the radical philosophical transformations, which the two myths under discussion here exhibit, they also prove that the philosophical problem, which they both face, remains similar.

The problem for both romantic and existential philosophers was to explain how things can come to mean anything at all without the assurance that God secures their meaning. This problem seems especially urgent for abstract concepts like the concept of truth and justice. Can these concepts mean anything without God guaranteeing what they mean? Or, can they simply mean anything at all? For the thinkers under consideration here, the solution to this problem was to be found in the myth. The ancient Greek and Roman mythology played a central role in the romantic philosophical investigation. For them, myth proved that meaning can produce itself from immanent sources. Hans Jonas, on the other hand, set forth the Gnostic myth. This myth also proved that meaning can come from within, even if in a radically different way.

No less importantly, juxtaposing the romantic and Gnostic myths exhibits the immediate proximity between religious thought and the philosophical discourse of the nineteenth and early twentieth century. More exact, the discussion below underlies the esoteric trends that underlie the Modern German philosophical tradition. Wouter Hanegraaff calls western esotericism:

> a field of research that (1) has been set apart by mainstream religious and intellectual culture as the 'other' by which it defines its own identity, and (2) is characterized by a strong emphasis on specific worldviews and epistemologies that are at odds with normative post-Enlightenment intellectual culture.[7]

As we shall see, both romantic and existentialist thinkers were searching for spirituality from within an imminent worldview. As such, they effectively take a critical stance against established and organized religion. Elad Lapidot makes a similar point when suggesting, "from a Christian anathema, Jonas turned Gnosticism into an element of universal intellectual history, which is called in German 'history of spirit' (Geistesgeschichte)."[8] The romantics made their stance by identifying with pagan traditions of the myth. And the existentialist thinker Hans Jonas did so by examining the Christian heretic position par excellence, the Gnostic myth.[9]

The discussion of the nineteenth-century romantic myth and the early twentieth Gnostic myth cannot be complete without noting that after World War Two, Jonas turned away from the spiritual salvation offered by Existentialism. As we shall see in conclusion, in the early 50s, Jonas criticized Existentialism and sought recourse to a notion reminiscent of the romantic yearning for nature. Jonas' later appreciation of Gnosticism serves here to validate the present interpretation of his early work. No less significantly, it points at the continuous importance of romantic imagination as it points in the direction that his philosophy will take in the later part of his career.

The Reintroduction of the Myth in the Secular Age

The distinction between mythology (myth) and revelation (logos) is a constitutive element of the Western Christian tradition. This is not to suggest that Jewish, Christian, or Islamic texts cannot be read as myth or that one cannot find mythic elements or themes within monotheist tradition. Nevertheless, for much of Christian history, especially its earlier part, the word of the revelation was considered superior to the petty drawings of pagan mythology. As Mircea Eliade notes, "The earliest Christian theologians took the word [myth] in the sense [of] 'fable,' 'fiction,' 'lie'."[10] It would indeed seem likely to suggest that the moral law, which was given to man directly by a unified, infinite, and invincible God is endlessly more powerful than the tales of hybrid monsters and odd transformations that fill Greek and Roman mythology. Also, the idea that gods walked among the people, that they were both powerful and weak, easy to seduce but hard to satisfy, that they were both benevolent and cruel, erratic and unpredictable, rendered them inferior to the mighty presence of the one and only God.

Scholars often understand the romantic turn to myth as a spiritual endeavor. In his book, *The Longing for Myth in Germany*, Williamson argues that German Romantic philosophers reacted to an increasingly de-spiritualized Protestant Christianity by turning to myth. In other words, romantic philosophers understood myth as an alternative to monotheist thought most emphatically. For example, the Schlegel brothers, Schelling, and others sought to create in symbolic literature, that is, in the myth, a replacement for what had been lost in the Protestant theology, now under the sway of scientific rigor. Scientific skepticism downplayed or marginalized central aspects of the traditional Christian world view like the belief in miracles and the notion of the "mystery of faith." In response, romantic thinkers reimagined the myth as a gateway to the awesome aspects of human existence. They tried, in other words, to create an alternative to what they perceived as the dwindling spirit of Protestantism by positing another option: a pathway to the fantastic, that is, something similar to that which the enlightened Protestant church downplayed.[11]

Talal Asad also identifies the growing interest in the myth in the late eighteenth and early nineteenth centuries as part of a larger process, the rise of what he calls "secularism."[12] Like Williamson, Asad understands the (re)invention of the myth in the eighteenth century as a solution to the dwindling spirituality of Modern organized religions. It was adopted first by the intellectual elite and then by members of the bourgeoisie, who increasingly understood the traditional sources of spirituality, most importantly the Bible, as subjects to rigorous scientific study. The search for a new mode of spiritual power, one that would replace the Bible and be above the reach of rational criticism, led many to the myth. As Asad writes,

> In general, the literary assault on mythic figures and events demonstrated a preference for a sensible life of happiness as opposed to the heroic ideal that was coming to be regarded as less and less reasonable in a bourgeois society.[13]

Serving as a counter-model, the non-monotheistic myth became a cornerstone for the construction of secularism.

The Beautiful, the Symbolic, and the Romantic Myth

It is in the wake of secularism that the separation between subject and object or the spiritual and the material became pressing. Indeed, the fact that human consciousness knows of things it cannot perceive with the senses is, philosophically speaking, infuriating. In so far as it can create knowledge without experience, consciousness has possession of the Absolute. For example, even though things like "God," "circle," or "the number three" cannot be sensed empirically, they have shaped human history, politics. As Frederick Beiser powerfully suggested, this problem is also central to Modern German thought:

> The post-Kantian idealists understood the absolute in transcendental terms as the fundamental condition of the possibility of experience; as such, they

refused to define it as either subjective or objective; rather, they argued that both subjectivity and objectivity fall within the experience.[14]

This then is the holy grail of German idealism: a position beyond the objective/subjective reality dichotomy or between the material/spiritual.

It is in this context that the myth came into its own as a solution of sorts. This solution often appears in concert with a string of other ideas that include, most prominently, the "beautiful" and the "symbol." These terms will be discussed in some detail presently. It should, however, be clear that that the historical record does not offer a definitive description of each term nor a succinct discussion of their interrelations. Different thinkers described these terms differently at different times and in different contexts. Still, some scholarly consensus exists and it offers general (somewhat inaccurate) principles, from which the discussion here is drawn. Generally, it may be suggested that the "beautiful" offered a way beyond dualism for its existence in both subjective and objective experiences, or as it appears simultaneously in both the spiritual and material realms. After all, the beautiful is a (material) thing that triggers a (spiritual) experience. The symbol is a special kind of signification that captures this subject–object dynamic within itself. It does not represent an idea or a thing but fully embodies what it means to be. And mythology was understood as symbolic literature, that is, a literary genus replete with symbols. As such, therefore, it seems to occupy a position beyond the subject–object divide.

The idea that the subject–object divide merges in the beautiful can already be seen in Kantian philosophy,[15] but was further developed by a group of thinkers, often referred to as the German romantics.[16] The beautiful was unique because it had both a spatial and non-spatial aspect. It appeared in the world as a painting or as a view of rolling hills. But the specific appearance of something beautiful is also strangely uplifting, even spiritual. The beautiful is more than a sight. It is an experience and as such, offers an opportunity for knowing in an entirely different form.

The ideas appear already in Friedrich Schiller's famous 1794 *Letters on the Aesthetic Education of Man*.[17] In letter fifteen, after discussing the dual nature of human experience, he reaches the point:

> To the extent that [beauty] deprives feelings and passions of their dynamic power, it will *bring them into harmony* with the ideas of reason; and to the extent that it deprives the laws of reason of their moral compulsion, it will reconcile them with the interests of the senses.[18]

For Schiller, feelings and passions represent the material aspect of the human mind and therefore stand alongside sense perceptions, that is, things real and material, also known as objects. Opposing the former, Schiller posits ideas of reason which go on to establish the laws of reason. The beautiful, however, subsumes both reason and the senses, that is, the spiritual and the material. And it is beauty that thus also frees humans from both the constraints of reason and the necessity of the natural world. It is beauty, Schiller suggests, that sets humans free.

128 *Amir Engel*

The liberating capacity of beauty is encompassed in "the symbol." The "symbol" becomes constitutive for the reinvention of the myth in Modern German philosophy and for Jonas' Gnostic myth. The symbol was the beautiful par excellence because it merged the two aspects of existence. One of the most influential definitions of the symbol was offered by Goethe, who famously distinguished it from allegory:

> There is a great difference, whether the poet seeks the particular for the sake of the general or sees the general in the particular. From the former procedure there ensues allegory, in which the particular serves only as illustration, as example of the general. The latter procedure, however, is genuinely the nature of poetry; it expresses something particular, without thinking of the general or pointing to it.[19]

The allegory and the symbol represent different things in different ways. Allegory holds fast to an underlying notion of adequacy. The word "tree," for example, is taken as an adequate word to represent a specific material "tree" just as scales adequately represent justice. This system of representation is kept simple (possibly naïve) by virtue of the fact that the signifier always points to something beyond itself.

The romantic symbol does not point to something beyond itself. It is a gateway to the abstract or spiritual realm. Concrete in appearance, a (beautiful) thing – a Greek statue or a poetic verse – offers a window into a new dimension of being. Schelling offers the following example for the symbol: "Mary Magdalene does not only signify repentance but is living repentance itself."[20] Here is a material reality, Schelling suggests, that is also purely spiritual. It is an idea. The symbol thus represents something beyond the dichotomy between subject and object. In his study of the romantic symbol, Nicholas Halmi writes, "the symbol was supposed to be the point of contact between the contingent and the absolute, the finite and the infinite, the sensuous and the supersensuous, the temporal and the eternal, the individual and the universal."[21]

Myth is often understood as symbolic literature. In other words, it is a literary form imbued with symbols. The reasons for this association are complex but can broadly be associated with the view that sees the myth as a result of a primordial meeting between humans and nature.[22] In this view, the primordial encounter forced humans to create primitive forms of representation (symbols) that were later formed into stories (myths). In any case, the notion that myth – in a way similar to the beauty and to the symbol – presented a position beyond the subject–object divide is commonly found in Modern German thought and literature. It comes to light brilliantly in one of the earliest and most concise formulations of the idea of "myth' known as the "Oldest Systematic Program of German Idealism." This obscure fragment composed around 1793, has variously been attributed to Hegel, Schelling, and Hölderlin.[23] One relevant passage from the fragment reads:

> I am convinced that the highest act of reason, which, in that it comprises all ideas, is an aesthetic act, and that *truth and goodness* are united like sisters

only in beauty – The philosopher must possess just as much aesthetic power as the poet.... Poetry thereby obtains a higher dignity; it becomes again in the end what it was in the beginning – *teacher* of *(history) the human race*.... Monotheism of reason and the heart, polytheism of the imagination and art, that is what we need! First I will speak about an idea here, which as far as I know, has never occurred to anyone's mind – we must have a new mythology; this mythology must, however, stand in the service of ideas, it must become a mythology of *reason*. Until we make ideas aesthetic, i.e., mythological, they hold no interest for the people.[24]

The piece is famously dense, metaphorical, and complex. It is nevertheless clear that the writers posit mythology as a model for a way of thinking that transcends the dichotomy of being. It exists somehow beyond religion, philosophy, and reason.[25] As such, it could also be read as esoteric.

The Gnostic Myth

Jonas signals both his commitment to and his departure from the Modern conception of myth in a myriad of forms. He does so by holding fast to many of the core ideas of Modern German thought, most importantly to the idea of the myth and its "symbols." As we shall see, he is also making use of these terms to discuss the central problem at hand, namely the subject–object or the spiritual–material divide. Indeed, the Gnostic myth, like the Greek myth, is devoted to solving this problem. A closer look shows, however, that Jonas uses the same themes and questions to prompt a radically new way of thinking.

The subversion of the philosophical dogma comes to light already in the titles Jonas chooses for the chapters and subjects. The title "Form of Myth," for example, or "The Logic of Gnosticism" undermines a very basic impulse in Modern German discourse. The "form" represents, already in Schiller's aesthetic writings, one of the sides of the spiritual–material divide. It denotes the spiritual ability to create order, to "form" the material world. The attempt to recreate the forms of the myth suggests familiarity with the language of Modern German thought. More importantly, it clearly takes a stance against it. If the myth has "forms," then it can no longer fulfill its imagined destiny, namely, the dissolution of form and matter.

The very opening of the first chapter of the first part of Jonas' work on Gnosticism represents his new approach to the study of the myth. In this work, the myth is built, so to speak, from the ground up.[26] The analysis focuses not on the essence of the myth or its appearance, but rather on its discourse or *Rede* (speech) to extrapolate recurring themes and reconstruct its central "symbols." As Jonas writes, "the vocabulary and imagery characteristic of the gnostic literature ...in as much as it provides its central unity of meaning, already portrays a system and the transcendental character of the gnostic myth."[27] Like the combination "mythic forms," Jonas' insistence on the "transcendental" character of the myth, or its "unity of meaning," and its underlying "system" indicate his aim to subvert the subject–object dichotomy.

A similar dynamic can be seen throughout Jonas' discussion of the Gnostic symbols that form the content of the early sections of the first volume. The chapter *Logos der Gnosis* (Logic of the Gnosticism) devotes its discussion to the analysis of eighteen different symbols that are central to the Gnostic mythological discourse. Taken in their entirety, the list of symbols offers a glimpse of the overall trajectory of the myth. The symbols that Jonas discusses can be grouped into thematic pairs that maintain a dialectic tension. Thus, for example, Jonas discusses "This" and "That" World, "Dwelling" and Beyond "Light and Darkness," "Singularity and Multiplicity." Clearly, light cannot be understood beyond darkness, and Dwelling here immediately assumes "Beyond." Essentially, however, Jonas' myth avoids synthesis or the relinquishing (*Aufhebung*) of the dialectic origin. On the face of things, therefore, the dialectic is maintained in its duality.[28]

Taken together, the symbols form a story. According to this story, the human being has fallen from a world of light and identity into a world of darkness and confusion. This story is conveyed by symbols like "The Strange."[29] The world of confusion also unfolds through time, augmenting the distance between the human being and its origin. This is implied by symbols like "The Worlds and Aeons."[30] And yet, within "The Noise of the World,"[31] this being still maintains some connection to "That World."[32] "The Call from the Beyond"[33] can, therefore, awaken being and inform it of its true existential status. It can also force it to turn back toward the light. The call from the beyond is an opportunity to reconfigure life in light of the truth of being. This is the story Jonas tells with his symbolic reading of the Gnostic myth. The story is not necessarily a beautiful one in the way the romantic myth is beautiful. It is rather complicated and uncertain. But as such, it holds a description of a state of being in its relation to the problem of Being, of man in his relation to creation and to the Creator. This is ostensibly the Gnostic way of being, but at the same time, it is also patently Modern.

The Gnostic symbols do not merely serve as critique of Romanticism, its yearning for immanent spirituality. Certainly, they tell a story that is radically dissimilar from the idea of the myth of Modern German thought discussed above. As noted, the romantic myth was meant to show how purely spirituality (and concepts and ideas) may come to light from within the world. It was, crudely put, the responsibility of the symbol to do so. Jonas' symbols, we have seen, suspend this solution by insisting that the dialectic is not relinquished in the symbol, but rather unfolds as a story. But these symbols are telling also for the way they reconstruct the philosophical question at hand. Rather than solving the subject–object divide, Jonas' Gnostic myth asks the question anew: what does it mean to be in the world? Or, what does it mean to be there (*Dasein*)?

Jonas' analysis of Dasein can be found throughout his work but nowhere more clearly than in his discussion of the symbols. The first symbol that Jonas discusses, "the strange" (*das Fremde*), may serve as an example. "The strange," Jonas writes, "is that which comes from somewhere else, that which does not belong here. As such, it is the foreign, the strange, the uncanny for the local: not at home here – but at home outside, inside one's self."[34] There is much to unpack in this convoluted statement. It is helpful to observe, firstly, how Jonas sets up the basic symbolic tension. The symbol does not ask whether the idea of "the strange" adequately represents something in the world. Neither is this symbol capable of overcoming the duality of the idea by virtue of its beauty. "The strange" is not beautiful in any immediate sense. Instead, Jonas' Gnostic symbol offers a matrix of signification, which precludes the subject–object divide altogether. "The strange" binds together places (here and afar), humans (local and foreign), ideas (about traveling and being-at-home), feelings (of belonging and longing), and personal histories (of travel, immigration, or exile). In short, it tells a story that depicts the entanglement of both ideas and objects.

"The strange" symbolizes a state of being. It is not an aesthetic symbol as the romantics imagined it. But, similar to the romantic project, it aims to recreate existence which is at once spiritual and material. The stranger is strange because she is in a strange land, about which she knows very little. But the land is strange primarily for being that place in which the stranger found herself unwittingly stranded. Neither the land nor the person belongs to any fixed idea. They become what they are in their interaction from which it is impossible to extract either one of them. As a state of being, "the strange" is more than a physical reality or ideology. It signifies a being, who forgot where she really belongs. It might be thus said that "the stranger" is one that thinks she belongs but does not. As Jonas notes,

> the stranger, who does not know his way around gets lost in the strange, he wanders around in it; but if he knows his way around too well, he forgets his own strangeness, he gets lost in the Strange in another sense, in to which he falls ...and alienates himself from his own origin.[35]

It turns out that "the stranger" is one that both makes life strange and feels lost in life.

The idea of the Gnostic symbol affirms and undermines the very assumptions of the Romantic symbol. To be sure, the symbol here is no longer an appearance, and it does not partake in the aesthetic discourse. It is also not a pure embodiment of an idea. It is rather a state of being, which, like the romantic symbol, exists beyond spiritual–material distinction. "The strange" is both ideological and factual. As such, it is also both the condition and the outcome of what it is: the state of being strange. In short, it is an existential symbol, clearly reliant on the romantic symbol but also reimagines it.

The Logic of Myth

The discussion of Jonas' Gnosticism, thus far, underscored the differences between his philosophy, the philosophy of being or Existentialism, and the philosophical current in Germany before the turn of the twentieth century, known as German idealism and German Romanticism. As we have seen, Jonas uses the vocabulary of myth and symbol, so central in the German philosophical tradition before him, but upends the meaning of these terms. These dissimilarities should not, however, avert our attention from the deep and abiding connections between Jonas and the

132 *Amir Engel*

tradition in which he worked. The myth, in both cases, addressed some of the most pressing issues in thought. More specifically, Jonas' use of the myth constitutes an attempt to supplant a spiritual worldview that failed to resolve central questions. At stake here is the very meaning of being. In the history of Modern German philosophy, the term being was often used for God. The question about the relation to being was thus a central theological concern. In both a fundamental and an obvious way, therefore, both Jonas' Gnosticism and the debate about the myth seem to belong in a theological framework. As noted above, the discussions about the myth coincide with the decline of Christianity in Europe.

Jonas' myth, like the romantic myth, attempts to address the problem of spirituality in a secular world. It aims, in other words, to describe spiritual presence without recourse to a transcendent God, to Judaism, Christianity, or any established religion. As such, Jonas' myth can be construed as an aspect of the esoteric tradition. It is a (twice) non-Orthodox view of spirituality. To a certain degree, Jonas shares this characteristic with the German Romantic myth.

It is in the form of heresy that Jonas unveils something that Heidegger's Existentialism keeps hidden.[36] Jonas offers a glimpse into the complicated ways by which Existentialism seeks to position itself between this world (being) and the next (death), between secular philosophy that avoids the metaphysical and theology. As we have seen, Jonas' Dasein is also stranded. It may sound secular but speaks the language of religious awakening. The Gnostic symbols make this point powerfully. Dasein awaits a call from the beyond, it sees itself as nothing less than fallen. Similar ideas can be intuited in Heidegger's philosophy, but Jonas makes them explicit. In his discussion of the last of eighteen symbols, under the title "The Answer to the Call," Jonas writes:

> How does the one, who received it, relate to the call and its content? [He] … is always the awakened from the deep slumber of the world. Then, however, the reaction of the one who just awoke to the revelation of his situation …and to the consequent imposition on his behavior varies greatly. It comes down to unique dialogues between the caller and the called one.[37]

Here, Jonas represents the Gnostic conception of self. However, as Jonas also notes, this representation also echoes Heidegger's conceptualization of Dasein, being called onto the question of being. It indeed follows closely upon what Judith Wolfe describes as Heidegger's theology,

> if human existence teaches us that we can never attain fulfillment but also that we seek it, that we can never find our ground but also that we crave it, then the phenomenological conclusion cannot simply be a denial of the object.[38]

Coda: Postwar Gnosis

Much changed between 1934, when Jonas published his book on Gnosticism, and 1952, when he revisited the topic in a much-discussed essay titled "Gnosticism and

Modern Nihilism."[39] In lieu of a conclusion, I offer a succinct reading of Jonas' postwar reflections on Gnosticism. This reading serves two objectives. It shows, firstly, that Jonas himself understood his early work in a way similar to the analysis above, that is, as an attempt to think existentially about the relationship between self, God, and the world. Secondly, Jonas' postwar Gnosticism shows how he changed his mind about these core issues. Before the war, Gnosticism served as a method of analysis and effectively propagated Heidegger's Existentialism. After the war, Jonas used Gnosticism to launch an attack on his onetime mentor and his philosophical system.[40] Jonas' postwar work on Gnosticism even advocates a return to nature and to the "beautiful." In other words, Jonas' later work returns to Romanticism, the very thing his younger self hoped to leave behind.

The essay "Gnosticism and Modern Nihilism" sets up a comparison between Gnosticism and Modern Existentialism. The ultimate purpose of this comparison was, as noted, to create a basis for a critique of Existentialism, more specifically, of Heidegger's philosophy. As Lapidot noted, "having used Heidegger's categories for conceptualizing late-antique Gnosticism, Jonas now turns in the opposite direction and takes the gnostic categories for interpreting Heidegger, who now becomes the embodiment of Modern Gnosticism."[41] In the context of the present discussion, however, the comparison yields foreseeable results. As was shown above, and as Jonas conceded in his 1952 essay, the two systems – Gnosticism and Existentialism – are similar. According to Jonas, the similarity is found in the historical context, in the problem these systems hoped to solve, and in the visions they offered their adherents. For Jonas, importantly, both systems were also deeply and woefully nihilistic.

Both Gnosticism and Existentialism, Jonas claimed, emerged in the context of deep political, social, and ideological crises. Gnosticism was precipitated by the disintegration of the Greco-Roman world; Existentialism came about, thanks to the decline of Christianity and the rise of Modern societies. These crises rendered the reigning metaphysical worldview obsolete. The disintegration of the Empire precipitated a deep sense of alienation, easily understood by Modern readers. As Jonas notes, "I leave it to the reader to draw whatever analogies …between this alienation …and the situation in atomized industrial societies."[42] The meaning of this insinuation is obvious. Those who hoped to find spiritual salvation in Gnosticism after the collapse of the Roman Empire are essentially similar to those who sought refuge from the anonymity of Modern urban industrial societies.

The historical sense of alienation, Jonas argues, gave rise to new and far-reaching philosophical visions. Whereas believers in late antiquity found solace in the idea of a supreme hidden God, Modern believers hoped that Nietzsche's Übermensch or Heidegger's Being-unto-Death would offer relief. Gnostic and Modern existentialist visions encouraged individuals to pursue their spiritual goals alone, given that existing norms, traditions, and institutions were now obsolete. Both systems discuss their philosophical worldviews in terms of personal beginning and end, origin and eschatology. "A famous formula of the Valentinian school," Jonas writes, "epitomizes the content of gnosis: What makes us free is the knowledge of who we were, what we have become; where we were, wherein we have been thrown, wherefrom we are redeemed; what is birth and what rebirth."[43] Jonas finds very similar rhetoric in Heidegger's Existentialism.

> All the relevant categories of existence ...fall in correlate pairs under the heads of either past or future: 'facticity,' necessity, having become, having been thrown, are existential modes of the past; being ahead of oneself, anticipation of death, care and resolve, are existential modes of the future.[44]

Both Gnosticism and Existentialism offered a similar solution to the problem of estrangement. In a fundamental way, they both fostered the individual's ability to draw from spiritual origins to remake the future, appreciate life anew, and bring about a redemption of sorts.

As we saw above, Jonas propagated these worldviews in his early work on Gnosticism, which he wrote under Heidegger's tutelage. Returning to the subject after the war, he admitted he was deeply drawn to Heidegger's Existentialism with temporal structure. "This breathless dynamism holds a tremendous appeal for the contemporary mind, and my generation in the twenties and early thirties succumbed to it."[45] It is easy to see how this invitation to examine the world in terms of origin and horizon offered an exciting alternative to a man in his twenties studying philosophy during the turbulent years of the Weimar Republic. These turbulent years, however, came to an end when the Republic crumbled.

Jonas fled Germany in 1933, mere weeks after Hitler came to power. After a short sojourn in London, Jonas immigrated to Palestine where he joined the British Army, serving first in an anti-aircraft battery then joining the newly minted Jewish Brigade. In this capacity, he was sent, in the final months of the war, to fight in Italy. In summer 1945, shortly after Germany capitulated, Jonas entered Germany, for the first time since he had left it, in the uniform of the occupying army. It was then that he learned his mother's fate: sent to Auschwitz, she met her death in the gas chambers.[46]

The horrors of the war and the Holocaust forced on Jonas a philosophical "revolution."[47] He realized that Existentialism did not resolve the fundamental problems it set out to solve. We have seen that Modern German philosophy understood the "beautiful," the "symbolic," and the "myth" as solutions to the problem of dualism, that is, the tension between the subject and the object or between the spiritual and the material. Before the war, Jonas made use of the same tropes – the symbol and the myth – to criticize this philosophical tradition. Unlike the Greek myth, the Gnostic myth produced a worldview that assumed the subject–object (or spiritual–material) divide and rendered it insignificant. Returning to the topic after the end of the war, Jonas was more skeptical.

By 1952, Jonas realized that while "Being-in-the-World" may have avoided the subject–object chasm, it opened a new one. This was the divide between the past–future structure of this being and the present tense. The loss of the present tense, furthermore, came at a considerable price.

> It is eternity not time that grants it a status of its own in the flux of time; and it is the loss of eternity which accounts for the loss of a genuine present. Such a loss of eternity is the disappearance of the world of ideas.[48]

In other words, the past–future structure of both Gnosticism and Existentialism may have filled hearts with radical hope but also relinquished much of what makes human life what it is. Life, Jonas now thought, was deeply tied to the notion of eternity. Without it, the very existence of a spiritual realm became questionable together with ideas in general, the law, and the possibility that human dealings somehow fall under general categories of good and bad. Also, nature, beauty, and love were lost. In his postwar reflections, Jonas concedes that Existentialism set the stage for radical nihilism. Experiencing World War Two firsthand, Jonas now thought that the price of losing the spiritual realm, held together by the notion of eternity and the care for the present, was too terrible to pay.

In his later work, Jonas confronted the problem of dualism once again. What is the relation, he asked, between Being-in-the-World and nature? What does it mean to be an ethical, politically minded, responsible Dasein? These questions forced Jonas to reevaluate his understanding of the Gnostic myth. Gnosticism was still useful after the war, of course, but only as a critique of the Modern mind. It would indeed become a cornerstone of his later pioneering work in the ethics of environmental ethics. However, as an attempt to propagate Existentialism, Jonas realized, it was a mistake. Nevertheless, it was still a milestone of scholarship. No less importantly, it shows how one concept – the myth – carries an entire array of philosophical considerations. And thus, it offers invaluable insights to the radical changes German intellectual tradition underwent in the volatile history of the long nineteenth century.

Notes

1 The project was developed in the mid-1920s and published in two volumes. Part one was published under the title *Gnosis und spätantiker Geist, Teil:1 Die mythologische Gnosis* in 1934. The second part *Gnosis und spätantiker Geist Teil 2: Von der Mythologie zur mystischen Philosophie* was written earlier but came out only in 1954. For more on this publication history, see Elad Lapidot's chapter in this volume on GSG II.
2 "Despite the almost cliché deprecation of Jonas's reconstruction of Gnosticism as typologically outdated and politically outmoded ... it is clear that Jonas's work – and especially, in the English-speaking world, his Gnostic Religion – is still remarkably influential." Jonathan Cahana-Blum, "Gnosis. Die Botschaft des fremden Gottes (1958)," in Bongardt et al., *Hans Jonas-Handbuch*, (Stuttgart: J.B. Metzler 2021), 96–103, here 102. I thank the author for sharing the original English version, from which this quote is taken. See also Section 14.2 about the book's reception in Rainer Kampling, "Gnosis und spätantiker Geist I: Die mythologische Gnosis (1934)," in Bongardt et al., *Hans Jonas-Handbuch*, 83–87, here 86.
3 The outstanding counter examples include Rainer Kampling, "Gnosis und spätantiker Geist I," 83–87; Elad Lapidot, "Hans Jonas's Work on Gnosticism as Counterhistory," *Philosophical Readings* ix, no. 1 (2017): 61–68. Otherwise, the most frequent comments on Jonas' early interpretation of Gnosticism relate it to Heidegger and his thought. For a recent appraisal of this relationship, see Daniel M. Herskowitz, "Reading Heidegger against the Grain: Hans Jonas on Existentialism, Gnosticism, and Modern Science," *Modern Intellectual History* 19, no. 2 (June 2022): 527–550. A few typical examples for the incorporation of Jonas' early work in larger discussions may include the role of Jonas' Gnosticism within the context of his oeuvre, of Zionism, of postwar German philosophy, and recently its influence on Jacob Taubes, see Christian Wiese, *The Life and Thought of Hans Jonas: Jewish Dimensions* (Lebanon: UPNE, 2007), 9; Kurt Rudolph, "Hans Jonas and Research on Gnosticism from a Contemporary Perspective," in *The*

Legacy of Hans Jonas: Judaism and the Phenomenon of Life, ed. Hava Tirosh-Samuelson and Christian Wiese (Leiden: Brill, 2008), 97–98; Yotam Hotam, *Modern Gnosis and Zionism: The Crisis of Culture, Life Philosophy and Jewish National Thought*, trans. Avner Greenberg (Abingdon: Routledge, 2013), 48–50; Willem Styfhals, *No Spiritual Investment in the World: Gnosticism and Postwar German Philosophy* (Ithaca, NY: Cornell University Press, 2019), 30–31; Jerry Z. Muller, *Professor of Apocalypse: The Many Lives of Jacob Taubes* (Princeton, NJ: Princeton University Press, 2022), 65–67.

4 Quoted in George S. Williamson, *The Longing for Myth in Germany: Religion and Aesthetic Culture from Romanticism to Nietzsche* (Chicago, IL: University of Chicago Press, 2004), 1.

5 Williamson, *Longing for Myth*, 3.

6 Michael Waldstein, "Hans Jonas' Construct 'Gnosticism': Analysis and Critique," *Journal of Early Christian Studies* 8, no. 3 (2000): 341–372, here 345.

7 Wouter J. Hanegraaff, *Western Esotericism: A Guide for the Perplexed* (London: Bloomsbury, 2013), 13–14.

8 Lapidot, "Hans Jonas's Work on Gnosticism as Counterhistory," 64.

9 Some scholars go so far as to suggest that the term is primarily used to distinguish the orthodox "we" from the heretic "they." See Karen L. King's *What Is Gnosticism?* in which she claims, for example, that "Gnosticism as a category served important intellectual aims, defining the boundaries of normative Christianity" and that "the language, themes, and strategies of orthodoxy and heresy proved to be a powerful discourse, persisting in various forms up to our own day" (Cambridge, MA: Harvard University Press, 2005), 7 and 54 respectively; Lapidot, "Hans Jonas's Work on Gnosticism as Counterhistory," 64.

10 Mircea Eliade, *Myth and Reality* (New York: Harper & Row, 1963), 162.

11 Williamson, *Longing for Myth*, 19–71.

12 Talal Asad, *Formations of the Secular: Christianity, Islam, Modernity* (Stanford, CA: Stanford University Press, 2003), 1.

13 Asad, *Formations of the Secular*, 29.

14 Frederick C. Beiser, *German Idealism: The Struggle against Subjectivism, 1781–1801* (Cambridge, MA: Harvard University Press, 2009), 5.

15 See for example, Klaus Düsing, "Beauty as the Transition from Nature to Freedom in Kant's Critique of Judgment," *Noûs* 24, no. 1 (1990): 79–92, https://doi.org/10.2307/2215614.

16 The scope of Romanticism is vigorously debated. Some scholars define it in accordance with its reception of the myth. George Williamson, for example, claims that German Romanticism desires "a new myth" in its center. He writes: "the Romantic nature of a 'new mythology' addressed long-standing problems in Aufklärung theology concerning biblical revelation, religious liturgy and the nature of God." Tzvetan Todorov associates Romanticism with the preoccupation with "Symbols." "Without exaggeration, we can say that if we had to condense the Romantic aesthetic into a single word, it would certainly be the word 'symbol'". And Frederik Beiser argues that Romanticism is a preoccupation with overcoming the dual nature of reality. "For the young Romantics, there was ultimately one fundamental malaise behind all forms of Modernity. They gave several names to this malaise: alienation (Entfremdung), estrangement (Entäusserung), division (Entzweiung), separation (Trennung), and reflection (Reflexion)." These three suggestions – the "myth," the "symbol," and overcoming "duality" – seem to point at deeply intertwined themes within the discourse in question. See, Williamson, *Longing for Myth*, 24; Tzvetan Todorov, *Theories of the Symbol* (Ithaca, NY: Cornell University Press, 1984), 198; Frederick C. Beiser, *The Romantic Imperative: The Concept of Early German Romanticism* (Cambridge, MA: Harvard University Press, 2003), 31.

17 For more on Schiller and his role in the development of Romantic and Idealist thought, see for example, Leonard P. Wessell, "Schiller and the Genesis of German Romanticism," *Studies in Romanticism* 10, no. 3 (1971): 176–198, https://doi.org/10.2307/25599803.
18 Friedrich Schiller, *Essays: Friedrich Schiller*, ed. Walter Hinderer, trans. Daniel O. Dahlstrom (New York: Continuum, 1993), 127. Emphasis added.
19 Johann Wolfgang von Goethe, *Maxims and Reflections* (London: Penguin, 2005), 33–34.
20 Friedrich Wilhelm Joseph Schelling, *Friedrich Wilhelm Joseph von Schellings sämmtliche Werke* (Stuttgart: J. G. Cotta, 1859), 5:555.
21 Nicholas Halmi, *The Genealogy of the Romantic Symbol* (New York: Oxford University Press, 2007), 2.
22 In his book on the history of the myth in German culture, George Williamson traces this position to the work of Christian Gottlob Heyne, who argued as early as the 1760s that "myth was not the invention of individual poets but rather a natural and necessary mode of expression during 'the childhood of the human race.'" Williamson, *Longing for Myth*, 32. Similar ideas may be also found in Giambattista Vico's *New Science* (1725). For more, see for example, Joseph Mali, *The Rehabilitation of Myth: Vico's "New Science"* (Cambridge: Cambridge University Press, 1992), 136–209.
23 For more about the authorship and the discovery of this fragment, see Christoph Jamme and Helmut Schneider, eds., *Mythologie der Vernunft: Hegels "Ältestes Systemprogramm des deutschen Idealismus"* (Frankfurt am Main: Suhrkamp, 1984), 21–78.
24 Ernst Behler, ed., "Oldest Systematic Program of German Idealism," in *Philosophy of German Idealism: Fichte, Jacobi, and Schelling*, trans. Diana I. Behler (New York: Continuum, 1987), 162.
25 The nineteenth-century philosopher most obviously associated with the myth is undoubtedly FWJ Schelling (1775–1854). A discussion of his work is beyond the purview of this essay, but his concept of myth does not stray dramatically from the positions presented above. For more, see for example, Louis Dupré, "The Role of Mythology in Schelling's Late Philosophy," *The Journal of Religion* 87, no. 1 (January 2007): 1–20, https://doi.org/10.1086/508384.
26 These terms appear in the opening chapter of Part 1, titled, Die Gnosis in ihrer mythischen Form. Jonas, *Mythologische Gnosis*, 1:92.
27 Hans Jonas, *Gnosis und spätantiker Geist: Die mythologische Gnosis* (Göttingen: Vandenhoeck & Ruprecht, 1934), 1:92.
28 In his essay in this volume on the second part of *Gnosticism and the Spirit of Late Antiquity*, Elad Lapidot briefly describes how, eventually, the Gnostic myth undoes itself, turning to philosophy.
29 Jonas, *Mythologische Gnosis*, 1:96.
30 Jonas, *Mythologische Gnosis*, 1:98.
31 Jonas, *Mythologische Gnosis*, 1:119.
32 Jonas, *Mythologische Gnosis*, 1:98.
33 Jonas, *Mythologische Gnosis*, 1:120.
34 Jonas, *Mythologische Gnosis*, 1:96.
35 Jonas, *Mythologische Gnosis*, 1:96.
36 This is not to suggest that readers have not noticed Heidegger's debt to Christian theology. On the contrary, this issue has yielded intense scholarly debate. Interesting in this context is a note made on Heidegger's reception among theologians. As John D. Caputo suggests, "When Christian theologians looked into the pages of Being and Time they found themselves staring at their own image – formalized, ontologized, or as Bultmann said 'demythologized'." John D. Caputo, "Heidegger and Theology," in *The Cambridge Companion to Heidegger*, ed. Charles Guignon, Cambridge Companions to Philosophy (Cambridge: Cambridge University Press, 1993), 274.
37 Jonas, *Gnosis und spätantiker Geist: Die mythologische Gnosis*, 1:134.

38 Judith Elisabeth Wolfe, *Heidegger and Theology* (London: Bloomsbury, 2014), 94.
39 Hans Jonas, "Gnosticism and Modern Nihilism," *Social Research* 19, no. 4 (December 1952): 430–452. Jonas appended this essay also to his English monograph on Gnosticism, see Hans Jonas, *The Gnostic Religion* (Boston, MA: Beacon Press, 1958), 320–340.
40 There is ample scholarly discussion about Jonas' critique of Heidegger. See, for example, Jonathan Cahana, "A Gnostic Critic of Modernity: Hans Jonas from Existentialism to Science," *Journal of the American Academy of Religion* 86, no. 1 (March 5, 2018): 158–180; Wiese, *Life and Thought*, esp. 95–102; Richard Wolin, *Heidegger's Children: Hannah Arendt, Karl Löwith, Hans Jonas, and Herbert Marcuse* (Princeton, NJ: Princeton University Press, 2003), 101–133.
41 Lapidot, "Gnosticism as Counterhistory," 66.
42 Jonas, "Gnosticism and Modern Nihilism," 440.
43 Jonas, "Gnosticism and Modern Nihilism," 445.
44 Jonas, "Gnosticism and Modern Nihilism," 448.
45 Jonas, "Gnosticism and Modern Nihilism," 448.
46 Jonas recounts his visit to Mönchengladbach in chilling clarity in Jonas, *Erinnerungen*, esp. 220–221.
47 In a letter to Leo Strauss from 1948, Jonas writes: "In my later soldiering years, far from books and thrown back upon the most direct contemplation …the apocalyptic nightmare slowly vented itself …and gave space to theoretical freedom; amidst the most enduring reflections of my life, there occurred an overhaul of my philosophical vision, a revolution …which determined my theoretical 'postwar program.'" Quoted in Wiese, *Life and Thought*, 29.
48 Jonas, "Gnosticism and Modern Nihilism," 450.

Bibliography

Asad, Talal. *Formations of the Secular: Christianity, Islam, Modernity*, Stanford, CA: Stanford University Press, 2003.
Behler, Ernst, ed. "Oldest Systematic Program of German Idealism Translated by Diane I. Behler." In *Philosophy of German Idealism: Fichte, Jacobi, and Schelling*, New York: Continuum, 1987, 119–140. The issue of authorship is much debated. For more, see footnote 23.
Beiser, Frederick C. *German Idealism: The Struggle against Subjectivism, 1781–1801*, Cambridge, MA: Harvard University Press, 2009.
Beiser, Frederick C. *The Romantic Imperative: The Concept of Early German Romanticism*, Cambridge, MA: Harvard University Press, 2003.
Cahana, Jonathan. "A Gnostic Critic of Modernity: Hans Jonas from Existentialism to Science," *Journal of the American Academy of Religion* 86, no. 1 (March 5, 2018): 158–180. https://doi.org/10.1093/jaarel/lfx035.
Cahana-Blum, Jonathan. "Gnosis. Die Botschaft des fremden Gottes (1958)." In *Hans Jonas-Handbuch: Leben – Werk – Wirkung*, edited by Michael Bongardt, Holger Burckhart, John-Stewart Gordon, and Jürgen Nielsen-Sikora, Stuttgart: J.B. Metzler, 2021, 96–103. https://doi.org/10.1007/978-3-476-05723-5_16.
Caputo, John D. "Heidegger and Theology." In *The Cambridge Companion to Heidegger*, edited by Charles Guignon, *Cambridge Companions to Heidegger*, Cambridge: Cambridge University Press, 1993, 270–288. https://doi.org/10.1017/CCOL0521385709.011.
Dupré, Louis. "The Role of Mythology in Schelling's Late Philosophy," *The Journal of Religion* 87, no. 1 (January 2007): 1–20. https://doi.org/10.1086/508384.
Düsing, Klaus. "Beauty as the Transition from Nature to Freedom in Kant's Critique of Judgment," *Noûs* 24, no. 1 (1990): 79–92. https://doi.org/10.2307/2215614.

Eliade, Mircea. *Myth and Reality*, New York: Harper & Row, 1963.
Goethe, Johann Wolfgang von. *Maxims and Reflections*, London: Penguin, 2005.
Halmi, Nicholas. *The Genealogy of the Romantic Symbol*, New York: Oxford University Press, 2007.
Hanegraaff, Wouter J. *Western Esotericism: A Guide for the Perplexed*, London: Bloomsbury, 2013.
Herskowitz, Daniel M. "Reading Heidegger against the Grain: Hans Jonas on Existentialism, Gnosticism, and Modern Science," *Modern Intellectual History* 19, no. 2 (June 2022): 527–550. https://doi.org/10.1017/S147924432100010X.
Hotam, Yotam. *Modern Gnosis and Zionism: The Crisis of Culture, Life Philosophy and Jewish National Thought*, translated by Avner Greenberg. Abingdon: Routledge, 2013.
Jonas, Hans. *Erinnerungen*, Frankfurt: Insel Verlag, 2003.
Jonas, Hans. *Gnosis und spätantiker Geist: Die mythologische Gnosis*, vol. 1. 2 vols. Göttingen: Vandenhoeck & Ruprecht, 1934.
Jonas, Hans. "Gnosticism and Modern Nihilism," *Social Research* 19, no. 4 (December 1952): 430–452.
Jonas, Hans. *The Gnostic Religion*, Boston, MA: Beacon Press, 1958.
Kampling, Rainer. "Gnosis und spätantiker Geist I: Die mythologische Gnosis (1934)." In *Hans Jonas-Handbuch: Leben – Werk – Wirkung*, edited by Michael Bongardt, Holger Burckhart, John-Stewart Gordon, and Jürgen Nielsen-Sikora, Stuttgart: J.B. Metzler, 2021, 83–87. https://doi.org/10.1007/978-3-476-05723-5_14.
King, Karen L. *What Is Gnosticism?* Cambridge, MA: Harvard University Press, 2005.
Lapidot, Elad. "Gnosis und spätantiker Geist II. Von der Mythologie zur mystischen Philosophie (1954)." In *Hans Jonas-Handbuch: Leben – Werk – Wirkung*, edited by Michael Bongardt, Holger Burckhart, John-Stewart Gordon, and Jürgen Nielsen-Sikora, Stuttgart: J.B. Metzler, 2021, 88–95. https://doi.org/10.1007/978-3-476-05723-5_15.
Lapidot, Elad. "Hans Jonas's Work on Gnosticism as Counterhistory," *Philosophical Readings* ix, no. 1 (2017): 61–68.
Mali, Joseph. *The Rehabilitation of Myth: Vico's "New Science,"* Cambridge: Cambridge University Press, 1992. https://www.cambridge.org/core/product/identifier/9780511558535/type/book.
Muller, Jerry Z. *Professor of Apocalypse: The Many Lives of Jacob Taubes*, Princeton, NJ: Princeton University Press, 2022.
Rudolph, Kurt. "Hans Jonas and Research on Gnosticism from a Contemporary Perspective." In *The Legacy of Hans Jonas: Judaism and the Phenomenon of Life*, edited by Hava Tirosh-Samuelson and Christian Wiese, Leiden: Brill, 2008, 91–106.
Schelling, Friedrich Wilhelm Joseph. *Friedrich Wilhelm Joseph von Schellings sämmtliche Werke*. Vol. 5. Stuttgart,: J.G. Cotta, 1859.
Schiller, Friedrich. *Essays: Friedrich Schiller*, Edited by Walter Hinderer and Daniel O. Dahlstrom. New York: Continuum, 1993.
Staudenmaier, Peter. *Between Occultism and Nazism: Anthroposophy and the Politics of Race in the Fascist Era*, Leiden: Brill, 2014.
Styfhals, Willem. *No Spiritual Investment in the World: Gnosticism and Postwar German Philosophy*, Ithaca, NY: Cornell University Press, 2019.
Todorov, Tzvetan. *Theories of the Symbol*, Ithaca, NY: Cornell University Press, 1984.
Waldstein, Michael. "Hans Jonas' Construct 'Gnosticism': Analysis and Critique," *Journal of Early Christian Studies* 8, no. 3 (2000): 341–372. https://doi.org/10.1353/earl.2000.0054.
Wessell, Leonard P. "Schiller and the Genesis of German Romanticism," *Studies in Romanticism* 10, no. 3 (1971): 176–198. https://doi.org/10.2307/25599803.

Wiese, Christian. *The Life and Thought of Hans Jonas: Jewish Dimensions*, Lebanon: UPNE, 2007.
Williamson, George S. *The Longing for Myth in Germany: Religion and Aesthetic Culture from Romanticism to Nietzsche*, Chicago, IL: University of Chicago Press, 2004.
Wolfe, Judith Elisabeth. *Heidegger and Theology*, London: Bloomsbury, 2014.
Wolin, Richard. *Heidegger's Children: Hannah Arendt, Karl Löwith, Hans Jonas, and Herbert Marcuse*, Princeton, NJ: Princeton University Press, 2003.
Zander, Helmut. *Die Anthroposophie: Rudolf Steiners Ideen Zwischen Esoterik, Weleda, Demeter Und Waldorfpädagogik*, Paderborn: Ferdinand Schöningh, 2019.

9 *Gnosis und spätantiker Geist. Teil II*
The Forgotten Book

Elad Lapidot

Gnosis und spätantiker Geist. Teil II (*GSG II*) is Jonas' unfinished book. The situation of this work is perplexing and confusing. Generally speaking, it has been to a large extent forgotten. Contemporary reception, perception and understanding of Jonas' work on Gnosticism have tended to draw on *The Gnostic Religion* of 1958, the most accessible presentation of Jonas' project, which mostly draws on *Gnosis und spätantiker Geist. Teil I*, published in 1934.[1] The effacement of *GSG II* was in fact carried out initially by Jonas himself. Already in the foreword to the unfinished book's first publication in 1954, twenty years after *GSG I*, he expressed his postwar distance from his earlier work on Gnosticism. Jonas' self-alienation from his "apprentice work," as he called it, was *eo ipso* his alienation from his prewar world: not least the world of German philosophy in the school of Heidegger.

If the repression of *GSG II* is thus understandable, it is nonetheless remarkable, insofar as *GSG II* contains the original nucleus of Jonas' project on Gnosticism. Provocatively speaking: it is the forgotten unfinished Part II that holds both the beginning and the end of Jonas' project. *GSG II*, even though published only in 1954, is in many respects a reproduction of Jonas' dissertation, *Der Begriff der Gnosis*, submitted in 1928.[2] Its introduction and first two chapters were published *verbatim* already in 1930 as a "partial print" (*Teildruck*) of the dissertation.[3] Part II was conceived and to a large extent written first.

This makes the oblivion of this work all the more interesting – and significant. Retrieving *GSG II* may, from today's perspective, shed a new light on Jonas' original prewar project on Gnosticism – partially contrasting the light Jonas himself has cast on it after the war. This revaluation will reconstruct Jonas' own original understanding of his apprentice work, in its relation to the work of his philosophical *Meister*, Heidegger.

In what follows, by way of introduction and contextualization within Jonas' oeuvre, this chapter first briefly recapitulates Jonas' famous post-WWII account of his prewar project on Gnosticism. Subsequently, with Jonas' later self-interpretation in mind, the main part of the chapter presents the book *GSG II* itself, its basic motivation, methodology, argument, and structure. The chapter concludes by indicating one provocative implication or perspective that a re-appreciation of *GSG II* could have for further research on Hans Jonas' early years.

DOI: 10.4324/9781003439882-9

GSG II in Context: Jonas' Self-Interpretation

In order to return to Part II, as the forgotten origin of Jonas' work on Gnosticism, it would be helpful first to briefly recall Jonas' own account of his work, as he initially outlined it in "Gnosticism Existentialism and Nihilism."[4] According to this text, Heidegger's philosophy originally provided a general theoretical framework for Jonas' attempt to analyze the historical phenomenon of ancient Gnosticism:

> When, many years ago, I turned to the study of Gnosticism, I found that the viewpoints, the optics as it were, which I had acquired in the school of Heidegger, enabled me to see aspects of gnostic thought that had been missed before.[5]

The encounter between Heideggerian philosophy and Gnosticism "started as the meeting of a method with a matter."[6] More specifically, the disciple Jonas used basic categories of his teacher Heidegger's account of human existence, *Daseinanalytik*, to describe the basic existential condition or state of mind from which Gnostic literature had presumably historically arisen.[7]

It was only later, so goes Jonas' 1958 account, that he discovered a deep affinity between ancient Gnosticism and Heidegger's modern existentialism: "In retrospect, I am inclined to believe that it was the thrill of this dimly felt affinity which had lured me into the gnostic labyrinth in the first place."[8] The affinity would lie in a similar problematic relation that both intellectual projects, both systems or forms of thinking or knowledge, that is to say gnosis and existential philosophy, have to practice, namely their *ethical* implication. This common ethical problem of Gnosticism and existentialism was designated by Jonas as "nihilism." "Nihilism" for Jonas, inspired on this point by Nietzsche (as was Heidegger), is the practical implication of a philosophy that precludes all possibility of acknowledging any laws, values, or ethics for guiding life in this world: "the denial of every objective norm of conduct."[9]

Interestingly, Jonas' understanding of the epistemic condition leading to nihilism, as described in his essay, in fact stands in contrast to Nietzsche. For Nietzsche, the seed of nihilism lies in determining the value of this world in reference to *another* world: subjecting physis to meta-physis. Jonas, in contrast, considered the acknowledgment of metaphysics, of transcendence, of a dualism of this world and another world, as the necessary condition for observation and observance of stable laws for stable ethics in human conduct within the flux of life. For Nietzsche, Platonism represented the *arche* of Western metaphysics and nihilism. Plato was "the sincerest 'other-worldly' [der 'Jenseitige'], the great slanderer of life."[10] In contrast, Jonas, in "Gnosticism, Nihilism and Existentialism," described Platonism as a paradigmatic non-nihilistic theory, in which a transcendent, metaphysical, ideal world of eternal Being serves as a model and practical guidance for life in this sensual–physical world of Becoming:

> If values are not beheld in vision as being (like the Good and the Beautiful of Plato), but are posited by the will as projects, then indeed existence is

committed to constant futurity, with death as the goal; and a merely formal resolution to be, without a *nomos* for that resolution, becomes a project from nothingness into nothingness.[11]

In contrast to Platonism, Jonas posited, as the historical prototype of nihilistic epistemology, what he called "ancient nihilism," Gnosticism.[12] As he showed in *GSG I*, the Gnostic myth does recognize, like Plato, beyond this world, another world; however, the Gnostic metaphysical world or cosmos is radically different, radically other, and foreign to this world, radically unworldly, in fact anti-worldly, such that Gnostic metaphysics is *negative* metaphysics, that is to say a-physics or a-cosmism – a transcendence of pure negation of the world, of *Entweltlichung*. Accordingly, Gnostic metaphysics, so was Jonas' argument, can offer purely negative, anti-worldly values and practice, ultimately amounting to "ancient nihilism."

The main thrust of Jonas' thesis in 1958 was the claim that Heidegger's existentialism, as the most accomplished form of modern epistemology, not only resembled Gnostic nihilism, but amplified and radicalized it. Whereas ancient Gnosticism devaluated this world in favor of another world, be it alien, hostile, transcendent, and inaccessible as it may, Sartre's and Heidegger's existentialism, so went Jonas' claim, devaluates this world without acknowledging *any* other world. Theirs is a "dualism without metaphysics,"[13] negation of this world without offering any other world. In Jonas' analysis, Heideggerian anti-worldly epistemology more specifically left no place for the solid objects of Platonic *theoria*, that is as "seeing," as vision of things. Denying human knowledge of any objectivity denies it of any possible normativity and so condemns human practice to pure "will to power."

This was the story of Jonas' involvement with Heidegger and Gnosticism as told by Jonas in 1958. It explains very well the reorientation of Jonas' work after the war, that is the shift in his interest from studies of ancient Gnosticism and contemporary existentialism, of ancient and modern nihilisms, to the philosophy of life.

GSG II. Philosophical Hermeneutics: *Entmythologisierung*

Gnosis und spätantiker Geist. Teil II reveals a more complex story than this later account. It offers the fundamental observation that, just like the retrospective essay of 1958, Jonas' original project on Gnosticism too was concerned from its early stages and basic conceptual foundations with the relation between knowledge and ethics. And it was Heidegger's philosophy that Jonas identified as favorable for this ethical concern.

This applies, first, to the question of methodology. Jonas referred to his methodology only briefly in the introduction to *GSG I*. He explained it in much more detail in the earlier introduction to *GSG II*, which echoed his even earlier book on Augustine.[14] According to Jonas' original explanation, Heidegger's philosophy did not provide his project with just categorical tools, as he claimed in 1958. Rather, Heidegger's philosophy inspired Jonas' work on Gnosticism with the basic method of philosophical hermeneutics applied to historical texts.

This method was for Jonas a counter-measure against the hermeneutics of what he called in *GSG I* "the historical motif research" (*motiv-geschichtliche Forschung*).[15] The latter, according to Jonas, treats historical texts as material objects – things devoid of ideas, matter without spirit, such that their study can only consist in the production of objective information. In the research of myth, such as the Gnostic one, historical research considers the myth only by its "material inventory [...], according to which the myth is just another available element within the material multiplicity and [...] an object of possible syntheses; it also presents itself as such to any solely objective-mythographic observation."[16] Historical research applies the perspective "of 'natural sciences' that pertains to thing-like elements."[17] This kind of knowledge, which is the only kind that the historical hermeneutics is able to produce, remains disconnected from any practical, ethical concerns.

In contrast, Jonas' philosophical hermeneutics deemed historical texts not as objects but as "objectivations." Jonas draws this term explicitly from Cassirer and Husserl. It means that texts, which appear to us as given objects in the world, originally arise from a subjective source, and should therefore be studied as objective expressions – "objectivations" – of a subjective or existential condition, as expressing a certain *Dasein*.

Jonas accordingly describes the historical, mythological text as "the objectifying exteriorizing utterance [Ver-Äußerung] of existential phenomena."[18] As Jonas read in Heidegger's *Sein und Zeit*, human existence consists in understanding its own being, and it understands itself by first projecting (and thus self-alienating itself) in the world as a world of things, of objects. Self-understanding takes place in a process of "the human becoming world."[19]

According to Jonas' methodological explanation, objects such as words, texts, and books feature an exceptional form of objectivation, in which the expression of the subject in objective means is done explicitly. These objects are explicitly referred to as "expressions." This applies in particular to the expressive form of the myth. "The comprehensive world-interpretation of the myth,"[20] Jonas explains, explicitly represents objective reality, depicts the world in words. We may say that this self-alienating objectivation of human existence is perfected by the application of historical philology to the mythical text and the specific knowledge – "objectivation" – that historical hermeneutics itself produces, which is modeled after the epistemology of modern natural sciences.

In contrast, philosophical hermeneutics performs the counter-movement of bringing back *Dasein* to itself. It does so by re-translating the objective terms of the dogmatic or mythical text back into existential categories, that is, the categories of subjective human condition. This is the basic project of Jonas in *Gnosis und spätantiker Geist*. This project is reflected in the structure of the work, which traces a movement going from *Part I. The Mythological Gnosis* to *Part II. From Mythology to Mystical Philosophy*, namely from myth to philosophy. To be sure, "mythology" and "philosophy" designate in these titles the genres of historical (gnostic) texts that they investigate. And yet, the passage from myth to philosophy in ancient Gnosticism, through which the myth becomes *entmythisiert*, de-mythified, as Jonas described it, also describes the hermeneutical principle of his own philosophical readings.

This hermeneutical operation will, under the title *Ent-mythologisierung*, de-mythologization, become Jonas' important contribution to twentieth-century theology.[21] The existential – and not just scholarly – significance of this operation, as Jonas described it in the first pages of *GSG II*, is the return of the textual objectivation back to the human subject, a process of "re-subjectivation."[22] Within the situation of knowledge referring to a historical text, re-subjectivation means re-converting the epistemic relation to the text as an object, a thing, a purely theoretical relation, into an epistemic relation to the text as an existential possibility, the text as a potential subjective performance. Re-subjectivation means shifting from knowledge as theory to knowledge as praxis.

The Concept of *Gnosis*: *Entweltlichung*

This general hermeneutical project is also mentioned, very concisely, in *GSG I*. What arises from the Introduction to *GSG II*, which was already published in 1930, is the great intimacy between Jonas' hermeneutical act and the text to which it is applied, namely ancient Gnostic literature. The act of de-mythologization performed by Jonas on this literature in *GSG I* in fact revealed, beneath the Gnostic myth, or beneath *gnosis* in its narrow, historical–philological meaning, in the sense of Gnosticism, a general existential principle, a historical human performance, which Jonas referred to as the "Gnostic movement,"[23] and that we can refer to as *gnosis* in its broader meaning. The basic existential performance of Gnosticism, as *GSG I* indicated, is a human tendency to distance or alienate oneself from the world, a world-negating tendency: *Ent-weltlichungs-tendenz*.[24]

What *GSG II* makes clear is that this Gnostic movement arises from the existential return of the human Dasein back from the subject's self-objectivation and self-alienation in the world. Gnosticism, as world-negation, arises from "elementary facts of Dasein,"[25] whereby Dasein "discovers, in its basic motion of fall [*Verfallen*], its being essentially captivated and absorbed by the world. The puzzlement of discovering one's total alienation emerges as uncanniness [*Un-Heimlichkeit*] of the world," and so to anxiety before the world [*Weltangst*] and to the "drive to redemption from the world."[26]

Jonas thus presents the Gnostic movement explicitly as the very same movement of Heideggerian hermeneutics, which Jonas adopted for his reading of historical Gnosticism. *Entweltlichung*, world-negation, is akin to *Entmythologisierung*, myth-negation or de-mythologization. Gnosis would accordingly constitute re-subjectivation ("*Rückgabe*"[27]): a return from the object to the subject. In terms of knowledge, gnosis features a return from objective knowledge to subjective knowledge, from theoretical to existential, practical knowledge.

Indeed, Jonas' seminal realization about Gnosticism was that conceptually the Greek term *gnosis*, in contrast to *episteme*, was used to designate a knowledge-relation to the world that is not just a relation to an object, not merely theory. Gnosis is a performative, practical relation to the world – knowledge as *Heilpraxis*, that is, as a salvific or therapeutic practice: "According to its content, the gnostic myth is eschatological; as such, it is not mere knowledge of being, but essentially knowledge of salvation. This provides an immediate *practical* relation back to the Dasein."[28]

It is by virtue of this practical essence of *gnosis* that it stands in contrast to mere contemplative *episteme* and *theoria*. In other words, Jonas' original project on Gnosticism could be situated within a broader intellectual project, which aimed at exposing and thus preparing a historical movement away from classical Greek, paradigmatically Platonic and Aristotelian reified knowledge, back to ethico-existential *gnosis*, "knowing good and bad," to quote Genesis 2:17 (γινώσκειν καλὸν καὶ πονηρόν). In this project, to formulate it provocatively, it was Plato who stood for reification, and ultimately nihilism, whereas Heideggerian thought would open the road to the ethical "Gnostic principle," which for Jonas was the foundation not only of Gnosticism, but of Christianity and Hellenistic Judaism as well.[29]

The Problem of Gnosticism: *Objektivation der Entweltlichung*

In order to further substantiate and fine-tune this observation, it is vital to understand the fundamental problem that Jonas originally identified in Gnosticism. If existential gnosis, the broader historical "Gnostic movement," was performing *Entweltlichung*, world-negation, as ethical re-subjectivation of knowledge, this performance was characterized by a deep and constitutive ambivalence: on the one hand, it was negating the world, on the other hand, this negation itself constituted a kind of praxis in and of the world, a form of ethics. Formulated concisely, Gnosticism featured the paradox of *Verweltlichung der Entweltlichungstendenz*, of "making worldly a world-negation tendency."[30]

The first two chapters of *GSG II* provide an articulation of this basic inner tension of all Gnostic movements through a synchronic typology of various Gnostic phenomena, as Jonas understood them. The typology is based on an evaluation of the practical or ethical quality of the different manifestations of gnosis, in relation to the basic Greek moral notion of ἀρετή, *arete*, commonly rendered "virtue." In fact, Jonas examined Gnostic ethics as a break with Hellenic moral virtue and an essential transformation of it.

Chapter 1 of *GSG II*, "The Dissolution of the Antique Concept of *Arete* in the Domain of Gnosis," asserted a fundamental negative operation of gnosis movements vis-à-vis classic Greek virtue. In a nutshell, it is Jonas' argument that the world-negating tendency of gnosis invalidates the essentially worldly Greek morals. Jonas portrayed different forms of this Gnostic negation of *arete* in the historical phenomena of the Hermetic abstinence (*Enthaltung*),[31] in the rejection of "works" in Christian gnosis,[32] in the "worldly renouncement of the self" in the early Christian community,[33] in the Mandean and Manichean "minimizing of worldly relations"[34] and in Philo, who Jonas describes as "equivocal," presenting an "inner corrosion of the Greek arete-concept through Jewish and so to speak crypto-Gnostic motifs."[35]

Chapter 2, "Anticipation of *eschaton* and the Formation of a Gnostic Concept of *Arete*," then focuses on the second, positive moment of the development of Gnostic ethics. In other words, following world-negation (*Entweltlichung*), including the negation of world-virtues, as explored in Chapter 1, Chapter 2 looks at the process in which this world-negating attitude itself becomes a "producible condition within this-worldly life."[36] This means that the Gnostic acosmic position nonetheless generates a system of praxis within the world, with its own world-negating worldly ethics. Jonas' typology examines the community ethics developed in early Christianity in response to its crisis of "anarchic individualism," which led Paul to omit *gnosis* from his list of virtues (*pistis, elpis, agape*) and to interpret "love" not as the individual's love of God, but as communal neighborly love.[37] He further discusses the mystical praxis of hermetic contemplation of God,[38] the meditative techniques of Mithras,[39] and the "real possibility of experiencing worldlessness" offered by the rituals of mystery religions.[40]

Based on this latter typology, Jonas' basic claim is that the inner tension of the Gnosis movement, that is the foundation of worldly praxis of world-negation, has been conceptually and historically performed in two basic alternative modes. One mode is based on the strict adherence to *gnosis*, while the other mode is based on the shift from gnosis to *pistis*, that is to faith. Jonas' argument was that the first mode, the way of gnosis, was adopted by what is known as proper Gnostic literature, *gnosis* in the narrow sense, namely Gnosticism. The main task of his project was to problematize this direction of the Gnostic movement.

Jonas based the distinction between gnosis and pistis, and the problematization of gnosis, among others, on a verse from the Epistles of Paul, 2 Corinthians 5:7, δια πιστεως γαρ περιπατουμεν ου δια ειδους, "For we live by faith, not by sight." The opposite of faith, pistis, which Jonas identified as the mode of gnosis, is described in this verse as "sight." The late-antique spiritual movements that developed, out of the basic Gnostic posture of world-negation, an ethics that is based on gnosis, were oriented by the principle of seeing. Paul understood this as a problematic turn, and Jonas accepted this diagnosis.

In fact, the problem that young Jonas originally observed in the narrowly gnostic, we may say gnosticist *Entweltlichungstendenz* is not, as it arises from "Gnosticism, Nihilism and Existentialism," that it went too far away from Plato. On the contrary, the problem with Gnosticism was that it remained epistemologically too Platonic, by conceptualizing the existential operation of de-objectivation and re-subjectivation in categories of objective knowledge – of *theoria*, of "sight." As Jonas concisely formulated the problem already in his dissertation, gnosticist *Verweltlichung of Entweltlichungstendenz* (that is the development of a worldly ethics that is based on the fundamental existential posture of world-negation) was carried out in the mode of *Objektivation einer Entweltlichungstendenz*, "objectivation of a world-negation tendency."[41]

From Mythology to Mystical Philosophy: Philo, Origen, Plotinus

The main bulk of *GSG II* is dedicated to the demonstration and further development of this basic claim in several antique and late-antique corpora, which according to Jonas represent Gnosticism in its narrow sense. As a primordial instance of gnosticist or proto-gnosticist discourse, which Jonas described as "crypto-gnostic,"[42]

Chapter 3 features "Knowledge of God, Intuition and Perfection in Philo." Philo was the first to formulate the basic configuration of Gnostic world-negation in the terminology of Greek worldliness: "gnostic idea of God in the categories of Greek thought, a foreign content in a pre-given form."[43] The Gnostic anticosmic, foreign God appeared in Philo, paradoxically, in the traditional Greek categories of worldly contemplation, "a foreign content in a pre-given form," in a process that Jonas termed, after Spengler, "psedumorphose."[44]

Generating "the first self-misunderstanding"[45] of the nascent Gnostic movement, Philo, so Jonas' claim, employed the Platonic "primate of intuition,"[46] that is to say knowledge conceived as vision of worldly objects, for the knowledge of the non-worldly God. This is how Philo produced the notion of God as a "supreme being," which is nothing but a super-object. "As a Jew," Jonas underlined, Philo's thought stands at a "radical distance" from Gnosticism. Philo's Jewish "anti-Gnosticism"[47] would nonetheless be "crypto-gnostic," insofar as Philo's "Israel" is literally (ישר-אל) "*der Gott schauende*," "the one who sees or contemplates God": knowledge of the non-worldly by means of worldly categories.[48]

The resulting form of knowledge, which according to Jonas arises from Philonic epistemology as the paradigm for all future Gnosticism, is the mystical knowledge of God. Mystical knowledge is not purely theoretical, no scientific *episteme*, but essentially praxis, since it aspires to *know* God in the sense of coming closer to God, ultimately by ecstatically transcending one's self and one's world. Philo thus introduced, Jonas argued, the first seed of gnosis in the narrow sense of knowledge as world-negating, proto-nihilistic praxis.

Chapter 4, "From the 2nd to the 3rd Century: from Mythological to Philosophical-Mystical Gnosis," is, as its title suggests, the core of the entire project of *Gnosis und spätantiker Geist* Part I and II. As I explained, this project presents and articulates the ethico-philosophical problem of Gnosticism in the form of a discursive genealogy, that is, by describing the development of Gnostic discourse from mythology to philosophy. Jonas' main thesis asserted an "inner genesis" (based on "morphological affinity" rather than on any "direct evidence" of actual influences) between the "gnosis of the second century and Neoplatonism of the third and following centuries."[49] It is in the third century that Jonas located the "consummation" of gnosticist discourse, where *gnosis* assumes the fully developed shape of knowledge with a "soteriological" function.[50]

The movement of Jonas' genealogy starts in the mythical form of Gnosticism, which Jonas considers as its "*uneigentlich*" form, that is the improper or inauthentic, the "external" form of Gnosticism.[51] The detailed analysis of Gnostic mythology was done by Jonas in *GSG I* of 1934. Having already formulated in his 1928 dissertation both the genealogical thesis and the analysis of Neoplatonic philosophy as the consummation of the genealogical process, *GSG I* provided retroactively the point of departure for this process, featured so to speak the prequel of Jonas' dissertation. *GSG I* distilled from the multiplicity of Gnostic mythologies a primordial Gnostic narrative of rupture between world immanence and godly transcendence, a story of "anticosmic eschatological dualism,"[52] which has become the canonic definition of Gnosticism after Jonas.

However, in the main part of *GSG II*, in Chapter 4, Jonas indicates how the underlying theoretical, objectifying Greek epistemology instilled (by Philo) in the foundation of the gnosticist narrative, which told of acosmic dualism, nevertheless generated a tendency to re-convert transcendence into immanence. The absolute static dualism (termed by Jonas "substantial dualism"[53]) was thus transformed into a dynamic, dialectical dualism, namely a dualism that functions as the internal tension within a *monistic* system.

Jonas illustrated this by contrasting the gnosticist myth (expressing the narrow, problematic, gnosis-based form of Gnostic posture) with the Jewish–Christian biblical myth (expressing the alternative, pistis-based mode of the Gnostic posture). Jewish and Christian mythology, he claimed, featured an absolute distance between the world and God as a "personal relation God-creation."[54] This constituted an absolute human relation to a "He," which is based on hearing *without* seeing, featuring a relation of *pistis*, of faith and open temporality. Gnosticist mythology, in contrast, so Jonas' observation, "de-personifies" dualism, such that the relation to the divine being is no longer a relation to a "He" but to an "It." Accordingly, the Gnosticist narrative inherently tends to undergo conceptualization and "rationalization."[55] In this myth, transcendence tends to become immanence, and mythical exteriority transforms into mystical interiority, *Innerlichkeit*.

This explains the fact, which is visible but remains inexplicable or even contradictory in *GSG I*, that the paradigmatic gnosticist – that is dualistic – myth for Jonas is rather provided by Valentinian monism, as the "proper gnostic speculation."[56] Monism is precisely where the objectifying tendency of Gnosticism leads its dualism, by converting "substantial dualism" into internal, dynamic, or dialectical dualism, which functions as the inner tension of a superior unified entity. Accordingly, Valentinian myth, the paradigm of Gnosticist myth, marks the liminal point of a mythology, whose plot actually portrays an event of pure immanence, less a temporal narrative than a process of logos. The gnosticist myth thus features for Jonas the "de-mythologization of intuitive entities,"[57] in other words, a myth that de-mythologizes itself.

The gnosticist myth spontaneously, by its own inner dynamic, transforms into gnosticist philosophy. De-mythologization ultimately converts all factual, historical, temporal objects into abstract concepts. Empirical or experiential knowledge is accordingly converted into a speculation of purely conceptual necessity and "autonomous reproducibility."[58] The basic elements of gnosticist thought were exposed by Jonas in his analysis of Philo (Chapter 3), as the crypto-Gnostic emergence of Gnosticism in Platonic categories. The actual, mature, revealed figure of gnosticist philosophy, however, is identified by Jonas later, in "The Systems of the 3rd Century," as announced in the title of Chapter 5, first and foremost in the works of Origen and Plotinus.

Chapter 5, the last of the unfinished *GSG II*, is dedicated to Origen, in whose thought Jonas recognized the emergence of the new form of the conceptual "system," never before operative in Greek philosophy. For Jonas, the philosophical system is the conceptual essence of Gnosticism's monistic myth. In Origen's *De Principiis*, Jonas observes a discursive configuration based on the premise of "absolute unity."[59] This configuration features a One that is simultaneously a *pleroma*, a multiplicity of spiritual entities, and so constitutes "unity in plurality."[60]

Jonas indicates that the Origenic system is not properly gnosticist since its foundational dynamics is not animated by *gnosis*, that is by the force of knowledge, but rather by the force of will. The primary dynamic principle in Origen's thought is not intellectual, but moral, its conceptual movement proceeds only secondarily between knowledge and ignorance, and primarily between good and evil, by powers such as "guilt," "justice," and "punishment."[61]

Nevertheless, Jonas deems Origen's discourse as gnosticist insofar as its moral cosmic scheme abstracts from all proper names, including Satan and Christ, such that it remains a configuration of mere "figures" or "functions," where "everything can become everything."[62] Origenic system therefore constitutes on Jonas' account a crucial milestone in the "progress towards *Entmythisierung*,"[63] since it transformed gnosticist myth into a conceptual instrument that may be used by the soteriological praxis of *theoria*, as it already emerged in Philo, namely by mystical contemplation. The actual application of Origenic thought in mystical praxis would only take place, Jonas notes, 150 years after Origin, in the work of the ascetic monk Evagrius Ponticus.

The last destination and full maturation of the gnosticist movement, as Jonas portrays it, from Greek virtue to ancient nihilism, was identified by him, from the early stages of his project, as the Neoplatonism of Plotinus, which featured the "complete liberation of mysticism to itself."[64] It is the absence of Plotinus from *GSG II* that left it unfinished. Nonetheless, in the years following the publication of *GSG II*, Jonas published several texts on Plotinus that presented central elements of his missing chapter. In light of Jonas' overall project on Gnosticism, as it was presented above, it is noteworthy that he deemed Plotinus (quoting Richard Harder) as "the visible symbol of the change of fronts in ethics."[65] In Plotinus' thought, "the retreat into the circle of the isolated subject provides a new concept of virtues or of virtue as such, which radically contradicts their original 'political' and action-oriented meaning. Their performance became utterly immanent and no longer needs any world."[66]

However, since Plotinus nonetheless continued "thinking in the style of Greek philosophy," that is to say guided by the primate of vision, the world-negation, the *Entweltlichung* that he carried out remained an "objectivation" that is subjected to "the ontology of worldly things."[67] As Jonas explained in an article on Plotinus from 1964, in Heideggerian terms, "the radical 'other' of the world, as Dasein ultimately finds itself to be (what *gnosis* discovered in the experience of foreignness, experienced as *Weltangst* and 'heard' as the call of the non-worldly) appears [in Plotinus] as hypostasized to a substantial 'what' in the metaphysical system."[68] Accordingly, and this summarizes Jonas' basic critique against Gnosticism, "on the theoretical level [Plotinus] already surrendered to what his practical intention wished to overcome: the world-bias of natural Dasein."[69]

A Perspective for Further Research: *Pistis*

This last quote from Jonas' article on Plotinus clearly confirms that Jonas' recognized the significance of the Gnostic movement "from the East" in overcoming the objectivizing tendency of Greek thought, its "world-bias." Jonas' project should therefore be understood not only in the context of Heideggerian critique of Western object-based ontology, but also in the context of contemporary Jewish thinkers, such as Hermann Cohen and Franz Rosenzweig, who were looking for alternative models in the archives of non-Greek, oriental, biblical discourse. They too found in this archive an intellectual heritage that is based not on worldliness but on transcendence, on a non-worldly God, and which, against Greek tendency to theory, featured an ethics-based thinking.

What Jonas problematized was not the basic break with the world, but the betrayal of this break by its re-inscription into Greek, worldly categories of vision and theory. This was the specific problem of Gnosticism, which for Jonas presented the historical source of Neoplatonic and in fact of any systematic speculative philosophy. It is striking to compare this to Rosenzweig's criticism in the *Star of Redemption* against the totalitarian systematicity of German idealism as arising from Neoplatonism.[70]

In conclusion, it may be instructive to point at what Jonas perceived as the alternative to Gnosticism, namely the other modality of *Entweltlichung* that Jonas identified but left undeveloped. As noted, for young Jonas, the alternative to the gnosis-based Gnosticism was not the Platonic (world-biased) idea, but pistis, "faith." Jonas identifies *pistis*, in Philo and then in Paul, as the non-objectifying, non-reifying relation to the non-objective, unworldly transcendence. This relation takes shape not as theory and contemplation, but as performance and action.

Whereas Gnosticism looked for transcendence as a world beyond or outside of the world, the traditions of *pistis* enact transcendence within this world as a non-theoretical, temporal, and ethical relation to a non-objectifiable other. In *GSG II*, Jonas identified the ethical practice of knowledge as *pistis* in the Christian Church, in Biblical Judaism and, among his contemporaries, in Heidegger's *Being and Time*. As noted, we may add to the list Franz Rosenzweig, Hermann Cohen, and Martin Buber.

Future research will need to reflect on the question of whether Jonas' critique of Heidegger in America of 1952 as a modern Gnostic nihilist was perhaps Jonas' less powerful intervention on his teacher's thought, in comparison to his attempt in Germany of the early 1930s to read Heidegger as an heir of Judeo-Christian ethics.

Notes

1 Hans Jonas, *The Gnostic Religion. The Message of the Alien God and The Beginnings of Christianity* (Boston, MA: Beacon Press, 1958); Hans Jonas, *Gnosis und spätantiker Geist I. Die Mythologische Gnosis* (Göttingen, Vandenhoeck & Ruprecht, 1934).
2 Hans Jonas, *Der Begriff der Gnosis*, Inaugural-Dissertation zur Erlangung der Doktorwürde einer Hohen Philosophischen Fakultät der Philipps-Universität Marburg/L. HJ-13-30-1, 1928.
3 Hans Jonas, *Der Begriff der Gnosis* (Göttingen, 1930).
4 Hans Jonas, "Gnosticism, Existentialism, Nihilism" in *The Gnostic Religion. The Message of the Alien God and The Beginnings of Christianity* (Boston, MA: Beacon Press, 1958), 320–341.
5 Jonas, *Nihilism*, 320.
6 Jonas, *Nihilism*, 321.

7   Cf. Jonas, *GSG I*, 90.
8   Jonas, *Nihilism*, 320.
9   Jonas, *Nihilism*, 331.
10 Friedrich Nietzsche, *Zur Genealogie der Moral*, KSA 5 (München [1887] ⁹2007), 402–403.
11 Jonas, *Nihilism*, 338.
12 Jonas, *Nihilism*, 320.
13 Jonas, *Nihilism*, 340.
14 Hans Jonas, *Augustinus und das paulinische Freiheitsproblem* KGA III/1 [1930], 59–176, Anhang I.
15 Jonas GSG I, 9.
16 Jonas GSG II, 1.
17 Jonas GSG II, 1 n. 2.
18 Jonas GSG II, 5.
19 Jonas GSG II, 6.
20 Jonas GSG II, 10.
21 Cf. the chapters of Luca Settimo and Andreas Grossman in this volume.
22 Jonas GSG II, 4.
23 Jonas GSG I, 43. "It appears everywhere in the movements coming from the East, and most conspicuously in that group of spiritual movements which are comprised under the name 'gnostic.' We can therefore take the latter as the most radical and uncompromising representatives of a new spirit, and may consequently call the general principle, which in less unequivocal representations extends beyond the area of gnostic literature proper, by way of analogy the 'gnostic principle.' Whatever the usefulness of such an extension of the meaning of the name, it is certain that the study of this particular group not only is highly interesting in itself but also can furnish, if not the key to the whole epoch, at least a vital contribution toward its understanding"; Jonas, *Gnostic Religion*, 26.
24 Jonas GSG I, 5.
25 Jonas GSG II, 12.
26 Jonas GSG II, 12.
27 Jonas GSG II, 18.
28 Jonas GSG II, 17.
29 Jonas, *Gnostic Religion*, 25.
30 Jonas GSG II, 13.
31 Jonas GSG II, 28.
32 Jonas GSG II, 29–39.
33 Jonas GSG II, 34.
34 Jonas GSG II, 36.
35 Jonas GSG II, 38.
36 Jonas GSG II, 42.
37 Jonas GSG II, 43–48.
38 Jonas GSG II, 49–51.
39 Jonas GSG II, 55.
40 Jonas GSG II, 60.
41 Jonas, Dissertation, 2.
42 Jonas GSG II, 98.
43 Jonas GSG II, 80.
44 Jonas GSG II, 81; GSG I, 43.
45 Jonas GSG II, 90.
46 Jonas GSG II, 92.
47 Jonas GSG II, 77.
48 Jonas GSG II, 70, 96.
49 Jonas GSG II, 131.
50 Jonas GSG II, 124, 149–150.

51 Jonas GSG II, 125–126.
52 Jonas, GSG I, 5.
53 Jonas, GSG II, 152–153.
54 Jonas, GSG II, 134.
55 Jonas, GSG II, 141.
56 Jonas, GSG I, 362.
57 Jonas, GSG II, 169.
58 Jonas, GSG II, 165.
59 Jonas, GSG II, 178.
60 Jonas, GSG II, 182.
61 Jonas, GSG II, 184–187.
62 Jonas, GSG II, 191–192.
63 Jonas, GSG II, 209.
64 Jonas, GSG II, 143.
65 Hans Jonas, „Plotins Tugendlehre: Analyse und Kritik," In Franz Wiedmann (ed.), *Die Sorge der Philosophie um den Menschen* (München 1964), 143–173.
66 Jonas, GSG II, 151.
67 Jonas, GSG II, 171–172.
68 Jonas, GSG II, 172.
69 Jonas, GSG II, 166.
70 Franz Rosenzweig, *Der Stern der Erlösung* (Frankfurt am Main: Suhrkamp, 2002 [1921]), Teil I, Buch II.

Bibliography

Brumlik, Micha, "Ressentiment – Über einige Motive in Hans Jonas's frühem Gnosisbuch," Christian Wiese and Eric Jacobson (Ed.), *Weiterwohnlichkeit der Welt. Zur Aktualität von Hans Jonas*, Berlin 2003, 127–144.
Cahana, Jonathan, "A Gnostic Critic of Modernity: Hans Jonas from Existentialism to Science," *Journal of the American Academy of Religion* 86/1 (2018): 158–180.
Heidegger, Martin, *Sein und Zeit* [1927], Tübingen, 2001.
Jonas, Hans, *Der Begriff der Gnosis. Inaugural-Dissertation zur Erlangung der Doktorwürde einer Hohen Philosophischen Fakultät der Philipps-Universität Marburg/L.* HJ-13-30-1 1928.
Jonas, Hans, *Augustinus und das paulinische Freiheitsproblem* [1930], KGA III/1, 59–176.
Jonas, Hans, *Der Begriff der Gnosis*, Göttingen 1930.
Jonas, Hans, *Gnosis und spätantiker Geist. Die mythologische Gnosis* [1934], Göttingen 1988.
Jonas, Hans, "Gnosticism and Modern Nihilism," *Social Research* 19/4 (1952): 430–452.
Jonas, Hans, *Gnosis und spätantiker Geist. Von der Mythologie zur mystischen Philosophie*, Göttingen 1954.
Jonas, Hans, *The Gnostic Religion. The Message of the Alien God and the Beginnings of Christianity* [1958], Boston, MA, 1991.
Jonas, Hans, "Plotins Tugendlehre: Analyse und Kritik," Franz Wiedmann (Ed.), *Die Sorge der Philosophie um den Menschen*, München 1964, 143–173.
Jonas, Hans, *Erinnerungen*, Frankfurt am Main 2003.
Lapidot, Elad, "Hans Jonas's Work on Gnosticism as Counterhistory," *Philosophical Readings* IX (2017): 61–69.
Lazier, Benjamin, *God Interrupted. Heresy and the European Imagination between the World Wars*, Princeton, NJ and Oxford, 2008.
Nietzsche, Friedrich, *Zur Genealogie der Moral* [1887], KSA 5. München, 2007, 245–412.

10 From *Gnosis und spätantiker Geist* to *The Gnostic Religion*

The Jerusalem Period in Hans Jonas' Intellectual Development

Daniel M. Herskowitz

Hans Jonas' book *The Gnostic Religion*, published in the United States in 1958, has left a decisive mark on the study of Gnosticism in the twentieth century. Its origins are found in an earlier study, written in Germany in the late 1920s as a dissertation supervised by the philosopher Martin Heidegger and the theologian and New Testament scholar Rudolf Bultmann.[1] Part I of this study was published in 1934 as *Gnosis und spätantiker Geist*: *Teil I*. *Teil II*, originally written before *Teil I*, appeared after it, in 1954.[2] This early German work, deeply entrenched in the intellectual scene of early twentieth century Marburg, was almost entirely overshadowed by its later and better-known English version and is often read in light of it.[3] There are, however, glaring differences between the two works. Indeed, the English version is not a translation of the original German version but a substantial reworking of its project. An account of this reworking, however, has yet to be offered in the extant scholarly literature on Jonas. This chapter seeks to contribute to filling this gap and illuminate some aspects of the transformation of Jonas' Gnosis study. It claims that the crucial intellectual developments that are exhibited in this transformation took place during Jonas' stay in Mandate Jerusalem throughout the 1930s, and thus it establishes the importance of the Jerusalem period in Jonas' intellectual trajectory.

In the preface to *The Gnostic Religion*, Jonas offers some brief thoughts on the differences between the two works. He writes:

> When, many years ago, under the guidance of Rudolf Bultmann, I first approached the study of Gnosticism [...] My aim, somewhat different from that of the preceding and still continuing research, but complementary to it, was a philosophic one: to understand the spirit speaking through these voices and in its light to store an intelligible unity to the baffling multiplicity of its expression.[4]

This in no longer the task of the present volume, he continues, which is "different in scope, in organization, and in literary intention." In comparison to the original *Gnosis und spätantiker Geist*, the current work is more conservative in its application of the category 'Gnosticism,' offers a more detailed interpretation of certain

DOI: 10.4324/9781003439882-10

texts, and includes a discussion of newly discovered materials. Another difference, particularly relevant to the present discussion, is that

> much of the more difficult philosophical elaboration, with its too technical language – the cause of much complaint in the German volumes – has been excluded from this treatment, which strives to reach the general educated reader as well as the scholar.[5]

What is implied here is that doing away with the convoluted and technical philosophical formulations of the original project was required to tailor the revised English edition to its new target audience, and that this revision took place as part of the preparation for this post-war publication.

However, a different source, the transcripts of a short lecture series on Gnosis that Jonas delivered at the Hebrew University in Jerusalem in the academic year of 1938/1939 – virtually unexplored in the scholarly literature on Jonas' life and thought – seems to complicate the stated motivation for the revision and its chronology. As we shall see, this lecture series anticipated the transformed shape his Gnosis study would later take in *The Gnostic Religion* in some important respects, suggesting that Jonas' self-distancing from the original project of *Gnosis und spätantiker Geist* did not take place initially in the post-war context of the preparation of his research for a North American audience, but earlier, in the pre-war setting of a Jewish and Zionist audience in Jerusalem.[6] Thus, an examination of the transcripts of these lectures will allow us to trace the origin and context of this shift, made more publicly evident in *The Gnostic Religion*, to his period in Jerusalem during the 1930s.

The discussion below begins with an examination of some of the key differences between Jonas' German and English publications on Gnosticism. It then turns to his Hebrew University lecture series, with the aim of showing that what appears to be a post-war shift in Jonas' approach toward Gnosticism can already be detected in these pre-war lectures in Jerusalem. It then proposes a number of reasons for this shift.

***

The conceptual departure point of Jonas' early study, *Gnosis und spätantiker Geist*, is that articulating the distinct existential attitude or posture of Gnosticism will reveal its essence and internal unity. The key to understanding this spiritual movement, he believed, was its particular experience of self and the world, the Gnostic manner of being-in-the-world by means of which the different content found in the various sources can be organized and made meaningful. Unlike previous scholarship, he did not believe that 'origin' equals 'essence' and thus did not seek to identify the moment of origination of Gnosticism, chart its historical or conceptual development, or reduce its multiple manifestations to a unified and formal definition. Rather, he sought to reconstruct its existential–ontological structure as a mode of experiencing and inhabiting the world. This does not mean Jonas did not build on the voluminous historical scholarship that preceded him.

Notwithstanding his fondness to criticize its conclusions, there is no question that he is indebted to the work of the History of Religions school. Yet his main intervention is predicated on the historical claim that Gnosticism reflected the emergence of a novel expression of existence, and that it was the task of the scholar to reconstruct and lay out its essential elements on the basis of historical, cultural, textual, and philosophical analyses. This historical claim is based on Oswald Spengler's *Der Untergang des Abendlandes* and its use of the geological concept of *pseudomorphosis* to explain the emergence and presentation of new ideas from the 'Orient' under the dominant albeit lethargic spiritual rule of Hellenism.[7] For Spengler, these ideas were forced to present themselves in the image of the prevalent Hellenistic structures of thought, even while they were fundamentally original. The decay of the spirit of late Greek antiquity was in fact the beginning of a new spiritual period that Spengler called 'the Magian' (or 'Arabian') period. Beyond a short analysis of what he calls 'the Mandean religion' which he considered the height of Arabian culture, Spengler did not discuss Gnosticism in much detail at all.

While Spengler provided Jonas with the historical framing for his study, Jonas' reliance on Heidegger is considerably more prevalent and decisive. The prime methodological and terminological tools with which Jonas grasped the meaning of the phenomenon of Gnosticism were developed by Heidegger. As Jonas announced in the Introduction to *Gnosis und spätantiker Geist I*, "our undertaking will draw to a large extent on an already crafted ontology of Dasein" that had been developed "especially in the work *Sein und Zeit*."[8] Indeed, Heidegger's philosophical vocabulary is crucial to the analysis of the existential world of Gnosticism. Among the Heideggerian notions employed by Jonas are 'fallenness' [*Verfallenheit*], 'dread' [*Angst*], 'being-abandoned' [*Verlorensein*], 'thrownness' [*Geworfenheit*], the 'call' [*Ruf*], and 'alienation' [*Überfremdung*], all which received an elaborate analysis in the first chapter of this work and all expressing different facets of the existential Gnostic experience, namely, the imprisonment in an alien and fallen world controlled by astral powers and evil deities actively obstructing the soul's ability to attain the redemptive knowledge, 'Gnosis.'

Yet Heidegger's role in *Gnosis und spätantiker Geist* goes far beyond matters of vocabulary. The Dasein analytic is vital to the hermeneutical method with which Jonas approaches the content and form of the ancient Gnostic texts as well as to the overarching ontological goal of his exploration. It is difficult to imagine his approach to Gnosticism without the impetus and content of Heidegger's ontological–existential phenomenology. While conducting an existential analysis, the 'object' of Jonas' study was not the ontic or 'empirical' existence of the Gnostic individual or even collective. It was, rather, the "original constitution" of the Gnostic world and mode of being,

> the basic position of Dasein in that primordial dimension [*Ursicht*] of the imaginative apperception of being [*Sein*], from which the overall constitution of the 'world' and of the Dasein relationship to the world, as a historical act, leads to an entire epoch.[9]

In other words, Jonas was directing his attention to the ontological 'spirit' [*Geist*] underlying and making possible the various empirical manifestations of concrete Gnostic forms of existence. History in Jonas' analysis is the history of *Geist*, that is, the instances of the realization of *Geist* as the existential posture of the particular epoch, through and as history. According to this schema, the emergence of Gnosticism in the Hellenistic period constituted an important stage in the dialectical movement of *Geist*. It reflected the end of one epoch and the breaking forth of a new self-understanding of *Geist* in history, and thus a new chapter in its history. It is, therefore, this existential posture, this Dasein, this *Geist*, that is imbued in the Gnostic texts, and it is *Geist* that was the focus of Jonas' early philosophical hermeneutics.

For Jonas, articulating the Dasein of Gnosticism required acknowledging not only its historicity but also its historical conditioning and contingency. He set out to identify "the transcendentally constitutive" factors of the Gnostic existential posture, but these are "respectively rooted in an actually historical fundamental state of 'Dasein'."[10] This means that some basic or originary *existentiell* features of Gnostic existence are to be outlined, such as "dependence on the world and freedom, life and death, care [*Sorge*], fear [*Angst*], protection and concealment [*Verdeckung*]."[11] But it would be a mistake to treat these *Urphänomene* as formal or ahistorical features of a general spiritual propensity called 'Gnosticism' which can be identified in diverse historical and cultural settings. As a spiritual movement and form of existence, Gnosticism for Jonas is very much determined by the particular historical setting of the epoch of 'Late Antiquity,' as it emerged from, encapsulated, and responded to the overall crisis ensuing from the conquests of Alexander the Great and the syncretistic results of the encounter between the Hellenistic and 'Oriental' cultures at the time.

Crucial to Jonas' existential focus on the Gnostic *Geist* is the notion of objectivation [*Objektivation*]. According to his Spenglerian understanding, the dominance of the Hellenistic spiritual framework led the 'Orient' to reformulate its ideas by means of a more universalized and abstract mold. While remaining in essence mythical and symbolic, these ideas adopted a form of expression more in accord with the Hellenistic dictates of *logos*. The Gnostic myth, at once 'primitive' and 'sophisticated,' is the fruit of this ideational–historical dynamic and the site of Jonas' exegetical attention. But while exploring the basic myth abstracted from the Gnostic texts, Jonas' study was not a literary study but an "existential analysis" of the Gnostic Dasein as a particular "fact of Dasein history."[12] He approached what he took to be the basic Gnostic myth with the purpose of extracting and uncovering from it the central existential posture that 'objectivates' itself in it. According to Jonas' understanding, myth is an external, objectified representation of an internal subjective state, the attribution of the existential situation of the human subject to the objective world. The process of objectivation is in fact dual: the objective world is subjectivized in accordance with the human's existential posture, but the process of subjectivation is also one of objectivation, because through its mythologization, the subjective existential posture is reformulated as an objective feature of reality.

Jonas' conception of objectivation is built on but is not identical with the Marburgian Neo-Kantian notion of 'objectification.'[13] One salient difference is that for the Neo-Kantians, it denotes the epistemological apprehension and construction of an object in accordance with the principle of law, while for Jonas objectivation is an ontological category, an "original phenomenon" of Dasein's "being-in-the-world" and of the "Dasein-*Welt* relation."[14] It is more than just a basic feature of human existence; it is an essential factor and necessary condition for the "being-able-to-be-real" *(Wirklichsein-konnens)* of *Existenz*.[15] Objectivation, Jonas wrote, is

> a condition of being of *Dasein* itself as a whole. We do not use the term 'world' here ontically, as the sum total of entities (therefore in the worldly sense), but ontologically, as the horizon of transcendence of *Dasein* (therefore in the existentialist sense, or to speak with Heidegger, as *Existenzial*).[16]

In this respect, objectivation is not simply a cognitive or interpretive instrument for making sense of the world, but "the destiny of *Existenz*."[17]

Objectivation, moreover, is a normatively charged notion. Myth is the expression of self-understanding in the form of world-understanding, whereby *Dasein* objectifies itself [*Sich-Objektivieren*] as being-at-hand [*Vorhandensein*].[18] Thus *Geist* comes into historical reality as something it is not, as "a transposition [*Übereignung*] of the deepest structure of our being into another mode of being."[19] Jonas called the transferring of subjective existential character to the objective language 'alienation' [*Überfremdung*]. This is because the objects of myth "are in the most comprehensive ontological sense that which is essentially alien to human existence [*das wesenhaft Daseinsfremde*]."[20] Objectivation involves, then, a certain disengagement from one's existential situation, reflecting an escape and withdrawal from the question of one's own existence. "*Dasein* has no longer to deal with the original real relation to itself," Jonas stated, "although this remains in the background, but now deals with it in its derived, objectified mode."[21] Myth therefore is a form of self-understanding expressed through the generality and mediation of an objectified construct. Another implicit duality becomes evident: objectivation is at once a necessary and essential form of expression of a specific understanding of existence *and* a process of alienation from its originary content and meaning.

In Part II of Jonas' early Gnosis study – the original part, written before Part I – the question of the alienation and authenticity of *Geist* takes central stage. Can human beings comprehend their true existential posture through their myths or does objectivation ultimately conceal their existential condition beyond retrieve? It is the task of the scholar, he maintained, to conduct a demythologization [*Entmythologisierung*] of the epochal existential posture that is objectified through mythical language and reveal its underlying Dasein. Indeed, it was Jonas who originally came up with the hermeneutical understanding of myth, objectivation, and demythologization that was soon to be picked up and developed by Bultmann in the context of his theological exploration of scripture, to much acclaim and controversy.[22]

Jonas held that the process of objectivation is a non-static, dynamic movement of the changing forms of *Geist* or *Dasein* throughout history, from radical inauthentic alienation to a gradual attainment of the authentic being of *Geist* itself. His own scholarly effort on Gnosticism was guided by the goal of retrieving the Spirit's existential self-understanding from its objectivated form in the Gnostic myth. His findings were that the unitary existential principle objectivated in the Gnostic myth was that of *Entweltlichung* and that it was Gnosticism, more than any other spiritual movement of the time, that best captured the Spirit of Late Antiquity – hence the title of his study, *Gnosis und spätantiker Geist*.

Profoundly reflecting the Marburgian context in which it was composed, *Gnosis und spätantiker Geist* is a thoroughly Heideggerian project in its vocabulary, method, framing, and guiding normative aims.[23] Years later, Jonas referred to it as an "interesting attempt, and a unique one" of an "application of Heidegger's philosophy, especially of existential analysis, with its particular interpretive methodology and its understanding of human existence, to a specific body of historical material, in this case Gnosticism of late antiquity."[24] However, that Jonas' debt to Heidegger is evident, acknowledged, and discernible does not mean he was a mindless disciple. His work exhibited remarkable originality, even brazenness, and was not infrequently at odds with the original meaning and purpose of his mentor's philosophical categories. The divergence is evident in numerous moments, not least in the very application of the existential hermeneutic to a set of textual sources, in his conception of myth and objectivation, in the way in which he framed the authentic/inauthentic distinction, and in the broad liberty with which he employed Heideggerian notions for his own aims.[25] Yet even when he departed from the spirit or the letter of the philosophical apparatus of *Sein und Zeit* or when he blended it with other intellectual impulse, it remained one of the main conceptual resources of Jonas' early scholarly enterprise. *Gnosis und spätantiker Geist* also bore the mark of Bultmann's occupation with myth and pivots on the consolidation of the process of objectivation, myth, and demythologization as it was developed in dialogue with the New Testament scholar. Overall, its own self-understanding partook in the grand Heideggerian narrative of the unfolding of the existential posture of *Geist*. Indeed, while it is remarkably informed by contemporary historical and philological scholarship and grounded its claims in careful textual analyses of Gnosticism material, these served the undeniably philosophical and normative aim of retrieving the authentic self-recognition of *Geist* from its self-imposed alienation.

***

Little of this original project is found in *The Gnostic Religion*.[26] No doubt, the historical framing and details of Jonas' earlier presentation of Gnosticism continued to inform his later account. He also repeated his general characterization of Gnosticism as a fundamentally religious phenomenon directed toward salvation and operating according to a framework of dualisms – between a transcendent God and the world, spirit and matter, soul and body, light and darkness, good and evil, and life and death – and he echoed his previous outline of its theology, cosmology, anthropology, eschatology, and (im)morality, basing his claims on largely the same prooftexts. But notwithstanding these important continuities, the methodology, aims, vocabulary, and style of the English study are different from the German original. Methodologically, *The Gnostic Religion* is a more straightforwardly typological–historical study.[27] Its main concern remained to disclose "the directing principle" that served as the uniting feature of the multiplicity of sources and expressions of Gnosticism – "Is there a one in the many, and what is it?" – but it no longer did this through a philosophical–existential examination of the Dasein underlying the differing manifestations of Gnosticism.[28] Instead, great emphasis is given to the exposition of the basic tenets of the Gnostic view of reality, and the 'essence' or 'principle' of Gnosticism is expressed typologically rather than philosophically. Jonas continued to reject the benefit of the search for origins as a way to identify the essence of Gnosticism, but instead of seeking to expose its "existential root itself," as he did before, he now wished to sketch its defining characteristics.[29] The prime aim is forthrightly historical, namely, to better understand the period of antiquity. As Jonas wrote, "the study of this particular group is not only highly interesting in itself but also can furnish, if not *the* key to the whole epoch, at least a vital contribution toward its understanding."[30] When compared with the original German version, the scholarly perspective taken in English version is more that of a historian of ancient religions proposing a unifying synthesis of a wide range of textual material than that of a philosopher seeking to uncover an original existential posture of *Geist* manifested in historical reality and expressed inauthentically in myth.

Corresponding to the minimizing of the philosophical and existential analysis is an overall reduction of Heidegger's mark and of the existential terminology more generally.[31] Instead of openly referring to the ontological features of the Gnostic 'being-in-the-world,' Jonas now prefers to speak of "certain characteristic mental attitudes" exhibited in the various Gnostic sources.[32] To be sure, Jonas does not entirely gloss over the Gnostic existential analysis. There are references to the ontic existential situation of the Gnostic person, but these are far removed from the initial exploration into the existential expression of *Geist*, dealt with in diminished depth, and occupied a significantly reduced place and purpose in this work. For example, Heideggerian echoes remain discernible in Jonas' outlining of the Gnostic characteristics of "anguish and homesickness" and "dread" of the Gnostic person, in what he called the soul's 'dispersal' or 'distraction' by the multiple concerns and lures of the world, in the motif of 'the call,' and in the Gnostic imagery of life as having been "cast (thrown) into the world and into the body."[33] Consider the following passage on the Gnostic image of life being 'thrown':

> The impact of the image has itself a symbolic value in the gnostic account of human existence. It would be of great interest to compare its use in Gnosticism with its use in a very recent philosophical analysis of existence, that of Martin Heidegger. All we wish to say here is that in both cases 'to have been thrown' is not merely a description of the past but an attribute qualifying the given existential situation as determined by the past.[34]

Such a comparison between the Heideggerian and Gnostic visions of thrownness is offered by Jonas himself in his essay "Gnosticism, Existentialism, and Nihilism" as part of a broader juxtaposition aimed to demonstrate the gravity of the nihilism of contemporary existentialism.[35] What is noteworthy in this context is the strikingly limited

From Gnosis und spätantiker Geist *to* The Gnostic Religion   161

application of the existential lexicon of *Sein und Zeit* in Jonas' updated presentation of Gnosticism. In fact, this passage is the only invocation of Heidegger's name in the entirety of *The Gnostic Religion*. This indexical fact about the number of appearances of the philosopher's name is indicative of the unequivocal shift in methodology, terminology, and normative aim that becomes clear when the spirited existential and ontological analyses of the German version of Jonas' Gnosis study is compared with the more sober analysis of the basic teachings of Gnosticism of its English adaptation. In the later work, the intense philosophical tone of the original German version almost entirely disappears, the existential analysis of the Dasein of the Gnostic *Geist* is absent, and the focus on the authenticity of *Geist* concerning the processes of objectivation and demythologization is altogether omitted. In this sense, *The Gnostic Religion* is a robust revision of the original project of *Gnosis und spätantiker Geist*.

As we saw above, Jonas did not offer much as an explanation for this shift, noting only that it was executed as part of the post-war preparation of the English publication. Turning now to examine the transcripts of the 1938/39 Hebrew University lecture series on Gnosis, we will see that its methodology, arrangement, and presentation of material better resembles what is found in *The Gnostic Religion*, published two decades later, than what is found in *Gnosis und spätantiker Geist*, published just four years before. What this suggests is that the roots for the transition from the original project of an existential analysis of the manifestation of *Geist* through the Gnostic myth to the later typological analysis of Gnosticism should be sought in Jonas' Jerusalem period.

***

Jonas emigrated to Palestine in the early 1930s and settled in Jerusalem with hope to secure a permanent academic position in the Hebrew University. There he formed the circle of German–Jewish intellectuals in Jerusalem called PILEGESH, together with the orientalist Hans J. Polotsky, the philologist Hans Lewy, and soon after, Gershom Scholem.[36] It quickly became clear that his prospects for securing a permanent academic job were dire.[37] Through his acquaintance with Hugo Bergmann, the first rector of the University, he managed to make some money from teaching philosophy courses on Mt Scopus as an adjunct professor. It is in this context that his lecture series on Gnosis took place.[38]

Jonas' 1938/1939 lecture series consisted of three lectures.[39] The first was dedicated to the historical background for the rise of Gnosticism. Like in the German original, Jonas' presentation was marked by vitalist imagery, interpreting the new forms of syncretism that resulted from the Greek–Orient encounter according to the Spenglerian paradigm, whereby cultures follow an organic life cycle of birth, vitality, depletion, and demise. The second lecture followed the historical thrust of the first and then turned to discuss 'the Gnostic principle' uniting the different manifestations of this syncretism, which was not a repackaging of old ideas but something genuinely new. It continued with a condensed presentation of his reconstruction of the core elements of Gnostic myth and belief system, including its perception of the nature, origin, and fate of the world, the path to salvation, its ontological, astrological, demonological, and magical underpinnings, its antinomism and rebellion against the world, and its transvaluation of contemporary values. The third lecture was dedicated to the Gnostic anthropology, soteriology, and doctrine of God, focusing on the salvific knowledge of the Gnostic secrets and its liberating effects on the soul, the Gnostic praxes of libertinism and asceticism – two opposing ways of denying the value and *nomos* of the world – and the opposition between the world and the good and just God of redemption. Great emphasis is given to the immoralism of the Gnostic 'ethics' and its assault on the natural order of the world through its championing of sinful activities.

Although Jonas struggled with lecturing in Hebrew at the time – in a letter from June 25, 1938, he complained to Scholem about his difficulties preparing for a Hebrew radio address to commemorate Edmund Husserl, who had just passed away – the clarity of presentation is noteworthy.[40] Moreover, the cultural and political setting in which these lectures were delivered left its mark on their content. As was common at the time, Jonas uses the first-person plural manner of speech, referring, for example, to Jewish history as "our history" (10). He also frequently alluded to Jewish sources and drew examples from Jewish history that are absent from his German study (and that were not included in his later English study either). For instance, he compared the process of spiritualization and generalization of particular Oriental traditions and ideas that ensued from the encounter with Hellenism to a similar process that took place in Judaism as a response to the Babylonian exile, as is reflected in the universal sensitivity of second Isaiah. Jonas immediately added, however, that "the Jewish development is, after all, unique. But parallel manifestations can, to some extent, be found elsewhere" (11). The discussion of the relationship between Gnosticism and Judaism is also relatively lengthy in comparison with both the German and the English publications, specifying how the Gnostic anti-creationism and anti-nomism was bound up with its anti-Judaism, as it identified the despised world and its demiurge with the Jewish creator God.

On the one hand, it is not difficult to see that the Hebrew University lecture is based on *Gnosis und spätantiker Geist*. The sources, many of the claims, and the overall descriptive image of Gnosticism clearly recall the German study. At the same time, these lectures are far from an abridged version of the German study or a translation of its main findings into Hebrew. They are, rather, a critical reworking of the recently published study, a reworking that is evident in a shift in method, focus, and style of presentation. Jonas' main and explicit aim in this lecture series was sketching an account of the 'Gnostic principle' that can serve as something like a definition or common denominator for a wide diversity of sources and details, and he pursued this aim with little philosophical analysis and jargon, minimal focus on the Gnostic *Daseinshaltung*, and no mention of the drama of the demythologization of the objectified existential posture of *Geist* exhibited in the Gnostic myth. In other words, what is found in these lectures is an early articulation of the shift that is discernible later on in *The Gnostic Religion*.

Some light can be shed on this shift from the second lecture, where Jonas surveyed the history of the scholarship of Gnosticism through its main milestones (Ferdinand Christian Bauer, Adolf von Harnack, Johann Lorenz Mosheim, and Richard August Reitzenstein) and the ideological factors embedded in them (Protestantism, Hegelianism, Historical Positivism, and Orientalism).[41] This survey is of great interest to anyone wishing to understand how Jonas positioned his own scholarly perspective and contribution vis-à-vis the broader German tradition of Gnosticism scholarship that preceded him.[42] As part of this survey, Jonas remarked that when he began his research, it became increasingly accepted that 'Gnosticism' was syncretistic and best understood as a 'principle' that can be identified in multiple locations, settings, and movements in antiquity. But once the precise content of this unifying spiritual principle was no longer presupposed from the outset – as he believed was common in past scholarship – but rather needed to be scientifically established on the basis of the sources, each scholar suggested his own unifying principle that resulted in a scholarly cacophony. The 'spiritual unity' of Gnosticism, and hence also the possibility of defining it, were in jeopardy, and the question of its 'essence' was subsequently abandoned. The task of his lecture series, Jonas declared, was to address this question anew. This, he openly admitted, constituted a shift from the aim of his recently published *Gnosis und spätantiker Geist*, where he sought to provide "a survey and philosophical analysis of all the available material of the Gnostic mythology" (38). The present lectures, in contrast, aimed to "sketch out some of the general lines of Gnostic thought" (38) and extract from the multiplicity of its manifestations an abstract and unified Gnostic worldview or 'principle.'

Another indication of this shift can be gleaned from how Jonas presented the original prompt for his Gnosis study. According to the account presented in this lecture series, what led him to research these ancient sources was neither Bultmann, whose seminar in Marburg introduced him to Gnosticism, nor Heidegger, who provided him with the existential framework and conceptuality for his study. Rather, the figure whom Jonas credited as the intellectual instigator of his study was Spengler. Speaking in first person, he related that for him, the chapters in *Der Untergang des Abendlandes* interpreting the decay of the spirit of late Greek antiquity and the beginning of a new spiritual period as a process of *pseudomorphosis* were "a real illumination" (38). Because he recognized that Spengler's thesis was posited dogmatically and lacked the appropriate historical evidence, he took it upon himself to prove its scientific veracity. Accordingly, the scholarly agenda driving his study of Gnosticism was not to disclose a crucial stage in the historical realization of *Geist* and help it reach transparency and authenticity, but to corroborate Spengler's historical thesis. Jonas added that Spengler led him to the additional insight that all the spiritual phenomena of this period were all essentially connected and nourished from a singular root. There is no denying Spengler's role in *Gnosis und spätantiker Geist*. But crowning him as the key stimulus for its scholarly intervention does more than just demote the roles of Bultmann and Heidegger in it – it obscures them altogether.[43] It also paints the main impulse of this early work in historical colors, obfuscating its deep philosophical fortitude. In fact, not only was Heidegger not credited for providing the impetus, conceptual framework, philosophical lexicon, and normative edge with which Jonas approached his subject matter, the philosopher goes entirely unmentioned in the lecture series.

To a certain degree, the omission of Heidegger's name in this context should not be entirely surprising. By the time these lectures were delivered, Heidegger's public endorsement of the National Socialist party in 1933 was widely known. It stands to reason that Jonas wished to leave such a tainted figure out of his lectures and conceal his close personal and scholarly affiliation with him, especially in front of a Jewish crowd. It is also likely that this omission reflected Jonas' personal offense to Heidegger's Nazism – a point to which we will return below.[44] But the key issue here, again, is not the number of times Heidegger's name is mentioned, but the broader and more substantial shift reflected by this omission. For not only is Heidegger's name absent, the entire existential framework and analysis of the Gnostic being-in-the-world that was cardinal to Jonas' original work on Gnosticism is absent too. A diligent search in the transcripts of these lectures detects only a few evocations of remnants of existential terminology, and these appear scarcely, in passing, and are marginal to the overall analysis. For example, the discussion of the structural opposition between God and the world devoted no more than a few very brief sentences within a single paragraph to the notion of 'thrownness.' The notion of 'fallenness' is evoked only once. Contrasting the Gnostic contempt toward the world with the Greek and Stoic appreciation of the *cosmos*, Jonas stated:

> All the admiration toward the cosmos that characterized the philosophical idolatry is founded on the feeling of affinity with the forces operating in the world, it is all an affinity between the soul and the cosmic principle; instead of this feeling there is now a complete sense of alienation – instead of the feeling of being at home in the world there is the feeling of being a foreigner in the world.
>
> (61)

Likewise, in the analysis of the Gnosis 'psychology,' he alluded without much elaboration to the soul's 'anxiety' of itself and the world, in contrast to the Stoic security within the realm of the self. In all these cases, the focus is not so much the experience of the Gnostic soul in the world but on how the lords of the celestial spheres govern every aspect of the world, including the internal realm of the self. The Gnostic existential situation as a whole receives only cursory attention in the general thematic and typological description of the Gnostic myth.

It is in fact noteworthy how little the presentation of Gnosticism in these lectures recall the existential apparatus that previously determined Jonas' approach to these sources. Allusions to the existential terminology of *Sein und Zeit* are so few and far between that they can go entirely unnoticed. If one wishes to account for this dramatic minimization of the place and role of existential conceptuality, it is unconvincing to propose that it happened because taught lectures demand a brevity that written scholarship does not – as if Heidegger's mark would have been more clearly recognizable, or an account of the process of objectivation of *Geist*'s subjectivity remained cardinal, had the lecture series consisted of more lectures. What is evident, rather, is that Jonas abandoned his original philosophical–existential methodology and aim in this lecture series and reframed his analysis of Gnosticism in accordance with a methodology, style, and aim that was altogether different from his earlier study.

Thus, in terms of methodology, vocabulary, and agenda, the key differences between *Gnosis und spätantiker Geist* and *The Gnostic Religion* are already found in Jonas' Hebrew University lectures. When this is taken into consideration, it seems justified to assert that the transformation of his approach to Gnosticism from the thoroughly Heideggerian existential project of the German work to the more historical–typological project of the later English work did not take place first in the late 1950s, as implied by the preface to *The Gnostic Religion*, but earlier, in the intellectual context of 1930s in Jerusalem. This does not mean that Jonas was misinforming the readers of the Preface that the specific intellectual and stylistic demands of the English-speaking readership dictated the revision that became *The Gnostic Religion*. What it means is, first, that the revision was not merely a tailoring of Jonas' account of Gnosticism to a new market but reflected an ideational shift in his approach to Gnosticism and philosophy more broadly; and second, that the ideational shift occurred earlier and in the entirely different context but was first publicly reflected in the production of *The Gnostic Religion*. It is unlikely that Jonas prepared his post-war English study on the basis of the notes from his Hebrew University lectures, but the blue-print for his new approach toward Gnosticism was already present in them.

***

The question that must be asked now is, what are the reasons for this transformation in Jonas' scholarly approach toward Gnosticism? Given that Jonas' early Gnosticism study was a doctoral project written under the auspices of two towering figures in Marburg, it is not inconceivable that different facets of the project would change and develop with the passing of time and shift in intellectual surrounding. This reason should certainly be taken into account, but the Jerusalem lectures testify to much more than a natural development from his earlier study; they bespeak a substantive changeover in methodology, terminology, and normative objective.

A number of additional factors should therefore be considered. One is Jonas' reaction to Heidegger's Nazism. Jonas' original project was deeply invested in his mentor's philosophy, but after Heidegger's public endorsement of National Socialism, Jonas reacted with more than just personal disappointment and offense. Claiming for an intimate bond between his mentor's philosophy and politics, he came to suspect the entire project of Heideggerian existential ontology, perceiving it as morally debased and nihilistic. Two decades or so would pass before Jonas published reflections on Heidegger's nihilism, but from 1933, he sought to distance himself from Heidegger and from his philosophy. This was not an easy task, and Jonas continued to grapple with Heidegger throughout his entire philosophical career. While a vocal critique of his philosophy, its mark can be discerned in Jonas' post-war thought, both as a constructive resource and as a negative foil.[45] This is intimately connected to a broader shift in Jonas' general philosophical disposition that can be traced to the mid- and late 1930s. As he himself attested, during this period, he resolved to shift away from an objectifying and theory-based

166 *Daniel M. Herskowitz*

philosophical perspective toward a more concrete, organic, and temporal perspective, one focused on life in its actual worldliness. This was not a shift away from philosophy, but away from a certain kind of abstract philosophy oriented toward spirit, and toward more concrete themes, such as ethics, life, and philosophical biology.[46] The transformation of his approach to Gnosticism may be part of this broader development in philosophical disposition. It is noteworthy that this turn toward a more concrete manner of philosophizing brought Jonas *back into* the vicinity of Heidegger's philosophical outlook, which can explain Jonas' continuous struggle with his thought.[47] But from the perspective of his approach toward Gnosticism, the Heidegger-inflected philosophical project of his original study was evidently abandoned.[48] Originally a philosophical–existential project, it became a historical–typological project in which Heideggerian (and Bultmannian) hues were substantially toned down.[49]

Another factor is the new context of the Jerusalem *intelligentsia* during the 1930s, and specifically the influence of Gershom Scholem. The long and unsteady personal relationship between Jonas and Scholem has been explored in considerable detail and this is not the place to recount it.[50] Pertinent to the present concern is that in 1932, a meeting between the two men took place at Jonas' hotel in London, and following the meeting, Jonas wrote to Scholem, who had returned to his home in Jerusalem, and appended to the letter two texts: his recently published study *Augustin und das paulinische Freiheitsproblem*, which originated in a 1928 seminar he took with Heidegger, and the Introduction and first chapter of his still unpublished Gnosis study. Jonas would later testify that Scholem was the only person to read chapters from his Gnosis study before it was published. He also reported Scholem said that "with each chapter my admiration for the work and its originality increased" (though there is reason to believe Scholem's real reaction was more ambiguous, as will be see below).[51] In another letter from London to Jerusalem, dated December 14, we find Jonas apologizing to Scholem for the overburdened jargon of Heideggerian terminology in his Gnostic research. Jonas had sent Scholem his work with a clear strategic aim: to seek assistance and support in securing an academic affiliation with the recently established Hebrew University where Scholem was a professor, in preparation for Jonas' planned move. It would be too strong a reading to claim that in this letter, Jonas was openly distancing himself from the particular Heideggerian tenor of his early Gnosis study, but it certainly suggests some form of self-reflection on Jonas' part, at least in front of Scholem.

What has not been noted in the well-known account of their relationship is that Scholem's spoken and unspoken presence hovered over Jonas' Hebrew University lectures. Scholem is the only figure mentioned by name in them who is not an ancient author or part of Jonas' survey of the scholarship on Gnosticism. He is mentioned twice. The first time is when Jonas points to similarities in content, style, and structure between a Gnostic adage by Theodotus the Gnostic and the Mishna from Tractate Hagigah 1:2: "Whoever looks at four matters, it would have been better for him had he never entered the world: what is above, what is below, what was before, and what will be after." The comparison between the two dictums, Jonas related to his audience, leaves no doubt as to the Mishnah's dialogue

From Gnosis und spätantiker Geist *to* The Gnostic Religion   167

with Gnostic views, but he does not proceed to develop the comparison between the two texts any further or to pursue the theme of Jewish Gnosticism. "I am not discussing in these lectures Jewish Gnosis at all," he explained, "because Prof. Scholem is dealing with this topic in his own lectures in this very semester" (52). The lecture courses to which Jonas was referring served as the basis for Scholem's *Major Trends in Jewish Mysticism*, where his view on the Gnostic characteristics in ancient Jewish mystical sources is fleshed out in much detail.[52] It is difficult to determine why Jonas devoted so little attention to Jewish Gnosis in these lectures. He certainly had what to say on the topic and it would have fit well with the broader themes he was addressing. The reason may be entirely mundane – lack of time or a preference to focus on other sources or what not – but it is also possible that Jonas was expressing deference toward Scholem as the indisputable authority on Jewish Gnosis and exercising caution not to tread unto his turf.

The second time Scholem is mentioned is in the discussion of the practical aspect of the Gnostic life. Jonas portrayed the Gnostic moral system as based on disdain toward the creator of the world, world negation, and the effort of emancipation from astral influence. It came, as noted above, in the seemingly contradictory forms of asceticism and libertinism. In its libertine expression, Jonas wrote, members of the Gnostic sects would hold secret "anarchical" orgies that would occasionally take the form of acts of licentiousness and promiscuity. The aim of these acts was to deliberately violate the *nomos* of the world and thus to liberate the Gnostic individual from the astral influence. It is in the context of this Gnostic logic, Jonas continued, that the Talmudic pronouncement that "Israel is immune from planetary influence" should be interpreted.[53] He then added:

> Here I take the liberty to quote a passage from my book that Prof. Scholem has translated in his study 'Redemption through Sin' because of the astounding similarities between the Gnostic doctrine of obscenity and the doctrine of obscenity expressed by Jacob Frank to his followers
>
> (106)

– which he then proceeded to do.[54] Scholem's presence is also felt when Jonas referred to medieval Jewish kabbalistic teachings as proof for his claim that the Gnosis ideal of knowledge of divine matters retained an important place in religious thought – a claim neither found in *Gnosis und spätantiker Geist* nor in *The Gnostic Religion* and which Jonas would soon be very hesitant to make, but which was in line with Scholem's scholarship.

Beyond the explicit presence of Scholem, it is noteworthy that the shift in Jonas' approach toward Gnosticism attested in this lecture series – from an existentially focused analysis centered on the objectivation in Gnostic myth and the march toward authenticity of *Geist* to a typological study more comfortably situated within the broad subfield of the history of ancient religions – was a methodological refashioning that better aligned him with the critical–historical methodological framework that governed the study of ancient religion at the Hebrew University at the time and which was particularly affirmed by Scholem. By 1938, Scholem had already published a long list of studies on Kabbalah as well as a number of critical appraisals of the work done by previous scholars on the subject. The common targets of his ire were nineteenth-century *Wissenschaft* scholars whose rationalistic biases and scorn toward Kabbala led to a lack of knowledge of the sources, mistaken judgments, and a dearth of 'objective research' as he saw it. In his own work, Scholem sought to cleanse scholarship from the excessive speculative nature of previous generations and from obvious ideological coloring – be it theological, anti-theological, or any other form of apologetics – and to secure its generalizations on valid academic foundations, based on rigorous historical and textual scholarship. As he stated in his monumental work *Major Trends in Jewish Mysticism* – published in 1941 on the basis of research and teaching he was doing in the Hebrew University in 1938 – "The time has come to reclaim this derelict area [of kabbalah scholarship] and to apply to it the strict standards of historical research."[55] In a later entry to the *Encyclopaedia Judaica* entitled "Scholarship and the Kabbalah," Scholem would identify his own approach toward Kabbalah as part of the 'school of historical criticism.'[56] While Scholem's claim for objectivity and neutrality masked a distinct ideological agenda, his historical–critical methodological approach, together with his general dismissal of excessive focus on subjective experience and the existential perspective more broadly, may have contributed to way in which Jonas modified his Gnosis study during this period in Jerusalem.[57]

But while Jonas drew closer to the methodological perspective guiding Scholem's work, it does not follow that he shared Scholem's understanding of Gnosticism. He did not, and this scholarly divergence would soon further strain their personal relationship. Jonas held what can be termed a minimalistic understanding of Gnosticism, perceiving it as a limited and historically contained spiritual movement that encapsulated the 'Spirit of Late Antiquity'; Scholem held what can be termed a maximalist understanding of Gnosticism, perceiving it as a formal spiritual tendency that can be identified in various different historical epochs and spiritual contexts. In a letter to Jonas, Scholem described their differences aptly: "Your definition of Gnosticism is not mine [...] For me gnosis is a constantly self-repeating structure within religious thinking, for you it is a unique historical-philosophical phenomenon."[58] While they shared some basic assumptions at the time, Scholem was evidently suspicious of the early methodological foundations of Jonas' scholarship on Gnosticism.[59] It is not without reason that when Scholem quoted the paragraph from Jonas' *Gnosis und spätantiker Geist* on the libertinism and licentiousness of Gnostic immorality in his essay "Redemption through Sin" which Jonas then quoted in his own lectures, he referred to him not as a scholar of Gnosticism or as a historian of ancient religions but as "the philosopher Hans Jonas." Thus, while in his later work on Gnosticism Jonas presented himself less like a philosopher and more like a historian of ancient religion – less like a Heidegger and more like a Scholem – he did not turn his back on philosophy. Jonas remained a philosopher, but he no longer approached Gnosticism *as* a philosopher but as a historian of religion. For Scholem, however, Jonas remained too much of a philosopher and not enough of a philologist–historian. In this, Scholem was not altogether wrong, as Heideggerian resonances were not entirely abolished

From Gnosis und spätantiker Geist *to* The Gnostic Religion   169

from Jonas' later approach toward Gnosticism and Jonas himself admitted to not being up to date with the latest developments in the relevant scholarship. In any event, the modification of Jonas' methodological approach toward Gnosticism can be partially explained by the personal and professional influence of Scholem and, perhaps, his hopes to land a permanent job at the Hebrew University.

***

This chapter has dealt with three texts on Gnosticism in three languages: one German, one English, and one Hebrew. The first has been basically neglected, the second is highly influential, the third entirely unknown. All three were written by Jonas in different locations and contexts: one in interwar Germany in the fermenting context of the Marburg intellectual world; one in the peripheral Jerusalem as part of the burgeoning intellectual culture in the Zionist *Yeshuv*; one in the more stable waters of post-war North America. The German and the Hebrew texts are closer to each other chronologically, but the projects they pursue are dramatically dissimilar, as the Hebrew betrays considerable proximity to the English. As a general statement, it can be said that Jonas' interpretation of Gnosticism in *Gnosis und spätantiker Geist* is governed by two hermeneutical nodes: the historical and the philosophical–existential, whereby the former is in service of the latter. In the English version, the historical node remains intact and is buttressed by a typological focus, while the philosophical–existential is markedly minimized. This shift constituted a major development in Jonas' intellectual attitude in general and in his approach toward Gnosticism in particular, one which amounts to an abandonment of one project and the installation of a rather different one. On the basis of the analysis above, it stands to reason to trace the period of this shift to Jonas' Jerusalem years, where it found its initial expression in his Hebrew University lectures. If so, then it can be concluded that the years in Jerusalem were not, as it is commonly supposed, a transitional and largely inconsequential period in Jonas' intellectual biography, stationed between the two philosophically fertile periods of his formative years in Marburg and his mature years in North America. Rather, Jonas' years in Jerusalem emerge as a fateful period, encompassing important developments and shifts that would leave a decisive mark on his intellectual trajectory.

Notes

1   On Jonas during this period, see Christian Wiese, *The Life and Thought of Hans Jonas: Jewish Dimensions* (Hanover, NH: University Press of New England, 2007); Steven M. Wasserstrom, "Hans Jonas in Marburg, 1928," *The Legacy of Hans Jonas: Judaism and the Phenomenon of Life*, eds. Hava Tirosh-Samuelson and Christian Wiese (Leiden: Brill, 2010), 39–72. On Bultmann and Heidegger in these early years, see Judith Wolfe, *Heidegger and Theology* (London: Bloomsbury, 2014), 152–155; Idem, *Heidegger's Eschatology: Theological Horizons in Martin Heidegger's Early Work* (Oxford: Oxford University Press, 2013); William D. Dennison, *The Young Bultmann: Context for his Understanding of God, 1884–1925* (New York: Peter Lang, 2008), 132–140; Rudolf Bultmann and Heidegger Martin, *Briefwechsel, 1925–1975*, eds. Andreas Großmann and Christof Landmesser (Tübingen: Mohr Siebeck, 2009).

2   Hans Jonas, *Gnosis und spätantiker Geist Teil I* (Göttingen: Vandenhoeck & Ruprecht, 1934); Hans Jonas, *Gnosis und spätantiker Geist II. Von der Mythologie zur mystischen Philosophie* (Göttingen: Vandenhoeck & Ruprecht, 1954). General overviews of these works can be found in Rainer Kampling, "Gnosis und spätantiker Geist I: Die mythologische Gnosis (1934)" and Elad Lapidot, "Gnosis und spätantiker Geist II. Von der Mythologie zur mystischen Philosophie (1954)", *Hans Jonas Handbuch: Leben, Werk, Wirkung*, eds. Michael Bongardt, Holger Burckhart, John-Stewart Gordon, Jürgen Nielsen-Sikora (J.B Meltzer, 2021), 83–87 and 88–95, respectively. On the second part of Jonas' early Gnosis study and on the journey of its publication, see James M. Robinson, "Introduction to Hans Jonas," in Jonas, *Gnosis und spätantiker Geist II*, 11–22.
3   One example of this tendency is the analysis of Jonas' account of Gnosticism in Karen L. King, *What Is Gnosticism?* (Cambridge, MA: Harvard University Press, 2003), 115–137.
4   Hans Jonas, *The Gnostic Religion: The Message of the Alien God and the Beginnings of Christianity* (Boston, MA: Beacon Press, 1958), xvii.
5   Jonas, *The Gnostic Religion*, xvii–xviii. Bultmann, who wrote the 'forward' for the first part of *Gnosis und spätantiker Geist*, felt that an apology to the reader was due for Jonas' extensive and dense recourse to Heideggerian terminology.
6   The Philosophical Archives of the University of Konstanz, Hans Jonas Papers, Call number HJ-38-1, Hans Jonas archive, University of Konstanz. I would like to thank Elad Lapidot for informing me of the existence of these transcripts and for the initial insight that prompted the research on this study. I would also like to thank Jonathan Cahana for providing me with the file of these transcripts.
7   For example, Jonas, *Gnosis I*, 70–74; Oswald Spengler, *Decline of the West*, vol. II (Oxford: Oxford University Press, 1991), 189.
8   Jonas, *Gnosis I*, 9.
9   Jonas, *Gnosis I*, 13.
10 Jonas, *Gnosis I*, 13.
11 Jonas, *Gnosis I*, 15. For an analysis of the relation between the historical and transcendental accounts of Jonas' description of Gnosticism, see in the present volume, Nathalie Frogneux, "A Historical Transcendental at the Heart of Jonas' Research on Gnosticism."
12 Jonas, *Gnosis I*, 89.
13 A good overview in English of this notion in Jonas' early study is Roger A. Johnson, *The Origins of Demythologization: Philosophy and Historiography in the Theology of Rudolf Bultmann* (Leiden: Brill, 1974), 169–231.
14 Jonas, *Gnosis II*, 4–5.
15 Jonas, *Gnosis I*, 88.
16 Jonas, *Gnosis II*, 6–7.
17 Jonas, *Gnosis I*, 88.
18 Jonas, *Gnosis II*, 12.
19 Hans Jonas, *Augustin und das paulinische Freihitsproblem: ein philosophischer Beitrag zur Genesis der christlich-abendlandischen Freiheitsidee* (Gottingen: Vandenhoeck & Ruprecht, 1930), 67.
20 Jonas, *Gnosis II*, 9.
21 Jonas, *Gnosis II*, 9.
22 Bultmann explicitly mentioned Jonas in the context of his own project of demythologization in his programmatic 1941 essay. See Bultmann, "New Testament and Mythology: The Problem of Demythologizing the New Testament Proclamation," *New Testament and Mythology and Other Basic Writing*, ed. Schubert M. Ogden (Philadelphia, PA: Fortress Press, 1984), 15. On the relation between Jonas and Bultmann, see the essays by Michael Bongardt, Andreas Grossmann, and Luca Settimo, in the present volume. A great deal has been written on Bultmann's notion of demythologization. For example, Johnson, *The Origins of Demythologization*; Schubert M. Ogden, *Christ without Myth: A Study Based on the Theology of Rudolf Bultmann* (New York: Harper, 1961), 45–46; Anthony C. Thiselton, *The Two Horizons: New Testament Hermeneutics and*

Philosophical Description with Special Reference to Heidegger, Bultmann, Gadamer, and Wittgenstein (Grand Rapids, MI: Eerdmans, 1980); David W. Congdon, *Mission of Demythologizing: Rudolf Bultmann's Dialectical Theology* (Minneapolis, MN: Fortress Press, 2015). A study of Bultmann that sheds light on Jonas' work as well is Michael Waldstein, "The Foundations of Bultmann's Work," *Communio* 14 (1987): 115–145.

23 On Jonas' place in the Marburg intellectual setting, see the essays collected in the volume *Hans Jonas Und Die Marburger Hermeneutik*, eds. Andreas Großmann and Malte Dominik Krüger (Frankfurt am Main: Vittorio Klostermann Verlag, 2023); Elad Lapidot "Geschichtsphilosophische Einleitung," *Kritische Gesamtausgabe der Werke von Hans Jonas*, Band IV/1, *Gnosis und spätantiker Geist*, hg. von E. Lapidot und R. Kampling (Freiburg/Berlin/Wien, forthcoming).

24 Hans Jonas, *Memoirs*, ed. Christian Wiese, trans. Krishna Winston (Waltham, MA: Brandeis University Press, 2008), 66.

25 Heidegger briefly discusses 'myth' in *Being and Time*, trans. John Macquarrie and Edward Robinson (New York: Harper & Row, 2008), 112–113; see also his review of Cassirer's work, Martin Heidegger, Review of *Philosophie der symbolischen Formen*, Vol. II, by Ernst Cassirer, *Deutsche Literaturzeitung*, V (1928), 1000–1012.

26 According to Jonas' testimony, Jacob Taubes was the person who got Beacon Press to commission him to write a book on Gnosticism in English. See Jonas, *Memoirs*, 168–169. On the publication history of Jonas' English book and its influence on American scholarship, see Jonathan Cahana-Blum, "Gnosis. Die Botschaft des fremden Gottes (1958)," *Hans Jonas-Handbuch: Leben–Werk–Wirkung*, eds. Michael Bongardt, Holger Burckhart, John-Stewart Gordon, and Jürgen Nielsen-Sikora (Berlin: J. B. Metzler Verlag, 2021), 96–103. See also Jerry Z. Muller, *Professor of Apocalypse: The Many Lives of Jacob Taubes* (Princeton, NJ: Princeton University, 2022), especially 181–236.

27 According to King, Jonas' greatest contribution to Gnosticism research was "to shift the discussion of Gnosticism away from genealogy to typology." King, *What Is Gnosticism?* 12. See also Jonas, "Delimitation of the Gnostic Phenomenon – Typological and Historical," *The Origins of Gnosticism / Le origini dello gnosticismo* (Leiden: Brill, 1967), 90–108. For a critique of Jonas' account of Gnosticism, see Michael Waldstein, "Hans Jonas' Construct 'Gnosticism': Analysis and Critique," *Journal of Early Christian Studies* 8.3 (2000): 341–372.

28 Jonas, *The Gnostic Religion*, 26.

29 Jonas, *Gnosis I*, 12.

30 Jonas, *The Gnostic Religion*, 26.

31 Scholars of religion in antiquity who describe Jonas' account of Gnosticism as 'Heideggerian' on the basis of *The Gnosic Religion* might be surprised to learn that it is a dramatically de-Heideggerized version in comparison with the original German study. An offshoot of the minimization of the existentialistic hermeneutic in Jonas' account of Gnosis is the lack of reference to the Nietzschean trope of *Ressentiment* in the English version of his study (an absence also characterizing the earlier Hebrew transcripts). Originally, he interpreted Gnosis as a 'revolutionary position resulting from the spirit of resentment' that was 'directed against the Jewish God of creation and of the law.' On this trope in Jonas' early study, see Micha Brumlik, "Ressentiment – A Few Motifs in Hans Jonas's Early Book on Gnosticism," *The Legacy of Hans Jonas*, 73–90. The Nietzschean notion of transvaluation remains operative in Jonas' understanding of the Gnostic revolt against the value systems of its time.

32 Jonas, *The Gnostic Religion*, 26.

33 Jonas, *The Gnostic Religion*, 149, 62, 63.

34 Jonas, *The Gnostic Religion*, 64.

35 This article was originally published as "Gnosticism and Modern Nihilism" in 1952 by the journal *Social Research*, and then republished, with some minor changes and a new introduction, under this title, as an epilogue to the second edition of *The Gnostic Religion*. It was then republished again, unchanged, as the ninth essay of Jonas' *The*

Phenomenon of Life: Toward a Philosophical Biology (Chicago, IL and London: Northwestern University Press, 1966), 211–234. The Jonas–Heidegger–Gnosticism triangle is probably the most explored area of research in the study of Jonas' thought. See for example Daniel M. Herskowitz, *Heidegger and His Jewish Reception* (Cambridge: Cambridge University Press, 2020), 103–108; idem, "Reading Heidegger Against the Grain: Hans Jonas on Existentialism, Gnosticism, and Modern Science," *Modern Intellectual History* 19.2 (June 2022): 527–550; Willem Styfhals, *No Spiritual Investment in the World: Gnosticism and Postwar German Philosophy* (Ithaca, NY: Cornell University Press, 2019); Benjamin Lazier, *God Interrupted: Heresy and the European Imagination between the World Wars* (Princeton, NJ: Princeton University Press, 2008), 27–59; Elad Lapidot, "Hans Jonas' Work on Gnosticism as Counterhistory," *Philosophical Readings* 9.1 (2017): 61–68; Yotam Hotam, "Overcoming the Mentor: Heidegger's Present and the Presence of Heidegger in Karl Löwith's and Hans Jonas' Postwar Thought," *History of European Ideas* 35 (2009): 253–264; Eric Jacob, *Martin Heidegger und Hans Jonas: Die Metaphysik der Subjektivität und die Krise der technologischen Zivilisation* (Tübingen/Basel: Francke, 1996); Christian Wiese, "'Revolt Against Escapism': Hans Jonas's Response to Martin Heidegger," in *Heidegger's Jewish Followers: Essays on Hannah Arendt, Leo Strauss, Hans Jonas, and Emmanuel Levinas*, ed. Samuel Fleischacker (Pittsburgh, PA, 2008), 151–177; Micha Brumlik, *Die Gnostiker. Der Traum von der Selbsterlösung des Menschen* (Frankfurt am Main, 1992); Lawrence Vogel, "Hans Jonas's Diagnosis of Nihilism: The Case of Heidegger," *International Journal of Philosophical Studies* 3.1 (1995): 55–72.

36 See Christian Wiese, "'For a Time I was Privileged to Enjoy his Friendship:' The Ambivalent Relationship between Hans Jonas and Gershom Scholem," *The Leo Baeck Institute Year Book* 49 (2004): 25–58; Wiese, *The Life and Thought of Hans Jonas*, 10-23; Noam Zadoff, "'Mit Witz in Ernst und Ernst in Witz'" – Der Jerusalemer PILEGESH-Kreis," *Jüdischer Almanach: Humor*, ed. Gisela Dachs (Frankfurt am Main: Jüdischer Verlag, 2004), 50–60.

37 Jonas was eventually offered a permanent position at the Hebrew University, but only many years later, in 1951, on Scholem's recommendation. By that time, he had already settled in Canada, and after much deliberation, decided to reject the offer. This decision strained his personal relationship with Scholem.

38 Information on the immediate background of this lecture series is scarce. In a short resume that is found in the personal file on Jonas in the Hebrew University Central Archive, dating 1947, it is said that "in 1938 Jonas was invited by the University to deliver the memorial lecture for his teacher Edmund Husserl upon his passing away. In the academic year of 1938/39 (Jonas) gave two consecutive series of guest-lectures, on Gnosticism and on Neo-Platonist philosophy." Hans Jonas, personal file, The Hebrew University Central Archive, 1947. The Hebrew University archive does not hold a file on Jonas from the 1930s. I'd like to thank Ofer Tzemach from the Hebrew University archive for his assistance.

39 The archival file of the lecture series consists of 130 or so pages of typed transcription of the three lectures, including a number of Hebrew translations of Gnostic texts and a few handwritten notes. All references in parentheses in the body of the text refer to the transcript page numbers as it is found in the archival file.

40 For this letter, see Weise, *Jonas: Jewish Dimensions*, 12. Jonas' address was published in Hebrew as "Husserl and the Problem of Ontology," *Moznayim* 7 (1938): 581–589. In English: Hans Jonas, "Edmund Husserl and the Ontological Question," *Études phénomenologiques* 17 (2001): 5–20. See also his piece in Hebrew Jochanan (Hans) Jonas, "Edmund Husserl," vol. 21, *Turim*, September 7, 1938, 2. An analysis of the different versions of this obituary can be found in the present volume, Elad Lapidot, "Hans Jonas from Husserl to Heidegger: in Search for Judeo-Christian Ethics." See also Daniel M. Herskowitz, "The Husserl-Heidegger Relationship in the Jewish Imagination," *Jewish Quarterly Review* 110 (2020): 491–522.

From Gnosis und spätantiker Geist *to* The Gnostic Religion   173

41 Interestingly, Jonas does not mention Bultmann in this august list of scholars of Gnosticism. The mark of Bultmann in Jonas' lectures is felt, however, in his discussion of the presence of Gnostic layers in the Gospel of John and in Paul's letters.
42 See Johannes Zachhuber, "Hans Jonas on Gnosis and Late Antiquity: In Search of the Spirit of an Epoch," in the present volume.
43 Jonas, *Gnosis I*, 9. See also Jonas, *Memoirs*, 86–87.
44 While Jonas broke ties with Heidegger after 1933 and kept his distance for decades, he remained in contact with Bultmann, toward whom he had great appreciation and respect, for the rest of his life, save the turbulent years between 1938 and 1952, parts of which Jonas served in the military. Some of Jonas's writings on Bultmann include Jonas, "Is Faith Still Possible? Memories of Rudolf Bultmann and Reflections on the Philosophical Aspects of His Work," *The Harvard Theological Review* 75.1 (1982): 1–23; Hans Jonas, "Myth and Mysticism," in *Philosophical Essays: From Ancient Creed to Technological Man* (Hoboken, NJ: Prentice Hall, 1974), 291–304; also relevant is his "Philosophische Meditation über Paulus, Römerbrief, Kapitel 7," *Zeit und Geschichte. Dankesgabe an Rudolf Bultmann*, ed. E. Dinkler (Tübingen 1964), 557–570. The Bultmann-Jonas correspondence has recently been published. See *Rudolf Bultmann, Hans Jonas: Briefwechsel 1928–1976*, ed. Andreas Grossman (Tübingen: Mohr Siebeck, 2020).
45 His unheralded assault on Heidegger's popularity among Christian theologians in a 1964 conference in Drew University, "Heidegger and Theology," was reported on by the *New York Times*. See Hans Jonas, "Heidegger and Theology," *The Review of Metaphysics* 18.2 (1964): 207–233. On this lecture and its reception, see Daniel M. Herskowitz, "Hans Jonas's 'Heidegger and Theology' as Text and Event," *Hans Jonas und die Marburger Hermeneutik*, 83–109; idem, "Secularization and de-legitimation: Hans Jonas and Karl Löwith on Martin Heidegger," *History of European Ideas* (forthcoming).
46 This is how Jonas put it: "Heidegger's conduct in the year 1933. Does that have anything to do with philosophy? In my opinion, yes. […] [W]hen the most profound thinker of my time fell into step with the thundering march of Hitler's brown battalions, it was not merely a bitter personal disappointment for me but in my eyes a debacle for philosophy. Philosophy itself, not only a man, had declared bankruptcy." See Hans Jonas, "Philosophy at the End of the Century: Retrospect and Prospect," *Mortality and Morality: A Search for the Good after Auschwitz* (Evanston, IL, 1996), 49.
47 In the present volume, Lapidot provides a complementary perspective on the shift in Jonas's philosophical attitude during this period to which I am calling attention. See Lapidot, "Hans Jonas from Husserl to Heidegger."
48 Together with the abandonment of the original Gnosticism project was an abandonment of the general sympathy to the Gnostic project which marked his early approach. In his 1952 "Gnosticism and Modern Nihilism" Jonas renounced both Gnosticism and Heidegger and he appended this essay to *The Gnostic Religion* in 1958 book to add a clear negative normative valuation to its historical-typological presentation. It is difficult to find any trace of sympathy for Gnosticism in the Hebrew University lectures either.
49 I stress the minimization and toning down of existential terminology, impulses, and aims, and the abandonment of the overall existential approach toward Gnosticism, but as noted, it would be a mistake to say that Heidegger's mark on Jonas's understanding of Gnosticism has been entirely eliminated. The abandonment of the original philosophical project concerning Gnosticism is also demonstrated by the fact that Jonas allowed the second part of his German Gnosticism work to be published in 1954 without ever actually finishing it or even doing any substantial work on it to prepare it for publication. This was typical of Jonas, who would frequently publish and republish texts he had written in the past without any serious reworking.
50 Wiese, "'For a Time I was Privileged to Enjoy his Friendship'."
51 Jonas, *Memoirs*, 86.
52 Gershom Scholem, *Major Trends in Jewish Mysticism* (New York: Schocken Books, 1941).
53 Babylonian Talmud, *Tractate Shabbat*, 156a.

54 No reference to Scholem appears in the discussion of the matter in *The Gnostic Religion*. In its English translation, see Scholem, "Redemption through Sin," 133.
55 Scholem, *Trends in Jewish Mysticism,* 2–3. In the Preface to the First Edition, Scholem wrote: "More than twenty years have passed since I began to devote my life to the study of Jewish mysticism and especially of Kabbalism. It was a beginning in more than one sense, for the task which confronted me necessitated a vast amount of spade-work in a field strewn with ruins and by no means ripe as yet for the constructive labours of the builder of a system. Both as to historical fact and philological analysis there was pioneer work to be done, often of the most primitive and elementary kind. Rapid bird's eye syntheses and elaborate speculations on shaky premises had to give way to the more modest work of laying the secure foundations of valid generalization." Scholem, *Major Trends in Jewish Mysticism,* vii. See also Amir Engel, *Gershom Scholem: An Intellectual Biography* (Chicago, IL: University of Chicago, 2017).
56 Scholem, "Scholarship and the Kabbalah," *Kabbalah* (Jerusalem, 1974), 201–203.
57 Shaul Magid, "Gershom Scholem's Ambivalence toward Mystical Experience and His Critique of Martin Buber in Light of Hans Jonas and Martin Heidegger," *The Journal of Jewish Thought and Philosophy* 4 (1995): 245–269. In an article on Scholem's early years in the Hebrew University, Katz urged scholars to differentiate between periods in Scholem's life and influence and not to retroject his later academic dominance and recognition onto earlier periods of his scholarly life. See Shaul Katz, "Gershom Shalom Ve'Techilat Darko Ba'Oniversita Ha'Ivrit," 3 *Katharsis* (Spring 2005): 1–16. This cautioning is duly noted, but even if Scholem had not yet achieved the academic-institutional success by this time, he was already a dominant and overbearing figure for Jonas personally as well as, potentially, his entry way into the Hebrew University. On Scholem's post-war rise to academic stardom, see Yaacob Dweck, "Gershom Scholem and America," *New German Critique* 132, 44.3 (November 2017): 61–82.
58 He would soon accuse Jonas's research on Gnosticism of being "too strongly inspired by Christianity." Gershom Scholem, "Letter to Hans Jonas of November 14, 1977," in *Briefe: 1971–1982,* ed. I. Shedletzky (Munich: C.H. Beck, 2000), 160. Jonas's critique of the French scholar Gilles Quispel is rightly understood as an indirect critique of Scholem. Jonas, "Response to G. Quispel's 'Gnosticism and the New Testament'," in J. Philip Hyatt (ed.), *The Bible in Modern Scholarship* (London: Carey Kingsgate Press, 1965), 279–293. For a comparison of their conceptions of Gnosticism, see Elisabeth Hamacher, *Gershom Scholem und die Allgemeine Religionsgeschichte* (Berlin, New York: de Gruyter, 1999), 184–195.
59 Moshe Idel, "Rabbinism Versus Kabbalism: On G. Scholem's Phenomenology of Judaism," *Modern Judaism* 11 (1991): 281–296; Moshe Idel, *Hasidism: Between Ecstasy and Magic* (Albany: 1995), 31–146.

Bibliography

Aland, Barbara (Ed.). *Gnosis: Festschrift für Hans Jonas*, Gottingen: Vandenhoeck und Ruprecht, 1978.
Bornkamm, Heinrich (Ed.). *Imago Dei: Beiträge zur theologischen Anthropologie*, Giessen: A. Töpelmann, 1932.
Brumlik, Micha. *Die Gnostiker. Der Traum von der Selbsterlösung des Menschen*, Frankfurt am Main: S. Fischer Verlag, 1992.
Brumlik, Micha. "Ressentiment – A Few Motifs in Hans Jonas's Early Book on Gnosticism," in Hava Tirosh-Samuelson and Christian Wiese (eds.), *The Legacy of Hans Jonas: Judaism and the Phenomenon of Life* (Leiden: Brill, 2010), 73–90.
Bultmann, Rudolf. *Glauben Und Verstehen*, Tübingen: Mohr, 1933.

Bultmann, Rudolf. *Kerygma and Myth: A Theological Debate*, ed. Hans Werner Bartsch. London: S.P.C.K., 1972.
Dennison, William D. *The Young Bultmann: Context for His Understanding of God, 1884–1925*, New York: Peter Lang, 2008.
Frogneux, Nathalie. "A Historical Transcendental at the Heart of Jonas' Research on Gnosticism." 102–122.
Grossman, Andreas, and Krüger, Malte Dominik (eds.), *Hans Jonas Und Die Marburger Hermeneutik*, Frankfurt am Main: Vittorio Klostermann Verlag, 2023.
Hamacher, Elisabeth. *Gershom Scholem und die Allgemeine Religionsgeschichte*, Berlin, New York: de Gruyter, 1999.
Herskowitz, Daniel M. "Hans Jonas's 'Heidegger and Theology' as Text and Event," in Grossman, Andreas, and Krüger, Malte Dominik (eds.), *Hans Jonas und die Marburger Hermeneutik* (Frankfurt am Main: Vittorio Klostermann Verlag, 2023), 83–109.
Herskowitz, Daniel M. *Heidegger and His Jewish Reception*, Cambridge: Cambridge University Press, 2020.
Herskowitz, Daniel M. "The Husserl-Heidegger Relationship in the Jewish Imagination," *Jewish Quarterly Review* 110 (2020): 491–522.
Herskowitz, Daniel M. "Reading Heidegger against the Grain: Hans Jonas on Existentialism, Gnosticism, and Modern Science," *Modern Intellectual History* 19.2 (June 2022): 527–550.
Hotam, Yotam. "Overcoming the Mentor: Heidegger's Present and the Presence of Heidegger in Karl Löwith's and Hans Jonas' Postwar Thought," *History of European Ideas* 35 (2009): 253–264.
Idel, Moshe. *Hasidism: Between Ecstasy and Magic*, Albany: State University of New York Press, 1995.
Idel, Moshe. "Rabbinism versus Kabbalism: On G. Scholem's Phenomenology of Judaism," *Modern Judaism* 11 (1991): 281–296.
Jacob, Eric. *Martin Heidegger und Hans Jonas: Die Metaphysik der Subjektivität und die Krise der technologischen Zivilisation*, Tübingen/Basel: Francke, 1996.
Johnson, Roger A. *The Origins of Demythologization: Philosophy and Historiography in the Theology of Rudolf Bultmann*, Leiden: Brill, 1974.
Jonas, Hans. "Delimitation of the Gnostic Phenomenon – Typological and Historical," in Ugo Bianchi (ed.), *The Origins of Gnosticism / Le origini dello gnosticismo* (Leiden: Brill, 1967), 90–108.
Jonas, Hans. *Gnosis und spätantiker Geist Teil I*, Göttingen: Vandenhoeck & Ruprecht, 1934.
Jonas, Hans. *Gnosis und spätantiker Geist II. Von der Mythologie zur mystischen Philosophie*, Göttingen: Vandenhoeck & Ruprecht, 1954.
Jonas, Hans. *The Gnostic Religion: The Message of the Alien God and the Beginnings of Christianity*, Boston, MA: Beacon Press, 1958.
Jonas, Hans. "Heidegger and Theology," *The Review of Metaphysics*, 18.2 (1964): 207–233.
Jonas, Hans. "Is Faith Still Possible? Memories of Rudolf Bultmann and Reflections on the Philosophical Aspects of His Work," *Harvard Theological Review*, 75.1 (1982): 1–23.
Jonas, Hans. *Memoirs*, ed. Christian Wiese, trans. Krishna Winston, Waltham, MA: Brandeis University Press, 2008.
Jonas, Hans. "Myth and Mysticism," *Philosophical Essays: From Ancient Creed to Technological Man* (Hoboken, NJ: Prentice Hall, 1974), 291–304.
Jonas, Hans. "Philosophische Meditation über Paulus, Römerbrief, Kapitel 7," in E. Dinkler (ed.), *Zeit und Geschichte. Dankesgabe an Rudolf Bultmann* (Tübingen: Mohr Siebeck, 1964), 557–570.

Jonas, Hans. "Philosophy at the End of the Century: Retrospect and Prospect," in Lawrence Vogel (ed.), *Mortality and Morality: A Search for the Good after Auschwitz* (Evanston, IL: Northwestern University Press, 1996), 41–55.

Jonas, Hans, and Scholem, Gershom. *Briefwechsel 1928–1976*, ed. Andreas Grossman, Tübingen: Mohr Siebeck, 2020.

Katz, Shaul. "Gershom Shalom Ve'Techilat Darko Ba'Oniversita Ha'Ivrit," *Katharsis* 3 (Spring 2005): 1–16.

King, Karen L. *What Is Gnosticism?* Cambridge, MA: Harvard University Press, 2003.

Lapidot, Elad. "Geschichtsphilosophische Einleitung," *Kritische Gesamtausgabe der Werke von Hans Jonas*, Band IV/1, *Gnosis und spätantiker Geist*, hg. von E. Lapidot und R. Kampling. Freiburg/Berlin/Wien, Forthcoming.

Lapidot, Elad. "Gnosis und spätantiker Geist II. Von der Mythologie zur mystischen Philosophie (1954)," in Michael Bongardt, Holger Burckhart, John-Stewart Gordon, and Jürgen Nielsen-Sikora (eds.), *Hans Jonas Handbuch: Leben, Werk, Wirkung* (Berlin: J.B Meltzer, 2021), 88–95.

Lapidot, Elad. "Hans Jonas' Work on Gnosticism as Counterhistory," *Philosophical Readings* 9.1 (2017): 61–68.

Magid, Shaul. "Gershom Scholem's Ambivalence toward Mystical Experience and His Critique of Martin Buber in Light of Hans Jonas and Martin Heidegger," *The Journal of Jewish Thought and Philosophy*, 4 (1995): 245–269.

Muller, Jerry Z. *Professor of Apocalypse: The Many Lives of Jacob Taubes*, Princeton, NJ: Princeton University, 2022.

Robinson, James M. "Introduction to Hans Jonas," in Hans Jonas (ed.), *Gnosis und spätantiker Geist II Von der Mythologie zur mystischen Philosophie* (Göttingen: Vandenhoeck & Ruprecht, 1954), 11–22.

Spengler, Oswald. *Decline of the West, vol. II*, Oxford: Oxford University Press, 1991.

Styfhals, Willem. *No Spiritual Investment in the World: Gnosticism and Postwar German Philosophy*, Ithaca, NY: Cornell University Press, 2019.

Thiselton, Anthony C. *The Two Horizons: New Testament Hermeneutics and Philosophical Description with Special Reference to Heidegger, Bultmann, Gadamer, and Wittgenstein*, Grand Rapids, MI: Eerdmans, 1980.

Vogel, Lawrence. "Hans Jonas's Diagnosis of Nihilism: The Case of Heidegger," *International Journal of Philosophical Studies* 3.1 (1995): 55–72.

Waldstein, Michael. "The Foundations of Bultmann's Work," *Communio* 14 (1987): 115–145.

Waldstein, Michael. "Hans Jonas' Construct 'Gnosticism': Analysis and Critique," *Journal of Early Christian Studies* 8.3 (2000): 341–372.

Wiese, Christian. "'For a Time I was Privileged to Enjoy his Friendship:' The Ambivalent Relationship between Hans Jonas and Gershom Scholem," *The Leo Baeck Institute Year Book* 49 (2004): 25–58.

Wiese, Christian. *The Life and Thought of Hans Jonas: Jewish Dimensions*, Hanover, NH: University Press of New England, 2007.

Wiese, Christian. "'Revolt Against Escapism': Hans Jonas's Response to Martin Heidegger," in Samuel Fleischacker (ed.), *Heidegger's Jewish Followers: Essays on Hannah Arendt, Leo Strauss, Hans Jonas, and Emmanuel Levinas* (Pittsburgh, PA: Duquesne University Press, 2008), 151–177.

Wolfe, Judith. *Heidegger and Theology*, London: Bloomsbury, 2014.

Wolfe, Judith. *Heidegger's Eschatology: Theological Horizons in Martin Heidegger's Early Work*, Oxford: Oxford University Press, 2013.

Zachhuber, Johannes. "Hans Jonas on Gnosis and Late Antiquity: In Search of the Spirit of an Epoch." Hans Jonas Papers, Call number HJ-38-1, Hans Jonas archive, University of Konstanz.

Zadoff, Noam. "'Mit Witz in Ernst und Ernst in Witz'" – Der Jerusalemer PILEGESH-Kreis," in Gisela Dachs (ed.), *Jüdischer Almanach: Humor* (Frankfurt am Main: Jüdischer Verlag, 2004), 50–60.

11 Once a Gnostic, Always a Gnostic

The Persistence of Gnosticism in Hans Jonas' Post-War Thought

Agata Bielik-Robson

Had Jonas ever overcome his fascination with Gnosis? According to the prevailing opinion among Jonas' scholars, his later reflections on responsibility to nature should be inscribed in the tendency characteristic of many thinkers called by Richard Wolin 'Heideggers children'[1]: initially marked by the Gnostic aura of the Weimar era, they all eventually put themselves to the task of 'overcoming Gnosticism,' which would leave the dualistic influence of Heidegger, Barth, and Harnack behind and attempt a return to the classical sense of participation in the natural cosmos. According to this Blumenbergian narrative, championed mostly by Benjamin Lazier in *God Interrupted*, the post-Gnostic trajectory of Jonas' thought can be compared to the similar one of Leo Strauss and other late-modern 'Aristotelians' who changed camps from Gnosticism to Naturalism. By pioneering the 'third overcoming of Gnosis' and turning toward the phenomenon of life, Jonas recreates a philosophy of *physis* that recuperates the Aristotelian notion of the spontaneous purposefulness of nature: "Jonas revisited the notion of teleology, and linked its rejection to a distrust of final causes as explanations for natural phenomena, a sensibility central to the anti-Aristotelian animus of modern science."[2] In the introduction to *Mortality and Morality*, Lawrence Vogel utters a similar diagnosis: "as a cure for modern nihilism Jonas provides an account of nature that is more in the spirit of Aristotle than Descartes, while still keeping in step with modern science."[3]

Yet, as demonstrated by Jonas' ample use of the Lurianic 'speculative mythology'[4] in his post-war period, the story cannot be that simple. Yes, it is true that Jonas attempts to overcome dualistic Gnosis, the most powerful modern manifestation of which he locates in Heidegger's doctrine of *Geworfenheit*, being-thrown into an alien world – and yes, he also advocates a return to nature as the one metaphysical house of man and things, mind and matter. But does it mean that what he thus wishes to recover is the Aristotelian eidetic teaching of the ontological good of being? Not necessarily.[5] By taking Jonas' 'tentative myth'[6] seriously, I will propose a different scenario of Jonas' 'overcoming of Gnosticism,' consisting in the following transformation: from the dualistic type of Gnosis, which he made an explicit object of his early studies, to a dialectical type of Gnosticism, which he implicitly assumed in his later period while borrowing heavily from as well as modernizing the kabbalistic doctrine of Isaac Luria. According to this alternative hypothesis, Jonas, despite his conviction that he left Gnosticism behind,[7]

DOI: 10.4324/9781003439882-11

would still remain within the Gnostic realm, merely shifting from the rigid dualistic framework of hostility to matter to a more dialectical position of truce/reconciliation, which perceives material universe as a necessary stage in the process of the formation of Being and its inner 'holy history.' I will thus attempt to show that the rule which Lazier reserves mostly for Gershom Scholem's variant of 'overcoming of Gnosticism' – "dualism – not so much; dialectic – yes"[8] – applies also to Jonas.

Yet, taking Jonas' Lurianic myth truly seriously, that is, as a *philosophical* proposition on its own and not just a speculative 'luxurious' *addendum* to his philosophy of biology, must also lead to a critical reappraisal of the conceptual integrity of Jonas' post-war project. Lawrence Vogel insists on the parallel structure of Jonas' multi-faceted thought: while his Luria inspired theology uses different conceptuality than his Aristotle-inspired naturalist philosophy, the results mirror one another and lead to the same conclusions.[9] I would like to take issues with this diagnosis and emphasize the unique nature of the philosophical implications deriving from Jonas' Jewish-theological engagement.[10] Although there are affinities on the abstract level – the idea of the reconnection with the natural totality as a source of meaning and value – the concrete execution of this idea in Jonas' writings takes two quite different paths. The meaning wrenched from the neo-Aristotelian view on nature is not the same as the meaning that hatches within the modernized Lurianic myth; there is an essential difference between the former's monistic teleology and the latter's 'theology of risk'[11] whose complex dialectics could have emerged solely on the basis of the former Gnostic dualism. True, Jonas refers to Aristotle's concept of teleology often, especially in his purely philosophical texts, but wherever he can *not* do it, he seems to prefer a more hazardous idiom of his Lurianic *Gott mit eigenem Risiko*, in which the teleological thrust of nature is much less assured.[12] On the one hand, therefore, he defends Aristotelianism as the only ontological doctrine capable of accounting for the rise of life in the universe: "That coming must be understood as actualisation, as 'telos,' as fulfillment of a movement tending toward it. In short, only in connection with a generally 'Aristotelian' ontology is the theory of emergence logically tenable."[13] On the other, however, he seems dissatisfied with Aristotle's 'safe teleology' which he tries to impregnate with a tacit 'theology of risk' also in his philosophical writings:

> Only with the superiority of mind and the inordinate powers of technical civilization eventually engendered by it has one form of life, man, lately acquired the ability to endanger all others (and therewith himself too). Nature could not have incurred a greater hazard than to produce man: with his emergence, it potentially upset its internal balance and left it to the gathering momentum of his career to do so actually. That actuality has now come to pass. Any 'Aristotelian' idea of a safe teleology of 'Nature' (*physis*) as a whole that attends to itself and automatically ensures the harmonizing of the many purposes into one is refuted by this latest turn, whose very possibility even an Aristotle could not yet have suspected.[14]

I will thus claim that while Jonas' return to Aristotle serves his plan to find a solid philosophy of *physis* that would be inherently immune to Gnostic dualism, his turn toward Luria spells something else: not a total rejection of the Gnostic-dualistic narrative of Fall and estrangement, but a conceptual reversal *within* this very narrative, which inverts the negative into the positive, precisely as in Lazier's perceptive description: "what began as a demythologization of the gnostic stranger God ended with a reworked myth of the *deus absconditus*. What began as a determined attempt to make him known ended with grateful praise for his absence."[15] This reversal constitutes the gist of Jonas' philosophical 'work on myth,' thanks to which the lapsarian narrative of the original Lurianic vision transforms into a new metaphysics of hope and responsibility.[16] As such – deeply modified – the Lurianic narrative offers a dialectical *tertium* between Jonas' secular philosophy and his religious commitment: a characteristically modern compromise that Gershom Scholem (with whom Jonas enjoyed an ambivalent friendship) called a 'pious atheism.'[17] By focusing on the world and world history, Jonas' myth follows the secular immanentist temper, yet, by constantly referring the immanence to the withdrawn God in *tsimtsum* in the background, it also retains an element of the traditional cosmic piety, the maintenance of which was Jonas' main concern in both his purely secular and more religiously oriented writings. This compromise is not always successful: there is a visible discrepancy in Jonas' appropriation of the Lurianic 'theology of risk,' on the one hand – and his appropriation of Aristotle's teleology, on the other, which reduces the hazard of 'unprejudiced becoming'[18] to minimum, by securing the emergence of life and mind as an ontological certainty, slowly but surely realizing the latent tendency of Being. I am not going to hide my own preference: I find Jonas' philosophical experimental return to the Lurianic theosophy far more promising than his supposed 'return to Aristotle.' I will thus attempt to develop a fuller *imago* of the doctrine that Jonas left in the embryonic form – 'a blurring of boundaries, a jumble, a mishmash; and for all that a myth of creation, life, and history of frequently stunning beauty'[19] – and oppose it to his Aristotelian tendencies, also in hope that it will help to resolve tensions and inconsistencies present in Jonas' late work.

The main issue at stake is, as already indicated, the non-negotiable difference between Aristotle's self-assured teleology and Luria's precarious theology of risk: a difference reflecting the perennial tension between Athens and Jerusalem, described by Jonas himself as the conflict between necessity and contingency.[20] In light of the latter, the freedom granted to the 'liberated creation'[21] is so great that it necessarily involves a risk of forfeiting all the stakes that might have been present at its inception: life and mind *could* thus have emerged within the shards of inorganic matter, but there was no metaphysical guarantee than they ever *should* have. In light of the former, on the other hand, the latent tendency to awaken the 'dormant mind' slumbering in matter is so powerful that it cannot meet an obstacle: life and mind not only could have, but most emphatically should, sooner or later, have emerged in the natural history of the universe – it was only a matter of time. It is precisely the tension between the contingent *could* and the semi-necessary *should* of life – a lucky 'seizing of the opportunity' in the risk-ridden universe versus a 'secret teleology' of the natural law[22] – which seems to plague Jonas' philosophy of biology, from its inception in the trenches of war to his latest essays from the 80s. I will try to ease this tension, by shifting Jonas' thought away from the realist influence and closer to both materialist and nominalistic revision of the Lurianic myth that then indeed could begin to evolve into a future metaphysics – if not itself a science (as Kant wished it to be), then at least compatible with modern science's immanentist temper.

In Praise of Limitation

The Lurianic school was the latest development in kabbalistic thought, originating in the 16th century in Safed, where the Spanish kabbalists found refuge after the expulsion of Jews from Spain. Its founder, Isaac Luria aka Ari (The Lion), created a highly original historical metaphysics that involves a radical transformation of the Godhead occurring in time: from the Infinite and All-Encompassing (*Ein Sof*), through the Nothingness of the ultimate self-withdrawal (*tsimtsum*), to the scattered God (*Shekhinah*), exiled and dispersed in the creation in the form of sparks of higher life (*hayim d'aziluth*), which, in the present state of the world, remain distorted and dormant. In Lurianic thought, the individual soul is the carrier of the spark of divine life in the least disfigured shape, so it is her prerogative to search for, gather, and lift other sparks, left in various stages of distortion and inertia, in order to form a redemptive constellation: a restituted countenance of God.

The fundamental category of the Lurianic myth is *tsimtsum* – meaning 'contraction,' 'limitation,' and 'withdrawal' – and it is also equally crucial for Jonas.[23] The concept of *tsimtsum* emerges explicitly only in Jonas' latest essays, but can be seen as implicitly operative already at the earliest stages of his philosophy of life ("The Problem of Life in the Theory of Being" was originally delivered as a series of lectures at the Hebrew University of Jerusalem in 1946/1947), where it is precisely life that undergoes what may indeed be called a *tsimtsum* – 'the contraction of life from the whole of nature into its distinct singularity'[24] – and becomes decisively finite. Thus, long before the concept of *tsimtsum* officially enters the stage of Jonas' theology after Auschwitz, it is already present *in nuce* in his first departures from the Gnostic pattern. While in his doctoral dissertation devoted to the Gnostic movements, Jonas focused on the idea of Life Infinite – the Great Life indestructible and immortal – the first sign of his later 'overcoming of Gnosis' is the acceptance of the contraction of life to the dimension of finitude: initially recognized as ontological necessity, it gradually gains significance to be finally emphatically affirmed as the 'blessing of mortality.' In the Gnostic narrative, it is precisely the contraction to finitude that is deplored as the 'affliction' and the metaphysical scandal of 'thrownness':

> Who has cast me into the affliction of the worlds, who transported me into the evil darkness?" asks the Life; and it implores, "Save us out of the darkness of this world into which we are thrown." To the question, the Great Life replies, "It is not according to the will of the Great Life that thou hast come there": "That house in which thou dwellest, not Life has built it": "This world was not created according to the wish of the Life.[25]

Just as Isaac Luria, therefore, who made the divine *tsimtsum* – the contraction of the original form of Godhead as the Infinite *Ein Sof* – the very condition of creation and thus a positive 'root of finitude,'[26] Jonas, in a parallel move, makes the contraction of life the *sine qua non* of life's emergence within the structures of Being. Assuming the nominalist stance against the Gnostic abstraction of pure Life Unbound, Jonas states: "But life does not bear distillation; it is somewhere between the purified aspects – in their *concretion*. The abstractions themselves do not live"[27].

Conceived in that manner, *tsimtsum* indeed bears strong affinities with the fundamental concept of the nominalist tradition: Duns Scotus' *contractio* as the positive principle of individuation. The most important feature of the Scotist *contractio* is that it is not privative. It is not an instantiation of the already existing universal (Great Life) in the concrete singular (the living organism), marked with the loss of infinity, but a full actualization of the primary 'uncontracted nature': by bestowing concrete limitation on the general potentiality, *contractio* creates a singularity (*singularitas*) which is more real than the common nature (*natura communis*). Contraction, therefore, does not signify a loss of reality together with the loss of infinity – as it would be in the realist doctrine granting a higher form of existence to the universals – but its gain, that is, an ontological promotion: the numerically one singularity is 'ultimately real' as opposed to the 'uncontracted nature' which does not yet exist and constitutes only a potential being. When collated with the Lurianic idiom, Scotus' doctrine of *contractio* sheds new light on the originary construct of *Ein Sof* – the Godhead Without Limits or Life Unbound – which can also be perceived as a merely potential 'uncontracted nature' (a simple presence, *metsiut*, or in Scotus' idiom, 'beingness') which must first undergo *tsimtsum* in order to actualize itself in concrete singularities that only then form the 'ultimate reality' of the world: the mere 'beingness' of *Ein Sof* does not yet exist, it is promoted to existence only in the actualizing process of finitization, that is, fragmentation and concretion. The same logic applies to Jonas' inversion of the Gnostic narrative of the Great Life, which inaugurates his new philosophy of biology: instead of glorifying it as the highest and most intense being, Jonas begins to treat it precisely as the Scotist 'uncontracted nature' which does not come into existence until it fleshes itself out in the concrete finite living being.

This affinity with the Scotist nominalism is far from accidental. The work on the Lurianic myth reveals that if there is or could be a philosophy behind it, it would follow the nominalist thrust of Scotus' conceptual revolution: "a new reversal of the field of metaphysics [with which] the primacy of the singular over the universal is established (on top of the reversal enacted by the primacy of contingency over necessity): 'The individual bears a certain perfection that the common does not [*individuum includit aliquem perfectionem quam non includit commune*]'."[28] Jonas participates in this pro-modern nominalistic upheaval or what he himself calls the Scotist 'reversal of the classical order'[29]: whenever he calls upon the Lurianic myth, his own realist/Aristotelian tendencies recede and the nominalist complex of *contractio/tsimtsum* comes stronger to the fore.[30] The solution, therefore, is not to go back to the 'classical order,' for it was its assumed primacy of the universal over the singular – even as attenuated as in Aristotle's moderate realism – that became responsible for the denigration of the material world, which culminated in the Gnostic dualism. In order to overcome it once and for all, the very root of the world's denigration must be eradicated in a more decisive reversal.[31] Thus, in Scotus, *contractio* does not diminish the perfect existence of the universal; on the contrary, it promotes general potentiality into an ultimately real concrete thing. In Luria, *tsimtsum* as the 'root of finitude' does not lead to the Fall of creation plunging deeper and deeper into *privatio essendi*: on the contrary, the contraction of the Infinite makes *esse* as such possible.[32] And finally in Jonas, *tsimtsum* as the contractor of the imaginary Great Life does not bring a curse of death and 'affliction of the worlds'; on the contrary, it constitutes a 'blessing of mortality' thanks to which life can say yes to itself and thus, through this act of self-affirmation, strengthen its own being.[33] In these three cases, it is the concept of *contractio/tsimtsum* as a different, non-catastrophic form of limitation, in which the Infinite is not so much destroyed or disturbed as rather emptied out into the world that allows to subvert the Gnostic paradigm from within and affirm the intrinsic value of finite life. *Tsimtsum* thus stands for an alternative model of positive finitization which is not privative, but bestowing: "individual existence, as the 'ultimate reality' is a perfection and not a defect."[34] It does not belong to the 'classical order': it is wholly based on its reversal. What the dualistic Gnosis as the extreme development of the 'classical order' deplores and vehemently rejects – the negation of the Infinity for the sake of the finite existence, forever marked with deficiency and privation – Scotus, Luria, and Jonas, who reads the Lurianic myth philosophically, accept as the necessary condition of any existence at all, most of all life.[35]

Yet, within the context of 'overcoming of Gnosticism,' *haecceitas* of a single living organism can also prove problematic; after all, 'the contraction of life from the whole of nature into its distinct singularity'[36] produces an individual living being, possessing its own dynamic form that affirms its 'thisness' *over against* 'the rest of things' –

> An identity which from moment to moment reasserts itself, achieves itself, and defies the equalizing forces of physical sameness all around, is *truly pitted against the rest of things*. In the hazardous polarization thus ventured upon by emerging life, that which is not itself and borders on the realm of internal identity from without assumes at once the character of absolute otherness. The challenge of selfhood qualifies all this beyond the boundaries of the organism as foreign and somehow opposite: *as 'world,' in which, by which, and against which it is committed to maintain itself.* Without this universal counterpart of otherness, there would be no 'self.' And in this polarity of self and world, of internal and external, complementing that of form and matter, the basic situation of freedom with all its daring and distress is potentially complete.[37]

For Jonas, the distinctness of the singular living 'thisness' pitted against the rest of things, forms the *eternal truth of Gnosticism*: the dualistic sense of alienation of the individual self from the totality of being may be an exaggerated expression of this truth, but it nonetheless reflects the 'hazardous polarization' of every contracted living being, which only intensifies in the human subject. If Gnosticism is to be overcome, therefore, then not via simple negation, but rather via the dialectical strategy of sublation/*Aufhebung* that preserves the moment of the dualistic truth (*singularitas* against 'the rest of things') in the post-dualistic metaphysics that Jonas wishes to construct.[38] In the 1958 epilogue to the English edition of *Gnostic Religion*, "Gnosticism, Nihilism and Existentialism," Jonas formulates the challenge of the new metaphysics as a dialectical navigation between the Scylla of nihilistic dualism, in which the agonistic position *against the rest of things* leads to a total isolation of the human self – and the Charybdis of monistic naturalism that wants to undo the dualistic error, by returning to the 'classical order':

> The disruption between man and total reality is at the bottom of nihilism. The illogicality of the rupture, that is, of a dualism without metaphysics, makes its fact no less real, nor its seeming alternative any more acceptable: the stare at isolated selfhood, to which it condemns man, may wish to exchange itself for a monistic naturalism which, along with the rupture, would abolish also the idea of man as man. Between that Scylla and this her twin Charybdis, the modern mind hovers. Whether a third road is open to it – *one by which the dualistic rift can be avoided and yet enough of the dualistic insight saved to uphold the humanity of man* – philosophy must find out.[39]

The challenge facing the third dialectical way consists thus in giving justice to the dualistic truth without giving in into dualistic metaphysics, that is, in facing the difficult condition of 'bi-unity': an excentric position of the finite living metabolism (only to be exacerbated by the human mind) toward the "world, in which, by which, and against which it is committed to maintain itself." *In, by*, and simultaneously *against* constitutes a relation that can be elucidated solely by the highest form of dialectics that makes room simultaneously for separation and relation, freedom and necessity, antithesis, and dependence. "The organic form stands in a dialectical relation of *needful freedom* to matter,"[40] which means that while biological singularity manifests its distinctness in the antithetical freedom from material necessities, it is also dependent on matter. No simple monism can ever capture this 'bi-unity' which constitutes the unsurpassable testimony of life and, at the same time, the greatest challenge for any future metaphysics that would have to explain its coming into existence. The organic fusion of inwardness and outwardness becomes thus for Jonas "the prime paradigm for philosophy of concrete, uncurtailed being – indeed the key to a reintegration of fragmented ontology into a uniform theory of being."[41]

Philosophical Work on the Lurianic Myth

"Myth taken symbolically is the glass through which we darkly see"[42]: by referring to the Pauline *in speculum et enigmate* as opposed to the absolute truth witnessed face to face, Jonas confirms that metaphysics can only develop in the semi-mythic medium of pure *speculation* that allows to see the truth only darkly, but nonetheless allows to *see*: it offers a fleeting glimpse into the nature of things. The appreciation of myth is the anti-positivistic sentiment that Jonas shares with Hans Blumenberg, and on a similar ground: they both believe that mythology is a necessary human tool in fighting the specter of Gnosticism that inescapably returns with every new manifestation of the 'absolutism of reality.'[43] Just as Blumenberg who, in *The Work on Myth*, revindicates mythic story-telling, so does Jonas insist on his metaphysical story, firmly convinced that the Kantian ban on metaphysics obliquely fosters the Gnostic recognition of the world as the abyssal *mysterium tremens*: the empty infinite space of the Newtonian science, so dreaded by Pascal. They both agree that the disappearance of myths in the age of radical disenchantment leads to the Gnostic recidivism in modernity, culminating in Heidegger's doctrine of *Eigentlichkeit*: "our disenchantment, eye-opening at first, is beginning to make us blind."[44] In Blumenberg's words:

> Human life is the result of a long history of congruence between [man's] environment and 'signification': congruence that is only shattered in its most recent phase. In this history, life itself continually deprives itself of an immediate relation to its abysses, to what would make it impossible, and thus refuses to obey the summons of its terrifying 'authenticity.'[45]

Jonas' farewell to Heidegger and his 'terrifying authenticity' of facing the naked and deadly truth of Being is thus at the same time a return to myth – and, more specifically, a *Gnostic* myth, which he thoroughly reworks into an anti-Gnostic metaphysical story.[46] We may call it Jonas' *philosophische Arbeit am Mythos* – a move partly parallel and partly alternative to *Überwindung der Gnosis* – that neutralizes Gnostic negativity and, by replacing dualism with dialectics, converts the Gnostic myth of the Fall into a wholly new narrative of tentative affirmation, more compatible with the immanentist 'modern temper.' This transformation, however, occurs in Jonas' thinking tacitly and implicitly – mostly because he adamantly refuses to acknowledge the existence of 'Jewish Gnosis' as such: this refusal comes to the fore most visibly in his heated polemic with Gilles Quispel, but had also become a bone of contention between him and Gershom Scholem.[47]

Why is Jonas so reluctant to call his 'tentative myth' a piece of Gnostic speculation? According to Scholem, Lurianic kabbalah constitutes the paradigmatic expression of 'Jewish Gnosis'[48] – for Jonas, however, the very term 'Jewish Gnosis' is a misnomer, at least still in 1964 when he composes "The Gnostic Syndrome," that is, few years after he first used Luria's canvas for his metaphysical sketch in "Immortality and Modern Temper" (1961). It is a misnomer, because in Jonas' view the essential teaching of Gnosticism is necessarily marked with 'metaphysical anti-Semitism'[49] that originates in the Gnostic hatred for creation and its Creator who is to be blamed for the creaturely errors. At the same time, however, most of the distinctive features of The Gnostic Syndrome listed by Jonas seem to fit Luria's original "mythological" vision perfectly well: (1) "a metaphysic of pure movement and event, the most determinedly 'historical' conception of universal being prior to Hegel (with whom it also shares the axiom [...] that 'substance is subject')"[50]; (2) "the pathomorphic form of emanationism" which involves "tragedy and drama, crisis and fall";[51] and (3) "irresolubly mythological character" as the only medium capable of capturing "the contingency of subjective affect and will,"[52] operative both on high, in the drama of the divine pleroma, and on low, in the drama of human slumber and subsequent awakening. The description – "The typical gnostic myth [...] starts with a doctrine of divine transcendence in its original purity; it then traces the genesis of the world from some primordial disruption of this blessed state, a loss of divine integrity which leads to the emergence of lower powers who become the makers and rulers of this world"[53] – could just as well be a gloss on Luria's account of the beginning of creation. For unknown reasons, the originary peace of *Ein Sof* gets suddenly disrupted, which results in Its contraction – *tsimtsum* – creating a void (*tehiru*) where the world emerges, yet not as an effectuation of the divine plan, but through a 'pathomorphic emanation' gone wrong because of the 'breaking of the vessels.' The history of the world, therefore, is a highly dramatic narrative of redemption that attempts to undo the catastrophic event of creation: in the more moderate approach, it is only the secondary catastrophe of *shvirat ha-kelim*, while in the more radical restorative messianic versions, it applies also to the originary catastrophe of *tsimtsum*.

But there is one difference that remains absolutely decisive for Jonas: in the Lurianic myth, there is no trace of the figure of the evil demiurge, nor a contempt for creation. There may be a sense that there is something deeply wrong with the created world which is in a need of redemptive action (even to the point of equating redemption with the total annihilation of this world for the sake of a new creation), but there is no ill will implied in the creaturely catastrophes; God is not to be blamed either for his contraction or for the breaking of the vessels. For Jonas, this absence of reverse theodicy, which accuses God for bringing evil into the world, is already enough *not* to call Luria's myth Gnostic. Here creation is not an object of snidy derision, but still an object of cosmic piety, although tinged with compassion and a messianic urge to mend the world. And when fused with Hegel's evolutionism, which downplays the lapsarian moment of the kabbalistic 'patomorphic emanation,' the Lurianic story turns into a dialectics of affirmation rather than negation: even if not *ki tov* now, *not-yet*, the world can nonetheless realize the divine will, which is present in it in a diasporic and distorted form.[54] The historical metaphysics may thus be a Gnostic invention, but in the Lurianic narrative fused with the Hegelian one, it serves a completely different purpose: it does not undo the error of being, it helps to mend it. Hence, if radical negation of the created world is the most defining feature of Gnosticism, Luria's myth is *not* Gnostic.

But – isn't it really? When reproaching Scholem for wrongly applying the term 'Jewish Gnosis' to the monotheistic mysticism of palaces (*hekhalot*), which will eventually evolve into kabbalah, Jonas again lists the distinctive features of Gnosis proper, which quite ironically form a perfect description of the Lurianic myth (or, at least, its most pessimistic variant):

> A Gnosticism without a fallen god, without benighted creator and sinister creation, without alien soul, cosmic captivity and acosmic salvation, without

the self-redeeming of the Deity – in short: a gnosis without divine tragedy will not meet specifications. For those are the things we have to account for when truly asking for the origins of Gnosticism.[55]

But, what is *Shehkinah* – the scattered and fragmented deity lost in the world – if not a 'fallen god' searching for self-redemption? Is not *tsimtsum* (in more radical variants) leading straight to the breaking of the vessels a case of divine tragedy? Is not the Hasidic post-Lurianic kabbalah of Nachman of Brestlav, which Jonas must have known from Martin Buber, full of images alluding to the cosmic captivity and acosmic salvation? And finally, is Jonas' own rendering of Luria's story free from the Gnostic elements he just listed – most of all, the suffering God? True, Jonas' 'tentative myth' will indeed neutralize most of the negative aspects of the Lurianic kabbalah – but only because it was Gnostic to the tee in the first place.[56]

One way of seeing this *Gnostizismusstreit* between Jonas and Scholem is to treat it as a question of nomenclature. This is Jonas' position, when he criticizes Scholem for doing a 'semantic disservice' in calling Jewish mystical tradition a 'Gnosis': "An innocent enough label in its literal meaning, it encourages the view of a smooth 'transition' instead of a decisive break, a mere mutation in the same genus."[57] Yet, by insisting on the absolute difference between Gnosticism and monotheism, Jonas shuts himself from the historical mutations of the Gnostic motives which – so claims Scholem – underwent evolution in order to adapt themselves to the monotheistic belief: they shed the dualistic framework in order to become *dialectical*, that is, locating the antithetical moment of negativity in the Godhead itself.[58] Jonas' refusal to acknowledge this kind of transition is all the more surprising that he himself makes full use of one such historical mutation in the form of the Lurianic kabbalah, the most dialectical account of the relation between God, Man, and World, which, according to Scholem, proved precursorial to the development of German Idealism. Sticking firmly (perhaps, too firmly) to his resolve to 'overcome Gnosticism,' which he defined once for all as 'metaphysical anti-Semitism,' Jonas finds himself in the position of Molier's Monsieur Jourdain: he is speaking the prose of dialectical Gnosis without being aware of it.

This denial and misrecognition continues for more than two decades – until the final rendition in 1984 of the Lurianic myth in "The Concept of God after Auschwitz," where 'the mighty undercurrent of the Kabbalah'[59] comes finally to the surface and gets an official mention. While Jonas admits that he felt immediately inspired by Isaac Luria's concept of *tsimtsum* the moment he read about it in Scholem's *Major Trends of Jewish Mysticism* (in 1942, Scholem gave Jonas a copy of his work with a dedication to the 'Gnostic colleague'), the explicit reference to the Lurianic doctrine appears only in the latest rendering of his myth, which incorporates large fragments of the earlier essay, sketched at the beginning of the 60s, "Immortality and Modern Temper":

And here let us remember that Jewish tradition itself is really not quite so monolithic in the matter of divine sovereignty as official doctrine makes it appear. The mighty undercurrent of the Kabbalah, which Gershom Scholem in our days has brought to light anew, knows about a divine fate bound up with the coming-to-be of a world. There we meet highly original, very unorthodox speculations in whose company mine would not appear so wayward after all. Thus, for example, my myth at bottom only pushes further the idea of the *tzimtzum*, that cosmogonic centerconcept of the Lurianic Kabbalah. Tzimtzum means contraction, withdrawal, self-limitation. To make room for the world, the *En-Sof* (Infinite; literally, No-End) of the beginning had to contract himself so that, vacated by him, empty space could expand outside of him: the 'Nothing' in which and from which God could then create the world. Without this retreat into himself, there could be no 'other' outside God, and only his continued holding-himself-in preserves the finite things from losing their separate being again in to the divine 'all in all.' *My myth goes farther still*. The contraction is total as far as power is concerned; as a whole has the Infinite ceded his power to the finite and thereby wholly delivered his cause into its hands.[60]

It is debatable whether Jonas' reception of *tsimtsum* "goes farther still" or whether the implication of the total contraction of power can be found already in Luria's original thought: Scholem himself seems hesitant on this point.[61] What matters here is a new understanding of divinity that steers away from the 'Hellenic' theological absolutism, which bestowed on God the attributes of immutability, eternity, and omnipotence, and restores the biblical image of vulnerable Godhead, which Scholem associated with the original 'Jewish Gnosis.' According to Christian Wiese, Jonas, initially inimical to the term itself, eventually yielded to Scholem's hypothesis, but only two years after his death. Hence Jonas' ultimate decision to inscribe his own private metaphysical myth not only into the Lurianic heritage, which emphasizes the hazardous enterprise of creation, but also into the Joban one, which accentuates vulnerability of all life.[62] In Jonas' philosophical biology, every living organism becomes an incarnation of Job: a highly precarious unit of life, constantly struggling for survival in the vast expanses of the universe ruled mostly by mechanical forces. If this were what the all-powerful Creator truly wanted, then he could indeed be accused of a pharaonic cruelty, as it was done by Ernst Bloch in his openly gnosticizing reading of the Book of Job.[63] But if the deity is as limited and precarious as his *tselem* in even the smallest unit of life, then the whole issue of theodicy simply dissolves:

> Every mortal answer to Job's question, too, cannot be more than that. Mine is the opposite to the one given by the Book of Job: this, for an answer, invoked the plenitude of God's power; mine, his chosen voidance of it.[64]

God without power, falling short of the 'Hellenic' eternal Absolute, is also inescapably a God in time: not as a 'Lord *of* history,' but rather as a subject *to* and *in* history, dependent on its contingent development. The most striking novelty of Jonas' reworking of the Lurianic Gnosis is thus a *metaphysics of temporality*, constituting a variant of what Karl Löwith called *Heilsgeschichte*: the Holy History as the metaphysical history of the Good, gradually evolving in Being as the *event of self-affirmation* – of Being saying yes to itself as being. This affirmation, which awakens for the first time with life, relies on what Walter Benjamin, also in an oblique reference to the Lurianic scenario, named a 'weak messianic force'[65]: while it cannot secure the ultimate triumph of the Good in the universe, it can and should work toward its realization in time. First Luria – and after him, Benjamin and Jonas – draw implicitly on the fundamental Jewish imperative of a weak responsibility, which was first formulated by Rabbi Tarphon: "you are not expected to complete the work, but neither can you desist from it."[66]

The Good, therefore, is *in the making*: it neither *is* (as in Aristotle) nor *is not* (as in the Gnostic-dualistic doctrine), but rather *makes itself true* in the process of the cosmic *self-verification*. The same applies to Jonas' version of the processual deity. God neither is, nor is not; God is becoming, aided by the weak messianic power of its creation to make Himself true. The Good/God does not exist, *not yet* – but He could and should have become in the future, in the time of fulfillment or *tikkun olam*.[67] According to Ciril O'Regan, the idea of the processual and vulnerable 'God in pain' who must pass through the ordeal of negativity in order to conquer it, is Gnostic *per se*, although already adopted to the monotheistic dialectics. While it originates in Valentinus (whom already Jonas, in the second part of his work on Gnosticism, calls a thinker of a new dynamic monism[68]), it enjoys a powerful "Gnostic return" in modernity, reiterated in the dialectical variants: starting from the Lurianic, then Christian kabbalah and culminating in *christliche Gnosis* of Hegel.[69] Similarly in Jonas, *Imago Dei* – the image of God in the making, completing itself in the course of history – emerges in his private myth as deriving originally from the dualistic Mani, but then also implicitly from the dialectical Luria in whose system the living souls strive toward the reconstitution of the Divine Countenance (*panim*). The common denominator of all those images of the becoming deity is the shift of responsibility from God, discharged from the providential control over his creation, to man as God's active helper: whether coming from Mani, Luria, or Etty Hillesum, Jonas' private myth stakes itself on the active 'weak messianism' of each and every human soul, capable of impacting the fate of the becoming God in the moment of 'metaphysical decision.' This is also Jonas' own version of *finitum capax infiniti*: although finite, the human soul not only can reach, but also determine the eternal realm. 'The infinite in the finite' is precisely the most fleeting moment of decision that affects *Imago Dei*, either by fostering or by hindering its completion:

> By forgoing its own inviolateness, the eternal ground allowed the world to be. To this self-denial all creation owes its existence and with it has received all there is to receive from beyond. Having given himself whole to the becoming world, God has no more to give: it is man's now to give to him.[70]

It would thus seem that, despite all his protestations to the contrary, Gnosticism never truly lost its appeal to Jonas.[71] In the preface to the collection of philosophical essays, he explains why he eventually dropped the study of Gnosticism – 'five years of soldiering in British army' cut him off from the libraries and turned his philosophical attention to the vulnerability of the living beings fighting for survival – but also admits that

> the new resolve had by no means relegated the fascination of the earlier subject to the memory of a youthful infatuation, or lessened my conviction of its philosophical relevance [...] Even secret philosophical connections of this unlikely topic with my new interests emerged in the latters' pursuit.[72]

Could the 'tentative myth,' first conceived in 1961, testify to this 'secret philosophical connection'? Instead of rupture or sudden turn, we should rather see Jonas' 'overcoming of Gnosticism' as an evolution of the Gnostic reasoning; while it abandons the starkly dualistic model – in modernity represented by Heidegger and his nihilistic existentialism that revived the motif of extreme alienation of man in the metaphor of *Geworfenheit* – it gradually strives toward a subtly dialectical scenario, where nature itself turns into the first arena of confrontation between the living forces of becoming and the dead forces of inorganic permanence, and then, already on the organic level, between the forces of cyclical self-preservation and the forces of creative diversity. Jonas' original contribution to the dialectical model offered by the Lurianic myth would thus not so much "go farther" than the original doctrine as rather offer its philosophical working-through, aiming at the *neutralization of the Gnostic moment of antagonism*, still very much active in Luria's narrative. I deliberately choose the term deriving from psychoanalysis: *Durcharbeiten*. Jonas' overcoming of Gnosticism does not consist in bidding farewell to the Gnostic stories and embracing Greek naturalism; it is rather a patient working-through the Joban trauma of the human sense of isolation in the stony cosmos, the goal of which is to ease up its traumatic aspect. Due to such philosophical *Durcharbeiten*, the trauma of the existential scandal, which found its original expression in the Gnostic lament over the injustice of creaturely order, is to appear more 'relaxed,' *gelassen*, rubbed off of its original 'mythological' intensity by the demythologizing philosophical logic.

In Conclusion: The Dialectical Shift

The secret, never fully avowed intuition that one Gnosis can only be overcome by another Gnosis – or that the aporias of the dualistic metaphysics can only be solved by a post-dualistic dialectical one – matures in Jonas in the decade separating the 1958 epilogue to *The Gnostic Religion*, and the 1961 Ingersoll lecture on "Immortality and Modern Temper," but becomes acknowledged as such only in the latest rendering of the Lurianic myth in 1984 "The Concept of God after Auschwitz." While in the earlier 1958 text, the dualistic separation 'between man and the world, and concurrently between the world and God' – a 'duality not of supplementary but of contrary terms'[73] – is still criticized as an exaggerated account of 'an absolute rift between man and that in which he finds himself lodged,'[74] in the later one, it becomes endorsed as a difference that allows the world to liberate itself from the divine plan and unleash the 'unprejudiced becoming.' And while in

1958, the Gnostic 'nihilistic conception,' where the hidden and transcendent God "has more of the *nihil* than the *ens* in his concept,"[75] is still strictly opposed by Jonas to the Greek realist vision of the meaningful and nomotropic *physis*, in 1961 and then in 1984, it re-emerges as a canvas of the story about God who withdraws from the world and human history in order to grant immanence full freedom of the hazardous 'odyssey of time.' What formerly appeared as a nihilistic context of abandonment (God hiding from the world in the act of hostile negation), now shows a different face as a positive, albeit risky, separation between God and the world, where creation inaugurated by the divine *tsimtsum* becomes a gamble whose stake is either a complete loss of the last traces of the Godhead in the material universe, or its gradual restitution – and if not completely *in integrum*, then at least in the finite form of *tselem*, the human mind as the 'likeness' of the God in retreat.[76]

This conceptual shift, resulting in the "frankly speculative theology",[77] occurred in Jonas' thought in response to the Lurianic myth that first reached him through Scholem, but perhaps mostly through Hannah Arendt who wrote an enthusiastic review of the English translation of Scholem's *Major Trends of Jewish Mysticism*, with a special attention paid to the Lurianic vision as – surprisingly – *procosmic*; after all, the Ingersoll essay is dedicated to 'H. A.' And although the name 'Luria' does not yet get mentioned here, the dedication may obliquely suggest Jonas' source of inspiration in Scholem's work on the kabbalah, mediated by Arendt's reading of it, which – somewhat pace Scholem – accentuated Luria's 'turn toward the worldly,' which, termed as *directio mundi*, also happens to be a characteristic feature of Scotist nominalism (and Duns Scotus was Arendt's favorite scholastic).[78] Perhaps, therefore, it was only Arendt's genuine positive surprise that Jewish mysticism does not have to be acosmic and quietistic – that is, conform to the type of the Gnostic-Pauline Weimar religiosity that she, together with Jonas, wished to leave behind – that ultimately prompted her friend to appropriate the Lurianic myth, despite its 'dubious' Gnostic origin. And although Jonas' immediate concern here was a possibility of a post-Holocaust theology that would be structurally free from the traps of theodicy – justifying God's ways to the victims of the Shoah – the positive elaboration of the Lurianic myth, originally belonging to the Gnostic archive, also pushed Jonas toward a new metaphysics, very different from the Aristotelian eidetic doctrine of *physis*. If before Jonas could sound quite Voegelinian in his critique of Gnosis as metaphysical nihilism, juxtaposed with the apology of the Greek 'nomos of the Earth,' his Lurianic meditation heads for something completely else: instead of a static image of law-abiding nature, it offers a dynamic story in which it is no longer *nomos* that plays major role, but an intentional *force*, a bio-tropic desire that runs throughout the material universe as a yet unfinished and precarious project laden with risks.

In late Jonas, therefore, the never abandoned Gnosis inevitably returns, but not with the vengeance; it heals the wound that it itself smote, by offering to the malaise of dualism a dialectics of negotiation, in which the world is no longer a terrifying alien realm – just *insecure*. This is why he could say in his *Memoirs*: "But to me, even though terrible things happen, the world has never been a hostile place."[79]

Notes

1. See Richard Wolin, *Heidegger's Children. Hannah Arendt, Karl Löwith, Hans Jonas, and Herbert Marcuse* (Princeton, NJ: Princeton University Press, 2001).
2. Benjamin Lazier quotes Strauss' letter to Jonas: "I would state it as follows: gnosticism is the most radical rebellion against *physis*. Our problem now is to recover *physis*": Benjamin Lazier, *God Interrupted: Heresy and the European Imagination between the World Wars* (Princeton, NJ: Princeton University Press, 2012), 54, and comments: "Gnosticism had presented the most radical challenge in Western history to the Greek notion of *physis*, Strauss argued, and he claimed to discover in Jonas a concerted attempt to save it […] Behind and beyond their apparent diversity there nonetheless remains the fact of their shared theological parentage. Both were born of an interwar encounter with the gnostic challenge writ large […] Jonas expended much effort in the attempt to revive Aristotelianism, if not its full cosmology, then at least the particulars most suited to a philosophy of the organism" (Lazier, *God Interrupted*, 111–112; 122–123).
3. Lawrence Vogel, "Hans Jonas's Exodus: from German Existentialism to Post-Holocaust Theology," in Hans Jonas, *Mortality and Morality. A Search for the Good after Auschwitz*, ed. Lawrence Vogel (Evanston, IL; Chicago, IL: Northwestern University Press, 1996), 2.
4. Jonas, *Mortality and Morality*, 131.
5. A similar point is made by Elad Lapidot in his essay on Husserl and Heidegger in this volume, which claims that "it was precisely Jonas's concern for ethics that originally led him, as a thinker, from classic, Greek-inspired philosophy to the archives of Judeo-Christian religion." While analysing the divergence between the two versions of Jonas' obituary to Husserl in 1938, Lapidot notices a "gap between, *on the one hand*, the narrative offered in the later, reworked version published in *Moznayim*, in which late antique, Gnostic or Judeo-Christian, non-Greek thought features as a precursor of modern acosmic nihilism that undermines Greek commitment to the world, a narrative that will become dominant after the war; and, *on the other hand*, the narrative offered by the original obituary, which criticizes the ethical corruption in modern science's worldliness and against it, as epistemo-ethical corrective, asserts Judeo-Christian ethics combined with transcendental conscience." (5). I will claim that Jonas' reworking of the Lurianic myth is in harmony with the latter narrative.
6. Jonas, *Mortality and Morality*, 132.
7. This disavowal, repeated on many occasions, comes to the fore particularly strongly in Jonas' memoirs. Jonas reduces his interest in Gnosis to a passing affair of the youth, when he was still deeply influenced by his teachers, Heidegger and Bultmann, and not yet a mature thinker on his own: "Any discussion of my philosophy should begin not with gnosticism but with my efforts to establish a philosophical biology. My work on gnosticism was just my journeyman's project, an application of Heidegger's philosophy, especially of existential analysis, with its particular interpretive methodology and its understanding of human existence, to a specific body of historical material, in this case gnosticism in late antiquity […] I wouldn't go so far as to say, however, that an independent Jonas philosophy manifested itself here": *Memoirs: Hans Jonas*, ed. Christian Wiese and Krishna Winston (Waltham, MA: Brandeis University Press, 2008), 65.
8. Lazier, *God Interrupted*, 160. In his 'existential' diagnosis of late Jonas, Lazier claims that "for all his efforts, Jonas never managed to banish the specter of the alien. The gospel of the alien God goaded him until the very end, and in some of his moods proved victorious" (Lazier, *God Interrupted*, 59).
9. Jonas, *Mortality and Morality*, 19.
10. I am seconded here by Lazier who opposes Vogel, by claiming that "If [Jonas's] theological engagements were philosophically extraneous, if they were supplements only – and I happen to disagree with this view – they were from an intellectual-historical standpoint nonetheless crucial, because foundational": Lazier, *God Interrupted*, 61.

11 This term, *die Theologie des Hasards*, was first used by Scholem in reference to the Sabbatian modification of the Lurianic kabbalah by Abraham Miguel Cardoso who accentuated the risk implied by the enterprise of creation based on the divine *tsimtsum*-witdrawal: Gershom Scholem, "Die Theologie des Sabbatianismus im Lichte Abraham Cardosos," in *Judaica 1* (Frankfurt am Main: Suhrkamp, 1997), 142.
12 Hans Jonas, *Der Gottesbegriff nach Auschwitz. Eine jüdische Stimme* (Frankfurt am Main: Suhrkamp, 2016), 45.
13 Hans Jonas, *The Imperative of Responsibility. In Search of an Ethics for the Technological Age*, trans. Hans Jonas and David Herr (Chicago, IL: The University of Chicago Press, 1984), 69.
14 Jonas, *The Imperative of Responsibility*, 138.
15 Lazier, *God Interrupted*, 64.
16 *Arbeit am Mythos* is the title of Hans Blumenberg's magisterial work on the place of mythology in modern thought (Frankfurt am Main: Suhrkamp, 1979). Jonas deeply respected Blumenberg (the feeling was mutual), and it is quite probable that his modernized variant of the Lurianic myth at least partly reflects the latter's effort to demonstrate the intimate relationship between mythology and philosophy, which, as Blumenberg shows, did not cease in the hyper-rational conditions of modernity. Yet, although both thinkers intensely read and respected one another, Blumenberg was not very appreciative of Jonas' philosophical reworking of the Lurianic myth. In a critical essay that appeared in 1985 in *Neuen Zürcher Zeitung*, Blumenberg found it inconsistent to demand a total responsibility of creatures for the enterprise of creation when the Creator abandoned himself so irresponsibly to the 'adventure of the world' (*Weltabenteuer*): "And should not the objection against human demiurgic activity be also directed against such adventurous God?": quot. in Hannes Bajohr, "Damals noch. Die Korrespondenz zwischen Hans Blumenberg und Hans Jonas," in *Hans Blumenberg/ Hans Jonas: Briefwechsel 1954–1978 und weitere Materialien*, ed. Hannes Bajohr (Frankfurt am Main: Suhrkamp, 2022), 26.
17 Gershom Scholem, *On Jews and Judaism in Crisis. Selected Essays*, ed. Werner Dannhauser (New York: Schocken Books, 1976), 283. Ron Margolin proposes yet another name for this compromise: 'secular religiosity'; Ron Margolin, "Hans Jonas and Secular Religiosity," in *The Legacy of Hans Jonas. Judaism and the Phenomenon of Life*, ed. Hava Tirosh-Samuelson and Christian Wiese (Leiden/Boston, MA: Brill 2010), 231–260.
18 Jonas, *Mortality and Morality*, 134.
19 Lazier, *God Interrupted*, 61.
20 "To put it as briefly as possible, the biblical doctrine pitted contingency against necessity, particularity against universality, will against intellect. It secured a place for the 'contingent' within philosophy, against the latter's original bias": Hans Jonas, *Philosophical Essays: From Contemporary Creed to Technological Man* (Evanston, IL: Northwestern University Press, 1974), 29. While I locate Jonas' philosophical thinking firmly on the side of 'Jerusalem,' Lawrence Vogel claims otherwise: "… an ontological grounding of the imperative of responsibility is true to the Greek idea that the human mind shares in the divine because reason is able to grasp the good-in-itself. It remains unclear, therefore, whether Jonas is a philosopher of nature whose project is informed by Judaism – or rather a philosopher who happens to be Jewish. The question is particularly pressing in the face of Leo Strauss's claim that the Hebrew people had no concept of nature as a measure available to human reason […] *Mustn't Jonas's project be seen as an essentially 'Athenian' move – contrary to the temper of 'Jerusalem'?*": Lawrence Vogel, "Natural-Law Judaism? The Genesis of Bioethics in Hans Jonas, Leo Strauss, and Leon Kass," in *The Legacy of Hans Jonas*, 293–294; emphasis added.
21 Comp. Scholem's most succinct account of the Lurianic myth: "Creation out of nothing, from the void, could be nothing other than creation of the void, that is, of the possibility of thinking of anything that was not God. Without such an act of self-limitation, after

all, there would be only God – and obviously nothing else. A being that is not God could only become possible and originate by virtue of such a contraction, such a paradoxical retreat of God into himself. By positing a negative factor in Himself, God liberates creation": Scholem, *On Jews and Judaism in Crisis*, 283.
22 Jonas, *Mortality and Morality*, 180.
23 "Most attractive for Jonas was the image of God's 'self-contraction' (*tzimtzum*) – the idea that God, before creation was possible, had to limit Himself in order to create space outside of the divine [...] In modern terms, the metaphor of *tzimtzum* may be understood as attempting to explain the autonomy of both the world and humanity, while providing the theological explanation for why there is evil in the world, as well as for the gift of human freedom and the demand of responsibility it entails": Christian Wiese, *The Life and Thought of Hans Jonas: Jewish Dimensions*, trans. Jeffrey Grossman and Christian Wiese (Waltham, MA: Brandeis University Press, 2007), 134.
24 Hans Jonas, *The Phenomenon of Life. Toward a Philosophical Biology* (Evanston, IL: Northwestern University Press, 2001), 19.
25 Hans Jonas, *The Gnostic Religion. The Message of the Alien God and The Beginnings of Christianity* (Boston, MA: Beacon Press, 2001), 64. The earlier German version quotes the same Mandean fragments, but does not contain critical reference to Heidegger and his notion of *die Geworfenheit*: Hans Jonas, *Gnosis und spätantiker Geist I. Die Mythologische Gnosis* (Göttingen: Vandenhoeck & Ruprecht, 1964), 108. There are many differences between the later English version and its earlier German basis, mostly relating to the influence of Heidegger on Jonas who grows more and more critical of his doctoral mentor, which also reflects on Jonas' increasingly negative view of the Gnostic mythology. On this, see Daniel M. Herskowitz's essay in this volume.
26 See Kenneth Seeskin, "*Tsimtsum* and the Root of Finitude," in *Tsimtsum and Modernity. Lurianic Heritage in Modern Philosophy and Theology*, ed. Agata Bielik-Robson and Daniel H. Weiss (Berlin: de Gruyter, 2021), 107–118.
27 Jonas, *Phenomenon of Life*, 22.
28 Emmanuel Falque, *God, the Flesh, and the Other. From Irenaeus to Duns Scotus*, trans. William Christian Hackett (Evanston, IL: Northwestern University Press, 2015), 265. Falque comments: "Before Scotus everyone thought that the epistemological primacy of the universal over the singular, or the common over the individual, was self-evident" (Falque, *God, the Flesh, and the Other*, 265).
29 Jonas, *Philosophical Essays*, 42.
30 In the essay, "Jewish and Christian Elements in Philosophy," Jonas confirms the importance of Duns Scotus for the formation of modernity, by claiming that "these changes also affected the whole concept of matter, with consequences that reach into the beginnings of modern science. From a mere, abstract complement of form, it becomes a thing in its own right – its creation opposing it to the *nihil* with the absolute difference of existence, compared to which all differences of essence become relative. For creation by God surely means production into reality. Thus matter, if created by God, must have a positive, actual being of its own and cannot be merely the potency for something else to be, the empty possibility of becoming. Called forth 'from nothing,' it must be something, *aliqua res actu*, as Duns Scotus says. This change in ontological status, closely related to that of the individual, prepared matter for the role it was to play in the modern theoretical scheme": Jonas, *Philosophical Essays*, 38. Duns Scotus's *haecceitas* is also adopted by Jonas as the "biological foundation of individuality," but with a proviso that makes even more nominalistic: "individuality in any serious sense, and not the merely formal sense of numerical singularity, that is, individuality as a substantial quality, is an organic and only an organic phenomenon" (Jonas, *Philosophical Essays*, 187). On the principle of *contractio* or "God's self-restriction" as inaugurating modern era, see also the last part of Hans Blumenberg's *Legitimacy of the Modern Age*, where he analyzes the doctrine of Nicholas of Cusa: here too the world of contingent creatures gains autonomical existence due to the self-restriction of the divine omnipotence and the retreat

of the Infinite for the sake of finite beings: Hans Blumenberg's *The Legitimacy of the Modern Age*, trans. Robert M. Wallace (Cambridge, MA: MIT Press, 1985), the chapter: "The Cusan: The World as God's Self-Restriction," 483–548.

31 Already in *Gnosis und spätantiker Geist II*, the unfinished second part of his work on Gnosticism, published in 1954, Jonas makes it clear that the successful overcoming of Gnosticism cannot proceed the way of the return to the 'classical order.'

32 See again Seeskin, "*Tsimtsum* and the Root of Finitude," 110, which strongly emphasizes the affirmative aspect of *tsimtsum* as the necessary precondition of all existence against its negative Gnostic interpretation as the catastrophic disruption of the divine pleroma that initiates the chain of events leading to the Fall. On the ambivalence of the Lurianic *tsimtsum* as lending itself to both readings, also in Gershom Scholem's account, see my "An Unhistorical History of Tsimtsum: A Break with Neoplatonism?," in *Tsimtsum and Modernity*, 1–37. In what follows, I will argue that Jonas leans towards the non-lapsarian – non-Neoplatonic and in this sense nominalist – understanding of the concept of *tsimtsum* as the conditioning contraction; a tendency that will come to the fore explicitly in his famous late essay on "The Concept of God after Auschwitz" (see the last section).

33 "The 'yes' of all striving is here sharpened by the active 'no' to not-being. Through the negated not-being, being becomes a positive concern, that is, a constant choosing of itself. Life as such, in the inherently co-present danger of not-being, is an expression of this choice. Thus it is only an apparent paradox that it should be death, that is, the being liable to die (being 'mortal') and being so at every moment, and its equally ceaseless deferment every moment by the act of self-preservation, which sets the seal upon the self-affirmation of being: in this contrapuntal pairing, *the self-affirmation of being turns into single efforts of individual beings*": Jonas, *Imperative of Responsibility*, 82; emphasis added.

34 Jonas, *Philosophical Essays*, 42.

35 It is perhaps for this reason that Jonas never fully invested in the 'Aristotelian cosmology,' accepting it mostly (only?) in the contracted form, limited to the autoteleology of a single organism. This seems also Lazier's view, more cautious in co-opting Jonas to the Neo-Aristotelian team: "Jonas expended much effort in the attempt to revive Aristotelianism, if not its full cosmology then at least the particulars most suited to a philosophy of the organism": Lazier, *God Interrupted*, 121–122.

36 Jonas, *Phenomenon of Life*, 19.

37 Jonas, *Phenomenon of Life*, 83; emphasis added.

38 While contemplating a possibility of a future metaphysical doctrine, Jonas emphasizes that "a new, integral, i.e., philosophical monism cannot undo the polarity: it must absorb it into a higher unity of existence from which the opposites issue as faces of its being or phases of its becoming. It must take up the problem which originally gave rise to dualism": Jonas, *Phenomenon of Life*, 17. According to Alan Rubenstein, this dualism takes in Jonas a quite specific form: "The key ontological divide is not between human beings and the rest of nature – it is between living nature and that which does not live and, so, cannot die": Alan Rubenstein, "Hans Jonas: A Study in Biology and Ethics," *Society*, 46 (2009), 165–166.

39 Jonas, *Gnostic Religion*, 340; emphasis added.

40 Jonas, *Phenomenon of Life*, 80.

41 Jonas, *Philosophical Essays*, xiii.

42 Jonas, *Phenomenon of Life*, 261.

43 On the continuing importance of the concept of myth in Jonas' early and late writings, see Amir Engel's chapter in this volume.

44 Jonas, *Mortality and Morality*, 77.

45 Hans Blumenberg, *The Work on Myth*, trans. Robert M. Wallace (Cambridge, MA: MIT Press, 1985), 110.

46 On departing from Heidegger in Jonas' take on Gnosticism, see: Jonathan Cahana, "A Gnostic Critic of Modernity: Hans Jonas from Existentialism to Science," *Journal*

of the American Academy of Religion, 86 (March 2018), 158–180, where Cahana describes Jonas' growing mistrust towards Heidegger as the "profoundly pagan" thinker with strong nihilistic leanings. Daniel Herskowitz, however, although not disagreeing with Cahana's presentation of *Being and Time* as pagan and nihilistic, protests against calling it Gnostic: Jonas' take on Heidegger, although noticing an affinity between his concept of *Geworfenheit* and the Gnostic sense of being thrown into a hostile universe, locates him rather in the legacy of the mechanistic science with its characteristic "dualism without metaphysics" (Jonas, *Gnostic Religion*, 340) as the "illogical" outcome of the Gnostic metaphysical dualism: "This wider context will allow us to see that Jonas's originality as a reader of Heidegger is not to be found in the link with Gnosticism, which was not an uncommon trope, but in arguing that Heidegger is the philosophical outcome of the seventeenth-century scientific revolution and a manifestation of its calculative, technological reasoning": Daniel M. Herskowitz, "Reading Heidegger against the Grain: Hans Jonas on Existentialism, Gnosticism, and Modern Science," *Modern Intellectual History*, 19, nr 2 (2021), 4.

47 See *"The Hymn of the Pearl*: Case Study of a Symbol, and the Claims for a Jewish Origin of Gnosticism," published originally in 1965 and then included in Jonas' *Philosophical Essays*.

48 "Gnosis, one of the last great manifestations of myth in religious thinking, conceived at least in part as a reaction against the Jewish conquerors of myth, gave the Jewish mystics their language [...] the old God whom Kabbalistic gnosis opposed to the God of the philosophers proves, when experienced in all His living richness, to be an even older and archaic one": Gershom Scholem, *On the Kabbalah and Its Symbolism* (New York: Schocken Books, 1969), 98; 119. For Scholem, the most powerful expression of such return is 'the Lurianic gnosis' (Scholem, *On the Kabbalah and Its Symbolism*, 114), which combines the most archaic vision of the Jewish deity with the most modern experience of universal displacement, exile, and the redemptive stake of history.

49 Jonas, *Philosophical Essays*, 286.
50 Jonas, *Philosophical Essays*, 265.
51 Jonas, *Philosophical Essays*, 266.
52 Jonas, *Philosophical Essays*, 266.
53 Jonas, *Philosophical Essays*, 267.
54 On the possible kabbalistic grounds of German Idealism, which facilitate the Jonasian fusion of Luria with Hegel, see my "God of Luria, Hegel, Schelling: The Divine Contraction and the Modern Metaphysics of Finitude," in *Mystical Theology and Continental Philosophy*, ed. David Lewin, Simon Podmore, and Duane Williams (London and New York: Routledge, 2017), 32–50.
55 Jonas, *Philosophical Essays*, 290.
56 The catastrophic aspect of the Lurianic myth is very strongly emphasized in Eric Jacobson's interpretation of Jonas' *Gottesbegriff nach Auschwitz*; according to Jacobson, it is precisely Luria's idea of the 'divine catastrophe,' which attracts Jonas' attention in his attempt to reconstitute Jewish theology after the Shoah: Eric Jacobson, "Hans Jonas und der Gottesbegriff nach Auschwitz," in *Weiterwohnlichkeit der Welt. Zur Aktualität von Hans Jonas*, ed. Eric Jacobson and Christian Wiese (Berlin-Wien: Philo Verlagsgesellschaft, 2003), 221. While reading the Lurianic *tsimtsum* in the pessimistic vein of the Sarugian school – as the cataclysmic contraction of God attempting to free himself from the intrinsic evil – he thus confirms the presence of 'Jewish Gnosis' in Jonas' thought: "contrary to Jonas's intentions, we cannot but come to the conclusion that his understanding of God is inescapably Gnostic" (Jacobson, "Hans Jonas und der Gottesbegriff nach Auschwitz," 203; in my translation). The fact that Jonas did not stop referring to the Gnostic symbols and myths, but rather reelaborated them for the sake of his procosmic argument did not escape Christian Wiese either: "Jonas nonetheless resorts to the Gnostic symbolic – though against the Gnostic negation of the world and ethical

indifference – in order to validate the transcendent significance of our action and the way we live our lives, that is, a responsibility not only for the creaturely life, but also for the fate of the Godhead whose face became distorted due to human iniquity": Christian Wiese, "*Weltabenteuer Gottes* und *Heiligkeit des Lebens*. Theologische Spekulation und Ethische Reflexion in der Philosophie von Hans Jonas," in *Weiterwohnlichkeit der Welt*, 253; in my translation. On the persistent presence of Gnostic motives in Jonas' post-war thought, see also: Catherine Chalier, *Dieu sans puissance en complément au livre de Hans Jonas, 'Le concept de Dieu après Auschwitz,'* (Paris: Payot et Rivages, 1994), 52.

57 Jonas, *Philosophical Essays*, 288.
58 It is precisely the issue of dialectics that caused the rift between Jonas and Scholem on the subject of Gnosticism. As Christian Wiese reports, after the 1965 publication of Jonas' polemic with Gilles Quispel, Scholem wrote a long letter in which he "reproached Jonas for treating him 'with poisonous scorn' without ever really having read his works, sarcastically observing that as a philosopher he should be able to understand his, Scholem's, 'dialectical' approach": Christian Wiese, "*For a Time I was Privileged to Enjoy his Friendship…*: The Ambivalent Relationship between Hans Jonas and Gershom Scholem," *The Leo Baeck Institute Year Book*, 49, (1/2004), 25–58; 56. At the same time, however, in the second part of his work on Gnosticism, Jonas himself notices a dialectical tendency inherent to the process of demythologisation that occurs in the transition from the Gnostic "mythology to mystical philosophy": an emergence of a dynamic monistic system in which the initial negation of the world leads to the new eschatological practice of redeeming-repairing the world, which Jonas calls "das Paradoxon der Verweltlichung der Entweltlichungstendenz": Hans Jonas, *Gnosis und spätantiker Geist II. Von der Mythologie zur mystischen Philosophie* (Göttingen: Vandenhoeck & Ruprecht, 1954), 13. See also Lapidot's comment in his chapter on GSG II: "If existential gnosis, the broader historical 'gnostic movement,' was performing *Entweltlichung*, world-negation, as ethical re-subjectivation of knowledge, this performance was characterized by a deep and constitutive ambivalence: on the one hand, it was negating the world, on the other hand, this negation itself constituted a kind of praxis in and of the world, a form of ethics". Elad Lapidot, "Gnosis und spätantiker Geist II. Von der Mythologie zur mystischen Philosophie (1954),"in *Hans Jonas-Handbuch*, ed. Michael Bongardt (Berlin: Springer-Verlag, 2021), 90, (88-95), in my translation.
59 Jonas, *Mortality and Morality*, 142.
60 Jonas, *Mortality and Morality*, 142; emphasis added.
61 According to Christian Wiese, the main difference between Jonas' and Scholem's takes on the Lurianic myth is that the former treats *tsimtsum* as a one-time event inaugurating metaphysical history, while the latter sticks to more Neoplatonic notion of *tsimtsum* as continuous withdrawal; Wiese, "*For a Time…*," 39. In fact, both these interpretative possibilities are present in Scholem's treatment of Luria as a borderline figure of kabbalistic emanationism: the sequence from *tsimtsum* to *shvirat ha-kelim* can also be read as a break with the Neoplatonic tradition, suggesting a much stricter separation between God and the world that becomes fully liberated from the divine influence and set on its own historical course. And while contraction of God may indeed be seen as a continual withdrawal, the breaking of the vessels is definitely a single catastrophe and a turning point in the history of creation. Wiese claims that "Scholem would have perceived this as a distortion of Lurianic Kabbalah" (Christian Wiese, "Zionism, the Holocaust, and Judaism in a Secular World: New Perspectives on Hans Jonas's Friendship with Gershom Scholem and Hannah Arendt," in *The Legacy of Hans Jonas*, 176), but considering Scholem's ambivalence on this point, we cannot be so sure about it.
62 For Scholem, the Book of Job is the paradigmatic case of *kinah*: a lamentation of a single creature over the order of creation, and as such adumbrates the existential mood of 'Jewish Gnosis'; Gershom Scholem, *Tagebücher nebst Aufsätzen und Entwürfen bis*

    1923, 2 vols., ed. Karlfried Gründer (Frankfurt am Main: Jüdischer Verlag im Suhrkamp, 1995–2000), 550.
63 See Ernst Bloch, *Atheism in Christianity*, trans. J. T. Swann (London: Verso, 2009), 79.
64 Jonas, *Mortality and Morality*, 142.
65 Benjamin, *Illuminations*, trans. Harry Zohn (New York: Schocken Books, 2007), 254.
66 *Pirke Aboth: The Sayings of the Fathers*, trans. Joseph Hertz (London: Behrman House, 1945) 2;21.
67 Christian Wiese notices too that "what stands behind these thoughts – as in the case of *tzimizum* – is an equally philosophically transformed and radicalized interpretation of the kabbalistic idea of *tikkun olam*, the ability and obligation of humankind to work as partners in God's creation": Wiese, *The Life and Thought*, 136. Yet, he is very reluctant to see any equivalent of the Lurianic messianism, which involves 'the interaction of God and man,' in Jonas's thought: "Jonas's interpretation necessarily divests the myth of this messianic component; since the powerless deity that he conceives of 'has nothing more to give.' This de-messianizing of *tikkun* sheds more light on the absence of the messianic element in Jonas's philosophy in general […] In place of redemption of the world, one finds the duty to preserve that which has been created and the need to accept responsibility for God" (Wiese, *The Life and Thought*, 136–137). But while it is true that Jonas is not a type of a hot messianist who would hope for the ultimate conquering of the world of matter (in the manner of Ernst Bloch whom he severely criticised), his principle of responsibility for creation can still be characterized as a manifestation of a 'weak messianic power' that does not desist from the work of lifting the sparks wherever possible.
68 Jonas, *Gnosis und Spätaniker Geist II*, 156.
69 See Cyril O'Regan, *The Gnostic Return in Modernity* (Albany, NY: SUNY Press, 2001).
70 Jonas, *Mortality and Morality*, 142.
71 On Jonas' ongoing interest in the 'Gnostic Syndrome,' see Nathalie Frogneux's contribution in this volume: "And when he was the object of criticism at the Messina colloquium in 1967, which led to a stabilization of the distinction between Gnosis and Gnosticism, he nevertheless published his contribution under the title "The Gnostic Syndrome" in the important collection of *Philosophical Essays*, using the adjective "gnostic" rather than choosing between the nouns *Gnosis* and *Gnosticism*, and the term "syndrome" to designate this historical phenomenon of great magnitude with vague contours but with an identifiable focus for those who manage to liberate the mind from forms (pseudomorphosis). Jonas will thus maintain his thesis from the 1930s until the 1990s and his reply to an apolitical and ethical thought" (104).
72 Jonas, *Philosophical Essays*, xiv.
73 Jonas, *Gnostic Religion*, 326.
74 Jonas, *Gnostic Religion*, 326.
75 Jonas, *Gnostic Religion*, 332.
76 In her essay, "Resisting Nihilism: The Motif of *Entwurzelung* in Jonas's Early Writings" (also in this volume), Libera Pisano rightly claims that it is not so much Gnosticism itself as rather nihilism, which pertains to the extreme Gnostic dualism, that Jonas ultimately sought to overcome: "in the first phase of his thought, Jonas was looking for strategies for facing the abyss and for withstanding nihilism […] I would define Jonas's account of nihilism as a way of inhabiting the world in a metaphysical uprootedness that entails an ethical and political rejection of any responsibility as well as a passive acceptance of fatalism." (201–202). In my reading, Jonas' dialectical reworking of the Lurianic myth retains the main tenets of Gnostic mythology, but deprives them of their potential nihilistic implications in political despondency and existential quietism.
77 Jonas, *Mortality and Morality*, 131.
78 Hannah Arendt, usually critical of mysticism as an anti-worldly and anti-political way of life, became fascinated with the Sabbatian application of the Lurianic metaphysics after she learned it from Scholem's *Major Trends*. In 1944, in an attempt to

promote the English translation of Scholem's work, Arendt wrote an essay, "Jewish Religion Revised," in which she perceives the Lurianic type of mysticism as a welcome exception leading to the active messianic concern about this world as opposed to the traditional forms of the acosmic religious attitude. On the reception of Scholem's writings on Jewish messianism by Arendt, before their fall-out after the publication of *Eichmann in Jerusalem*, see most of all: Vivian Liska, *German-Jewish Thought and Its Afterlife. A Tenuous Legacy* (Bloomington: Indiana University Press, 2017), the chapter "Tradition and the Hidden: Arendt Reading Scholem," 17–25. Duns Scotus' *directio mundi* is widely appreciated in Arendt's last work: Hannah Arendt, *The Life of the Mind. Thinking & Willing (One-Volume Edition)* (New York: A Harvest Book, Harcourt, 1977), 196.
79 *Memoirs: Hans Jonas*, 107–108.

Bibliography

Arendt, Hannah. *The Life of the Mind. Thinking & Willing (One-Volume Edition)*. New York: A Harvest Book, Harcourt, 1977.
Bajohr, Hannes, *Hans Blumenberg/ Hans Jonas: Briefwechsel 1954–1978 und weitere Materialien*, ed. Hannes Bajohr. Frankfurt am Main: Suhrkamp, 2022.
Benjamin, Walter, *Illuminations*, trans. Harry Zohn. New York: Schocken Books, 2007.
Bielik-Robson, Agata, "God of Luria, Hegel, Schelling: The Divine Contraction and the Modern Metaphysics of Finitude," in *Mystical Theology and Continental Philosophy*, ed. David Lewin, Simon Podmore, and Duane Williams. London: Routledge, 2017, 32–50.
Bielik-Robson, Agata, "An Unhistorical History of Tsimtsum: A Break with Neoplatonism?," in *Tsimtsum and Modernity. Lurianic Heritage in Modern Philosophy and Theology*, ed. Agata Bielik-Robson and Daniel H. Weiss. Berlin: de Gruyter, 2021, 1–37.
Bloch, Ernst, *Atheism in Christianity*, trans. J. T. Swann. London: Verso, 2009.
Blumenberg, Hans, *Arbeit am Mythos*. Frankfurt am Main: Suhrkamp, 1979.
Blumenberg, Hans, *The Legitimacy of the Modern Age*, trans. Robert M. Wallace. Cambridge, MA: MIT Press, 1985.
Blumenberg, Hans, *The Work on Myth*, trans. Robert M. Wallace. Cambridge, MA: MIT Press, 1985.
Chalier, Catherine, *Dieu sans puissance en complément au livre de Hans Jonas, 'Le concept de Dieu après Auschwitz.'* Paris: Payot et Rivages, 1994.
Falque, Emmanuel, *God, the Flesh, and the Other. From Irenaeus to Duns Scotus*, trans. William Christian Hackett. Evanston, IL: Northwestern University Press, 2015.
Herskowitz, Daniel M., "Reading Heidegger against the Grain: Hans Jonas on Existentialism, Gnosticism, and Modern Science," *Modern Intellectual History*, 19, nr 2 (2021), 1–24.
Jacobson, Eric and Wiese, Christian, *Weiterwohnlichkeit der Welt. Zur Aktualität von Hans Jonas*. Berlin-Wien: Philo Verlagsgesellschaft, 2003.
Jonas, Hans, *Gnosis und spätantiker Geist I. Die Mythologische Gnosis*. Göttingen, Vandenhoeck & Ruprecht, 1934.
Jonas, Hans, *Gnosis und spätantiker Geist II. Von der Mythologie zur mystischen Philosophie*. Göttingen, Vandenhoeck & Ruprecht, 1954.
Jonas, Hans, *Philosophical Essays: From Contemporary Creed to Technological Man*. Evanston, IL: Northwestern University Press, 1974.
Jonas, Hans, *The Imperative of Responsibility. In Search of an Ethics for the Technological Age*, trans. Hans Jonas and David Herr. Chicago, IL: The University of Chicago Press, 1984.

Jonas, Hans, *Mortality and Morality. A Search for the Good after Auschwitz*, ed. Lawrence Vogel. Evanston, IL: Northwestern University Press, 1996.
Jonas, Hans, *The Gnostic Religion. The Message of the Alien God and The Beginnings of Christianity*. Boston, MA: Beacon Press, 2001.
Jonas, Hans, *The Phenomenon of Life. Toward a Philosophical Biology*. Evanston, IL: Northwestern University Press, 2001.
Jonas, Hans, *Memoirs: Hans Jonas*, ed. Christian Wiese and Krishna Winston. Waltham, MA: Brandeis University Press, 2008.
Jonas, Hans, *Der Gottesbegriff nach Auschwitz Eine jüdische Stimme*. Frankfurt am Main: Suhrkamp, 2016.
Lapidot, Elad. "Gnosis und spätantiker Geist II. Von der Mythologie zur mystischen Philosophie (1954)." In *Hans Jonas-Handbuch*. Ed. Michael Bongardt. Berlin: Springer-Verlag, 2021, 88–95.
Lazier, Benjamin, *God Interrupted: Heresy and the European Imagination between the World Wars*. Princeton, NJ: Princeton University Press, 2012.
Liska, Vivian, *German-Jewish Thought and Its Afterlife. A Tenuous Legacy*. Bloomington: Indiana University Press, 2017.
O'Regan, Cyril, *The Gnostic Return in Modernity*. Albany, NY: SUNY Press, 2001.
O'Regan, Cyril, *Pirke Aboth: The Sayings of the Fathers*, trans. Joseph Hertz. London: Behrman House, 1945.
Rubenstein, Alan, "Hans Jonas: A Study in Biology and Ethics," *Society*, 46 (2009), 160–167.
Scholem, Gershom, *On Jews and Judaism in Crisis. Selected Essays.* ed. Werner Dannhauser. New York: Schocken, 1976.
Scholem, Gershom, *Judaica 1*. Frankfurt am Main: Suhrkamp, 1997.
Scholem, Gershom, *On the Kabbalah and Its Symbolism*. New York: Schocken, 1969.
Scholem, Gershom, *Tagebücher nebst Aufsätzen und Entwürfen bis 1923*, 2 vols., ed. Karlfried Gründer. Frankfurt am Main: Jüdischer Verlag im Suhrkamp, 1995–2000.
Seeskin, Kenneth, "*Tsimtsum* and the Root of Finitude," in *Tsimtsum and Modernity. Lurianic Heritage in Modern Philosophy and Theology*, ed. Agata Bielik-Robson and Daniel H. Weiss. Berlin: de Gruyter, 2021, 107–118.
Tirosh-Samuelson, Hava and Wiese, Christian, eds., *The Legacy of Hans Jonas. Judaism and the Phenomenon of Life*. Leiden/Boston, MA: Brill 2010.
Vogel, Lawrence, "Hans Jonas's Exodus: from German Existentialism to Post-Holocaust Theology," in Hans Jonas, *Mortality and Morality. A Search for the Good after Auschwitz*, ed. Lawrence Vogel. Evanston, IL: Nortwestern University Press, 1996, 1–40.
Wiese, Christian, "*For a Time I was Privileged to Enjoy his Friendship...*: The Ambivalent Relationship between Hans Jonas and Gershom Scholem," *The Leo Baeck Institute Year Book*, 49 (1/2004), 25–58.
Wiese, Christian, *The Life and Thought of Hans Jonas: Jewish Dimensions*, trans. Jeffrey Grossman and Christian Wiese. Waltham, MA: Brandeis University Press, 2007.
Wolin, Richard, *Heidegger's Children. Hannah Arendt, Karl Löwith, Hans Jonas, and Herbert Marcuse*. Princeton, NJ: Princeton University Press, 2001.

12 Resisting Nihilism

The Motif of *Entwurzelung* in Jonas' Early Writings

Libera Pisano

In his famous and somewhat controversial essay "Gnosticism and Modern Nihilism," written in 1952, Hans Jonas describes the Gnostic heart of modern nihilism and existentialism as the radical foreignness and *Heimatlosigkeit* that characterize the human condition.[1] At the outset of this essay, he quotes Nietzsche's poem *Vereinsamt*, whose last line is: "Woe unto him who has no home!" This is the hermeneutic trace that I want to follow in this contribution in order to read Jonas' philosophical project through the prism of uprootedness from the vantage point of his earlier works. My claim is that his thought can be broadly defined as a challenge to a philosophical and political *Heimatlosigkeit* that manifests as a Zionistic commitment in the first phase of his thought and in the second phase as a development of a philosophy that argues for a harmonious relationship between humanity and nature. According to my interpretation, Jonas' early writings can be seen as a passionate reaction to a nihilistic disposition inherent in the uprootedness embodied by Diasporic Judaism, a disposition that – as we will see – bears similarities to a Gnostic attitude.

As is well known, in the preface to the third edition of his English book *The Gnostic Religion*, Jonas interpreted his *Kehre* after the war and emphasized it perhaps a little too much, revealing a certain unease.[2] However, this was not a real farewell to Gnosticism, or better to the topic that Gnosticism represents, since at the end of this preface, he drew a line from his early research to his most recent studies. I argue that while the first phase of Jonas' thought can be considered a critical analysis of the uprootedness of the human being, the most glaring examples of which are Diasporic Judaism and Gnosticism,[3] the second phase can be defined as a *pars construens* of a philosophical attempt to overcome this uprootedness. Jonas' statement in his *Memoirs* that "any discussion of my philosophy should begin not with Gnosticism but with my efforts to establish a philosophical biology" is therefore correct.[4]

Gnosticism thus represents both the negative on which Jonas is able to build his own proposal[5] and a philosophical phenomenon that clearly epitomizes some features of the time in which he lived. In the first phase of his thought, he was looking for strategies for facing the abyss and for withstanding nihilism that – as we will see – can be interpreted in many ways. It is possible to tentatively define Jonas' early conception of nihilism – even though he will not use this term until

DOI: 10.4324/9781003439882-12

later – in the context of his initial writings as a mode of existence characterized by metaphysical rootlessness that leads to a lack of ethical and political responsibility.[6]

The structure of my chapter will be as follows. First, I will analyze Jonas' commitment to overcoming nihilism and uprootedness through both his early Zionist writings, in particular his historical interpretation of the Prophets, and his work on Gnosticism. Then I will explore his theoretical and practical commitment to opposing uprootedness as a prism through which it is possible to interpret his philosophical project. Finally, I will discuss the fine line between politics and philosophy in Jonas' thought, whose anti-utopian and anti-messianic features allow him to reject the notion of an ontological and ethical void and perhaps even to question the very concept of politics.

The Jewish Alternative to Nihilism

The reaction to the spiritual and practical *Heimatlosigkeit* that is present in Jonas' writings allows us to situate him in his *Zeitgeist* as well as in the constellation of German-Jewish thinkers of the twentieth century.[7] At this time, such thinkers were looking for ways to understand the political turmoil in Germany between the two wars and the philosophical crisis of a whole set of values, which starts with Nietzsche's thought, the collapse of classical reasoning, the failure of the teleological understanding of history,[8] and a social and epistemological need for new models in order to find another approach to the world. This attempt was a collective effort that characterized the intellectual work of a generation of German-Jewish thinkers – such as, for instance, Landauer, Benjamin, Buber, and Rosenzweig – and drew on the reserve of Judaism as a heterodox tradition. For this generation, the Jewish alternative was a guiding image that allowed them to rethink the philosophical and political challenges of the time; namely, the bond between politics, history, and redemption. Even though they had different solutions, Judaism offered them a hermeneutical horizon and a *Gegen-bild* in a particular historical moment, which was the incubation of the end of German-Jewish history.

Jonas' works fit squarely within the collective effort of this generation of German-Jewish writers. In this nihilistic crisis in which all the assumptions fading out of significance could lead either to fatalism or to a radical indifference toward the world, it is no coincidence that "something in Gnosticism knocks at the door of our Being and of our 20th century Being in particular."[9] I argue that what Hans Jonas later calls "cosmic nihilism,"[10] along with concepts like *Entwurzelung*, *Heimatlosigkeit*, exile, and *Weltfremdheit*, which are frequently mentioned in Jonas' early works in various contexts, serves as a *terminus negativus* to which his philosophy responds. This response begins with his first essay on the Prophets and continues in his first book on Gnosticism, published in 1934.

Proactive Zionism as a Historical Commitment

In his *Memoirs*, Jonas emphasized the moment he discovered his Jewishness,[11] which was after World War One when people were divided between Rosa

Luxemburg and Gustav Noske. He depicted Zionism as a third view between left and right. However, he admitted that in the 1920s, his only concern was the overcoming of Galut by means of a Zionistic solution.[12] As we will see in the last section of this chapter, this concern was not religious or political in a broader sense, but rather mostly philosophical. In fact, Jonas' Zionism was not due to a religious conviction – he said that "although I was deeply moved by the Bible, I wasn't a believer"[13] – or to a messianic hope. Rather, it was as *sachlich*, factual, as possible.[14] This emerges in his essay on the Prophets as well as in an essay on education in Palestine published in the *Zionistisches Handbuch* in 1923, both of which stress the importance of a practical interest and a determined approach.

Jonas' anti-ideological way of conceiving politics has to do with his proactive attitude and his particular engagement with history. According to him – in a manner that was completely antithetical to that of Franz Rosenzweig[15] – the European Jews had to become political subjects and thus enter history. This historical commitment is evident when he speaks about the Prophets in his *Memoirs*, as well as in his first essay, "*Die Idee der Zerstreuung und Wiedersammlung bei den Propheten*," which was written while he was a member of the Maccabea Zionist student association and published in *Der jüdische Student* in 1922. Jonas admits that his fascination with the Prophets of Israel was not a "timeless revelation of the divine truth," but an event that needs to be interpreted "through the lens of modern historical scholarship."[16] It was precisely the living legacy of the Prophets that struck him the most: "Their voice spoke powerfully to me, and made Israel's legacy come alive for me in a way that no service or religious instruction had been able to do."[17]

According to Jonas, the voice of the Prophets was a translation of the word of God into human language.[18] This discovery led him to an important assumption that shaped his entire life; namely, "that the word of God can be uttered only by human mouths."[19] The manifestation and expression of the divine occurs through the voices of human beings. However, the voices of the Prophets were not welcome at first. Their unpopular message interfered with social norms, and only later – after the catastrophe was over – their task changed. It could be argued that Jonas saw his own Zionist involvement as a prophetic calling, since he was among the earliest advocates to stress the need to leave Germany and to warn of the real dangers of National Socialism before it came to power.[20]

There is one particular aspect of Jonas' account of the Prophets that needs to be mentioned. According to an idea of revelation not received through the eye, but through the ear, "a person's inner ear,"[21] the Prophets could not act differently, but felt obliged to proclaim what they heard: "Anyone who heard that couldn't help proclaiming it." He considered this "the essence of revelation," and I would describe it as the essence of his commitment: that he could not back down, as is also evident in his resolute call "Our Part in This War: A Word to Jewish Men."[22] This was Jonas' manifesto, which was presented for the first time at Gustav Krojanker's house in Jerusalem in 1939. Here, he emphasized the need for a historical commitment from the Jewish people, "the Nazis' metaphysical enemy" in this "total war."[23] Jonas depicts the war in its "mythological dimension"[24] and calls on the Jewish people to remain committed against the fatalism that was paralyzing them: "A fatalistic certainty that this fate was inescapable was spreading, i.e., a certainty that the *death sentence imposed on us as a people could not be reversed.*"[25] The war was a political and moral opportunity "to feel at home again in this world."[26] Instead of playing the pariah role or adopting a ghetto attitude, seen as "an attitude in which we duck our heads to let the storms of history pass over them," the *bellum judaicum* forced Jewish people to take "the risk of an *autonomous historical existence.*"[27] This urge to enter history was at the heart of Jonas' decision to become a soldier in the Jewish Brigade. The same urge is also found in his first writing on the Prophets.

Diasporic Verworfenheit

Jonas' essay "*Die Idee der Zerstreuung und Wiedersammlung bei den Propheten*" starts with a "gloomy prediction" [*düstere Verkündigung*] made by the Prophets; namely, an "uprooting from the native soil and dispersion among the peoples" [*Entwurzelung aus der Heimaterde und der Zerstreuung unter die Völker*].[28] *Verbannung, Zerstreuung,* and *Heimatlosigkeit* were the worst threat and danger to a people, as the disturbing content of this prophetic prediction was paradoxically opposed to the population's eudemonic vision. While on the one hand, the uprootedness has to be interpreted as the worst divine punishment and vengeance [*die letzte Grenzmöglichkeit göttlicher Rache*],[29] on the other, it was a common practice in antiquity, especially among the Assyrians, to exile at least most – if not all – of the conquered nation. However, according to Jonas, the transition from nomadic to settled life is closely connected with the entire Israelite legal system [*die gesamte israelitische Gesetzgebung*].[30]

Living in the promised land was a "special gift" [*besonderes Geschenk des Ewigen*], and therefore the possession of the land relied on a particular condition. A counter-image, "Gegenbild,"[31] of the scattering as a catastrophe is offered by Ezekiel's prophecy, which is usually interpreted as a praise of the exile. In fact, according to Ezekiel, the Jews in exile were a living testimony of human decadence and divine justice among other peoples:[32] "Their thrownness (*Verworfenheit*) should be a justification of divine action and their fate an unprecedented manifestation of the punishing and revenging power of the Eternal."[33]

Before Gnosticism and Heidegger's *Sein und Zeit*, *Verworfenheit* was the destiny of the Jewish people in Galut. In other words, terms such as "night," "thrownness," and *Entwurzelung* represent the Gnostic elements of Galut Judaism and are symptoms of what we might call an ontological and ethical nihilism. It was precisely this aspect that Jonas sought to overcome by offering an alternative hermeneutic of the prophetic writings. In fact, this is where his counter-move took place. He stated that the Prophets – even Amos, as the most tragic – could not renounce the idea of reuniting the Jewish people with their land. According to him, the reason for this was that all the Prophets were Jews and thus the eternal scattering was also unbearable to them. The prospect of a return was an opportunity to keep their own belief alive. It is not by chance that *Wiedersammlung* occurs many times in the writings of Amos, Hosea, and Micah, along with the idea of return and reconstruction: *bauen und pflanzen*, build and plant.[34]

In his analysis, Jonas deals with different forms that assumed a conjunction between dispersion and reunion, interpreted as the biggest dramas in the relationship between God and human beings. The first way is the "most philosophically primitive idea" based on a "required act of grace by God."[35] This is also the most anthropomorphic idea, in which a God can punish his people, but this punishment can only be overcome by an act of love. Prophetic thought tends to offer an ethical representation of God and interprets the chain of events as a result of the "ethical causality" [*ethische Kausalität*][36] that governs human actions. However, according to Jonas, this is not the only way of reading the conception of the punishment and destiny of the Jewish people. In fact, there is a higher one that interprets the events in a teleological way, where "ethical conditioning and ethical goal-determinism entangle themselves in history."[37] This means that historical events are not merely the result of ethical causes and effects. Rather, they are guided by a broader teleological purpose in which ethical considerations play a role in achieving an ultimate goal. While prophetic thought emphasizes ethical causality as a central aspect of human history, Jonas points to a broader perspective in which ethics and destiny are interwoven to serve a larger plan.

Even Deutero-Isaiah, the prophet of the exile, retrospectively (*rückschauend*) sees the need for the proof, education, and purification – three concepts at the heart of *Völkergeschichte* – that God requires from the Jewish people. This retrospective sight is already a historical interpretation; therefore, Jonas admits that the Prophets conceived and developed "*die erste Geschichtsphilosophie.*"[38] This hermeneutic twist, which entails an anticipation of the future, is what is at stake in Jonas' analysis.[39] Exile and scattering are not only seen as a punishment, but rather as a precondition for a reunion: the passage from the night of the Galut to its *Heimat*.[40]

According to Jonas, the belief in "a God-filled human community of the end times"[41] should be replaced by a possible historical experience; this means a passage from miracle to reality, from abstraction to realization, from messianism to history. At the end of the exile, there is a community to build. However, as the idea of the return of an entire people can be seen as far too optimistic, it can be replaced by the meaningful idea of the "Rest-idee." Some Jews were not ready to leave the Galut in order to plant again and settle down in the promised land; therefore, his pragmatic solution was that "*ein Rest wird umkehren*":[42] only a few people will come back, not everybody.

For Jonas, *Einkehr* and *Umkehr* represent a return to unity in the Jewish people determined by the hermeneutics of the Prophets. This ancient idea is like a thread that connects Isaiah and Amos to Herzl's *Judenstaat*, prophets to Zionists. This call for unity can be defined as the *Streben nach Einheit* for which Martin Buber strives in his discourses on Judaism.[43] In fact, in his famous *Reden*, Buber states that in the books of the Prophets, the book of Job, and the Psalms, it is possible to find the experience of being divided as well as the struggle for unity. This struggle is the most important part of Judaism, *der Weg zum Einswerden*, which is also the antidote to radical dualism that can only be repaired through unity and with a resolute answer.[44] Buber recalls this call to commitment and action at the end of his third discourse, and after quoting – and this is no coincidence – Isaiah, he states: "To be ready means to prepare" [*Bereit sein heiß: bereiten*].[45]

Like Buber, Jonas reads the texts of the Prophets as a hermeneutic tool for Judaism's present needs, but he offers a more historical interpretation of them. For him, the Prophets offer a model for a philosophy of history, but they can also provide some strategies to overcome the situation of Galut. If the uprootedness is the catastrophe and the danger, there is still a possibility of salvation:

> Before the exile, the mood of doom prevails almost exclusively; but after the catastrophe has occurred, it represents the living phenomenon of reacting against the apathetic condition of the defeated body politic and gives ever wider space to expectations of salvation.[46]

Salvation means showing a way to resist the thrownness that Jonas had detected in Diaspora Judaism, but also in Gnosticism, depicted as a radical exile. In fact, the Gnostic could be associated with the figure of Ahasuerus, the perpetual wanderer condemned to an eternal state of banishment. The Gnostic *Entweltlichung*, the deprivation of the world, is antithetical to the Greek idea of belonging to a cosmos, but also to the disposition to take action that is required – for instance – in Jonas' proactive Zionism and his later philosophical commitment.

Gnostic Heimatlosigkeit

Jonas' book on Gnosticism – especially its first volume – is an exilic book for many reasons: firstly because of its circumstances, as the final draft was written in exile in London, "the first stop of my émigré life";[47] secondly because of its method, as Jonas remarks on the outsiderness of his approach for philosophers and theologians alike;[48] and thirdly for its content, as Gnosticism epitomizes a radical exile in this world.

At the outset of *Gnosis* I, Jonas defines the Gnostic terrestrial existence as a "*Knechtschaft in der Fremde.*"[49] *Fremd*, "alien," is the constant connotation of life, and *fremdes Leben* is "one of the great impressive word-symbols"[50] of Gnosticism. However, Jonas also operates a hermeneutic twist in his interpretation of the alien:

> The alien is that which stems from elsewhere and does not belong here. To those who do belong here it is thus the strange, the unfamiliar and incomprehensible; but their world on its part is just as incomprehensible to the alien that comes to dwell here, and like a foreign land where it is far from home.[51]

The stranger is lonely and unprotected, exposed in a situation that is full of danger, but the danger also makes it possible for him to be at ease in the world and to forget his own origin: "If he learns its ways too well, he forgets that he is a stranger and gets lost in a different sense by succumbing to the lure of the alien world and becoming estranged from his own origin."[52] There is likewise ambiguity in the alien's *Aufenthalt*, the cosmic habitation in the world. In fact, on the one hand, dwelling in this world is something contingent and temporary, but on the other, the dwelling place depends on the place and surroundings that are fundamental to the inhabitant. A life thrown into the world – which is actually "*die Gefahr des Wohnens*"[53] – could consider himself "a son of the house" even if "his root was not of the world."[54]

The radical opposition between the present world, which is seen as a negative element, and a positive outside world is the backbone of Gnostic radical anti-cosmism. The "culmination of the stranger's tragedy" is the "awakened homesickness" – the knowledge of his nature – through which "the beginning of the return"[55] to his native realm, outside the world, can start. Gnosis, in its capacity as knowledge and awareness of this alienation, already entails the first step toward the positive world. It becomes the tool to free the human being from the prison of the world in view of the union with the otherworldly divinity. For Jonas, however, the Gnostic transcendence is not "the essence of that world, but its negation and cancellation."[56] Therefore, this knowledge cannot have a soteriological value: "Since the cosmos is contrary to life, the saving knowledge cannot aim at the knower's integration into the cosmic whole, cannot aim at compliance with the laws of the universe."[57]

Like the Diasporic Jew who conceives the world as a homeless and unredeemed place,[58] the Gnostic uprootedness means an alienated way of inhabiting the world that entails an "antagonistic, anti-divine and, therefore, anti-human nature."[59] In fact, the Gnostic pneumatic self – whose destiny depends on the *pneuma*, which is not of this world – can dispose the natural realm as he wishes and be indifferent to everything. This alienated indifference toward the world also has moral implications and leads to what Jonas – after the war – calls "nihilism of mundane norms."[60] In his *Gnostic Religion*, the absence of a doctrine of *arete* means that negativity becomes praxis, as is particularly evident in libertinism and askesis, two attitudes determined by hostility toward the world and disregard of all human actions.[61] For the pneuma as well as for the God – both of whom are hidden – there is no nomos, no law of nature or human conduct, and therefore they correspond to a "nihilistic conception."[62] Living "outside the mundane norms"[63] is another formula for defining nihilism. In fact, even if it is not a metaphysical nihilism, since Gnosis as knowledge provides a foundational and eschatological myth,[64] it is a sort of nihilism of responsibility toward the world and thus the most dangerous one.

This Gnostic *Heimatlosigkeit* does indeed have decisive political implications. In his *Memoirs*, Jonas writes that his dissertation on Gnosticism "was potentially a thousand times more political than Hannah Arendt's, the concept of love in Augustine."[65] Moreover, he said that the political drive in his work had also been detected by the conservative Leo Strauss, who was shocked by this secret revolutionary element.[66] The covert political component hidden in this text has to do with nihilism being seen as "the purest and most radical expression of the metaphysical revolt"[67] that deals not with creation, but only with destruction. Even if Gnosticism is not political in itself, it is derivatively political, since it has to do – according to my interpretation – with the Hegelian "*verkehrte Welt*" that also holds a political significance: "Instead of taking over the value-system of the traditional myth, it proves the deeper 'knowledge' by reversing the roles of good and evil, sublime and base, blest and accursed, found in the original."[68]

This inversion of contents is not just semantic – as Jonas underlines in the Gnostic allegories or in the Gnostic vocabulary, for instance, when describing Cain as a "pneumatic symbol"[69] – but it is also hermeneutic: Gnosticism is a radical resemantization of a particular *Weltordnung*.[70] In the Gnostic attitude, there is a profound negation and degradation of the world that has to do with fatalism.[71] However, Gnostic fatalism is completely different from the Greek *Ananke*; while the latter was "the metaphysical crowning of the whole *Seinsbildes*,"[72] the former is devoid of any metaphysical meaning. The Gnostic's fundamentally negative attitude toward the cosmos does not culminate in political revolt or revolution, but in the rejection of a positive worldview that could serve as the ontological basis for any ethical or political commitment.

The Danger of Political Nihilism

At this point, it is necessary to consider the narrow ridge between politics and philosophy in Jonas' thought. In his *Memoirs*, it is almost surprising to learn that during his years in the Heideggerian circle, Jonas was under the spell of pure philosophy. When he told Heidegger about the sixteenth Zionist congress in Basel in 1929 – which was the subject of the only conversation they had about Zionism – he was shocked to find that his mentor was not aware that this was a political gathering, but instead imagined the congress taking place "in a big tent."[73] However, Jonas justified Heidegger's attitude as that of one who has no clue about "the burning problems in contemporary society and politics."[74] This apolitical approach was shared by all the members of Heidegger's circle – even Arendt – with the exception of Günther Stern, who was engaged in social criticism. The philosophers in this circle were removed from the world and this "fateful situation"[75] was extremely apolitical. Jonas' explanation for this is that they had been captured by philosophy as a spiritual realm "that removed one from the hustle and bustle of ordinary life,"[76] which was the reason why Arendt considered Jonas' political Zionism as a "lovable weakness."[77] This political *Entweltlichung* is another aspect that the Heideggerians shared with Gnosticism. Their negation to the mundane world, which is another way of saying nihilism, means indifference to history and is also the common denominator of Diaspora Judaism, Gnosticism, and the Heideggerian apolitical attitude.

Jonas' account of politics was also ambiguous, since he defined himself as an apolitical Zionist. He was not interested in politics as a broader "formula that would solve the problem of the world."[78] Even if he acknowledged that socialism and the Russian Revolution held "a certain fascination" for him, he defined himself as a moderate – he voted for the German Democratic Party – but also as one who was not very involved in political matters in Germany or in the world in general. He only had one interest: "Namely that the Jewish existence in the Galut – in a human, psychological, and political sense – was untenable in the long run and had to be overcome by means of the Zionist solution."[79] He defined his approach as apolitical since it was not moved by a universal issue; rather, it was exclusively devoted to the destiny of the Jews. However, his rejection of politics was not a rejection of political practices, but rather of political ideologies and abstractions – in a nutshell, of political ideology.

There is an illuminating passage in Jonas' *Memoirs* where he defines philosophy in a Kantian way as "the realm of practical reason."[80] When describing the later shift of his philosophical project to the nature of human beings, he said of himself that he had "slid irreversibly into the role of a philosopher who not only commented on current practical questions but sometimes even intervened to prescribe or warn against a course of action."[81] He claimed that this was an original view, since in his case, the philosophical aspect comes first, in contrast to Marxism, where the political aspect is most important: "Philosophy wasn't simply an expression of a political position, as it was for the Marxist philosophers, but that as a philosopher one had an obligation to make an independent contribution to the things of this world and human affairs."[82] After the war – as he emphasized many times – Jonas decided to devote himself to the understanding of "our organic Being, [...] life in general."[83]

The attempt to overcome the split between human beings and nature in its radical form is the most important urge in Jonas' philosophical thought, which proposes a coalescence between ethics and ontology.[84] Human responsibility has to be deeply connected to the ontological structure of reality and the world as a living world. Jonas conceived his theoretical endeavors as a mission that brings us to a different self-understanding of philosophy by answering a long-neglected question: "How the human being should behave toward nature [...], how can we live with nature – or how nature can survive together with us."[85] The focal point of his philosophy is nature, not human relationships; it is cosmic, not political.[86] In this regard, one can say that he remains a member of the Heideggerian circle.

However, how is it possible to conceive of this question as politically neutral? How can our way of inhabiting the world not be also and above all political? Or does every political project call for an anti-cosmism? My claim is that Jonas' rejection of politics on an ideological level has to do with the nihilistic danger that can be hidden in any ideological, poetic, utopic, and messianic approach. On the one hand, Jonas rejects the messianic belief that would resolve the imperfection of human beings on earth.[87] In fact, messianism would have meant admitting to seeing time as an empty space to be filled. This also has moral implications, in a similar way to what Gershom Scholem calls *Leben im Aufschub*, "a life lived in deferment," as a result of the messianic idea of Judaism that corresponds to the "powerlessness of Jewish history during the years of the exile."[88] On the other hand, Jonas also rejected utopias:

> The only form of political philosophy that I really rejected was utopianism. We can't afford a utopian notion of individual fulfillment, of achieving an ideal society; it's simply too dangerous. First of all, such a goal is overreaching, and second, under current conditions it can lead straight to destruction – by raising people's expectations instead of moderating them.[89]

Utopia's "no-place" cannot be included in Jonas' thought, which is, on the contrary, a thought of the place, of the topos, not of its negation or alienation.[90]

There is an interesting similarity between utopianism and Gnosticism, as Scholem underlines in a short passage in his autobiography *Vom Berlin nach Jerusalem*. Here,

Scholem – who on another occasion quoted Jonas on Gnosticism in order to describe the dissolution of human behavior[91] – uses the adjective "pneumatic" in order to describe the anarchic atmosphere of the Forte Kreis to which Buber, Florens Christian Rang, Gustav Landauer, and Walther Rathenau belonged, a concrete attempt driven by a utopian urge to change society.[92] "Pneumatic" fits perfectly, for instance, with Landauer's idea of an anarchistic spiritual community to be realized as the negation of the contemporary state.[93] It can be said that the emptiness of pneuma is the (too fragile) *arche* of anarchic thought. It is not by coincidence that both the opening and the closing sentence of Max Stirner's *The Ego and His Own* are: "On nothing have I set my heart [*Ich hab' mein Sach' auf nichts gestellt*]."[94] This nothingness is synonymous with anarchy, as a rejection and abandonment of fixed identities. Both the individual and the world are permanently becoming, a flux of potentialities based on an abyss of nothingness that, far from being an inert element or metaphysical entity, is a creative void from which a constant self-becoming emerges.

Jonas conceived his philosophy as an antidote to this nothingness.[95] He directed his efforts first as a Zionist and later as a philosopher not only against an existential indifference to this world, but also against this attitude based on political, anarchic, and creative *nihil*. The "insurmountably empty" [*unüberwindlich leer*][96] that Buber saw in Heidegger's philosophy is what Jonas sees in the detached existence of Diasporic Judaism, in Gnosticism's anti-cosmism, in the anarchic project, and in the utopian-messianic way of conceiving politics. In its attempt to avoid alienation, which is the core of any political project, Jonas' philosophy is pro-cosmic, metaphysically full, and does not tolerate the vacuum of nihilism.

As a modern prophet of belonging to this world driven by an unshakable faith, Jonas possessed an unwavering and resolute attitude, quite incompatible with abstract and utopian notions. He recognized the dangers of political nihilism and viewed it as a form of escapism that resembled utopian and messianic ideologies. Therefore, he deliberately chose an affirmative stance. Despite terrible things, for Jonas, the world was not a "hostile place."[97] However, his struggle against nihilism led him to adopt a too narrow and too rooted idea of politics that is supposed to, but cannot be anchored to reality and to refuse a more philosophical conception of politics that risks the failure of utopian visions and messianic promises.

Acknowledgments

This research was funded by FCT—Fundação para a Ciência e a Tecnologia, I.P., under project reference 2020.01845 CEECIND, with DOI identifier 10.54499/2020.01845.CEECIND/CP1586/CT0009 (https://doi.org/10.54499/2020.01845.CEECIND/CP1586/CT0009)

Notes

1 Hans Jonas, "Gnosticism and Modern Nihilism," *Social Research* 19, no. 4 (1952): 430–452.
2 See Hans Jonas, "Preface to the Third Edition," in *The Gnostic Religion: The Message of the Alien God & the Beginnings of Christianity* (Boston, MA: Beacon Press,

2001), xiii–xxviii. This preface must be dated to 1963. See Jonathan Cahana-Blum, "Gnosis. Die Botschaft des fremden Gottes (1958)," in *Hans Jonas Handbuch. Leben – Werk – Wirkung*, ed. Michael Bongardt, Holger Burckhart, John-Stewart Gordon, and Jürgen Nielsen-Sikora (Berlin: Metzler, 2021), 96–103, 99. Jonas had a tendency to dismiss his work on Gnosis as his "journeyman's project, an application of Heidegger's philosophy, especially of existential analysis, with its particular interpretive methodology and its understanding of human existence, to a specific body of historical material." Cf. Hans Jonas, *Memoirs*, ed. Christian Wiese, trans. Krishna Winston (Lebanon, NH: Brandeis University Press, 2008), 65.

3 In "Gnosticism and Modern Nihilism," Jonas said that Gnosticism is "one situation, and one only that I know of in the history of Western man, where – on a level untouched by anything resembling modern scientific thought – that condition [of estrangement between man and the world] has been realized and lived out with all the vehemence of a cataclysmic event." See Jonas, "Gnosticism and Modern Nihilism," 433.

4 Jonas, *Memoirs*, 65.

5 This statement in no way diminishes the importance of Gnosticism in Jonas' thought; on the contrary, it reinforces it. There is an abundance of hidden traces of Gnosticism in his later philosophy due to his longstanding preoccupation with it. On this aspect, see Fabio Fossa, "Nihilism, Existentialism, – and Gnosticism? Reassessing the Role of the Gnostic Religion in Hans Jonas's Thought," *Philosophy and Social Criticism* 46, no. 1 (2020): 64–90.

6 One can say that nihilism appears in many forms in Jonas' philosophy. For instance, Elad Lapidot defined it as the practical implication of a philosophy that excludes any possibility of recognizing law, values, or ethics in order to live life in this world. See Elad Lapidot, "Gnosis und spätantiker Geist II. Von der Mythologie zur mystischen Philosophie (1954)," in *Hans Jonas Handbuch*, 88–95, here 94; or Fossa, who writes: "Jonas seems to define nihilism as a practical attitude centered on the creative, self-affirmative power of will. In addition, such attitude is explicitly linked to the recognition of being's value neutrality, which serves as ontological support to the attitude itself." Fossa, "Nihilism, Existentialism, – and Gnosticism?" 71.

7 See the work of Pierre Bouretz, *Témoins du futur. Philosophie et messianism* (Paris: Gallimard, 2003).

8 It is no coincidence that Jonas recalls Spengler's *Untergang des Abendlandes* on several occasions. Cf. Hans Jonas, *Gnosis und späteantiker Geist. Erster Teil: Die mythologische Gnosis*, 4th ed. (Göttingen: Vandhoeck & Ruprecht, 1988), 73: "Ein großer Aussenseiter der Wissenschaft: Oswald Spengler."

9 Jonas remarks on the contemporary aspects of Gnosticism, stating that it could be particularly useful for understanding our human existence by offering a "strange and even shocking form of an extreme option about the meaning of Being, the situation of man, the absolute importance of selfhood and the wrestling with the saving of this selfhood from all the powers of alienation that impinge on man." See Jonas, *The Gnostic Religion*, xxvi. On the "neo-gnostic" spirit in the Weimar Republic, see Paul Mendes-Flohr, "Gnostic Anxieties: Jewish Intellectuals and Weimar Neo-Marcionism," *Modern Theology* 35, no. 1 (2019): 71–81.

10 Jonas, "Gnosticism and Modern Nihilism," 433.

11 See Jonas, *Memoirs*, 25.

12 See Jonas, *Memoirs*, 69.

13 Jonas, *Memoirs*, 214.

14 In the collective volume entitled *Vom Judentum*, which was edited in 1913 by the Bar Kochba association, a Zionist organization based in Prague, Hans Kohn wrote: "Zionism ist keine Wissenschaft, kein logisches Begriffsystem […]. Er ist kein Wissen, sondern Leben. Leben war stets Kampf, so ist es auch unsere Aufgabe mit diesem Volke zu ringen, um es zu neuem, reinem freiem Dasein zu führen." See Kohn, "Geleitwort," in *Vom Judentum*, ed. Bar Kochba (Leipzig: Kurt Wolff Verlag, 1913), viii.

212 Libera Pisano

15 In the *Star of Redemption*, Rosenzweig argues that the Jews are already at the goal, *am Ziel*, outside of historical time and do not need to enter history. Cf. Franz Rosenzweig, *The Star of Redemption* [1921], trans. Barbara E. Galli (Madison: Wisconsin Press, 2005), 351–354. Also, in the essay "Geist und Epochen der jüdischen Geschichte," Rosenzweig argues that the Jewish people are outside the historical vice and that they are free of the violence of time. See Franz Rosenzweig, *Der Mensch und sein Werk. Gesammelte Schriften 3. Zweistromland. Kleinere Schriften zu Glauben und Denken*, ed. Reinhold and Annemarie Mayer (Dordrecht: Martinus Nijhoff, 1984), 538: "The Jewish spirit breaks the chains of the epochs. Because he himself is eternal and wants eternity, he denies the omnipotence of time. He goes untouched through history. No wonder that history and what lives in it are resentful of him, because the time wants everything that lives to reimburse the duty of temporality" (my translation).
16 Jonas, *Memoirs*, 30.
17 Jonas, *Memoirs*, 30.
18 As for the importance of the prophets, it would be interesting to compare Jonas' position with that of Margarete Susman, who shared Goethe's idea that the prophets were the founders of a philosophy of history. Unlike Jonas, however, Susman uses the prophets, especially Ezekiel, who is defined as a prophet of exile, to defend a Diasporic Judaism. See Margarete Susman, "Ezechiel, der Prophet der Umkehr, und die Bestimmung des jüdischen Volkes," *Neue Wege* 36 (1942): 8–23. Another important reference to the role of the prophets is found in Hermann Cohen's thought, especially in his 1901 speech "Der Stil der Propheten." See Hermann Cohen, *Jüdische Schriften*, 3 vols., *Ethische und religiose Grundfragen* (Berlin: Schwetschke & Sohn, 1924), I: 262–330. On Cohen's account of the prophets, see also the work of Daniel H. Weiss, *Paradox and the Prophets: Hermann Cohen and the Indirect Communication of Religion* (Oxford: Oxford University Press, 2012).
19 Jonas, *Memoirs*, 30.
20 After the Jewish boycott on April 1, 1933, during which many German Jews considered Zionism as a betrayal, Jonas gave a speech on the necessity of emigration that was not well received. In his *Memoirs*, he remembers the world of a lady who told his mother: "Your son was right; he was a real prophet" (Jonas, *Memoirs*, 35).
21 Jonas, *Memoirs*, 31.
22 His manifesto is reported verbatim in his *Memoirs*, 111–120.
23 Jonas, *Memoirs*, 112.
24 Jonas, *Memoirs*, 112.
25 Jonas, *Memoirs*, 115; italics in original.
26 Jonas, *Memoirs*, 115.
27 Jonas, *Memoirs*, 116.
28 Hans Jonas, *Herausforderungen und Profile. Jüdisch-deutscher Geist in der Zeit-gegen die Zeit*, ed. Sebastian Lalla, Florian Preußger, and Dietrich Böhler, vol. 3.2 of Jonas, *Kritische Gesamtausgabe der Werke von Hans Jonas*, ed. Dietrich Böhler, Michael Bongardt, Holger Burckhart, and Walther C. Zimmerli (Freiburg im Breisgau, Berlin, and Vienna: Rombach Verlag, 2013), 3.
29 Jonas, *Herausforderungen und Profile*, 3–4.
30 Jonas, *Herausforderungen und Profile*, 4.
31 Jonas, *Herausforderungen und Profile*, 6.
32 This idea – as Jonas rightly points out – is defended by the modern Jewish liberal *Missionsidee*, which was espoused by thinkers like Leo Baeck and Hermann Cohen. Cf. Christian Wiese, *The Life and Thought of Hans Jonas: Jewish Dimensions*, trans. Jeffrey Grossman and Christian Wiese (Waltham, MA: Brandeis University Press, 2007), 6–7.
33 Jonas, *Herausforderungen und Profile*, 7: "Ihre Verworfenheit solle eine Rechtfertigung des göttlichen Tuns und ihr Schicksal eine beispiellose Kundbarmachung der strafenden und rächenden Macht des Ewigen."

34 See Jonas, *Herausforderungen und Profile*, 7–8.
35 Jonas, *Herausforderungen und Profile*, 11.
36 Jonas, *Herausforderungen und Profile*, 12.
37 Jonas, *Herausforderungen und Profile*, 12; "Ethische Bedingtheit und ethische Zielbestimmtheit verweben sich zur Geschichte."
38 Jonas, *Herausforderungen und Profile*, 12.
39 The young Jonas had also had a great need for this alternative narration of history in his account of Gnosticism, as Lapidot underlined. See Elad Lapidot, "Hans Jonas' Work on Gnosticism as Counterhistory," *Philosophical Readings* 9 (2017): 61–69, here 61: "On the conceptual level, it means an alternative narration of history, which does not simply tell a completely different story, but re-reads the same facts in a different manner, thereby ascribing to them a new meaning, which runs counter, opposite to the traditionally accepted one. On a deeper level, in question here is a certain type of intellectual project, of philosophical project, whose fundamental act of conceptual re- thinking is inherently intertwined with an act of counter-history, of re-narration of history." It is worth noting that this hermeneutic twist also involves his interpretation of Heidegger. While in his *Gnosis I*, Heidegger's *Being and Time* was the hermeneutic tool and the theoretical framework through which Jonas interpreted Gnosticism, later on, existentialism, including in this label Heideggerian philosophy, as a radicalization of "Gnostic antinomism." Although Jonas points out several similarities between existentialism and modern Gnosticism, the main difference is that "Gnostic man is thrown into an antagonistic, anti-divine, and therefore anti-human nature, modern man into an indifferent one." This difference leads to two versions of nihilism, the modern one – characterized by such indifference that leads to the "true abyss"– being "infinitely more radical and more desperate than Gnostic nihilism ever could be." Jonas, "Gnosticism and Modern Nihilism," 450–451.On this aspect, see Daniel M. Herskowitz, "Reading Heidegger against the Grain: Hans Jonas on Existentialism, Gnosticism and Modern Science," *Modern Intellectual History* 19 (2022): 527–550, doi:10.1017/S147924432100010X
40 A Hegelian conception of history – it is not by chance that Jonas uses the verb "*sich selbst aufhebe*" – can be glimpsed in the background, where the chains of historical events can be a *Schlachtbank*, slaughter bank, but at the same time can be sublated as a necessary step for the self-realization of the spirit.
41 Jonas, *Herausforderungen und Profile*, 13: "Eine gotterfüllte Menschengemeinschaft der Endzeit."
42 Jonas, *Herausforderungen und Profile*, 14. See Petr Frantik, "Die Idee der Zerstreeung und Wiedersammlung bei den Propheten (1922)," in Bongardt, Burckhart, Gordon, and Nielsen-Sikora, *Hans Jonas Handbuch*, 160–163, here 162: "Wird die Rückkehr als ein Fortschritt gegenüber der Zeit vor der Diaspora gesehen, sodass die Diaspora eine notwendige Leidenszeit ist, von der aber letztlich die jüdische Gemeinschaft ebenso profitiert wie die Gemeinschaften, unter denen diese leben und das Wort und Gesetz Gottes übermitteln."
43 On the strong influence Buber also had on Jonas' early writing on the school system in Palestine, see Petr Frantik, "Das jüdische Schulwesen in Palästina (1923)," in Bongardt, Burckhart, Gordon, and Nielsen-Sikora, *Hans Jonas Handbuch*, 164–166, here 165: "Hier wird der starke Einfluss von Buber auf Jonas sichtbar, dessen *Drei Reden* über das Judentum ihn in jungen Jahren begeisterten. Hier beschreibt Buber die jüdische Gemeinschaft als eine Mischung unterschiedlicher Kulturen, und dieser Mischung soll sie sich auch gewahr sein. Das Judentum sei ein mehrdeutiges, von Widersprüchen und Gegensätzen erfülltes, polare Phänomen. Aus dieser desorientierenden Widersprüchlichkeit entsteht nach Buber eine Dynamik, die zu einem Streben nach Einheit auf einer tieferen Ebene führt." While the young Jonas was influenced by Buber's *Reden*, later on he was almost skeptical about Buber and Rosenzweig's vision of the future of German Judaism. In his *Memoirs*, he commented on their translation of the *Tanach* into German:

214 Libera Pisano

"Even before that I had a prophetic sense that German Jewry had no future, and accordingly there was no pressing need to translate the Bible into German again – the whole thing struck me as anachronistic. While Buber and Rosenzweig were proceeding on the assumption that German Jewry continued to have a mission, I tended to share the view of Feliz Theilhaber and others who predicted the disappearance of German Jewry." See Jonas, *Memoirs*, 52.

44 Thanks to its unity, action, and future, Judaism could even overcome the dualism between good and evil. See Martin Buber, *Drei Reden über das Judentum* (Frankfurt am Main: Rütten & Loening, 1916), 53: "Es gilt hier die Sache zwischen […] Zielmenschen und Zweckmenschen, Schaffenden und Zersetzenden, Urjuden und Galuthjuden."

45 Buber, *Drei Reden über das Judentum*, 102.

46 Jonas, *Herausforderungen und Profile*, 16: "Vor dem Exil herrscht fast ausschließlich die Unheilsstimmung vor; aber nach Eintritt der Katastrophe stellen sie die lebendige Reaktionserscheinung gegen den apathischen Zustand des geschlagenen Volkskorpers dar und geben den Heilserwartungen immer breiteren Raum."

47 Jonas, *The Gnostic Religion*, xx.

48 See Lapidot, "Hans Jonas' Work on Gnosticism as Counterhistory," 63: "Gnosticism would be the paradigmatic 'foreign' of the two major Western intellectual historiographies: religion and philosophy."

49 Jonas, *Gnosis und späteantiker Geist*, 5.

50 Jonas, *The Gnostic Religion*, 49.

51 Jonas, *The Gnostic Religion*, 49.

52 Jonas, *The Gnostic Religion*, 49.

53 Jonas, *Gnosis und späteantiker Geist*, 101.

54 Jonas, *The Gnostic Religion*, 55.

55 Jonas, *The Gnostic Religion*, 50.

56 Jonas, *The Gnostic Religion*, 271.

57 Jonas, "Gnosticism and Modern Nihilism," 438.

58 In *Gnosis II*, the alternative to Gnosticism's theoretical and anti-cosmic attitude is *pistis*. See Lapidot, "Gnosis und spätantiker Geist II," 93: "Die Alternative zur Gnosis war für Jonas keine platonische Idee, sondern Pistis. […] Währen die 'Gnosis' die Transzendenz, als eine Welt jenseits oder außerhalb der Welt suchte, vollzieht 'Pistis' die Transzendenz innerhalb dieser Welt als eine nicht theoretische, zeitliche Beziehung zu einem nicht objektivierten Anderen."

59 Jonas, "Gnosticism and Modern Nihilism," 450.

60 Cf. Jonas, *The Gnostic Religion*, xxvi. As Elad Lapidot pointed out, there is a shift in Jonas' account of the Gnostic *arete*. If in his dissertation and in *Gnosis und spätantiker Geist II* he shows how the Gnostics developed their own arete, in the postwar period he defined it as nihilistic. See Lapidot, "Gnosis und spätantiker Geist II," 90–91.

61 Cf. Jonas, *The Gnostic Religion*, 275: "Freedom by abuse and freedom by non-use, equal in their indiscriminateness, are only alternative expressions of the same acosmism." On Gnostic nihilism, cf. Claudio Bonaldi, *Jonas* (Rome: Carocci, 2009), 57–58.

62 Jonas, *The Gnostic Religion*, 271.

63 Jonas, *The Gnostic Religion*, 274.

64 The kind of nihilism that Jonas detects in Gnosticism has to do with the denial of the current world. However, I agree with Fossa, who claims that the dualistic ontology of Gnosticism is a "non-nihilist form of dualism." Fossa, "Nihilism, Existentialism, – and Gnosticism?," 72.

65 Jonas, *Memoirs*, 70. See Almong's contribution in this volume. Yael Almong, "Hans Jonas and Hannah Arendt's Variations on St. Augustine."

66 See Jonas, *Memoirs*, 161: "The antirevolutionary Strauss was so conservative that when he read my Gnosticism book, he instinctively sensed the Gnosticism contained a revolutionary element, and wrote to me that despite his personal acquaintance with me he hadn't realized that I was a secret revolutionary."

67 Jonas, *The Gnostic Religion*, 270.
68 Jonas, *The Gnostic Religion*, 92.
69 Jonas, *The Gnostic Religion*, 95.
70 Jonas, *Gnosis und späteantiker Geist*, 214.
71 Jonas, *Gnosis und späteantiker Geist*, 224.
72 Jonas, *Gnosis und späteantiker Geist*, 225.
73 Jonas, *Memoirs*, 67–68.
74 Jonas, *Memoirs*, 69.
75 Jonas, *Memoirs*, 70.
76 Jonas, *Memoirs*, 69.
77 Jonas, *Memoirs*, 69.
78 Jonas, *Memoirs*, 69.
79 Jonas, *Memoirs*, 69.
80 Jonas, *Memoirs*, 201.
81 Jonas, *Memoirs*, 201.
82 Jonas, *Memoirs*, 202.
83 Jonas, *The Gnostic Religion*, xxii.
84 See Avishag Zafrani, "Jüdische Philosophie," in Bongardt, Burckhart, Gordon, and Nielsen-Sikora, *Hans Jonas Handbuch*, 49–53, here 50: "Außerdem wissen wir, dass für Jonas die ethischen Konsequenzen aus der Ontologie, d.h. aus der Natur des Seins, abgeleitet werden müssen. Die Ontologie soll die Ethik legitimieren, menschliche Handlungen unterstützen und anleiten."
85 Jonas, *Memoirs*, 210.
86 See Lapidot, "Hans Jonas' Work on Gnosticism as Counterhistory," 69: "Jonas' post- and anti-Gnostic project is not formulated as proceeding from cosmology to history, but from history to cosmology. I wonder if this project could not be described as countering history itself, as returning from the oriental *mythos* to Athenian *physis*."
87 In his interview with Herlinde Koelbl, Jonas stated: "I do not share in messianic belief. On the contrary, I am convinced that man and the condition on earth will always remain imperfect and problematic. […] The sudden intervention, as announced by the Jewish religion, of such a [messianic] figure, with all the divine powers that will then be available to him […] – I do not believe that it will be like that." Quoted in Wiese, *The Life and Thought of Hans Jonas*, 69. Wiese adds: "Jonas' antimessianic and anti-utopian attitude hinges above all on his strong emphasis on the idea of a value inherent in life itself – in religious-philosophical terms: the goodness of the creation" (70).
88 See Gershom Scholem, *Toward an Understanding of the Messianic Idea*, trans. Michael A. Meyer, in Scholem, *The Messianic Idea in Judaism and Other Essays on Jewish Spirituality* (New York: Schocken Books, 1971), 1–36, here 35.
89 Jonas, *Memoirs*, 211. In a letter to Adolph Lowe on the occasion of Bloch's death in 1977, Jonas writes: "It became clear to me how much I must reject utopian philosophy as a fundamental anthropological error, a fundamental illusion about the nature of man (and, by the way, of power, too)." See his critique of Bloch's "ontology of not-yet-being." Cf. Wiese, *The Life and Thought of Hans Jonas*, 105–107.
90 Cf. Wiese, *The Life and Thought of Hans Jonas*, xxvi: "What emerges as one of the *leitmotifs* of his philosophy in his turn against all nihilistic negation of the world, all escapism."
91 See, for instance, Gershom Scholem, "Der Nihilismus als religiöses Phänomen," in *Norms in a Changing World*, ed. Adolf Portmann and Rudolf Ritsema [Eranos Jahrbuch 1974, vol. 43] (Leiden: Brill, 1977), 1–50, here 7.
92 See Gershom Scholem, *Von Berlin nach Jerusalem* (Frankfurt am Main: Suhrkamp, 1997), 88.
93 On Landauer, see Libera Pisano, "The Desert and the Garden: Gustav Landauer's Anarchistic Translation of Fritz Mauthner's *Sprachskepsis*," in *Skepsis and Antipolitics: The Alternative of Gustav Landauer*, ed. Cedric Cohen-Skalli and Libera Pisano (Leiden: Brill, 2022), 3–30.

94 See Max Stirner, *The Ego and His Own*, ed. David Leopold (Cambridge: Cambridge University Press, 1995). Stirner's line "On nothing have I set my heart" is the opening line of Goethe's poem "Vanitas! vanitatum vanitas!," which in turn echoes the famous refrain from Ecclesiastes: "All is vanity" (Eccl 1:2). See Johann Wolfgang von Goethe, *Goethe's sämmtliche Werke* (Stuttgart, 1840), 1/2:145.
95 See Zafrani, *Jüdische Philosophie*, 50: "Für Jonas ist diese Verantwortung eine Haltung gegenüber dem Nichts […]. Die Verantwortung des Menschen bestehe darin, dem Nihilismus zu wehren, und für Jonas konkret darin, die Lebensbedingungen der Menschheit, d.h. die Natur, zu erhalten, die durch die technologischen Exzesse des Menschen bedroht sei."
96 See Martin Buber, *Eclipse of God: Studies in the Relation between Religion and Philosophy* (Princeton, NJ, and Oxford: Princeton University Press, 2016), 61: "I shall only confess that for me a concept of being that means anything other than the inherent fact of all existing being, namely, that it exists, remains insurmountably empty."
97 Jonas, *Memoirs*, 108.

Bibliography

Bonaldi, Claudio. *Jonas*, Rome: Carocci, 2009.
Bouretz, Pierre. *Témoins du futur. Philosophie et messianism*, Paris: Gallimard, 2003.
Buber, Martin. *Drei Reden über das Judentum*, Frankfurt am Main: Rütten & Loening, 1916.
Buber, Martin. *Eclipse of God: Studies in the Relation between Religion and Philosophy*, Princeton, NJ, and Oxford: Princeton University Press, 2016.
Cohen, Hermann. *Jüdische Schriften*, 3 vols., *Ethische und religiose Grundfragen*, Berlin: Schwetschke & Sohn, 1924.
Fossa, Fabio. "Nihilism, Existentialism, – and Gnosticism? Reassessing the Role of the Gnostic Religion in Hans Jonas's Thought," *Philosophy and Social Criticism* 46, no. 1 (2020): 64–90.
Hans Jonas Handbuch. Leben – Werk – Wirkung, ed. M. Bongardt, H. Burckhart, J.-S. Gordon, and J. Nielsen-Sikora, Berlin: Metzler, 2021.
Herskowitz, Daniel M. "Reading Heidegger against the Grain: Hans Jonas on Existentialism, Gnosticism and Modern Science," *Modern Intellectual History* 19 (2022): 527–550, doi:10.1017/S147924432100010X
Jonas, Hans. *Gnosis und spätantiker Geist. Erster Teil: Die mythologische Gnosis*, 4th ed. Göttingen: Vandhoeck & Ruprecht, 1988.
Jonas, Hans. *The Gnostic Religion: The Message of the Alien God & the Beginnings of Christianity*, Boston, MA: Beacon Press, 2001.
Jonas, Hans. "Gnosticism and Modern Nihilism," *Social Research* 19, no. 4 (1952): 430–452.
Jonas, Hans. *Herausforderungen und Profile. Jüdisch-deutscher Geist in der Zeit-gegen die Zeit*, ed. S. Lalla, F. Preußger, and D. Böhler, vol. 3.2 of Jonas, *Kritische Gesamtausgabe der Werke von Hans Jonas*, ed. D. Böhler, M. Bongardt, H. Burckhart, and W.C. Zimmerli. Freiburg im Breisgau, Berlin, and Vienna: Rombach Verlag, 2013.
Jonas, Hans. *Memoirs*, ed. Ch. Wiese, trans. K. Winston. Lebanon, NH: Brandeis University Press, 2008.
Lapidot, Elad. "Hans Jonas' Work on Gnosticism as Counterhistory," *Philosophical Readings* 9 (2017): 61–69.
Mendes-Flohr, Paul. "Gnostic Anxieties: Jewish Intellectuals and Weimar Neo-Marcionism," *Modern Theology* 35, no. 1 (2019): 71–81.
Pisano, Libera. "The Desert and the Garden: Gustav Landauer's Anarchistic Translation of Fritz Mauthner's *Sprachskepsis*," *Skepsis and Antipolitics: The Alternative of Gustav Landauer*, ed. C. Cohen-Skalli and L. Pisano, 3–30. Leiden: Brill, 2022.

Rosenzweig, Franz. *Der Mensch und sein Werk. Gesammelte Schriften 3. Zweistromland. Kleinere Schriften zu Glauben und Denken*, ed. R. and A. Mayer. Dordrecht: Martinus Nijhoff, 1984.
Rosenzweig, Franz. *The Star of Redemption* [1921], trans. B. E. Galli. Madison: Wisconsin Press, 2005.
Scholem, Gershom. "Der Nihilismus als religiöses Phänomenon," In *Norms in a Changing World*, ed. A. Portmann and R. Ritsema [Eranos Jahrbuch 1974, vol. 43], 1–50. Leiden: Brill, 1977.
Scholem, Gershom. *The Messianic Idea in Judaism and Other Essays on Jewish Spirituality*, New York: Schocken Books, 1971.
Scholem, Gershom. *Von Berlin nach Jerusalem*, Frankfurt am Main: Suhrkamp, 1997.
Stirner, Max. *The Ego and His Own*, ed. D. Leopold, Cambridge: Cambridge University Press, 1995.
Susman, Margarete. "Ezechiel, der Prophet der Umkehr, und die Bestimmung des jüdischen Volkes," *Neue Wege* 36 (1942): 8–23.
Vom Judentum, ed. Bar Kochba, Leipzig: Kurt Wolff Verlag, 1913.
Weiss, Daniel H. *Paradox and the Prophets: Hermann Cohen and the Indirect Communication of Religion*, Oxford: Oxford University Press, 2012.
Wiese, Christian. *The Life and Thought of Hans Jonas: Jewish Dimensions*, trans. J. Grossman and Ch. Wiese. Waltham, MA: Brandeis University Press, 2007.

Index

alienation 6, 16, 96, 133, 136, 141, 145, 156, 158–59, 164, 183, 207, 209–11
Alien God 84, 98, 100, 151, 153, 170, 175, 192, 194, 200, 210, 216
amor 74
Arendt, Hannah viii, 69–70, 73–80, 82–83, 119, 122, 138, 140, 172, 176, 191–92, 197–200, 207–8
Aristotle 23, 178–79, 183, 189
Augustine 14–15, 18–22, 24, 26–27, 39, 41, 45–47, 49–50, 53–54, 59–61, 63–65, 67, 69–83, 90, 99, 117–18, 214
Auschwitz 14, 120, 134, 173, 176, 181, 187, 193, 195–97, 199–200

Benjamin, Walter 189
Bergmann, Hugo 161
Bloch, Ernst 188, 198
Blumenberg, Hans 185, 193–95, 199
Brentano, Franz 3
Buber, Martin viii–ix, 151, 174, 176, 187, 202, 205–6, 210, 213–14, 216
Bultmann, Rudolf viii, 14–61, 63–64, 67, 73–74, 81, 84, 99, 102–4, 117–18, 120, 137, 154, 158, 163, 169–71, 173–76, 192

caritas 41, 70, 72, 74–75
Cassirer, Ernst 45, 52, 119, 144, 171
Cohen, Hermann 26, 50, 151, 212, 217

Dasein 7–9, 11, 15, 19–20, 22, 24, 30–31, 42, 80, 104–8, 111, 113, 115, 130, 132, 144–46, 150, 156–58, 160–61
demythologization 17–21, 24, 28–30, 32–33, 36–38, 40–41, 43–53, 55, 57, 62, 65, 103, 105, 117–18, 158–59, 161, 170–71, 175, 180, 197

Diasporic Judaism 201, 206, 208, 210, 212
Dilthey, Wilhelm 28, 40–44, 50–52, 80, 105, 118–20

Eichmann in Jerusalem 69, 73, 77, 80, 82, 199
Enlightenment 69, 75, 77, 86, 125
Entweltlichung 45, 52, 124, 143–46, 150–51, 159, 197, 206, 208
existentialism 7, 19, 24, 33–34, 37, 39–40, 44, 48, 60, 62, 74, 80, 96, 99–100, 107, 113, 120–21, 125, 131–35, 138, 142, 144, 147, 151, 153, 156–61, 164, 172–73, 175, 184, 192, 196, 201, 211, 213–14, 216

Geist 30–31, 40, 141, 154–55, 157–64, 167, 212
German idealism 127–28, 131, 136–38, 151, 187, 196
Gnosis, Gnosticism 1–5, 7, 10–14, 23–24, 28, 30–32, 35–36, 44, 46–48, 54, 59, 61, 70–71, 78, 84–202, 204, 206–11, 213–16
Goethe, Johann Wolfgang 123, 137, 139

Hebrew University viii, 2, 155, 161–62, 165–69, 172–74, 181
Hegel, Georg Wilhelm Friedrich ix, 46, 79, 128, 137, 185, 189, 196, 199, 213
Heidegger, Martin viii, 1–9, 11–13, 16, 18, 20–26, 28, 32, 34, 40–44, 46, 48–53, 56, 64, 66–67, 70–71, 74, 79–82, 93, 96, 99, 102–3, 106, 113–15, 119–22, 133, 135, 137–38, 140–44, 151, 156, 158–60, 163–66, 168–69, 171–76, 178, 185, 190, 192, 194, 196, 204, 208, 213

220 Index

hermeneutics 1, 7, 18, 24, 27, 32, 43–44, 103, 105, 118–19, 144, 205, 208
Herrmann, Wilhelm 17–18, 26, 43, 50
historical Jesus 15, 33–34, 47, 54
Holocaust 9, 134, 191–92, 197, 200
Husserl, Edmund 1–13, 23, 66–67, 71, 80, 144, 172–73, 175, 192

Jerusalem 2, 64, 68–69, 73, 77, 80, 82, 155, 161, 165–66, 168–69, 174, 180–81, 193, 199, 203, 209, 215, 217
Jonas, Hans viii–x, 1–51, 53–87, 89, 91–111, 113–25, 129–51, 153–217

Kabbalah 168, 174, 186–87, 191, 196, 200
Kant, Immanuel 20, 51, 57, 66, 68, 79, 127, 136, 138, 157, 181, 209
Kierkegaard, Søren 22–23, 27, 31, 56–57, 64, 68

Luria, Isaac 178–94, 196–99
Luther, Martin 15, 17–18, 22–24, 27, 50

Manichaeism 45, 103–4, 146, 208
Marburg 11, 14, 17, 28, 38, 44–45, 50, 163, 165, 169, 171
myth viii, 14, 17–21, 24, 28–32, 34, 37, 39, 44–49, 51, 60–61, 65, 92, 99–100, 123–32, 134–37, 139–40, 144–45, 149, 157–60, 170–71, 175, 180, 184–85, 187–88, 195–96, 198–99
mythology 19, 24, 29, 31, 33, 38, 44–45, 50–51, 125, 127, 129, 137–38, 144–45, 147, 149, 157, 170, 185, 193

Nazism 9, 77, 104, 139, 164–65, 203
Nietzsche, Friedrich 96, 133, 136, 140, 142, 153
Nihilism 1, 3–4, 9, 66, 120–21, 142, 151, 160, 176, 184, 198, 201–2, 204, 207–8, 210–11, 213–14, 216

objectivation 15–17, 20, 28–29, 31–35, 37–45, 47–48, 50–51, 57–58, 105–6, 115, 144–45, 147, 150, 157–59, 164, 167
Ogden, Schubert 29, 35, 45, 48, 51, 53, 170

Origen 30, 114, 119, 147, 149–50
original sin 28, 31, 33, 38–40, 44–45, 49, 56–57, 64

Paul 7, 9, 12, 14–16, 18, 20, 24, 27, 33–40, 44–45, 47–49, 53–60, 62, 67, 72, 81–82, 147, 151, 173, 216
Pelagianism 26, 32, 39, 45, 49, 53, 59, 61, 67, 70–72, 117, 121
Philo viii, 29, 49, 56, 60, 130, 146–51, 159, 163, 193, 202
PILEGESH 161, 172, 177
Plato 5, 75, 88, 94, 99, 115, 142–43, 146–48, 151
Platonism 70, 80, 82, 142–43
Plotinus 30, 147, 149–50

Rosenzweig, Franz viii, 151, 203, 212, 217

Schiller, Friedrich 127, 137, 139
Scholem, Gershom viii, 161–62, 166–69, 172–76, 179–80, 185, 187–88, 191, 193–200, 209–10, 215, 217
Scotus, Duns 182, 191, 194, 199
Second World War 54, 95
secular, secularism 80, 83, 126, 136, 138, 180
Spengler, Oswald 87–89, 95–98, 101, 105, 148, 156, 161, 163, 170, 176, 211
Stoicism 15, 65, 71–72, 81, 164
Strauss, Leo 80, 83, 138, 172, 176, 178, 193

Talmud ix, 167
Taubes, Jacob viii, 135–36, 139, 171, 176
technology 45, 62, 67, 69, 75, 77, 96, 100, 116–17, 119–21, 172–73, 175, 193, 199
Tillich, Paul 24
tsimtsum 180–83, 186–88, 191, 194–97, 199–200

Valentinian school 133, 149, 189

worldliness 2, 5, 7–9, 80, 151, 166, 192, 201

Zionism 73, 135–36, 139, 155, 169, 197, 203, 205, 208, 210–12